ESSAYS ON
MAIMONIDES

ESSAYS ON
MAIMONIDES

An Octocentennial Volume

EDITED BY

SALO WITTMAYER BARON

AMS Press, Inc.
New York
1966

PREFACE

OVER five years have passed since the world-wide celebration of the eight-hundredth anniversary of the birth of Moses ben Maimon. A great deal has happened in the world at large, as well as in the Jewish world, during these eventful years. Nevertheless, the addresses given at the celebration held under the auspices of Columbia University and the essays, for the most part written shortly thereafter, despite the delay caused by unavoidable circumstances, appear here without any substantive alteration. That they seem as valid today, and valid essentially in the same form, as they were in the period of the more leisurely transformations a few years ago, is but another sign of the vitality of the Maimonidean approach to the riddles of existence and of its adaptability to ever-changing conditions.

Nonetheless, the outbreak of the second world war has left its mark also upon the present volume. Two of the contributors, living in war-torn Europe and Africa, respectively, have been inaccessible during the final stages of its preparation: Professor Gilson, residing in occupied France, could not be given the opportunity of checking the English translation of his essay, originally written in French, and of revising it in galley proof. Dr. Meyerhof, of Cairo, Egypt, brought his essay up to date in 1938, but could not see it in its final edited form. Professor Alexander Marx, President of the Alexander Kohut Memorial Foundation, through the generous collaboration of which the publication of this volume has been made possible, kindly consented to read the manuscript and to revise it, not only in the light of his own expert knowledge of the subject, but also on the basis of his correspondence with the author over a period of many years. Dr. Joshua Finkel had the kindness to revise the manuscript of the late Professor Gottheil, while Dr. Leo Strauss, serving in 1937–38 as Research Fellow on the Miller Foundation, at Columbia University, has proved very helpful in the preparation of the manuscript for the press. I am also much obliged to the staff of the Columbia University Press for its fine editorial work and its preparation of the Index.

SALO W. BARON

New York
January 2, 1941

CONTENTS

ABBREVIATIONS

b. The Babylonian Talmud (the individual tractates are cited in the customary abbreviated form)

C. M. Maimonides' Commentary on the Mishnah (in the usual Hebrew translations, unless a special Arabic edition is indicated)

H. M. Joseph Karo's Shulhan aruk, Section Hoshen mishpat

j. The Palestinian Talmud

JQR The Jewish Quarterly Review

Kobeṣ Kobeṣ teshubot ha-Rambam, edited by A. L. Lichtenfeld, 3 parts, Leipzig, 1859

M. Mishnah

MbM Moses ben Maimon by Jacob Guttmann et al., 2 vols., Leipzig, 1908–14

M. N. Maimonides' Moreh Nebuchim, or Guide for the Perplexed (the English quotations are taken from the Friedlaender translation, or are variations thereof)

M. T. Maimonides' Mishneh Torah, or Code of Laws

Outlook "The Historical Outlook of Maimonides" by Salo W. Baron, Proceedings of the American Academy for Jewish Research, VI (1934–35), 5–113

RABD Rabbi Abraham ben David

Resp. Maimonides' Teshubot (Responsa), edited by A. H. Freimann, Jerusalem, 1934

S. M. Maimonides' Sefer ha-Miṣvot (Book of Precepts), Hebrew translation ed. by Chaim Heller, Piotrkow, 1914 (unless the Arabic original, edited by M. Bloch, Paris, 1888, is indicated)

Tos. Tosefta, edited by M. S. Zuckermandel

Y. D. Joseph Karo's Shulhan aruk, Section Yoreh deah

CHAPTER ONE

THE EIGHT-HUNDREDTH ANNIVERSARY OF THE BIRTH OF MOSES MAIMONIDES

PROFESSOR Federico de Onís opened the celebration at the Casa de las Españas, Columbia University, March 30, 1935, by welcoming the members of the Columbia fraternity and their guests to the Casa de las Españas and by introducing the chairman of the evening, President Nicholas Murray Butler.

INTRODUCTION

BY NICHOLAS MURRAY BUTLER

Eight hundred years ago on this very day there was born at Cordova in Spain one of the most powerful and most influential intellects that the world has known. It is characteristic of that superficiality which so sadly dominates the generation through which we are passing, that those who in centuries past have laid the lasting foundations of our civilization and have given most penetrating interpretation of the highest human ideals, should be passed by as if they had never existed. The ancient Hebrews, the ancient Greeks, the ancient Romans and the intellectual monarchs of the Middle Ages are the builders of our modern civilization. Without knowledge of them, of their thought and of their insights, any reasonable understanding of what is going on in the world today, or of what is likely to go on in the immediate future is quite impossible. We are to celebrate tonight one of the great captains of the mind.

There are recorded in history few movements of men so important and of so lasting significance as that of the Mohammedans and their Hebrew companions from Asia Minor across North

Africa to the Straits of Gibraltar and then into Spain, where the fires were lighted on new altars of the soul and of the mind and kept burning and alight for several centuries. Doubtless, Charles Martel did a good job for the civilization which we call Western when he checked and turned back the Arabs near Poitiers, but we cannot be too grateful for these very Arabs and the Hebrews who accompanied them for what they accomplished during their long hegemony in Spain.

It has been said of Maimonides that his influence was incalculable. At a time when dogmatism was rampant he upheld the part which reason must play in examining and strengthening all faith which is to be really intelligent, and at a time of persecution he defended toleration in matters theological. His *Guide for the Perplexed* is one of the classics of philosophy and morals. He found ways and means to unite in more common causes than one Judaism, Mohammedanism and Christianity.

The contact established between Greek thought and the Jewish mind was brought about at the time of Philo of Alexandria. It has been said of Philo that he knew Greek philosophy thoroughly and that he was an orthodox Jew of his own time. He was able to reconcile, after his own fashion, the philosophy of the Greeks and the faith of the Jews. More than ten centuries later Maimonides did just this, and in a most striking and persuasive fashion.

In this clamorous and drifting age it is fine indeed to turn to the celebration of a great personality of world-wide influence, always on the side of reflection, of understanding and of constructive progress.

MOSES MAIMONIDES, THE PHILOSOPHER

BY RICHARD McKEON

On this occasion, dedicated to the celebration of the eighthundredth anniversary of the birth of a great philosopher, it is fitting that we recall his contributions to philosophy and the influence of his ideas on philosophers who came after him. Yet there is an inescapable contradiction in such acts of honor, for like most philosophers, ancient or modern, Maimonides labored long and strenuously to separate the truths accessible to reason from the mere probabilities familiar to imagination and opinion.

His work shows the influence of previous opinion no less than the mark of contemporary discussion, and it has not been unaffected by centuries of later interpretation; yet his endeavor, as a philosopher, was to attain, by effort of thought and with divine aid, to truths that are eternal. If we place the truths of the philosopher in the sequence of time to specify in what particulars Maimonides' doctrines derived from those of Aristotle and the Peripatetics or how they influenced later philosophers, we reduce philosophic ideas by that pious and historical act to the rank of opinion and subject to the processes of change what was set forth as eternal. Even the admirer of Maimonides might be tempted to say, as has frequently been said of many philosophers, that the spirit of his thought is fresh, but the matter on which it was exercised is obsolete, for the philosophy of Maimonides is based on a physics and a metaphysics, and it might be thought that the physics has been out of date for 300 years or that we have no need today for a metaphysics.

The philosopher who aspired to changeless truths, not the man who fell in with some opinions of the day, should be the subject of our consideration tonight. Philosophy is properly celebrated in the person of a philosopher, since the eternal, if it is to be celebrated, must have a local habitat and time, and Moses Maimonides is of the brief list of persons through whom philosophy has spoken clearly. Not the philosophy, but the expression of the problems of his philosophy is of his time, for philosophers borrow their language and their instances from the problems of their day. In much the manner in which we have been accustomed to go to the books of the scientists for our conception of nature, Maimonides and the philosophers of his time went to the books of the prophets.

You are no doubt aware [he said] that the Almighty, desiring to lead us to perfection and to improve our state of society, has revealed to us laws which are to regulate our actions. These laws, however, presuppose an advanced state of intellectual culture. We must first form a conception of the Existence of the Creator according to our capacities; that is, we must have a knowledge of Metaphysics. But this discipline can only be approached after the study of Physics; for the science of Physics borders on Metaphysics, and must even precede it in the course of our studies.[1]

[1] The *Guide for the Perplexed*, "Introduction," trans. by M. Friedlander (London, 1904), p. 4.

There is much that is strange to modern ears in this statement of the nature and purpose of philosophy. Science has been opposed to theology, and metaphysics no longer seems closely proximate to physics. Yet as Maimonides would have interpreted it, the statement of their relationship does much to clarify the problems of philosophy, even those of modern philosophy. Maimonides' great philosophic masterpiece, the *Guide for the Perplexed*, closes with a chapter on "True Wisdom," in which he states his conception of the sequence and contents of philosophy. First, one learns the truths of tradition; second, one learns to prove them philosophically; third, one derives from them rules to direct one's conduct.[2] The difficulties through which Maimonides sought to guide the perplexed are all contained in that sequence: (1) the clear and unambiguous statement of what is believed, (2) the statement of the rational grounds of that belief, (3) the derivation of the practical consequences of that doctrine as found in ethics and politics. Maimonides' entire philosophic effort was devoted to these three tasks, and the *Guide for the Perplexed* is divided into three corresponding parts; this is the whole of philosophy, and, conversely, Maimonides says, there is nothing superfluous in his work.

The *Guide for the Perplexed*, as its title implies, is addressed, not to the novice in philosophy, but to one who, already learned in the law and in the true sciences, is perplexed by that knowledge and by the interrelations of its parts. The sources of perplexity, which Maimonides considers may all be treated in terms of misunderstanding of words, are found particularly in the inconsistencies and contradictions of the literal with the analogical and allegorical significances of words.[3] The entire first part of the *Guide* may be said to be a treatise on the meanings of important words in the Bible and the Talmud, on homonyms, and on the dangers of persistently literal interpretations of such words. But the interest is not in a mere verbal precision. A metaphysical purpose is apparent constantly behind this examination of words, and the motivation which turned the philosopher to words is unmistakable, for Maimonides pauses from time to time to observe that Scriptures and sages have couched their truths in allegorical language. All the branches of science necessary for the interpretation of

[2] The *Guide for the Perplexed*, Vol. III, chap. 54, p. 394.
[3] The *Guide for the Perplexed*, Vol. I, Introd., pp. 9–11.

Scripture were cultivated by the ancient Jews, but in the periods of persecution science and literature had been endangered. At best Metaphysics can never be popular, for five reasons which Maimonides is at pains to enumerate, and should therefore never be taught to the young and uninitiated.[4] Physics is in a predicament which is almost as extreme as that of metaphysics, but whereas it must not be fully explained nor be expounded in the presence of two, metaphysics must not be fully expounded in the presence of a single student unless he be especially trained and endowed.[5] Both sciences are therefore referred to and developed in allegory and enigma. The peculiar place of physics in the doctrine of Maimonides may be seen clearly in his famous refutation of the Mutakallemim, a sect of Mohammedan philosophers whose error is reduced to a fallacy of method contrary to the method of Maimonides. Instead of beginning their discussion as he did with physics, they began with some point of doctrine or creed, considered what properties things would have if that doctrine were true, and thereupon asserted that things were endowed with those properties.[6]

Inquiry into the meanings of words and the use of the allegorical interpretation are constant devices in the philosophic method of Maimonides. The interest in words is already conspicuous in the first philosophic work he wrote, the *Terminology of Logic*, which according to some critics was written when Maimonides was sixteen; in that work Maimonides explains in 14 short chapters the meanings of 176 terms in logic, metaphysics, physics, ethics, and politics. The interpretation of words is a conspicuous device in his treatises on theology and law, in the *Commentary on the Mishnah*, and in the *Mishneh Torah*. To penetrate the meaning of the Scriptures and the Talmud required a fully elaborated technique of interpretation. It is fitting that this method guide us in our reading of Maimonides, for to make a literal or historical list of the contents of the *Guide for the Perplexed* would be to commit the very error against which Maimonides cautions in the first part of the *Guide*. We have, perhaps, other words to substitute for the words which are crucial in his treatise. We have in the centuries

---

[4] The *Guide for the Perplexed*, Vol. I, chaps. 33–34, pp. 43–49.
[5] The *Guide for the Perplexed*, Vol. I, Introd., pp. 2–3.
[6] The *Guide for the Perplexed*, Vol. I, chap. 71, pp. 109–10.

amassed other traditions and we may tend to other sources of belief, but the changes are more frequently verbal than real, and we do the past an injustice if we read what was written in a literal sense which we superimpose on words.

The second stage of Maimonides' philosophy, and the second part of the *Guide* consist in the rational demonstration of what we believe or of the traditional law. As the first part of the method required explanation to prepare it for modern ears, since concern with words and concern with truth are contrasted, rather than associated in our minds, so too this second part may seem at first to have a sophistical sound. For Maimonides, knowledge of the Law and philosophy were totally distinct, although philosophy consists in confirming the truths of the Law by true speculation. This conviction that knowledge is distinct from belief, yet consistent with it, does not imply either that anything you may wish can be believed, nor that anything you may believe can be proved. Yet, for many things which are true and which are suggested by tradition, proof can be found in an impartial examination of nature. The Law has communicated to us, inviting us to believe in them, several points of metaphysical importance: the existence of God, his unity, his knowledge, his power, his will, his eternity. These are the final end of science and can be understood completely and in detail only after preparatory knowledge. To the wise, however, they can be proved by reason and on the basis of physics.

The Second Part of the *Guide for the Perplexed* therefore begins with twenty-six propositions of the Aristotelian physics and metaphysics; on the basis of these propositions Maimonides constructs four proofs of the existence of God, and further demonstrates God's incorporeality and unity, and discusses the nature of angels, creation *ex nihilo*, prophecy. Like the first part of his method, the interpretation of words, this second part, the discovery of rational grounds for doctrines, is constant in Maimonides' thought. The famous treatise called *Eight Chapters*, which he wrote as preface to the moral precepts of Abboth, serves such a function by supplying psychological and ethical bases to those precepts.

The final aspect of Maimonides' method is to be found in his constant concern with the practical consequences of philosophy. Ethics for him has a metaphysical foundation, and metaphysics has ethical consequences. As he found the science of physics in the Bible, for he interprets the talmudic "Maaseh Bereshith," the account of creation, to mean physics, so he finds a metaphysics there too, for "Maaseh Mercabah," the description of the chariot, means metaphysics. The Third Part of the *Guide for the Perplexed*, therefore, opens with an interpretation of Ezekiel's vision of the chariot and proceeds from metaphysics to a discussion of moral questions: the nature of evil and providence, the fourteen classes of precepts, the fear of God and true wisdom. Maimonides' endeavor, repeated several times in his work, is to organize the precepts of the Mosaic law in logically distinct groups and to show how they proceed from self-evident principles.

The thought of Maimonides presents a double aspect, which may be found in many of the great philosophies of men of all faiths. The wisdom and science which he undertook to teach to such men as were prepared to understand was, according to him, as old as Judaism; it was not difficult for him to find the same wisdom and science in the prophets and the sages, and even in the philosophers of Greece and Islam and Christendom. Yet what he taught he properly said he had learned from no master; he had arrived at it by no divine inspiration, but by rational investigation. The concern of philosophy is with timeless truths, but the philosopher must find them in time and may at any point or moment be mistaken. Broadly based upon a tradition, Maimonides' thought was widely influential in Jewish, Christian, and Mohammedan thought; but rational in approach to that tradition, his doctrines have seemed novel in each age in which he has been quoted. Christian theologians at the University of Paris during the thirteenth century, William of Auvergne, Alexander of Hales, Albertus Magnus, Thomas Aquinas, could quote him on such points as the relation of metaphysics and physics, the proofs of the existence of God, the attributes of God, the creation of the world; theologians at the same university could publish a list of the errors of Rabbi Moyses.[7] In the seventeenth century Spinoza was greatly influenced by Maimonides, particularly in his analyses of the nature and attributes of God, the eternity of the soul, prophets, miracles, and angels; for precisely those doctrines Spinoza

[7] Incerti auctoris Tractatus de erroribus philosophorum Aristotelis, Averrois, Avicennae, Algazelis, Alkindi et Rabbi Moysis, capitulum xii. Edited among the texts of *Siger de Brabant et l'Averroïsme latin au XIIIme siècle* by P. Mandonnet (Louvain, 1908), II, 21–24.

was considered by his contemporaries a dangerous rationalist and atheist. To us today the sense of tradition is not strong, not so much because we have no tradition but because we have mixed many traditions, and the work of Maimonides may seem remote. But we should remember that to the men of his own time he seemed to be a second Moses. Like the first Moses, he gave a law to his people which has become part of the history of the Jews, and, like the law of the first Moses, his law had such scope and depth that its influence extended far beyond the limits of race and time. Perhaps the time has come for a third Moses, whose task would be to write a new Guide for the Perplexed of more recent times. Such a guide might well be divided, as was the earlier *Guide*, into three parts, one to examine the meanings of words we use today, that we might understand each other before we disagree and refute each other; a second to examine the fundamentals of our current beliefs, to order them, and reduce them to the metaphysical principles on which they depend; a third to bring our actions into some relation with our science, and to subject our manner of conduct to rigid scrutiny. Until such a third Moses appears, however, the second Moses is still, for all the changes that might have been introduced into physics since his time, an unexcelled Guide for the Perplexed.

MAIMONIDES, THE SCIENTIST

BY RICHARD GOTTHEIL

Whenever I have wandered through the streets of Cordova, or Fez, or Old Cairo, my thoughts have perforce turned to the great man who lived in those places, who wrote his wonderful treatises there, and who was at once an authority on Jewish law, on philosophy and ethics, on astronomy, and especially on medicine. Ibn Abi Usaibia, the distinguished Arabic biographer of Arabic medical scientists, speaking of Musa ibn Maimun (Maimonides) says: "He was the leading man of his time in the art of medicine," and he cites some verses of the Kadi al-Said ibn Sina al-Mulk, the first line of which can be translated somewhat freely as: "I have seen that Galen busied himself only with the body of man:

but Abu Imran [i.e., Maimonides] with the mind of man as well as with his body." It seems to me that this it is that places the man whom we honor here so far above his contemporaries. It is peculiar that the other celebrated Cordovan, Ibn Rushd — commonly called Averroes — wrote also on philosophical as well as scientific subjects. Sarton, in his *Introduction to the History of Science*, discussing these men, says: "These two giants not only dominated the thought of their age; they are still alive today."

I have been asked why the celebration in honor of Maimonides was held in the Casa de las Españas, seeing that Maimonides was obliged to leave the Peninsula when he was only thirteen years of age. But in Arabic sources, Ibn al-Kifti, the Arabic biographer, who lived a century previous to Ibn Abi Usaibia, and at the very time of Maimonides, speaks of him as the Andalusian; while Ibn Abi Usaibia is more specific and calls him "al-Kurtubi," i.e., the Cordovan. He was proud of his Spanish birth, and even in Egypt he speaks of himself as an Andalusian; for the dread days of the Inquisition had not yet come to make life for the Jew so intolerable that, even though he were a famous scholar, he would have had to leave Spain. Maimonides studied medicine with Averroes — who was only nine years his senior — at the same time pursuing his philosophical studies under Ibn Tufail and his Hebrew studies in the Bible, Mishnah, and Talmud under his father, himself a distinguished scholar.

Why, then, were Maimonides and his family forced to leave Cordova, which was then the intellectual capital of Europe? The reason is to be found in the condition of Islam in Northern Africa and in the Iberian Peninsula at that time. The al-Moravid dynasty had held the Maghreb in its power for nearly a hundred years. Under them a scholasticism had been evolved which that learned man, Goldziher, characterizes as "a casuistic prating indulged in by people who in their canonical disputes and their juridical subtleties pretend to be dealing with the science of religion." A young man named Ibn Tumart, of the Berber tribe of Masmuda, saw whither this was leading. He became the founder of the Almohades, or Unitarians, who, after conquering Western Africa, crossed over into Spain and fought the Almoravids at the point of the sword. They must also have been fanatical in their way; for Maimonides, one would think, would, with his clearness of vision and his love for directness of thought, and with his orderly mental habit, have

preferred to side with the Almohades rather than with the Almoravids. It is evident, however, that the former desired to clear the
Peninsula of all that was not Islamic according to their own way
of thinking. For twelve years the family of Maimonides wandered
about in Spain, until life there became impossible, and they then
crossed the straits and landed in Fez, though it is peculiar that
Ibn al Kifti says that they went directly from Spain to Cairo.

Now, in the words of the very Ibn Abi Usaibia whom I have
already quoted,

It is reported that the latter Musa had become a Moslem in
the Maghrab, that he knew the Koran by heart, and that he
occupied himself with Mohammedan law. Then when he went to
Egypt and lived in Fostat [Old Cairo], he relapsed into his former
faith.

Aside from the fact that Ibn Abi Usaibia prefaces this story with
the words "It is said," Professor Margoliouth of Oxford has shown
how impossible the tale is. Islam would not permit a proselyte to
revert to his former faith. It would have had him beheaded.
Baidawi, the great commentator of the Koran, says distinctly:
"Whosoever turns back from his people openly or secretly, take
him and kill him wheresoever ye find him like any other infidel."
There are other stories which say that Maimonides led in reading
the Ramadan prayers on board ship. But he was, we know, at
sea on May 16, 1165, and Ramadan in that year did not come
before July 1. It is impossible to believe that he was at sea all this
time; and we must therefore conclude that the whole story is a
legend.

From the above it will be seen that Maimonides and his family
found it impossible to remain in Fez, as the Almohades were as
powerful there as in the southern part of the Spanish Peninsula.
They resolved to go to Cairo by way of Acre and Jerusalem. It
was there in Fostat, or Old Cairo, that Maimonides began his real
practice as a physician. He was forced to this step because of the
death of his brother David, who had been a dealer in precious
stones, the two having decided to earn their living together. He
not only practiced, but in Old Cairo he composed the works that
made his name known as a writer on medicine and brought him
his post as Physician in Ordinary to Al-Afdal nur al-Din Ali, the
oldest son of the famous Saladin. His job was no sinecure. He
himself tells us:

My daily life is as follows: the Sultan lives in Cairo [2.5 kilometers from Fostat]. I must visit him every morning. If he, or one of his children or one of his wives is ill, I must remain there the whole day. When there is nothing the matter, I do not get home until the afternoon.

In addition, he had a great many patients to attend in Fostat itself; and on the Sabbath day he was busy with matters relating to the congregation. No wonder that he died at the comparatively early age of sixty-nine.

In regard to his medical attainments, it is said by those who know more about this than I, that he drew his knowledge mainly from al-Razi, Avicenna, and Ibn Sina-al-Wafid, who, on their part, were dependent upon translations of the Greek medical writers, especially Galen. He knew that he owed a debt to Galen; for he had collected from him and from Hippocrates as many as 1,500 medical aphorisms. It is true that he was influenced by his Greek teachers, but he in turn influenced not only Jewish, but Moslem and Christian science as well, Henri de Mondeville in the thirteenth century and Guy de Chauliac in the fourteenth century being especially mentioned in regard to the latter.

The medical works of Maimonides were all written in Arabic, though at a very early date the Arabic was translated into Hebrew, and some of the works from Hebrew into Latin. We know that Maimonides composed nine works dealing with medical topics. Some of them are mere compendia, as, e.g., his *Extracts* (*Mukhtasarat*), and a number of works on Galen, who was perhaps the most famous physician and writer on medicine of the Graeco-Roman period. It is supposed that Maimonides made these extracts in order to facilitate the understanding of the rather difficult Greek in which Galen's treatises were written — although I must confess that they are equally difficult to understand in their Arabic dress.[8]

The influence of Maimonides in medical matters was important, as I have said, not only among the Moslems and the Jews of both the Orient and the Occident, but also among the Christians; and we know that his works, in Latin translations, were studied at the universities of Padua and Montpellier. One can only echo the

---

[8] A few paragraphs of Professor Gottheil's address containing a brief description of Maimonides' medical treatises have been omitted here, in view of the more elaborate analysis of the same subject in Dr. Meyerhof's paper. Ed.

hope of Dr. Meyerhof that a complete set of his medical writings
be published — I would add, together with an English translation.

Nor must we forget that in his nonmedical works — especially
his philosophic and juridic writings, as well as in his medical
treatises — he has a good deal to say about general hygiene, for
the body and the soul of man are equally influenced by these
hygienic principles. He discusses climate, houses, manner of dress,
baths, sleep needed, and bodily exercise — as well as the proper
food, as regards both quantity and quality. An old man should
see that he nourishes himself properly, that he has three repasts a
day — not too much and not too little.

So great was the scholar's reputation in Cairo that the synagogue in the Old City which bears his name and which I have had
the pleasure of visiting and photographing several times, still
receives sick people who are carried there. They pass the night in
an underground chamber supposed to have been Maimonides'
room, in the hope that healing may come to them from their mere
presence there, a practice contrary to all Maimonides taught in
his fight against superstition.

But, apart from that, his diatetic treatises made quite a sensa-
tion in both the West and the East, and caused Arabic medicine
to become most influential in Western Europe. I am told that as
late as the seventeenth century we find citations prefaced by the
words: "Dixit Rabbi Moyses."

I cannot close without quoting the words of the master himself
in his *Guide for the Perplexed*. He says: "It is our great advantage
that man who knows his station should not imagine that the whole
universe exists for him alone."

MAIMONIDES, THE LEADER AND LAWGIVER

BY SALO W. BARON

The Jewish people all over the world commemorate on this day
not only Maimonides, the great scientist and philosopher, but also
Maimonides, their own unforgettable leader and lawgiver. They
also revere him as a living illustration of the unity of the human
mind, which even in an age of great religious intolerance permitted
Muslim students to gather in special groups to study his works,

under the direction of Jewish teachers, and allowed the greatest minds of medieval Christendom to embody many of his teachings in their own systems of Catholic theology. In these days of rampant nationalist intolerance, the Jews view with special gratification celebrations like those held in Spain and like ours here, which bear witness to the persistence of the undying springs of human solidarity.

Maimonides appeared at a critical juncture of Jewish history. In the gigantic struggle between Christendom and Islam the Jewish people suffered severely. Religious fanaticism, which had subsided after the first century of Islam's expansion, was reawakened in the age of the Crusades, and in the twelfth century it reigned supreme in both the Christian and the Muslim worlds. Maimonides himself, during his brief sojourn in the Holy Land, had an opportunity to obtain first-hand acquaintance with the desolate conditions of Palestine Jewry, brought about by the massacres and the repressive legislation of the Latin invaders. A part of the Muslim world responded with equal ruthlessness. Maimonides' entire family spent many years in wandering from place to place, because the Almohades of Spain and Morocco had preached violent "unification" of all mankind under the aegis of Islam. Even under the more tolerant rule of Egypt he had to face a grave accusation. One of his Muslim enemies denounced him as a backsliding convert, since, according to rumors, he had adopted Islam in his youth, under Almohade compulsion. In Muslim law such a relapse, even in the case of forcible conversion, constituted a capital crime. Although Maimonides seems to have had no difficulty in disproving that accusation, such a climax to decades of suffering vividly demonstrated to him the insecurity pervading the life of his people. As a result of the dissolution of the great caliphate into small, mutually hostile kingdoms, the formerly flourishing Jewries of the Near East suffered considerable loss in their political and legal status. Having become in the ninth and tenth centuries the great commercial mediators between East and West, linking Marseilles and Cologne with India and China, the Jews now saw their position dwindle to relative insignificance, inasmuch as they could not possibly compete with the heavily armed merchant marine of the Italian republics. To clinch it all came the widespread anarchy in Jewish communal life, since the disjointed Jewries of the dispersion could no longer look for authoritative guidance to the Prince of Captivity and the heads of the two Babylonian academies.

Under these circumstances, Maimonides felt obliged to assume the leadership of the people. Personally of a scholarly and retiring nature, extremely busy with his growing medical practice, for many years in poor health, he nevertheless devoted himself unsparingly to the task of rebuilding Jewish inner life in Egypt, his country of adoption. Although firmly convinced that, in view of the many dangers threatening the survival of Jewry, "all the House of Israel are in duty bound to be united in one indivisible whole, and there should be among them no conflict whatsoever," he could not help being dragged into the controversy raging over the position of the *nagid*, the official head of Egyptian Jewry. It was largely due to his efforts that the iniquitous chief, Zutta, was removed from office a few years after his arrival in Fostat. In contrast to Spain, where the expansion of Karaism had long been held in check, this powerful sect still weakened the cohesive forces of Jewish life in the eastern Mediterranean. Maimonides, always insisting upon humane personal relations with individual sectarians, successfully combated this heresy in Egypt and its environs. He issued many an appeal to distant coreligionists for the ransom of Jewish captives who had fallen into the hands of pirates. In his famous *responsa* to numerous inquirers the world over he not only issued authoritative decisions with respect to the application of individual laws, but established for them broad principles of ethical and legal conduct. Under his direction many a community succeeded in steering clear of difficulties arising from controversial points of law or conflicting social situations. As early as 1172, when Maimonides was only thirty-six years of age, his fame spread even to distant Yemen, whose learned rabbi appealed to him for advice in a difficult case. In his answer, the renowned *Epistle to Yemen*, he dealt primarily with the interrelated problems of Islamic persecution and the Jewish messianic movements. This *Epistle* earned for him the gratitude of the Yemenite Jews to such an extent that they soon included the name of Moses ben Maimon in their daily commemorative prayer, a distinction formerly bestowed only upon the Prince of Captivity as the embodiment of world Jewry's leadership. Far beyond his predecessor Isaac Alfasi, he thus inherited the mantle of the Babylonian masters and became the recognized teacher of all Jewry.

It was to counteract the centrifugal forces in the dispersion that Maimuni undertook the greatest of his life works: the reinterpretation and codification of Jewish law. Like the medieval Muslim and Canon jurists and like his own talmudic predecessors confronted with the problem of reformulating ancient God-given law, he could employ only the method of successive interpretation rather than legislative enactment or abrogation. To achieve this goal he pursued three distinct lines of approach. He first proceeded to reinterpret the entire body of talmudic law in his extensive Arabic commentary on the Mishnah, that basic code of talmudic Judaism. Not confining himself to the elucidation of obscure passages, he prefaced many discussions with elaborate investigations of the underlying principles. Some of these prefatory statements (e.g., his introduction to the commentary on the *Sayings of the Fathers*) have become independent monographs, widely read, frequently translated, and extensively commented upon in subsequent generations. Maimonides soon realized, however, that the orthodox method of heaping explanations upon the utterances of earlier authorities, although extremely popular among his Jewish and Arab predecessors (incidentally also among the Western glossators), did not enable him to present a clean-cut and well organized summary of Jewish law. Following in the footsteps of Ahai of Shabha, an eighth-century authority, he then tried to lay down the basic 613 commandments of Judaism and to point out their numerous ramifications. To this task he devoted another Arabic work, the so-called *Book of Precepts*. These preliminary compilations were finally crowned by his *magnum opus* (*hibbur gadol*), as he himself frequently styled it. Its title was little short of a program: *The Second Torah*. "I have called this work *Mishneh Torah*," the author asserted in a much debated passage of his introduction, "because everybody who has read the written Torah [the five Books of Moses] and then reads this book will know the entire oral law and will not have to study any intervening book." It was a truly monumental attempt to reorganize completely the mass of legal material which had accumulated in a millennial growth, through custom, precedent, and judicial, as well as academic interpretation. To serve its double purpose of a scholarly summary of the entire legal tradition and a practical guide for the rabbi and judge, it was made to embrace the totality of law, no matter how obsolete certain of its parts had already become. The critical reader, however, had no difficulty in separating the anti-quated from the valid norms, theory from practice. He could utilize the theory at least for purposes of juridical analogy. Written with convincing clarity, in a lucid neo-Hebraic style, unparalleled since the days of the Mishnah, all-embracing in subject matter and nevertheless reliable in every legal minutia, the Maimonidean code has become a masterpiece of Hebrew letters and a classic in the history of codification. By virtue of its content it appealed primarily to Jews and to a few Muslim or Christian students of Jewish law. Unlike the *Guide*, it had little influence upon Western medieval letters. Only modern jurists and theologians, such as Hugo Grotius and John Spencer, consulted the work in their researches, while others translated certain chapters of more general interest into Latin and other European languages. But its influ-ence upon medieval Jewish life and literature far transcended that of any other work. Notwithstanding the heated controversy it provoked through its purported attempt to supplant the Talmud, and notwithstanding the recurrent opposition to any kind of codification on the part of those who feared that it might tend to crystallize Jewish law at a particular stage of its development, *The Second Torah* has helped, as did no other medieval book, to illumine the road for the wandering people in the darkest centuries of its history.

One of the main objectives of the Maimonidean codification undoubtedly was to supply a uniform law to the various countries of the dispersion. It was doubly important in that period of great stress, when few people had the leisure to immerse themselves wholeheartedly in the study of the vast talmudic literature and when the forces of provincial separatism threatened to disrupt the body of Israel. Maimonides emphatically proclaimed the basic unity of Jewish law, repeatedly invoking "the common consent of all Israel" or "the spread of the law in all Israel" as a sufficient argument for the undisputed validity of all talmudic regulations. He thereby motivated their strict observance, even in the face of contradictory evidence of more advanced scientific research. For the sake of uniformity he also demanded that the entire people recognize the supremacy of the Babylonian Talmud in all con-troversial matters. As a son of Spain deeply attached to the Babylonian tradition, he realized with serious misgivings that the majority of Egyptian Jewry tenaciously clung to Palestinian rather than Babylonian customs. But this realization merely stimulated his enthusiasm for conformity. Although recognizing the importance of the Palestinian Talmud in a higher degree than any of his Spanish or Babylonian predecessors, Maimuni bluntly declared that "all of Israel are bound to follow everything found in the Babylonian Talmud, and we should force the Jews of every city and country to adhere to all customs established by the talmudic sages."

This anti-Palestinian orientation had, of course, no bearing upon his deep love for the Palestine of the past, his recognition of the exceptional position of the Holy Land in Jewish law, and his firm hope of Israel's ultimate restoration to it in the messianic era (Maimonides himself counted the messianic ideal among the thirteen cardinal principles of Judaism). But it accentuates the underlying Maimonidean philosophy of law, which so radically differs from the modern conception of the inherent nexus between law and state. In Maimonides' opinion, Jewish law, being divinely ordained, is wholly independent of its territorial origin and of the state for which it was first enacted. Both the church and Islam likewise gloried in the supernatural origin of their respective legal systems, Canon jurists in particular stressing the *ius divinum* and the law of nature, which they often identified with the fundamentals of Old Testament law. But for the medieval Jew, far more than for the medieval Christian, the state was the result of sin, although at the same time a remedy for sin. He saw in the loss of his national independence but a well-deserved punishment for his forefathers' sins. On the other hand, he believed that the Exile, as such, expiates for those sins and paves the way for the coming of the redeemer. Maimonides takes pains to emphasize the difference between the messianic age and the hereafter. Jewish messianism, in his opinion, would be realized in this world of ours with the restoration of the Jews to Palestine and the establishment of universal peace between men. In sharp contrast to many antinomian trends in the history of Judaism, moreover, he does not expect the invalidation of Jewish law in the messianic age. On the contrary, in a remarkable passage he explains the messianic hope mainly as the yearning of Israel's prophets and sages to devote themselves unreservedly to the study of the law and to the observance of the divine commandments, without outside interference.

Much in the Maimonidean code may appear abstruse and inconsequential to modern men. Even the orthodox Jew has since replaced it by a sixteenth-century compilation and has found that under the novel conditions of our day, many more sections than originally intended (those treating of civil law, for instance) are of but theoretical value. The liberal Jew repudiates not only the binding force of ceremonial law, but denies to the law, as such, the supreme position in the Jewish religion assigned to it by Maimonides. Many, non-Jews and Jews alike, will differ from the great codifier in his basic outlook on authority and obedience, in his social evaluation of the intellectual minority, perhaps even in his dualistic distinction between body and soul. Few, however, will refrain from admiring the magnificent architectonic structure erected by the great legal systematizer and from appreciating his honest endeavor to find a rational basis for the totality of law and for each individual part. Even today many will take note of passages like the following, taken from the *Guide*, which render certain ultimate objectives of Maimonides, the codifier:

The general object of the law is twofold: the well-being of the soul and the well-being of the body. The well-being of the soul is promoted by correct opinions communicated to the people according to their capacity. Some of these opinions are therefore imparted in a plain form, others allegorically; because certain opinions are in their plain form too strong for the capacity of the common people. The well-being of the body is established by proper management of the relations in which we live one to another. This we can attain in two ways: First by removing all violence from our midst; that is to say, that we do not do everyone as he pleases, desires and is able to do; but everyone of us does that which contributes toward the common welfare. Secondly, by teaching everyone of us such good morals as must produce a good social state. Of these two objects, the one, the well-being of the soul, or the communication of correct opinions, comes undoubtedly first in rank, but the other, the well-being of the body, the government of the state and the establishment of the best possible relations among men, is anterior in nature and time.

CHAPTER TWO

HOMAGE TO MAIMONIDES

By ETIENNE GILSON

TO UNDERSTAND a writer of past ages, it is not enough to give an account of his ideas or of the expression which he had lent them. It is not even sufficient, perhaps, by using the method suggested by Bergson, to approach as closely as possible that simple intuition which underlies his entire doctrine in its mental images and conceptions. In the totality of an author we find much more than the final elaboration of his work, and even much more than its basic initial conception. Innumerable thinkers, perhaps not always of lesser distinction, have carried with them into their graves the secret of their thoughts. In order to become an author, the thinker must have a motive for breaking his silence and for taking that strange and mysterious step, often quite distasteful to him, of taking the public into his confidence. If one were to go back to the source of this decision, I believe that one would find in most cases what Descartes has called "the law which compels us to provide, to the extent of our ability, for the general good of all men." That is why this man who "hated the profession of making books," nevertheless wrote books which have deeply impressed the world.

If there is a case in which the validity of this explanation is no less subject to doubt, it is that of Moses Maimonides. Moses ben Maimon was born March 30, 1135 (fourteenth of Nissan 4895) in Cordova. As the son of a talmudist who combined knowledge of Scripture with that of mathematics and astronomy, Maimonides received from his father a comprehensive education which gave free play to his natural talents. We ought the more readily to

Note: An anniversary lecture delivered in Paris, at the invitation of a Jewish society.

include the father in the tribute rendered the son today, when we consider the extremely difficult conditions under which he lived and taught. Forced by the persecution of the Almohades constantly to change his domicile, Maimon and his three children for twelve years (1148–59) wandered throughout Spain. These hardships did not prevent the young Maimonides, however, from publishing a treatise on *Logic* and, in 1158, an essay on the Hebrew calendar. In 1159 the family fled to Fez, where the situation was but slightly more favorable. It was there that Maimonides wrote his *Epistle on Apostasy*, in order to bring back to the truth those Jews who had allowed themselves to be drawn into Islam, or rather who had succumbed to an almost irresistible pressure. The dangerous repercussions of this publication forced him to leave Morocco with his family on April 18, 1165. After a brief stay in Palestine he went to Alexandria. It is in the Egyptian city of Fustat that the family finally settled down in peace.

Or shall we rather say that it would have found peace if the old father, resembling therein those ancient patriarchs who reached the goal of their journeys only to perish there, had not passed away soon after their arrival in Fustat; and if a brother, upon whose mercantile activities depended their livelihood, had not died in a shipwreck. Left without means, Maimonides decided to practice medicine. He found time, nevertheless, for his literary work and completed in those years his *Luminary*, or commentary on the Mishnah.

This commentary, in the opinion of all historians of Judaism, marks an important date in the history of rabbinic literature. Here Maimonides' whole personality comes to the fore. Not satisfied with merely explaining the literal meaning of the text, he attempts to bring order into its content and on every occasion discusses the scientific problems arising therefrom. It is in this work in particular that, prompted by his characteristic drive toward simplicity and clarity, he has formulated the first "Credo of Judaism," to employ Louis-Germain Lévy's striking expression. May I be permitted to refer, with the same author, to the thirteen articles which, if I am not grievously mistaken, form that part of Maimonides' work which he valued most? God exists; he is unique; he is incorporeal; he is eternal; he alone is to be worshiped; what the prophets have said is true; Moses is the greatest of prophets; the Torah is of divine origin; it is unchangeable; God knows of all our thoughts and all

our deeds; He punishes the wicked and rewards the just; some day
the Messiah will come; and the dead will be resuscitated. Maimonides devoted the rest of his life to the explanation and, wherever
feasible, to the justification of these thirteen articles, at least nine of
which, we must not forget, are common to Judaism and Christianity.

Those who undertake to bring order into ideas must not expect
gratitude from their contemporaries, and usually the very men
whose ideas they try to organize become their worst enemies.
Maimonides' adversaries protested against what they called his
pretension in attempting to regulate the creed for others. Most
remarkably this reproach is still being repeated today. One of his
most renowned interpreters writes that "Maimonides, sensing
heresy in the rejection of any article of the creed formulated by
him, deeply misunderstood the spirit of Judaism, which favors
liberty of thought." I should make myself extremely ridiculous
if I attempted to intervene in this dispute, which has all the earmarks of a family argument. But since I happen to have the great
honor of speaking of our indebtedness to Maimonides, such a
reproach, I dare say, is quite "Hebrew" to me.

Here is a rabbi, the son of a rabbi, who has passed his youth in
Spain, in a country from which he was forced to flee because, on
account of his religion, he was subjected to severe persecution; he
was also obliged to quit Morocco, and even Palestine. Wherever
he went, he saw his coreligionists in hiding, denying their faith,
and outwardly adopting rites and symbols which were not theirs.
How many among them still knew what they were to believe, in
order to remain faithful to their ancestral creed? Even among the
better informed, how many could resist that other pressure, exerted
by Arabic philosophy upon the most cultivated minds of the time?
In this universal confusion, which was more urgent, to encourage
liberty of thought or to save Judaism? I gladly admit that Judaism
may favor liberty of thought, but was it its task to champion such
liberty at a time when its very existence was at stake? For Maimonides this question was far more urgent and less abstract than
it may appear to us today. What he wished to remind his contemporaries was that Judaism is first of all a religion; that a religion
is not based upon liberty of thought, but upon a free acceptance of
a certain way of thinking; that one is perfectly free not to accept
this way of thinking, but that one is not free to repudiate it, if one
pretends to profess that religion.

I allow myself to insist upon this point, because it seems to me that Maimonides' *Commentary* introduces us to the very core of his thought. When nowadays we wish to render him the honor which is his due, we must neither reproach him for not having been a freethinker, nor on the contrary try to prove that he was one. In fact he never cared to be a freethinker, but wished to be, or rather naturally was something entirely different. The basis of all his philosophy, it seems to me, that which accounts for his greatness and which has assured him authority far beyond the sphere of Judaism, was not an ambition to think freely, but a determination always to think of matters as they actually are. I do not know of any other ambition, however modest this may appear, which could be more productive, nor which would be more difficult of attainment.

The high regard in which Maimonides was soon generally held was essentially due to this persistent attitude, which inspired absolute confidence in the integrity of his judgment. One could feel confident that, whatever the circumstances, he would betray nothing, i.e., not that he would never betray any cause or party, but on the contrary that he himself would never accept the point of view of a party or cause. He always spontaneously adopted a standpoint representative of the facts. Holding a prominent position in the Jewish community of Cairo since 1171, he published about 1180 his *Mishneh Torah*, a talmudic code, in which everyone could find, under their proper classification and distinction, the obligatory religious truths, the interpretations of the sages, the moral and philosophic concepts implied in these beliefs, and their authoritative comments. For what purpose this new effort? In order to define the essence of Judaism; in brief, to delimit the confines within which one belongs to that creed, and outside of which one may be whatever one chooses but is not a faithful Jew. Maimonides would have been amazed to learn the praise subsequently showered upon his opponents, because they allegedly upheld against him "the right of the quest for truth and individual investigation." Truth? But he had searched only for truth. Individual investigation? But when he published his work he had offered to his contemporaries the result of twelve years of constant effort and the experience of a lifetime. We may add without hesitation that his adversaries themselves would have been much shocked by our approval. What they defended against Maimonides was not the right of "individual investigation," of which he had given them such a splendid example, but the authenticity of Jewish tradition, that is, the very thing which Maimonides wished to represent. Between them and him there was no question of freethinking but one of correct thinking, i.e., of using the freedom of thought only in order to represent matters as they really are.

This consideration will also help us to obtain a true understanding of Maimonides' most famous work, the *Moreh Nebukim*. The very title of this book, the *Guide for the Perplexed*, as it is rendered in the French translation by the renowned Solomon Munk — to whom I am happy to express, at this juncture, the gratitude owed by all students of medieval thought — or the *Guide for the Irresolute*, which would seem to be the more adequate translation, wonderfully expresses the author's anxious effort, to which I have previously alluded, to write with the aim of assisting men to resolve their perplexities. But who are these perplexed, confused, and irresolute men?

Maimonides knew them well. He had thought of them for a long time before he decided to write his book, but a final stimulus was given him by the case of a young man to whom he was greatly attached and about whom he tells us at the beginning of his work. When the young Joseph ben Yehudah came from far away, as Maimonides says "from the end of the world," to study in Fustat, he was no longer a beginner. As the author of poems revealing a marked predilection for philosophic speculation and of short treatises and *novellae*, he was evidently endowed with very rare qualities. In spite of his prepossession in favor of the young student, the master reserved judgment. To ascertain whether his desire for knowledge was not greater than his capacities, Maimonides applied a special method which is truly illuminating.

Having to do with a poet, he began by guiding him to serious studies in mathematics and astronomy. As young Joseph proved very successful in these studies and even took great pleasure in them, the master left him free to continue them, turning his attention to the study of logic. Only then Maimonides judged him fit to receive "an exposition of the esoteric ideas contained in the prophetic books,"[1] and to be led to the comprehension of what

[1] The *Guide for the Perplexed*, I, Introd. This, as well as all forthcoming quotations, are from M. Friedlaender's English translation.

perfect men ought to understand. The master was then faced by a problem, the difficulties of which he knew all too well, but the solution of which he could no longer delay. Joseph had had other teachers besides Maimonides, and as soon as one began giving him an inkling of certain paramount problems, he wished to learn more about them. The Mutakallimun, Arabic philosophers who played in Islam a role similar to that of the scholastics in Christianity, had raised many grave problems of metaphysics, and their way of solving them must have troubled the conscience of any young, educated, and religious Jew. Of what value were their proofs? Did they offer necessary and convincing evidence, or merely probabilities? So long as they were together, the master tried to satisfy the curiosity of the young man and to appease his inner unrest. Moreover, and there is nothing more revealing about the philosopher himself, he tried to dissuade his pupil from following this line of reasoning. He did not wish to prevent him from raising questions, but to teach him "to continue his studies systematically," so that "the truth should present itself in connected order, and that you should not hit upon it by mere chance." In short, the pupil who wished to find a solution for the philosophic problems arising from Scripture was told that, for their understanding, he must first acquire a thorough grounding in both the Bible and philosophy.

Joseph was still far from reaching this goal when he left his master. It was with him and his like in mind, however small their number, that Maimonides wrote his *Guide for the Irresolute*, a guide for those who, accepting revelation as a matter of faith, do not know how to reconcile it with the teachings of reason. Dedicated to Joseph ben Yehudah, the *Moreh Nebukim* appeared in 1190. In the introduction the author has formulated with remarkable clarity the main problem which, in his opinion, awaited solution.

Arriving now at what I consider the greatest achievement of Maimonides, I should not like to have it thought that the ardor with which I express my admiration is merely a reflection of that official approval which a panegyrist owes to the man whose life and thoughts he describes. We deal here with a problem which is no less vital today than in the time of Maimonides, for you who share his faith; for me, whose faith was born from yours, wherefore I cannot consider myself merely a stranger in your midst; and also (I might say, in particular) for those among us who do not render allegiance to any faith. We deal here with a question as to whether, with respect to religion as well as nature, the proper function of reason is to create its object or merely to understand it. When reason insists upon believing that it creates nature, it wrongs science alone, since nature does not therefore cease to exist. But when reason pretends to regulate religion or, in the words of Kant, to hold it "within the limits of reason," it threatens the very existence of religion. Now religion, that feeling of being "tied up," together with the wholeness of nature, to a mysterious and divine source of life, this is, for the believer, life itself in its deepest meaning. From it he derives his entire way of thinking, feeling, and acting; it determines his attitude toward men, events, and things. In the presence of this reality, to which he adheres with his whole soul but which far transcends him, what can his reason do? It can neither give up itself, nor give up reality; it merely may attach itself to reality as to the highest of its objects and to try to understand it, without measuring it by its own standards. It is the mark of great intelligence, applying itself to whatever order of reality, to respect that reality.

It is this respect which accounts for the greatness of Maimonides. He was surrounded by a great number of religious men who lived according to the law and were not bothered by any problem. What would have been the purpose of disturbing those? He saw other men who devoted themselves, either by avocation or professionally, to the study of the law and of its traditional interpretation by the sages. Nor is it to these men that he addressed himself, except when he reminded them of the fundamentals taught by the law, neglect of which was tantamount to its betrayal. But he also knew of a third group of men who, like young Joseph, were at once believers and students of philosophy and, as such, exposed to the twofold danger of losing their faith and their philosophy, since they could not lose one without the other. How can a philosopher believe in his law, if he must sacrifice for it what his reason tells him to be true? But how can a true believer have any confidence in his philosophy, if he can uphold it only by renouncing his law? Hence comes, says Maimonides in various connections, the indecision and confusion of these men; hence also his desire to come to their assistance and his decision to write the *Guide* so as to help them overcome their difficulties.

Let us consider for a moment the attitude of this great thinker, for it is possible that many among us are very much puzzled by it.

Faced with the same problem, what would one of our contemporaries do, or rather what is he likely to do? We know very well: he will sacrifice his faith, often even without the slightest hesitation. Is it not the absolute duty of man to follow the demands of his reason in every instance? Maimonides will thus appear to the majority of our contemporaries, and especially to those who claim to be scientists or philosophers, as the representative of a bygone era, perhaps even as a dangerous example of those reactionary minds of the past who tried with the aid of formulas to reconcile mythical beliefs with the conclusions of reason.

I am not here to plead the cause of Maimonides, but I should like at least to make his attitude understandable, for we would be grievously mistaken if we assumed that he had failed to see this objection. Not only did he see it, but he examined it from all angles, and, were he in our midst today, I believe that after assimilating the last conclusions of our science and philosophy he would have no reason for changing any of his conclusions. What is his first advice to the "irresolute" reader? Thoroughly to study the sciences, beginning with physics, because in the final analysis the first book of the Bible is nothing but a physical interpretation of the universe, written in pictorial and simple terms for the use of ignorant persons. However, he immediately adds, if the Bible is obscure, physics is no less so, a circumstance of which the scientists of any historical period are not always sufficiently aware. The obscurity of physics is exceeded by that of philosophy. If Maimonides could observe us teaching these sciences today, he would greatly question our understanding of the necessary prerequisites for both teachers and pupils. Do we take sufficient cognizance of the psychological, as well as the social consequences of universal instruction in the highest ranges of knowledge, as if we would be entitled to expect from everyone to be able to understand the results of these sciences without having previously studied them?

This was of supreme interest to Maimonides, and I wonder whether we, too, ought not seriously to consider the question. First of all, there is no instruction without a preparatory, as well as a parallel, moral education: "a man, when he commences to speculate, ought not to embark at once on a subject so vast and important; he should previously adapt himself to the study of the several branches of science and knowledge, should most thoroughly refine his moral character and subdue his passions and desire, the offspring of his imagination." Moreover, Maimonides, like all medieval thinkers, is convinced that not all objects of knowledge are equally accessible to reason, and that the higher the objects the more prudence and restraint we ought to exercise in voicing our opinions. Man should "not decide any question by the first idea that suggests itself to his mind or at once direct his thoughts and force them to obtain a knowledge of the Creator; he must wait modestly and patiently, and advance step by step. In this sense we must understand the words: 'And Moses hid his face, for he was afraid to look upon God'" (Exod. 3:6).[2] What Maimonides demands from us is not that we give up science but, on the contrary, that we thoroughly investigate the nature of the evidence presented by our reason. To be sure, from time to time some prophets appear among us, men who see light in the darkness engulfing all others, but very rarely do they perceive such a new lightning flash more than once in a lifetime. The majority of us are not even among those to whom "the flashes of lightning appear with varying intervals." They are "in the condition of men, whose darkness is illumined not by lightning, but by some kind of crystal or similar stone, or other substances that possess the property of shining during the night; and to them even this small amount of light is not continuous, but now it shines and now it vanishes, as if it were 'the flame of the rotating sword'."[3]

Maimonides would gladly say, with Henri Poincaré — or rather, he said it before him — that thought is but a flash of light in a long night. He would not admit, however, that it is this flash alone that matters. No, it is the night that matters, that mysterious night of existence, full of dark potentialities, which surrounds us who see just enough to perceive the night, but not enough to bring light to bear upon it. What the flash rending the night for a moment unveils, the glittering of the stones which our eye perceives, was not created by our reason; it merely perceives them. It is salutary, indeed, for reason to remember the darkness in which it found them.

This intellectual modesty, which differs alike from presumption and skepticism, was, if I am not mistaken, the paramount quality of Maimonides. If I did not fear to give it a name debased through

[2] The *Guide for the Perplexed*, I, 5.
[3] The *Guide for the Perplexed*, I, Introd., with reference to Gen. 3:24.

usage, I should say that it was common sense, for I know of no rarer or more necessary quality. Let us consider, for instance, how Maimonides deals with the philosophers whose works had disturbed his pupil's mind. He does not question whether their philosophy has the right to exist, but whether it is philosophy. Have they proved what they contend to be true? Have they demonstrated that the opposite of their contention is false? That is the only question. "Our beliefs are contradicted by what philosophy has proved," complained the young men of his circle. This may be so, Maimonides quietly replied, but do you know exactly what philosophy does prove? Do you even know exactly what it is that you believe?

Hence arises the twofold aspect of his *Guide.* Here he first explains that the assertion of Scripture concerning God must not be taken literally. The law was not written to teach experts in physics or metaphysics; it addresses itself to all men and therefore uses a simple and picturesque language which is clear to all men. That is why a theologian's work must properly begin with the search for the spiritual and rational meaning which is hidden behind the letter of the law. This is, indeed, the task accomplished by Maimonides, in a manner wonderfully displaying his deliberate method. The quest for the spiritual meaning does not consist in reading whatever one wishes into a text; on the contrary, the more one wishes to understand the spiritual, the surer must one be of the literal term. Maimonides always first ascertains the precise meaning of the words by tracing them back to their original roots. Wherever he suspects some ambiguity, he compares the Hebrew term with its Arabic equivalent. Only after completing this preparatory work, incessantly repeated with respect to every name given to God in the Bible, does our exegete indicate the spiritual meaning of the word under discussion. At this juncture the theologian succeeds the philologist, and it is a pleasure to observe in every case with what masterly assurance he draws out of the literal term the meaning hidden behind it.

In order to understand the full implication of this part of his work, one must remember Maimonides' evaluation of the greatness of man, or rather his definition of human nature. We read in the Bible that God created man "in our image, after our likeness." A great subject for meditation by our author! A scholarly exegete had once remarked to him that, according to the revealed text, the knowledge of good and evil seems to have come to man as a consequence of his sin. "And ye shall be as gods knowing good and evil" (Gen. 3:5). If I cite this example of the Maimonidean exegesis, it is because it introduces us to the very core of his thought. He is profoundly shocked by such an interpretation, which assumes that

man was originally intended to be perfectly equal to the rest of the animal creation which is not endowed with intellect, reason or power of distinguishing between good and evil: but that Adam's disobedience to the command of God procured him the great perfection which is the peculiarity of man, viz., the power of distinguishing between good and evil — the noblest of all the faculties of our nature, the essential characteristic of the human race. It thus appears strange that the punishment for rebelliousness should be the means of elevating man to a pinnacle of perfection to which he had not attained previously. This is equivalent to saying that a certain man was rebellious and extremely wicked, wherefore his nature was changed for the better, and he was made to shine as a star in the heavens.[4]

For Maimonides, man was not merely an animal like other animals, endowed, *in addition*, with reason; if God has created man in his image and likeness, he did it precisely by endowing him with reason. This term is to be understood, moreover, in its deepest sense. Reason "which God granted to man," and which constitutes his ultimate perfection, is only, as it appears to us today, a capacity to choose the most probable among various probabilities. Adam's reason, the reason of a man who had just come from the hand of God, is true reason, reason as such, which discriminates between true and false and recognizes no intermediary truth between what is evidently true or evidently false. We may say, by way of historic phantasy (which contains however, an element of truth), that human reason before the fall was precisely such as Descartes still believed man to possess, namely that "he [Adam] was not able to follow or to understand the principles of apparent truths," or mere probabilities.[5]

Reason is more than an ornament of man, it is man himself; although injured by the fall, it still remains the essence of humanity. We are still obliged to cultivate it, in order to bring it to the perfection of which it remains capable. It would be a fatal error to

[4] The *Guide for the Perplexed*, I, 2.
[5] The *Guide for the Perplexed*, I, 2.

believe that man carries in himself the image of God through the mere fact of his existence. For what is intelligence without knowledge? Adam had begotten many sons before Seth, says our exegete, but Seth was the first to be begotten "in his own likeness" (Gen. 5:3), because Seth was the first whom Adam "instructed, enlightened and brought to human perfection." What are, in reality, men deprived of knowledge?

It is acknowledged that a man who does not possess this "form" (the nature of which has just been explained) is not human, but a mere animal in human shape and form. Yet such a creature has the power of causing harm and injury . . . as though he merely resembled man, or simulated his outward appearance.[6]

This deep feeling that it is only reason which accounts for the greatness of man and that its possession also proves the divine nature of our origin furnishes us an essential link assuring the unity of the Maimonidean doctrine. Maimonides is neither an eclectic nor a harmonizer counseling faith to live with reason, or reason to live with faith. Every effort of reason to know the truth attests God's presence in us and may hence be rightly considered as on an equality with prayer. What our theologian styles "to be with God," is also what he calls "comprehension by intelligence." Where we might be tempted to see but a naive or a calculated effort to bring into agreement opposing points of view, Maimonides sees only the unity of reason, in which speculation blends with meditation. How must we admire the grandeur of this life, once we comprehend the mainsprings of its inspiration!

We do not sit, move, and occupy ourselves when we are alone and at home, in the same manner as we do in the presence of a great king; we speak and open our mouth as we please when we are with the people of our own household and with our relatives, but not so when we are in a royal assembly. If we therefore desire to attain human perfection, and to be truly men of God, we must awake from our sleep and bear in mind that the great king that is over us, and is always joined to us, is greater than any earthly king, greater than David and Solomon. The king that cleaves to us and embraces us is the Intellect that influences us, and forms the link between us and God.

6 The *Guide for the Perplexed*, I, 7.

It is by means of this light that God sees us and that we see God; hence that chastity in our daily life, born of the feeling of being always in the presence of the divine majesty. Hence also that noble pride which finds expression in the sage's conduct and appearance. He may be exiled, persecuted, insulted, but he will not uncover his head, because, as Maimonides says, God's glory "is round him and above him."[7] Therein also we shall unmistakably find the secret of his philosophic attitude and of the extraordinary freedom of thought which it reveals. Maimonides knows what God has said, and he knows that it is true; it is quite another matter in regard to what men might say. We might formulate it in this way: he is freed from the human word by the word of God. That is why, far from hastening to accept as so many evident truths everything the philosophers have said about God or even in honor of God, he reveals a constant anxiety not to compromise the law by placing it in the service of philosophy. But for the same reason he absolutely distrusts that particular brand of philosophy which might be designated the pietist philosophy, for if God is present in us through our intelligence, the purest form of worship which we can offer him is the worship of truth.

A pietist philosophy is something akin to the doctrine of the Mutakallimun, the study of which had caused much confusion in the heads of his pupils. Maimonides was perfectly aware of its origin; he has even left us some lines about it which our modern historians could profitably apply in their investigations. Maimonides tells us in essence that philosophy has come from the Greeks and that when the Christian church had been embraced by the Greeks and the Syrians, the sages of these nations then living realized that their philosophy did not agree with their faith. Consequently they tried to refute the philosophers, in order to put an end to this great and conspicuous contradiction. They laid the foundation for this science of dogmatics (Kalam); they "commenced by putting forth such propositions as would support their doctrines, and be useful for the refutation of opinions opposed to the fundamental principles of the Christian religion." Among these Christian sages was, for example, Philoponus. The Arabs at first merely

[7] The *Guide for the Perplexed*, III, 52.

became the disciples of the sages in answering the philosophic arguments advanced by the adversaries of their creed. In short, stated in modern terms, Maimonides suggests that Christian apologetics was the main source for the Muslim Kalam. [8]

Two significant qualifications must be made, in Maimonides' opinion, showing his truly remarkable historic insight. From the beginning, Muslim theology, born of the Christian reaction against the philosophers, found itself much further removed from the plane of Greek philosophy than that of the latter's Christian assailants. Little wonder, then, that it soon pursued a devious course, which neither the Greek philosophers nor their Christian opponents, still very close to the Greeks, had even envisaged. Subsequently this newborn speculation forgot its apologetic origin and began to view itself as pure philosophy:

This course was followed by able men who originated this method, and adopted it in their writings, they professed to be free from preconceived opinions, and to have been led to a stated result by actual research. Therefore when philosophers of a subsequent date studied the same writings they did not perceive the true character of the arguments, on the contrary, they found in the ancient works strong proofs and a valuable support for the acceptance or the rejection of certain opinions, and thus thought that, so far as religious principles were concerned, there was no necessity whatever to prove or refute any of their propositions, and that the first Mutakallemim had discussed those subjects with the sole object of defeating certain views of the philosophers, and demonstrating the insufficiency of their proofs. [9]

This ignorance of the true nature of their work was also an initial mistake of those Arab theologians, greatly vitiating their doctrines. One might say that the essential point for them was to show that things are as they are only by virtue of reality and, as it were, of habit, but that the opposite would be equally possible from the standpoint of reason. These theologians, and the Jewish theologians who had followed them, thus tried to safeguard God's rights by curtailing the necessity of nature. They believed they would thus be able to prove the creation in time, and hence the existence of God, *qua* creator, his being unique, permanent, eternal, and distinguished by the other attributes of the first cause. Mai-

---

[8] The *Guide for the Perplexed*, I, 71.
[9] The *Guide for the Perplexed*, I, 71.

monides wondered: no philosopher had ever proved that the world was created in time. On the contrary, the concept of creation in time, i.e., the idea that the world had a beginning, contradicts our ideas of both the necessity and the stability of the laws of nature. Incidentally, that is why these theologians have taught a conception of the world in which nothing seems to follow a necessary course, but in which all matters reduce themselves to a succession of momentary and disrupted phenomena which do not last nor follow a particular order, nor seem to react upon one another except by the sole will of God.

What have these theologians achieved by taking such a stand? They have created a poor philosophy by eliminating the natural order, but theirs was also a poor theology because they had tried to build the knowledge of God on the foundation of a worthless philosophy. Maimonides' great merit consisted in putting everything back to its legitimate place, and that is why his influence rightly extended beyond his coreligionists, to whom he addressed himself directly, to all the great Christian theologians of the thirteenth century. Because Maimonides had worked for them as well, it is perhaps among them that he found his most brilliant disciples, at least in this particular period. In his remarkable book on Maimonides, Louis-Germain Lévy has well demonstrated the influence wielded by "Rabbi Moyses," as he was then called, upon the Christian Middle Ages. Alexander of Hales, Vincent de Beauvais, Albert the Great, St. Thomas Aquinas, and Duns Scotus quoted him as an authority and borrowed from him more than one idea. But rather than to enumerate the texts, the reading of which might prove tiresome and which would reveal the spread rather than the profundity of Maimonides' influence, we ought to examine here the causes and the nature of this influence.

What the Christian Middle Ages owe to Maimonides more than this or that particular doctrine is the example set and the encouragement given by his admirable intellectual integrity. Like Jewish theology, that of the Christian world was deeply menaced by the formidable temptation of confusing the two legitimate domains of philosophy and religion, and of falsifying philosophy in order to derive from it proofs for the authenticity of one's faith. The unavoidable result would have been the possession of neither philosophy nor faith, since to act in this manner is to reveal complete ignorance of both the nature of faith and of that of evidence.

The mark of true wisdom, on the contrary, is to believe firmly in what one believes and to know well what one knows. One soon realizes that true knowledge, if we do not allow our imagination to lose itself in unverifiable hypotheses, well harmonizes with a belief which cannot be proved. By adopting this attitude, Maimonides bequeathed to our western Middle Ages the example of a theology in which belief has retained its transcendence, while philosophy, utilized for the explanation of belief, has remained a true philosophy.

This doctrine, which sacrifices nothing indispensable for human life, for in it everything is differentiated and put in its proper place, sets an example from which our own time, too, could greatly benefit. For the first time since the beginning of the world, or at least since the beginning of civilization, we witness today the spectacle of man's reasoned attempt to live without religion. This experiment, for a long time conducted only by philosophers, is now being tried out by entire nations — you all know but too well with what success. Is it too late for the great theologians of Judaism and Christianity to remind us of the mystery of our existence, within the framework of our universe? Is it altogether impossible for a Maimonides still to teach us to perceive not only the provisional limits of our science and philosophy, but also those eternal limits imposed upon us by the profound mystery of existence all around us? We would not have to sacrifice any dictate of reason; on the contrary, we would merely rid reason of those vain imaginations which we mistake for science, but which are only the fictitious extensions of what little knowledge man really has. We would thus learn to respect in faith that charitable and creative force which, far beyond man's knowledge by which he cannot live, guides him toward those elements of hope and love which are indispensable for his survival.

In suggesting to you this example, I am perfectly aware of the diffidence of many among you toward what I have said, as well as toward what I may appear to be doing. But allow me to say in conclusion that I believe I know very well what I have done. I have tried to warn you against the widespread prejudice that progress of knowledge is identical with human progress, from which position it is but one step to the belief that knowledge may dispense with everything else — a credo of scientific barbarism. This prejudice is as dangerous as it is erroneous. To be sure, in comparison with a student armed with an elementary textbook today Maimonides knew very little of the facts of our world, but he possessed the most important thing besides knowledge, namely the true quality of the knowing mind and the knowledge of how to utilize available information. To put it in a nutshell, there exists a type of wisdom which, while of necessity reconciled with a measure of ignorance (and is not the science of the most advanced period only the ignorance of tomorrow?), radically excludes all and any barbarisms. This wisdom, I believe, would permit Rabbi Moyses to appreciate at its true value if not our science, at least the use to which we put it. It is this wisdom alone which I have wished to describe and to offer as an example, because I see in Maimonides' teaching nothing that could be more beneficial, nothing that could be greater, even for our time.

The best way to pay Maimonides the homage we owe is to accept him simply for what he really was — a man of God. Fourteen years after the publication of his *Guide* (December 13, 1204) Maimonides died, mourned by Muslims and Jews alike. A legend tells us that at his funeral the reading of a passage in Leviticus was followed by one taken from I Samuel 4, and ending with the words: "The glory is departed from Israel; for the ark of God is taken." No, this ark was not taken; it will never be taken, so long as we Christians and Jews remain there to guard it in unison. May the great personality of Maimonides remain among us as the living symbol of everything that binds us! In order better to feel this unity, let us recollect the great teaching bequeathed to us by him, summarized by him in the following injunction: to be "with our heart constantly near God, even whilst our body is in the society of men."[10] In 1935, as in 1135, there is no sage, no philosopher, and no saint who could propose to us a nobler formula for living.

[10] The *Guide for the Perplexed*, III, 51.

CHAPTER THREE

THE LITERARY CHARACTER OF THE
GUIDE FOR THE PERPLEXED

By LEO STRAUSS

ἡ γὰρ ὕστερον εὐπορία λύσις τῶν πρότερον ἀπορουμένων ἐστί, λύειν δ'οὐκ
ἔστιν ἀγνοοῦντας τὸν δεσμόν.   ARISTOTLE

AMONG the many historians who have interpreted Maimonides'
teaching, or who are making efforts to interpret it, there is
scarcely one who would not agree to the principle that that teaching, being essentially medieval, cannot be understood by starting
from modern presuppositions. The differences of view between
students of Maimonides have thus to be traced back, not necessarily to a disagreement concerning the principle itself, but rather
to its different interpretation, or to a difference of attitude in its
application. The present essay is based on the assumption that
only through its most thoroughgoing application can we arrive
at our goal, the true and exact understanding of Maimonides'
teaching.[1]

1. THE SUBJECT MATTER

The interpreter of the *Guide for the Perplexed* ought to raise, to
begin with, the following question: To which science or sciences
does the subject matter of the work belong? Maimonides answers
it almost at the very beginning of his work by saying that it is
devoted to the true science of the law.

[1] In the footnotes Roman and Arabic figures before the parentheses indicate
the part and chapter of the *Guide*, respectively. The figures in the parentheses
before the semicolon indicate the page in Munk's edition, and figures following
the semicolon indicate pages and lines in Joel's edition. For the first book of
the *Mishneh Torah*, I have used M. Hyamson's edition (New York, 1937).

The true science of the law is distinguished from the science of the law in the usual sense, i. e., the *fiqh*.[2] While the term *fiqh* naturally occurs in the *Guide* on more than one occasion, the explanation of its meaning has been reserved for almost the very end of the work. *Fiqh* is the exact determination, by way of "deduction" from the authoritative statements of the law, of those actions by means of which man's life becomes noble, and especially of the actions of worship.[3] Its most scientific treatment would consist in a coherent and lucid codification of the law, such as achieved by Maimonides in his *Mishneh Torah*, which he calls "our great work on the *fiqh*." In contradistinction to the legalistic study of the law, which is concerned with what man ought to do, the true science of the law is concerned with what man ought to think and to believe.[4] One may say that the science of the law in general is divided into two parts: a practical part which is treated in the *Mishneh Torah*, and a theoretical part which is treated in the *Guide*. This view is confirmed by the fact that the former work deals with beliefs and opinions only insofar as they are implied in prohibitions and commands, whereas the *Guide* deals with commands and prohibitions only in order to explain their reasons.

The relation between the two parts, or kinds, of the science of the law, may be described in a somewhat different way by saying that, whereas science of the law in the usual sense is the study of the halakah, the true science of the law corresponds to the aggadah. As a matter of fact, the *Guide* is a substitute for two books, planned by Maimonides, on the nonlegal sections of the Bible and the Talmud. But, above all, its most important feature, which distinguishes it from all philosophic as well as halakic books, is also characteristic of a part of the aggadic literature.[5]

Since Maimonides, however, uses an Islamic term to designate the ordinary science of the law, it may be worth while to consider what Islamic term would supply the most proper designation for that science of the law which is the subject of the *Guide*. Students of the *fiqh* deal with the actions prescribed by the law, but do not

---

[2] I, Introd. (3a; 2, 14 f., 26 f.).

[3] III, 54 (132b; 467, 20–25); cf. III, 27 (59b; 371, 29); 51 (123b; 455, 21–22).

[4] II, 10 (22b; 190, 14); I, Introd. (11a–b; 13, 3–5). Cf. the passages quoted in note 3.

[5] I, Introd. (5b and 11b; 5, 18 ff. and 13, 12–15). Cf. I, 70 (92b; 120, 4–8); 71 (94a; 121, 25–28).

deal with the "roots of religion," i.e., they do not attempt to prove the opinions or beliefs taught by the law. There seems to be little doubt that the science dealing with those roots is identical with the true science of the law.[6] Since the students of the roots are identified by Maimonides with the *Mutakallimûn*, the students of the *kalâm*, we shall say that the true science of the law is the *kalâm*.[7] It is true that Maimonides vigorously attacks the *kalâm*; yet in spite of his ruthless opposition to the assumptions and methods of the *Mutakallimûn*, he professes to be in perfect harmony with their intention.[8] The intention of the science of *kalâm* is to defend the law, especially against the opinions of philosophers.[9] And the central section of the *Guide* is admittedly devoted to the defense of the principal root of the law, the belief in creation, against the contention of the philosophers that the visible world is eternal.[10] What distinguishes Maimonides' *kalâm* from the *kalâm* proper is his insistence on the fundamental difference between intelligence and imagination, whereas, as he asserts, the *Mutakallimûn* mistake imagination for intelligence. In other words, Maimonides insists on the necessity of starting from evident presuppositions, which are in accordance with the nature of things, whereas the *kalâm* proper starts from arbitrary presuppositions, which are chosen not because they are true but because they make it easy to prove the beliefs taught by the law. Maimonides' true science of the law and the *kalâm* thus belong to the same genus,[11] the specific difference between them being that the *kalâm* proper is imaginative, whereas that of Maimonides is an intelligent, or enlightened *kalâm*.

The tentative descriptions of the true science of the law which have been set forth thus far are useful, and even indispensable, for the purpose of counteracting certain views more commonly held of

[6] III, 51 (123b–124a; 455, 21–23). Cf. III, 54 (132a–b; 467, 7–9) with I, Introd. (3a; 2, 12–14).

[7] I, 71 (96b–97a; 125, 12). Cf. I, 73 (105b; 136, 2). Maimonides was called a שרשי by Messer Leon; see Steinschneider, *Jewish Literature*, p. 310.

[8] II, 19 (40a; 211, 24–25); I, 71 (97b; 126, 4–5). Cf. also I, 73 (111b; 143, 6).

[9] Farabi, *'Iḥṣâ al-'ulûm*, chap. 5. (See the Hebrew translation in Falakera's *Reshit Hokmah*, ed. David, pp. 59 ff.) Farabi's discussion of the *kalâm*, and the framework of that discussion, are of decisive importance for the understanding of the *Guide*. Cf. also Plato's *Laws*, X, 887b8 and 890d4–6. I, 71 (94b, 95a; 122, 19–22; 123, 2–3).

[10] I, 71 (96a; 124, 18–19); II, 17 (37a; 207, 27–28).

[11] Cf. Aristotle, *Eth. Nic.*, 1098a8–10.

the character of the *Guide*. In order to arrive at a more definitive description of the subject matter of that work, we have to make a fresh start by reminding ourselves again of the authoritative statements with which it opens.

Maimonides states that the intention of his work is to explain the meaning of biblical words of various kinds, as well as of biblical parables. Such an explanation is necessary, because the external meaning of both lends itself to grave misunderstanding. Since the internal meaning, being hidden, is a secret, the explanation of each such word or parable is the revelation of a secret. The *Guide* as a whole is thus devoted to the revelation of the secrets of the Bible.[12] *Secret*, however, has manifold meanings. It may refer to the secret hidden by a parable or word, but it also may mean the parable or word itself which hides a secret. With reference to the second meaning, the *Guide* may more conveniently be said to be devoted to the explanation of the secrets of the Bible. Thus the true science of the law is nothing other than the explanation of the secrets of the Bible, and in particular of the Torah.

There are as many secrets of the Torah as there are passages in it requiring explanation.[13] Nevertheless, it is possible to enumerate at least the most momentous secret topics. According to one enumeration, these topics are: divine attributes, creation, providence, divine will and knowledge, prophecy, names of God. Another enumeration, which seems to be more lucid, presents the following order: *Ma'aseh bereshit* (the account of creation), *ma'aseh merkabah* (the account of the chariot, Ezekiel 1 and 10), prophecy, and the knowledge of God.[14] Whatever may be the relation between those two enumerations, it is certain that *ma'aseh bereshit* and *ma'aseh merkabah* occupy the highest rank among the secrets of the Bible. Therefore, Maimonides can say that the first intention, or the chief intention of the *Guide* is the explanation of *ma'aseh bereshit* and *ma'aseh merkabah*. The true science of the law is concerned with the explanation of the secrets of the Bible, and especially with the explanation of *ma'aseh bereshit* and of *ma'aseh merkabah*.[15]

[12] I, Introd. (2b–3b, 6a, 6b–7a; 2, 6–29; 6, 12–19; 7, 10–8, 3). Cf. *ibid*. (2a, 8a; 1, 14; 9, 6).

[13] See in particular III, 50 *in princ*.

[14] I, 35 (42a; 54, 20–26); II, 2 (11a–b; 176, 18–23).

[15] II, 29 (65b; 243, 17–19); III, Introd. (2a; 297, 5–7). Cf. the distinction between *fiqh* and secrets of the Torah in I, 71 (93b; 121, 20–22) with the dis-

2. A PHILOSOPHIC WORK?

The finding that the *Guide* is devoted to the explanation of the secret teaching of the Bible seems to be a truism. Yet it is pregnant with the consequence that the *Guide* is not a philosophic book.

The fact that we are inclined to call it a philosophic book is derived from the circumstance that we use the word "philosophy" in a rather broad sense. We commonly do not hesitate, for example, to count the Greek Sophists among the philosophers and we even speak of philosophies underlying mass movements. The present usage may be traced back to the separation of philosophy from science — a separation which has taken place during the modern centuries. For Maimonides, who knew nothing of "systems of philosophy" and consequently nothing of the emancipation of sober science from those lofty systems, philosophy has a much narrower, or a much more exact meaning than it has at the present time. It is not an exaggeration to say that for him philosophy is practically identical with the teaching as well as the methods of Aristotle, "the prince of the philosophers," and of the Aristotelians.[16] And he is an adversary of philosophy thus understood. It is against the opinions of "*the* philosophers"[17] that he defends the Jewish creed. And what he opposes to the wrong opinions of *the* philosophers is not a true philosophy, and in particular not a religious philosophy, or a philosophy of religion, but "our opinion, i.e., the opinion of our law," or the opinion of "us, the community of the adherents of the law," or the opinion of the "followers of the law of our teacher Moses."[18] He obviously assumes that the philosophers form a

---

tinction between *fiqh* and the true science of the law at the beginning of the work. For an interpretation, see A. Altmann, "Das Verhältnis Maimunis zur jüdischen Mystik," *Monatsschrift für Geschichte und Wissenschaft des Judentums,* LXXX (1936), 305–30.

[16] I, 5 *in princ.*; II, 23 (51a; 225, 4). I. Heinemann goes too far, however, in stating (*Die Lehre von der Zweckbestimmung des Menschen im griechisch-römischen Altertum und im jüdischen Mittelalter* [Breslau, 1926], p. 99, n. 1) that "*Failasûf* heisst nicht Philosoph, sondern steht für Aristoteles oder Aristoteliker." Cf. I, 17, 71 (94b; 122, 26–28); II, 21 (47b; 220, 20); III, 16 (31a; 334, 22–24), where *falsafa* or *falâsifa* other than Aristotelian are mentioned.

[17] Cf., for instance, III, 16 *in princ.*

[18] Cf., for instance, II, 21 (47a; 220, 17 f.); II, 26 (56a; 230, 30); III, 17 (34b; 338, 21), 21 (44b; 351, 17–18).

group[19] distinguished from the group of adherents of the law and that both groups are mutually exclusive. Since he himself is an adherent of the law, he cannot possibly be a philosopher, and consequently a book of his in which he explains his views concerning all important topics cannot possibly be a philosophic book. This is not to deny that he acknowledges, and even stresses, the accordance which exists between the philosophers and the adherents of the law in every respect except as regards the question (which, however, is the decisive question) of the creation of the world. For certainly such an accordance between two groups proves their nonidentity.

There is, perhaps, no greater service that the historian can render to the philosopher of our time than to supply the latter with the materials necessary for the reconstruction of an adequate terminology. Consequently, the historian is likely to deprive himself of the greatest benefit which he can grant both to others and to himself, if he is ashamed to be a micrologist. We shall, then, not hesitate to refrain from calling the *Guide* a philosophic book. To justify fully our procedure we only have to consider Maimonides' division of philosophy. According to him, philosophy consists of two parts, theoretical philosophy and practical philosophy; theoretical philosophy in its turn is subdivided into mathematics, physics, and metaphysics; and practical philosophy consists of ethics, economics, "government of the city," and "government of the great nation or of the nations."[20] It is obvious that the *Guide* is not a work on mathematics or economics; and there is practically complete agreement among the students of Maimonides that it is not devoted to political science of either kind. Nor is it an ethical treatise, since Maimonides expressly excludes ethical topics from the *Guide*.[21] The only sciences, then, to which that work could possibly be devoted are physics and metaphysics, which occupy

---

[19] That kind of group, one individual case of which is the group of the philosophers, is called by Maimonides פרקה or פריק (Ibn Tibbon: כת. The Greek equivalent is αἵρεσις; cf. G. Bergsträsser, *Hunain ibn Ishâq über die syrischen und arabischen Galen-Uebersetzungen*, Leipzig, 1925, p. 3 of the Arabic text); cf. II, 15 (33a; 203, 17 f.); III, 20 (42a; 348, 16).

[20] *Millot ha-higgayon*, ch. 14. Cf. H. A. Wolfson, "The Classification of the Sciences in Mediaeval Jewish Philosophy," *Hebrew Union College Jubilee Volume*, 1925, pp. 263–315.

[21] III, 8 *in fine*. Cf. I, Introd. (11a–b; 13, 3–5).

the highest rank among the sciences.[22] This view seems to be confirmed by Maimonides' professions (1) that the chief intention of the *Guide* is to explain *ma'aseh bereshit* and *ma'aseh merkabah*, and (2) that *ma'aseh bereshit* is identical with physics, and *ma'aseh merkabah* with metaphysics.[23] For these two statements seem to lead to the inference that the chief intention of the *Guide* is to treat of physics and metaphysics. This inference is contradicted, however, by another express statement of Maimonides, according to which all physics and an unlimited number of metaphysical topics are excluded from the *Guide*. He mentions in this connection particularly the doctrine of separate intelligences.[24] Thus the only philosophic subject treated, as such, in the *Guide* seems to be the doctrine of God.[25] But Maimonides excludes further all subjects proved, or otherwise satisfactorily treated by the philosophers and leaves no doubt that the philosophers succeeded in proving the existence of God as well as his unity and incorporeity.[26] In accordance with this, Maimonides clearly states that these three doctrines do not belong to the secrets of the Torah,[27] and hence neither to *ma'aseh bereshit* nor to *ma'aseh merkabah*, the principal subjects of the *Guide*. Thus we are led to the conclusion that no philosophic topic of any kind is, as such, the subject matter of the *Guide*.

We are then confronted with the perplexing contradiction that Maimonides, on the one hand, identifies the main subjects of the *Guide* with physics and metaphysics, the most exalted topics of philosophy, while on the other hand he excludes from the field of his investigation every subject satisfactorily treated by the philosophers. To solve that contradiction one might suggest that the *Guide* is devoted to the discussion of such "physical" and "metaphysical" topics as are not satisfactorily treated by the philosophers. This would amount to saying that the subjects of the *Guide* are

[22] III, 51 (124a; 456, 1–4).

[23] I, Introd. (3b; 3, 8–9). Cf. n. 15.

[24] II, 2 (11a–12a; 176, 3–27). Cf. also I, 71 (97b; 126, 13–15). As regards the philosophic doctrine of the sublunary world, cf. II, 22 (49b–50a; 223, 15–17); for that of the soul, cf., I, 68 *in princ.*

[25] Notice the identification of *ma'aseh merkabah*, or metaphysics, with the doctrine of God in I, 34 (40b; 52, 24–25).

[26] I, 71 (96b; 124, 29–125, 6); II, 2 (11a–12a; 176, 3–27). Cf. II, 33 (75a; 256, 21–25).

[27] I, 35.

"physics" and "metaphysics," insofar as these transcend philosophy, and consequently that the *Guide* is not a philosophic book.

Yet the objection may be raised that this suggestion disregards Maimonides' explicit and unqualified identification of *ma'aseh bereshit* with physics and of *ma'aseh merkabah* with metaphysics. If we assume for the time being that this objection is sound, we seem to have no choice but to admit that the question of the subject matter of the *Guide* does not allow of any answer whatsoever. But, as a matter of fact, the very obviousness of the only possible answer[28] is the reason why that answer could escape our notice. The apparently contradictory facts that (1) the subject matter of the *Guide* are *ma'aseh bereshit* and *ma'aseh merkabah*, and that (2) Maimonides, in spite of his identifying *ma'aseh bereshit* with physics and *ma'aseh merkabah* with metaphysics, excludes physics and metaphysics from the *Guide*, may be reconciled by the formula that the intention of the *Guide* is to prove the identity, which to begin with was asserted only, of *ma'aseh bereshit* with physics and of *ma'aseh merkabah* with metaphysics. Physics and metaphysics are indeed philosophic disciplines, and a book devoted to them is indeed a philosophic book. But Maimonides does not intend to treat physics and metaphysics; his intention is to show that the teaching of these philosophic disciplines, which is presupposed, is identical with the secret teaching of the Bible.[29] The demonstration of such identity is no longer the duty of the philosopher, but is incumbent upon the student of the true science of the law. The *Guide* is then under no circumstances a philosophic book.[30]

As a corollary we have to add that the *Guide* cannot be called a theological work, for Maimonides does not know of theology as a discipline distinct from metaphysics. Nor is it a book of religion, for he expressly excludes religious, together with ethical topics from the subject matter of his work.[31] Until we shall have rediscovered a body of terms which are flexible enough to fit Maimonides'

[28] That is to say, the only answer which could be given if the suggestion made in the foregoing paragraph is ruled out. Cf., however, pp. 55 f. below.

[29] As regards the identification of the teaching of revelation with the teaching of reason in medieval Jewish philosophy, cf. Julius Guttmann, *Die Philosophie des Judentums* (Munich, 1933), pp. 71 f.

[30] Cf. also above p. 38 (and n. 5), and below pp. 53 (and n. 60), 55 (and n. 64).

[31] III, 8 *in fine*.

thought, the safest course will be to limit the description of the *Guide* to the statement that it is a book devoted to the explanation of the secret teaching of the Bible.

3. THE CONFLICT BETWEEN LAW AND NECESSITY

When Maimonides embarked upon the explanation of the secrets of the Torah, he was confronted with the apparently overwhelming difficulty created by the "legal prohibition"[32] against explaining those secrets. The very same law, the secrets of which Maimonides attempted to explain, forbids their explanation. According to the ordinance of the talmudic sages, *ma'aseh merkabah* ought not to be taught even to one man, except if he be wise and able to understand by himself, and even to such a one only the "chapter headings" may be transmitted. As regards the other secrets of the Bible, their revelation to many people met with scarcely less definite disapproval in the Talmud.[33] Explaining secrets in a book is tantamount to transmitting those secrets to thousands of men. Consequently, the talmudic prohibition mentioned implies the prohibition of writing a book devoted to their explanation.[34]

This prohibition was accepted by Maimonides not only as legally binding, but also as evidently wise; it was in full accordance with his own considered judgment that oral teaching in general is superior to teaching by writing. This view may be traced back to an old philosophic tradition.[35] The works of Aristotle, which were known to Maimonides, are "acroamatic" and not "exoteric," and his method of expounding things betrays more often than not its provenance from Platonic or Socratic dialectics. Even *the* classical statement about the danger inherent in all writing may have been known to Maimonides, for the famous doctrine of Plato's *Phaedrus* had been summarized by Farabi in his treatise on Plato's philosophy.[36] Be this as it may, not the ambiguous advice of the

---

[32] III, Introd. (2a and b; 297, 16 and 25).

[33] I, Introd. (3b–4a; 3, 9–19); 33 (36a; 48, 19–21); 34 (40b; 52, 24–53, 3); III, Introd.

[34] I, Introd. (4a; 3, 19–20); III, Introd. (2a; 297, 15–16).

[35] I, 71 (93b; 121, 14–24); III, Introd. (2b; 297, 25–26). Cf. I, 17 and Introd. (4a; 3, 19–20).

[36] Cf. Falakera's Hebrew translation of Farabi's treatise in *Reshit hokmah*, ed. David, p. 75 bottom.

philosophers but the unequivocal command of the law was of primary importance to Maimonides.[37]

If a book devoted to the explanation of the secrets of the Bible is prohibited by law, how then can the *Guide*, being the work of an observant Jew, be a book? It is noteworthy that Maimonides himself in the *Guide* never calls it a book, but consistently refers to it as a *maqâla (ma'amar)*.[38] *Maqâla* (just as *ma'amar*) has several meanings. It may mean a treatise; it is used in that sense when Maimonides speaks, for instance, of the *Treatise on Government* by Alexander of Aphrodisias. But it may also mean — and this is its original connotation — a speech. Maimonides, by refraining from calling the *Guide* a book and by calling it a *maqâla*, hints at the essentially oral character of its teaching. Since, in a book such as the *Guide*, hints are more important than explicit statements, Maimonides' contentions concerning the superiority of oral teaching very probably have to be taken quite literally.

If the *Guide* is, in a sense, not a book at all, if it is merely a substitute for conversations or speeches, then it cannot be read in the way we may read, for instance, Ibn Sina's *Al-Shifâ*, or Thomas Aquinas's *Summa theologiae*. To begin with, we may assume rather that the proper way of studying it is somehow similar to the way in which traditional Judaism studies the law.[39] This would mean that if we wish to know what Maimonides thinks, say, about the prophecy of Moses, it would not be sufficient to look up that chapter of his work which is explicitly devoted to that subject, and in which we might find perfectly clear and apparently final statements about it; nor would it be sufficient to contrast the latter with divergent statements unexpectedly occurring in other chapters. We would also have to take into account analogous "decisions" given by Maimonides with regard to entirely different "cases," and to make ourselves familiar with the general rules of analogy which obtain in oral discussions of that kind. Producing a clear

[37] The inferiority of writing is also indicated by the designation of those biblical works which had not been composed by prophets proper as "writings." Cf. II, 45 (94a, 95b; 283, 1–5; 284, 21–285, 3).

[38] This fact is pointed out by Abravanel in his *Ma'amar ḳaṣer bebi'ur sod ha-moreh*. Ibn Tibbon, in his preface to his translation of the *Guide*, calls it הספר הנכבד הזה מאמר מורה נבוכים.

[39] Cf. H. A. Wolfson, *Crescas' Critique of Aristotle* (Cambridge, 1929), pp. 22 ff. Maimonides indicates the similarity between the prohibition of writing down the oral law and that of writing down the secret teaching of the law; see I, 71 *in princ.*

statement of the author, in the case of a book like the *Guide*, is tantamount to raising a question; his answer can be ascertained only by a lengthy discussion, the result of which may again be open, and intended to be open, to new "difficulties." If it is true that the *Mishneh Torah* is but the greatest post-talmudic contribution to the oral discussions of the halakah, then it may be asserted with equal right that Maimonides, while writing the *Guide*, continued the aggadic discussions of the Talmud. And just as the *Mishneh Torah*, far from terminating the halakic discussions, actually served as a new starting point for them, in the same way the *Guide*, far from offering a final interpretation of the secret teaching of the Bible,[40] may actually have been an attempt to revive the oral discussion thereof by raising difficulties which intentionally were left unsolved.

But although the method employed by Maimonides in the *Guide* may come as near as is humanly possible to the method of oral teaching, the *Guide* does not for that reason cease to be a book. Consequently the very existence of the *Guide* implies a conscious transgression of an unambiguous prohibition. It seems that Maimonides for a while intended to steer a middle course between oral and confidential teaching, which is permitted, and teaching in writing, which is forbidden. That kind of writing which comes nearest to confidential conversation is private correspondence with a close friend. As a matter of fact, the *Guide* is written in the form of letters addressed to a friend and favorite pupil, Joseph ibn Aknin.[41] By addressing his book to one man, Maimonides made sure that he did not transgress the prohibition against explaining *ma'aseh merkabah* to more than one man. Moreover, in the *Epistula dedicatoria* addressed to Joseph, he mentions, as it were in passing and quite unintentionally, that Joseph possessed all the qualities required of a student of the secret lore and explains the necessity of written communication by his pupil's departure.[42] This justification

[40] Cf., for instance, III, Introd. (2b; 298, 1–2); I, 21 (26b; 34, 10–12).
[41] Cf. in particular II, 24.
[42] These observations on the *Ep. ded.* cannot furnish a sufficient interpretation of that remarkable piece of literature, but deal merely with its more superficial meaning. Maimonides mentions Joseph's poems in order to show that the latter possessed the indispensable ability of expressing himself beautifully; cf. I, 34 (41a; 53, 14) with I, Introd. (7a–b; 8, 7–8). As regards the other qualities of Joseph, see Shem Tob's commentary on the *Ep. ded.*

would have held good if Maimonides had refrained from making public these private "letters to a friend." In spite of this inconsistency and in spite of his evident determination to write the *Guide* even if he had never met Joseph, or if Joseph had never left him,[43] it would be a mistake to assume that the dedicatory epistle is wholly ironical. For we need only ask ourselves: what was the ultimate reason for Joseph's premature departure, and we are going over from the sphere of private and playful things to the sphere of public and serious matters. Joseph's departure, we may say, was the consequence of his being a Jew in the Diaspora. Not a private need but only an urgent necessity of nation-wide bearing can have driven Maimonides to transgressing an explicit prohibition. Only the necessity of saving the law can have caused him to break the law.[44]

The necessity of taking such an extraordinary measure was a consequence of the long duration of the Diaspora. The secrets of the Torah, "the fountainhead of ancient Greek, and, consequently, also of Arabian wisdom,"[45] had been handed down from time immemorial by oral tradition. Even when the oral law, which likewise ought not to have been written down, was finally compiled in written form, the talmudic sages wisely insisted on the secret teaching being transmitted to posterity only by word of mouth from one scholar to another. Their command was obeyed; there is not a single book extant which contains the secret teaching in whole or in part. What had come down to Maimonides were only slight intimations and allusions in Talmud and Midrash.[46] However,

[43] It is controversial whether Maimonides finished the *Guide* before he made the acquaintance of Joseph or thereafter. According to Z. Diesendruck, "On the Date of the Completion of the Moreh Nebukim," *Hebrew Union College Annual*, XII–XIII, 496, the *Guide* was finished in 1185, i.e., at about the time when Joseph's sojourn with Maimonides began. Even if the *Guide* was not finished before the year 1190, which is the latest possible date (see *ibid.*, pp. 461, 470), it certainly had been conceived and partly elaborated before Joseph's arrival.

[44] I, Introd. (9b; 10, 28–29) in the interpretation of Fürstenthal and Munk.

[45] Baron, *Outlook*, p. 105, with reference to I, 71 *in princ*. Cf. also II, 11 (24a–b; 192, 17–29).

[46] I, Introd. (9b; 10, 26–27); 71 (93b–94a; 121, 9–26) [the words *tanbîhât yasîra wa-ishârât* recall the title of Ibn Sînâ's book *Ishârât wa-tanbîhât*; cf. also also II, 29 (46a; 244, 8)]; III, Introd. (2a–b; 297, 15–20). Maimonides here tacitly denies any authenticity or value to books such as the *Sefer ha-Yeṣirah* or *She'ur ḳomah*; cf. Baron, *Outlook*, p. 89.

continuity of oral tradition presupposes a certain normality of political conditions. That is why the secrets of the Torah were perfectly understood only as long as Israel lived in its own country in freedom, not subjugated by the ignorant nations of the world.[47] Particularly happy was the period when the supreme political authority rested in the hands of King Solomon, who had an almost complete understanding of the secret reasons of the commandments.[48] After Solomon, wisdom and political power were no longer united; decline and finally loss of freedom followed. When the nation was led into captivity, it sustained further loss in the perfect knowledge of the secrets. Whereas Isaiah's contemporaries understood his brief hints, the contemporaries of Ezekiel required many more details in order to grasp the sacred doctrine. The decline of knowledge became even more marked with the discontinuation of prophecy itself.[49] Still more disastrous was the victory of the Romans, since the new Diaspora was to last so much longer than the first.[50] As time went on, the external conditions for oral communication of the secrets of the Torah became increasingly precarious. The moment seemed imminent when it would become altogether impossible. Confronted with that prospect, Maimonides decided to write down the secret teaching.

The question naturally arises as to how Maimonides came into its possession. Once, in suggesting a date for the coming of the Messiah (in *Iggeret Teiman*), he refers to a tradition, obviously oral, which he had received from his father, who in turn had received it from his father and grandfather, and which in that way went back to the very beginning of the Diaspora. If we were to generalize from this remark, we would have to assume that he owed his entire knowledge of the secrets of the Torah to an uninterrupted oral tradition going back to the time of the second temple. We would then not only have to accept the legend of his conversion to the Kabbalah in his old age, but we would be forced to admit that he was a Kabbalist throughout his mature life, since the content of the *Guide* would be nothing but a secret teaching based on (oral) tradition. Indeed, as it seems that there had existed no Kabbalah,

---

[47] I, 71 (93b; 121, 10–11).
[48] III, 26 (58a; 369, 14–16). Cf. Baron, *Outlook*, pp. 51–54.
[49] III, 6 (9b; 307, 12–15); II, 32 (73b; 254, 23–24), 36 (80a; 263, 19–26).
[50] Cf. I, 71 (93b; 121, 10). Cf. also M.T., Introd.

strictly speaking, before the completion of the *Guide*,[51] one might suggest that Maimonides was the first Kabbalist.

Such venturesome hypotheses are, however, ruled out by his express statements. He not only disclaims the privilege of having had a special revelation about the hidden meaning of *ma'aseh merkabah*, but also disavows his indebtedness to any (human) teacher for his knowledge of the secret doctrine.[52] He apparently believes that the oral tradition of the secret teaching had been interrupted long before his time. That is also why he could not find any traces of a genuine Jewish secret tradition in the Gaonic literature, whereas he claims to have found such traces in the Talmud and in the Midrash. Neither was he able to detect any remnant of the holy doctrine still living in the nation.[53] He was, then, not the last heir of an age-old tradition, but rather its first rediscoverer after it had been lost for a long time. He rediscovered the secret teaching by following the indications which are met with in the Bible and in the words of the sages but also by making use of speculative premises.[54] Since the Bible and the Talmud had been studied no less thoroughly by his predecessors than by him, his rediscovery must have been due to a particularly deep understanding of the "speculative premises," i.e., of philosophy. He did not feel conscious of thereby introducing a foreign element into Judaism, for long before his time the "Andalusian" Jews had accepted the teachings of the philosophers as far as these were consonant with the basis of the Torah.[55] Philosophic teachings thus belonged, in a sense, to the tradition of Maimonides' family. Perhaps he even believed that the resurgence of philosophic studies in the Middle Ages more or less coincided with the disappearance of the secret teaching of Judaism and that thus the chain of tradition never was interrupted. After all, the defensible part of the philosophic teaching appeared to him as but a last residue of Israel's own lost inheritance.[56]

[51] "Zur Bezeichnung der Mystik wurde der Terminus [Kabbala] erst sehr spät verwandt, und ist zuerst bei Isaak dem Blinden (ca. 1200) nachweisbar." G. Scholem, *Encyclopaedia Judaica*, IX, 632.

[52] III, Introd. (2b; 297, 27–28). Cf., however, III, 22 (46a; 353, 21–22). Cf. also the allusion to a spurious "mystical" tradition in I, 62 (80b; 104, 26).

[53] I, 71 (94a; 121, 25–122, 3); III, Introd. (2b; 297, 17–18).

[54] III, Introd. (2b; 297, 28–29).

[55] I, 71 (94a; 122, 9–10).

[56] See above pp. 48 f. Cf. Altmann, *op. cit.*, pp. 315 ff.

The philosophic tradition of enlightened Andalusia thus gave Maimonides the first impulse to search the Bible for its secrets. Owing to his exertions during the greater part of his life, he succeeded in detecting a great many of them. At the same time he clearly realized that his achievement was not likely to be repeated by many others, if by any. For the age of philosophy in Muslim countries was drawing to its close. Fearing, therefore, that the precious doctrine might again be lost for centuries, he decided to commit it to writing, notwithstanding the talmudic prohibition. But he did not act imprudently. He insisted on taking a middle course[57] between impossible obedience and flagrant transgression. He thought it his duty to give such a written explanation of the biblical secrets as would meet all the conditions required from an oral explanation. In other words, he had to become a master of the art of revealing by not revealing and of not revealing by revealing.

The law requires that only the "chapter headings" be transmitted. Maimonides decided to abide by that precept. But the law goes further: it requires that even those "chapter headings" be not transmitted even to one, except he be wise and able to understand by himself. As long as the secret teaching was transmitted by oral instruction, that requirement was easily complied with: if the teacher had not known the pupil for a long time beforehand, as probably was almost always the case, he could test the pupil's intellectual capacities by having a talk with him on indifferent subjects before he started to explain to him some of the secrets of the Bible. But how can the author of a book examine his readers, by far the greater part of whom may not yet be born when the book is published? Or does there exist some sort of examination by proxy, which would allow the author to prevent incompetent readers not only from understanding his book — this does not require any special measure — but even from finding out the very formulation of the "chapter headings"? To see that such a device does exist, we have only to remind ourselves of how a superior man proceeds if he wishes to impart a truth, which he thinks not to be fit for everybody's use, to another man, who may or may not be able to become reconciled to it. He will give him a hint by casting some doubt on a remote and apparently insignificant consequence or premise of the accepted opinion. If the listener

[57] Cf. III, Introd. (3a; 298, 8–9).

understands the hint, the teacher may explain his doubts more
fully and thus gradually lead him to a view which is of necessity
nearer the truth (since it presupposes a certain reflection) than is
the current opinion. But how does he proceed, if the pupil fails to
understand the hint? He will simply stop. This does not mean
that he will stop talking. On the contrary, since by suddenly
becoming silent he would only perplex the pupil without being of
any help to him, he will continue talking by giving the first, rather
revealing sentence a more conventional meaning and thus gradually
lead him back to the safe region of accepted views. Now this
method of stopping can be practiced in writing as well as in speech,
the only difference being that the writer must stop in any case,
since certainly the majority of readers must be prevented from
finding out the "chapter headings." That is to say, the writer has
to interrupt his short hints by long stretches of silence, i.e., of
insignificant talk. But a good author will never submit to the
ordeal of indulging in insignificant talk. Consequently, after having
given a hint which refers to a certain chapter of the secret teaching,
he will write some sentences which at first glance seem to be conventional, but which on closer examination prove to contain a new
hint, referring to another chapter of the secret teaching. By thus
proceeding, he will prevent the secret teaching being prematurely
perceived and therefore inadequately understood; even those readers
who not only noticed but even understood the first hint and might
understand further hints directly connected with it, would experience considerable difficulty even in suspecting the second hint,
which refers to a different section of the argument. It is hardly
necessary to add that there are as many groups of hints as there
are chapters, or subdivisions of chapters, of the secret teaching, and
that in consequence an ingenious author has at his disposal almost
infinite possibilities of alternatively using hints of different groups.

We are now in a position to appreciate the bearing of the
following statement of Maimonides: "You will not demand from
me here [in the *Guide*] anything except chapter headings; and even
those headings are, in this treatise, not arranged according to their
intrinsic order or according to any sequence whatsoever, but they
are scattered and intermingled with other subjects, the explanation
of which is intended."[58] It is true Maimonides makes this state-

[58] I, Introd. (3b; 3, 11–14).

ment with regard to his explanation of *ma'aseh merkabah* only. But there can be no doubt that he has followed the same method in his explanation of *ma'aseh bereshit* and, indeed, of all the secrets of the Torah.[59] It is for this reason that the whole work has to be read with particular care, with a care, that is, which would not be required for the understanding of a scientific book.[60] Since the whole teaching characteristic of the *Guide* is of a secret nature, we are not surprised to observe Maimonides entreating the reader in the most emphatic manner not to explain any part of it to others, unless the particular doctrine had already been clearly elucidated by famous teachers of the law,[61] i.e., unless it is a popular topic, a topic only occasionally mentioned in the *Guide*.

The *Guide* is devoted to the explanation of an esoteric doctrine. But this explanation is itself of an esoteric character. The *Guide* is, then, devoted to the esoteric explanation of an esoteric doctrine. Consequently it is a book with seven seals. How can we unseal it?

4. A MORAL DILEMMA

No historian who has a sense of decency and therefore a sense of respect for a superior man such as Maimonides will disregard light-heartedly the latter's emphatic entreaty not to explain the secret teaching of the *Guide*. It may fairly be said that an interpreter who does not feel pangs of conscience when attempting to explain that secret teaching and perhaps when perceiving for the first time its existence and bearing lacks that closeness to the subject which is indispensable for the true understanding of any book. Thus the question of adequate interpretation of the *Guide* is primarily a moral question.

We are, however, entitled to object to raising that moral question because the historical situation in which we find ourselves is fundamentally different from that of the twelfth century, and therefore we ought to be justified in not taking too personally, so to speak, Maimonides' will. It is true, at first glance, that objection

[59] II, 29 (46a; 244, 10 f.). Cf. I, Introd. (3b–4b; 3, 17–4, 22), 17, 35 (42a; 54, 20–28). See also III, 41 (88b; 409, 16).

[60] I, Introd. (8b; 9, 26–10, 2), *ibid.* (3b; 3, 11–14); *ibid.* (4b; 4, 12–15).

[61] I, Introd. (9a; 10, 4–8).

seems to beg the question: it is based on the assumption that it is possible to have a sufficient knowledge of the historical situation of the twelfth century without having a true and adequate knowledge of the secret teaching of Maimonides. Yet, if one looks more closely, one sees that by the historical situation no historian understands the secret thoughts of an individual, but rather the obvious facts or opinions which, being common to a period, give that period its specific coloring. We happen to be excellently informed by competent historians about the opinions prevalent in the twelfth century, and each of us can see that they are fundamentally different from those prevalent in our time. Public opinion was then ruled by the belief in the revealed character of the Torah or the existence of an eternal and unchangeable law, whereas public opinion today is ruled by historic consciousness. Maimonides himself justified his transgression of the talmudic injunction against writing on the esoteric teaching of the Bible by the necessity of saving the law. In the same way we may justify our disregard of Maimonides' entreaty not to explain the esoteric teaching of the *Guide* by appealing to the requirements of historic research. For both the history of Judaism and the history of medieval philosophy remain deplorably incomplete, as long as the secret teaching of Maimonides has not been brought to light. The force of this argument will become even stronger if we take into consideration that basic condition of historic research, namely, freedom of thought. Freedom of thought, too, seems to be incomplete as long as we recognize the validity of any prohibition to explain any teaching whatsoever. Freedom of thought being menaced in our time more than for several centuries, we have not only the right but even the duty to explain the teaching of Maimonides, in order to contribute to a better understanding of what freedom of thought means, i.e., what attitude it presupposes and what sacrifices it requires.

The position of Maimonides' interpreter is, then, to some extent identical with that of Maimonides himself. Both are confronted with a prohibition against explaining a secret teaching and with the necessity of explaining it. Consequently, one might think it advisable for the interpreter to imitate Maimonides also with regard to the solution of the dilemma i.e., to steer a middle course between impossible obedience and flagrant transgression by attempting an esoteric interpretation of the esoteric teaching of the *Guide*. Since the *Guide* contains an esoteric interpretation of an esoteric teaching, an adequate interpretation of the *Guide* would thus have to take the form of an esoteric interpretation of an esoteric interpretation of an esoteric teaching.

This suggestion may sound paradoxical and even ridiculous. Yet it would not have appeared absurd to such a competent reader of the *Guide* as Joseph ibn Kaspi, who did write an esoteric commentary on it. Above all, an esoteric interpretation of the *Guide* seems to be not only advisable, but even necessary.

When Maimonides, through his work, exposed the secret teaching of the Bible to a larger number of men, some of whom might not be as obedient to the talmudic ordinance nor as wise as he was, he did not rely entirely on those readers' compliance with the law or with his own emphatic entreaty. For the explanation of secrets is, as he asserts, not only forbidden by law, but also impossible by nature:[62] the very nature of the secrets prevents their being divulged. We are then confronted with a third meaning of the word "secret": secret may mean not only the biblical word or parable which has an inner meaning, and the hidden meaning itself, but also, and perhaps primarily, the thing to which that hidden meaning refers.[63] The things spoken of by the prophets are secret, since they are not constantly accessible, as are the things described by the ordinary sciences,[64] but only during more or less short and rare intervals of spiritual daylight which interrupt an almost continuous spiritual darkness; indeed they are accessible not to natural reason, but only to prophetic vision. Consequently, ordinary language is utterly insufficient for their description; the only possible way of describing them is by parabolic and enigmatic speech.[65]

[62] I, Introd. (3b; 3, 15). Cf. I, 31 *in princ.*

[63] "Secrets of the being and secrets of the Torah," II, 26 (56b; 232, 5). For the distinction between various meanings of "secret," cf. Bacon, *Advancement of Learning*, ed. G. W. Kitchin, p. 205.

[64] I, Introd. (4b; 4, 15). This passage implies a fundamental distinction between esoteric and exoteric sciences. As regards such distinctions, cf. I. Goldziher, *Kitâb ma'ânî al-nafs* (Berlin, 1907), pp. 28*–31.* According to a usual distinction, "the exterior science" (*al-'ilm al-barrânî*) is identical with Aristotelian philosophy and also with the *Kalâm*; "the interior philosophy" (*al-falsafa al-dâḫila* or *al-falsafa al-ḫâṣṣa*), treated by the *muhakkikûn*, deals with "the secrets of nature." The teaching of esoteric science is the knowledge *al-maḍnûn bihi.* Cf. I, 17 *in princ.*, 35 (41b; 54, 4), 71 (93b; 121, 20).

[65] I, Introd. (4a; 4, 4–7). See the commentaries of Ephodi and Shem Tob on the passage. I, Introd. (4a-b; 3, 23–4, 20).

Even the interpretation of prophetic teaching cannot but be parabolic and enigmatic, which is equally true of the interpretation of such an interpretation, since both the secondary and the primary interpretation deal with the same secret subject matter. Hence the interpretation of the *Guide* cannot be given in ordinary language, but only in parabolic and enigmatic speech. That is why, according to Maimonides, the student of those secrets is required not only to be of mature age, to have a sagacious and subtle mind, to possess perfect command of the art of political government and the speculative sciences, and to be able to understand the allusive speech of others, but also to be capable of presenting things allusively himself.[66]

If each student actually had to meet all these conditions, we should have to admit at once, i.e., before any serious attempt has been made to elucidate the esoteric teaching of the *Guide*, that the interpretation of that work is wholly impossible for the modern historian. The very intention of interpreting the *Guide* would imply an unbearable degree of presumption on the part of the would-be interpreter; for he would implicitly claim to be endowed with all the qualities of a Platonic philosopher-king. Yet, while a modest man, confronted with the requirements which we have indicated, will be inclined to give up the attempt to understand the whole *Guide*, he may hope to make some contribution to its understanding by becoming a subservient part of the community of scholars who devote themselves to the interpretation of the *Guide*. If that book cannot be understood by the exertions of one man, it may be understood by the collaboration of many, in particular of Arabists, Judaists, and students of the history of philosophy. It is true that when speaking of the conditions to be fulfilled by students of the secret teaching, Maimonides does not mention disciplines such as those just alluded to; as a matter of fact, he thought very slightly of history in general.[67] But in all justice it may be said that he did not know, and could not know history in the modern sense of the word, a discipline which, in a sense, provides the synthesis, indispensable for the adequate understanding of the secret doctrine, of philosophy and politics. Yet, however greatly we may think of the qualities of the modern historian, he certainly is neither per

---

[66] I, 34 (41a; 53, 12–19), 33 (37b; 48, 22–25).
[67] Cf. Baron, *Outlook*, pp. 3–4.

se able to understand esoteric texts nor is he an esoteric writer. Indeed the rise of modern historic consciousness came simultaneously with the interruption of the tradition of esotericism. Hence all present-day students of Maimonides necessarily lack the specific training required for understanding, to say nothing of writing an esoteric book or commentary. Is, then, an interpretation of the *Guide* altogether impossible under the present circumstances?

Let us examine somewhat more closely the basic assumption underlying the conclusion at which we have just arrived, or rather upon which we have just come to grief. Maimonides, it is true, states in unambiguous terms that direct and plain communication of the secrets of the things, or of the secrets of the Torah, is impossible by nature. But he also asserts in no less unambiguous terms that such a communication is forbidden by law. Now a rational law does not forbid things which are impossible in themselves and which therefore are not subject to human deliberation or action; and the Torah is the rational law *par excellence*.[68] Consequently the two statements appear to be contradictory. Since we are not yet in a position to decide which of them is to be discarded as merely exoteric, it will be wise to leave the question open for the time being and not to go beyond briefly discussing the possibilities of an answer. There are three possible solutions (1) Maimonides may actually have believed in the unavoidable necessity of speaking enigmatically of secrets; (2) he may have conceded the possibility of plainly discussing them; (3) he may have approved some unknown intermediary position. There is, then, certainly a prima facie probability in the ratio of two to three that the first solution, which is wholly incompatible with our desire to understand the *Guide*, has to be ruled out. But even if the first solution had to be ultimately accepted, we need not be altogether despondent, since we may very well reject that view as erroneous. Esotericism, one might say, is based on the assumption that there is a rigid division of mankind into an inspired or intelligent minority and an uninspired or foolish majority. But are there no transitions of various kinds between the two groups? Has not each man been given freedom of will, so that he may become wise or foolish according to his exertions?[69] However important may be the natural

[68] III, 26. Cf. III, 17 (33a–b; 337, 8–15).
[69] M.T. Teshubah 5, 2.

faculty of understanding, is not the use of this faculty or, in other words, method, equally important? And method, almost by its very definition, bridges the gulf which separates the two unequal groups. Indeed, the methods of modern historical research, which have proved to be sufficient for the deciphering of hieroglyphs and cuneiforms, ought certainly to be sufficient also for the deciphering of a book such as the *Guide*, to which access could be had in an excellent translation into a modern language. Our problem reduces itself, therefore, to detecting the specific method which will enable us to decipher the *Guide*. What are, then, the general rules and the most important special rules according to which this book is to be read?

5. SECRETS AND CONTRADICTIONS

The clue to the true understanding of the *Guide* is provided by the very feature of that book which, at first glance, seems to make it for all modern generations a book sealed with seven seals. I am referring to the fact that it is devoted to the esoteric explanation of an esoteric text. For it is merely a popular fallacy to assume that such an explanation is an esoteric work of the second power, or at least twice as esoteric, and consequently twice as difficult to understand as is the esoteric text itself. Actually, any explanation, however esoteric, of a text is intended to be helpful for its understanding; and, provided the author is not a man of exceptional inability, the explanation is bound to be helpful. Now, if by the help of Maimonides, we understand the esoteric teaching of the Bible, we understand at the same time the esoteric teaching of the *Guide*, since Maimonides must have accepted the esoteric teaching of the law as the true teaching. Or, to put it somewhat differently, we may say that, thanks to Maimonides, the secret teaching is accessible to us in two different versions: in the original biblical version, and in the derivative version of the *Guide*. Each version by itself might be wholly incomprehensible; but we may become able to decipher both by using the light which one sheds on the other. Our position resembles then that of an archeologist confronted with an inscription in an unknown language, who subsequently discovers another inscription reproducing the translation of that text into another unknown language. It matters little whether or not we accept Maimonides' two assumptions, rejected by modern criticism, that the Bible is an esoteric text, and that its esoteric teaching is closely akin to that of Aristotle. As far as Maimonides is concerned, the Bible *is* an esoteric book, and even the most perfect esoteric book ever written. Consequently, when setting out to write an esoteric book himself, he had no choice but to take the Bible as his model. That is to say, he wrote the *Guide* according to the rules which he was wont to follow in reading the Bible. Therefore, if we wish to understand the *Guide*, we must read it according to the rules which Maimonides applies in that work to the explanation of the Bible.

How did Maimonides read the Bible, or rather the Torah? He read it as the work of a single author, that author being not so much Moses as God himself. Consequently, the Torah was for him the most perfect book ever written as regards both content and form. In particular, he did not believe (as we are told to believe by modern biblical criticism) that its formal deficiencies — for instance, the abrupt changes of subject matter, or repetitions with greater or slighter variations — were due to its having been compiled by unknown redactors from divergent sources. These deficiencies were for him purposeful irregularities, intended to hide and betray a deeper order, a deep, nay, divine meaning. It was precisely this intentional disorder which he took as his model when writing the *Guide*. Or, if we accept the thesis of modern biblical criticism, we have to say that he took as his model a book which unintentionally lacks order and that by so doing he wrote a book which intentionally lacks order. At any rate the *Guide* certainly and admittedly is a book which intentionally lacks order. The "chapter headings" of the secret teaching which it transmits "are not arranged according to their intrinsic order or according to any sequence whatsoever, but they are scattered and intermingled with other subjects."[70] Instances of apparently bad composition are so numerous in the *Guide* and so familiar to its students that we need not mention here more than one example. Maimonides interrupts his explanation of biblical expressions attributing to God place, local movement, and so on (I, 8–26) by an exposition of the meaning of *man* (I, 14) and by a discussion of the necessity of teaching *ma'aseh bereshit* esoterically (I, 17), just as the Bible itself interrupts the story of Joseph by inserting into it the story of Judah and

[70] I, Introd. (3b; 3, 11–14).

Tamar. Consequently, whenever we are confronted in the *Guide* with an abrupt change of subject matter, we have to follow the same rule of interpretation which Maimonides was wont to follow whenever he had to face a similar apparent deficiency of the Bible: we have to find out, by guessing, the hidden reason of the apparent deficiency. For it is precisely that hidden reason, accessible only to guesswork, which furnishes a link between the scattered "chapter headings," if not a "chapter heading" itself. Certainly the chains of reasoning connecting the scattered "chapter headings," and possibly even some "chapter headings" themselves, are not stated within the chapters, but are written with invisible ink in the empty spaces between the chapters, between the sentences, or between the parts of the *Guide*.

Another kind of irregularity occurs, for example, in his explanation of the various groups of biblical commandments (III, 36–49). At the beginning of each chapter reference is made to the book or books of the *Mishneh Torah* in which the laws under review had been codified. Maimonides deviates from that rule in the case of one chapter only (Chapter 41). That this is not a matter of chance can easily be seen from the context. There he points out with unusual clarity the difference between the text of the biblical commands and their traditional interpretation; his intention is, as he expressly states, to explain the "texts," and not the *fiqh*.[71] The *Mishneh Torah* is devoted to the *fiqh*. Consequently, it would have been most misleading if he had referred, at the beginning of that chapter, to the corresponding "book" of the *Mishneh Torah*, i.e., to the "Book of Judges." It may be added in passing that a full discussion of this irregularity, which space does not here permit, would help explain the scarcely less perplexing difficulty of the inclusion in the "Book of Judges" of the laws concerning mourning.

As a last instance of those devices, which may be called intentional perplexities, suggested to Maimonides by his model, we may mention here repetitions of the same subject with apparently no, or only insignificant variations. He observes that Ezekiel had twice the same vision of the celestial chariot, the most secret subject, and that both visions, in their turn, were but repetitions of the corresponding vision of Isaiah.[72] Hardly less important was for him

[71] III, 41 (88b; 409, 15–16).
[72] III, 3 *in princ.*, 6.

the realization that in the Book of Job all interlocutors apparently repeat continually one another's statements; in particular Elihu, supposedly superior in wisdom to Job, Eliphaz, Bildad, and Zophar, does not seem to add anything of weight to what the others had said before him.[73] Maimonides naturally asserts that these repetitions are apparent rather than real, and that closer examination will reveal that the opinions of Job, Eliphaz, Bildad and Zophar, as well as Elihu, differ materially from one another, and that the report of Ezekiel's second vision makes important additions to that of the first.[74] This method of repeating the same thing with apparently insignificant, but actually highly important variations was extremely helpful for Maimonides' purposes. An outstanding example may be found in his repeating in the *Guide*, with certain variations, the division of the biblical laws into 14 groups, an arrangement which had determined the whole plan of the *Mishneh Torah*.[75] He thus created the impression of merely repeating the division made in the code, whereas actually the two divisions greatly differ from each other. As further obvious examples of the application of the same method, one may cite the differences between the arrangement of the 248 affirmative precepts in the enumeration at the beginning of *Mishneh Torah* (or in *Sefer ha-miṣvot*) on the one hand, and that in the body of that code on the other; the differences between the enumeration of the 5 opinions concerning providence in the *Guide*, III, 17, on the one hand, and that in the same work, III, 23, on the other;[76] and the differences between the enumeration of the 3 opinions concerning creation in the *Guide*, II, 13, on the one hand, and that in the same work, II, 32, on the other. In all these cases Maimonides apparently merely repeats himself by speaking twice of the same number, but actually he introduces in the repetitions new points of view which had not even been hinted at in the first statements. His aim in so doing is clearly revealed by his explanation of the method employed by the first 4 interlocutors in the Book of Job (Job, Eliphaz, Bildad, and Zophar): "Each one of them repeats the subject of which the other had spoken . . . in order to hide the

---

[73] III, 23 (50a; 359, 4–9 and 14–15). Cf. also III, 24 (52b; 362, 22–23).

[74] III, 23 (50a; 359, 9–15); 1 (3a; 298, 23–24), 3 (6b and 7a; 303, 5, 19; 304, 4–5). Cf. M.T. Introd., 186th and 187th prohibition.

[75] Cf. also the fourteen principles in S. M.

[76] Notice also the three opinions on Providence indicated in III, 17 (37b; 342, 20 f.), as well as the two opinions indicated in III, 21 (44b; 351, 17–18).

subject peculiar to the opinion of each, so that it should appear to the vulgar that the opinion of all of them is one opinion generally agreed upon."[77] That is to say, the purpose of repeating conventional statements is to hide the disclosure, in the repetition, of unconventional views. What matters is, then, not the conventional view, constantly repeated, which may or may not be true, but the slight additions to, or omissions from the conventional view which occur in the repetition and which transmit "chapter headings" of the secret and true teaching. This is what Maimonides rather clearly intimates by saying that closer examination of Elihu's repetitious speech brings to light "the additional subject which he introduced, and this subject was the intention."[78] The question as to whether and to what extent Maimonides has generally employed this method of making hardly discernible additions to the "first statement" *par excellence*, i.e., to the biblical text itself, must remain unanswered in the present discussion.[79]

Since these rules of interpretation seem to confer excessive importance on every word used by Maimonides, we must have recourse again to our initial assumption that the *Guide* is an imitation of the Bible, and in particular of the Torah. Maimonides read the Torah as a book, every word of which was of divine origin and, consequently, of the greatest importance.[80] How conscientiously he strove to detect the full significance of each biblical term, however indifferent it might seem to be in its context, is known to every reader of the *Guide*, the first intention of which was to explain certain groups of biblical words.[81] He expressly applied the same principle of reading, or writing, to his own work:

if you wish to grasp the totality of what this treatise contains, so that nothing of it will escape you, then you must connect its

[77] III, 23 (50a; 359, 11–14).

[78] III, 23 (50a; 359, 9–10).

[79] Cf. III, Introd. (2b–3a; 298, 3–9). The method of "repetition" was certainly not invented by Maimonides; it was applied before him on a large scale by Farabi, who "repeated" the same teaching by making additions to it or omissions from it, in *Al-siyâsât al-madaniyya*, in *Al-madîna al-fâḍila*, and in *Al-milla al-fâḍila*. And let us not forget Plato, who (to mention only two examples) "repeated" the teachings of the *Republic* in the *Laws*, and in the *Apology* "reiterated" the defense of Socrates as well as the charge brought against him three times.

[80] M.T. *Teshubah* 3, 17.

[81] I, Introd. (2b; 2, 6 ff.).

chapters one with another;[82] and when reading a given chapter, your intention must be not only to understand the totality of the subject of that chapter, but also to grasp each word which occurs in it in the course of the speech, even if that word does not belong to the intention of the chapter. For the diction of this treatise has not been chosen by haphazard, but with great exactness and exceeding precision.[83]

Maimonides naturally read the Torah as a book which is in no way frivolous. Since he considered histories and poems to be frivolous writings, he was compelled to conceive of the biblical stories as of "secrets of the Torah."[84] As he had such a contempt for stories, it is most unlikely that the few stories which he inserted into the *Guide* have to be accepted at their face value: some necessity must have driven him to tell those stories in order to instill either some true opinion or some good moral habit into the minds of his readers.[85] In one case he tells us the story of how, "many years ago," a scientist had put to him a certain question, and how he had answered it.[86] Since the *Guide* is written "with great exactness and exceeding precision," it is safe to say that the framework of the story conveys some teaching which is not transmitted by the content of the discussion with the scientist. We find in the *Guide* more stories of things which happened "many years ago," such as the history of the science of *kalâm* and the story of the two books which Maimonides had begun to write on the parables of the prophets and of the Midrashim.[87] We do not hesitate to call also the "dedicatory epistle" a story, i.e., to assume that it, too, is one of the "secrets" of the *Guide*. Quotations from Maimonides' Commentary on the Mishnah and his code, indeed all quotations in the *Guide*, belong to the same class of hints.

[82] That is to say, you must do with the chapters of the *Guide* what Solomon did with the words and parables of the Bible; just as Solomon found out the secret teaching of the Bible by connecting word with word, and parable with parable, in the same way we may find out the secret teaching of the *Guide* by connecting chapter with chapter, and, indeed, secret word with secret word. Cf. I, Introd. (6b; 6, 26–7, 2).

[83] I, Introd. (8b; 9, 26–30).

[84] I, 2 (13b; 16, 9–11); III, 50. Cf. Baron, *Outlook*, p. 8, n. 4.

[85] Cf. III, 50 (120a; 451, 1–3).

[86] I, 2.

[87] I, 71. I, Introd. (5b; 5, 17 ff.); III, 19 (40a; 346, 3 ff.). Cf. III, 32 (70a–b; 385, 13–20).

After these preliminary remarks, we must try to place the method of reading the *Guide* on a firmer basis. In order to arrive at rules which would relieve us of the burdensome necessity of guessing Maimonides' secret thoughts, we must make a fresh start by discussing more exactly the relation between the model, the Bible, and its imitation or repetition, the *Guide*. What is the literary genus including the Bible and the *Guide*, and what is the specific difference giving the *Guide* its peculiar character?

Both the Bible, as Maimonides was wont to understand it, and the *Guide* are esoteric books. To cite but one other assertion of the author, his intention in writing the *Guide* was that the truths should flash up and then disappear again.[88] The purpose of the *Guide* is, then, not only to reveal the truth, but also to hide it. Or, to express the same thing in terms of quantity, a considerable number of statements are made in order to hide the truth rather than to teach it.

But what is the difference between the esoteric method of the Bible and that of the *Guide*? The authors of the Bible chose, in order to reveal the truth by not revealing it, and not to reveal it by revealing it, the use of words of certain kinds and of parables and enigmas.[89] Parables seem to be the more important vehicle, for Maimonides speaks of them much more fully than he does of the kinds of words in question.[90] Thus the suspicion arises that the species of esoteric books to which the Bible belongs is parabolic literature. That suspicion leads us to raise the question whether parables and enigmas are indispensable for esoteric teaching. As a matter of fact, that question is raised by Maimonides himself. After asserting that nobody is capable of completely explaining the secrets and that therefore every teacher speaks of them by using parables and enigmas, he goes on to say that, if someone wishes to teach the secrets without using parables and enigmas, he cannot help substituting for them obscurity and briefness of speech.[91] This remark may refer to an extreme case which is not likely to occur, but it also may suggest a possible innovation. Whether or not that case is likely and whether Maimonides is willing to make the inno-

[88] I, Introd. (3b; 3, 14).
[89] I, Introd. (5a; 5, 11 and 16).
[90] Cf. the index to Munk's *Guide*, *s.vv.* "allégories" and "noms."
[91] I, Introd. (4b–5a; 4, 11–13, 17–19, 26–28).

vation,[92] the substitution indicated by him is certainly possible. Thus his remark implies the admission that there exists a species of unparabolic esoteric literature and, consequently, that the species of esoteric books to which the Bible belongs may rightly be described as parabolic literature.

The question of how to avoid parables and enigmas when speaking of the secrets is taken up again by Maimonides a little further on in the general introduction to his work, in his discussion of the explanation of parables. He discusses that question by telling us a story. He narrates that once upon a time he had intended to write two books in order to explain the parables of the Bible and those of the Midrashim, but that when attempting to write these books he was faced by a dilemma. Either he could give the explanation in the form of parables, which procedure would merely exchange one individual for another of the same species, or he could explain the parables in unparabolic speech, in which case the explanation would not be suitable for the vulgar. Since the explanations given in the *Guide* are not addressed to the vulgar, but to scholars,[93] we may expect from the outset that they would be of an unparabolic character. Moreover, we know from Maimonides' earlier statement that parabolic and enigmatic representation of the secret teaching can be avoided: it can be replaced by obscurity and briefness of speech, i.e., by ways of expression which are suitable exclusively to scholars who, besides, are able to understand of themselves. Above all, in the case of an explanation of parabolic texts, it is not only possible, but even necessary to avoid parabolic speech: a parabolic explanation would be open to the objection, so aptly made by Maimonides himself, that it merely replaces one individual by another individual of the same species, or, in other words, that it is no explanation at all. What is then, the species of speech, different from that of parabolic speech, the use of which Maimonides had to learn after he had decided to write the *Guide* instead of the two popular books? What is the species, of which all expositions of the truth, given in the *Guide*, are individuals? To answer this question, we must first raise the more general question as to what is the genus which includes the species, hitherto unknown, of the expositions of the truth characteristic of the *Guide*, as well as of the

[92] I, Introd. (9b; 10, 24–28).
[93] Cf. I, Introd. (5b; 5, 18–25) with *ibid.* (3a and 4b; 2, 11 ff. and 4, 8–12).

species of parabolic expositions? The answer to this question, which no careful student of the *Guide* can help raising, is given by Maimonides in the last section of the general introduction to his work, where he quite abruptly and unexpectedly introduces a new subject: the various reasons for contradictions occurring in various kinds of books. We already know the hidden motive underlying this sudden change of subject matter; that hidden motive is the somewhat disguised question of the method characteristic of the *Guide* or, to speak more generally and vaguely, the question of the genus including the esoteric methods of both the Bible and the *Guide*. To the latter question, Maimonides gives here the rather undisguised answer that the genus looked for is contradictory speech. To the former question, he answers with equal clarity that the contradictions met with in the *Guide* are to be traced back to two reasons: to the requirements of teaching obscure matters, i.e., of making them understood, and to the requirements of speaking, or writing, of such matters. The contradictions caused by the former are bound to be known to the teacher (provided he did not make them deliberately), and they escape the pupil until he has reached an advanced stage of training; that is to say, they certainly escape the vulgar. But as regards the contradictions caused by the latter requirements, they always are deliberately made, and the author must take the utmost care to hide them completely from the vulgar.[94] Those disclosures of Maimonides enable us to describe the form of the esoteric teaching of the *Guide*: Maimonides teaches the truth not by inventing parables (or by using contradictions between parabolic statements), but by using conscious and intentional contradictions, hidden from the vulgar, between unparabolic and unenigmatic statements.[95]

From this result the inference must be drawn that no interpreter of the *Guide* is entitled to attempt a personal explanation of its contradictions. For example, he must not try to trace them back to the fact, or assumption, that the two traditions which Maimonides intended to reconcile, i.e., the biblical tradition and the philosophic tradition, are actually irreconcilable; or, more philosophically but scarcely more adequately, to explain them by assuming that

---

[94] I, Introd. (10a, 10b, 11b; 11, 19–26 and 12, 7–12 and 13, 13–15).

[95] Cf. I, Introd. (10a; 11, 13–16). Cf. the somewhat different interpretation followed by Altmann, *op. cit.*, pp. 310 f.

Maimonides was on the track of philosophic problems transcending the horizon of the philosophic tradition, but was unable to free himself sufficiently from its shackles. Such attempts would serve a useful purpose if meant to explain highly complicated and artificial reconciliations of contradictions. They are both erroneous and superfluous if they are destined to explain contradictions which, if unintentional, would betray not the failure of a superior intellect in the face of problems either insoluble or very difficult to solve, but rather scandalous incompetence.[96] All these attempts would tacitly or expressly presuppose that the contradictions had escaped Maimonides' notice, an assumption which is refuted by his unequivocal statements. Therefore, until the contrary has been proved, it must be maintained that he was fully aware of every contradiction in the *Guide*, at the very time of writing the contradictory sentences. And if the objection is made that we ought to allow for the possibility that unconscious and unintentional contradictions have crept into the *Guide*, since philosophers hardly inferior to Maimonides have been found guilty of such contradictions, we answer by referring to Maimonides' emphatic declaration concerning the extreme care with which he had written every single word of his book and by asking the objectors to produce similar declarations from those books of other philosophers which they may have in mind. Therefore the duty of the interpreter is not to explain the contradictions, but to find out in each case which of the two statements was considered by Maimonides to be true and which he merely used as a means of hiding the truth.

Maimonides has raised the question whether contradictions caused by the requirements of speaking, or writing, of obscure matters are also to be found in the Bible: he demands that this question be very carefully studied.[97] In fact, it reveals itself as being the decisive question, once one has looked beneath the surface of the teaching of the *Guide*. Since he does not answer it explicitly, it must here be left open. Neither can we discuss here the related questions as to whether the Maimonidean method of teaching the truth was influenced by a philosophic tradition; whether it is characteristic of a particular kind of philosophic literature; and whether, in accordance with the terminology of the philosophic tradition, the

[96] Cf. I, Introd. (10b; 12, 4–7).
[97] I, Introd. (11b; 13, 6–8).

Guide ought not to be described rather as an exoteric work. If this description should ultimately prove correct, the meaning of the term "addition" would have to undergo a profound change: it would not mean the decisively important secret teaching which is added to the conventional view, but rather the imaginative representation which is added to the undisguised truth.[98]

Since the contradictions in the *Guide* are concealed, we must briefly consider at least some of the ways of hiding contradictions: (1) The most obvious method is to speak of the same subject in a contradictory manner on pages far apart from each other. The symbol of this method is: $a=b$ (page 15) — $a \neq b$ (page 379). Considering, however, the carelessness with which we usually read, one may reduce the distance between the pages to any positive number. (2) A variation of this method is to make one of the two contradictory statements in passing, as it were. A good example is Maimonides' incidental denial of the obligatory character of the entire sacrificial legislation.[99] (3) A third method is to contradict the first statement not directly, but by contradicting its implications. The symbol of this method is: $a=b$ — $b=c$ — $[a=c]$ — $a \neq c$ — $[a \neq b]$, the brackets indicating propositions which are not to be pronounced. It may be illustrated by the contradiction between the statements that "one of the main subjects of the *Guide* is *ma'aseh bereshit*" and that "*ma'aseh bereshit* is physics" on the one hand, and that "physics is not a subject of the *Guide*" on the other; or by the contradiction between the contentions that "explanation of the secrets is impossible by nature" and that "explanation of the secrets is forbidden by the law." (4) Another method is to contradict the first statement not directly, but by seemingly repeating it while actually adding to it, or omitting from it, an apparently negligible expression. The symbol of that method is: $a=b$ — $[b = \beta + \epsilon]$ — $a = \beta$ — $[a \neq b]$. (5) Another method is to introduce between the two contradictory statements an intermediary assertion, which, by itself not contradictory to the first statement, becomes contradictory to it by the

---

[98] For the two meanings of *addition*, cf. I, Introd. (7a–b; 8, 6, 15), on the one hand, and *ibid.* (8a; 9, 8), on the other. Cf. also in the *Treatise on Resurrection* the beginning of the treatise proper. The importance of the term "addition," for instance, for the doctrine of attributes may be indicated here in passing.

[99] III, 46 (102a–b; 427, 14–16). Cf. Munk, *Guide*, III, 364, n. 5. An allusion to this statement is implied in Joseph ibn Kaspi's commentaries on Deut. 17:14 f. and I Sam. 8:6.

addition, or the omission, of an apparently negligible expression; the contradictory statement creeps in as a repetition of the intermediary statement. The symbol of this method is: $a = b — a \neq \beta — [b = \beta + \epsilon] — a \neq b$. (6) To use ambiguous words. The symbol is: $a = c — [c \overset{=}{\underset{\neq}{}} b \!\! \overset{a = b}{\underset{a \neq b}{\big\langle}}\!\!]$. For example, the sentence, "a certain statement is an addition," may mean a true addition to an untruth, or an untrue addition to the truth.

While on the subject of ambiguous words, we may indicate their great importance for the reader of the *Guide*. According to Maimonides, the Bible teaches the truth by using certain kinds of words, as well as by parables. While excluding the latter from his own work, he nowhere indicates his intention of avoiding the former, and in particular ambiguous words. The expression "ambiguous word" is itself ambiguous. Used as a technical term, it means a word which is applied to "two objects between which there is a similarity with regard to some thing which is accidental to both and which does not constitute the essence of either of them."[100] In another less technical, but scarcely less important sense, it means "a word fitly spoken" (Proverbs 25:11). For, according to Maimonides, this biblical expression describes "a speech spoken according to its two faces," or "a speech which has two faces, i.e., which has an exterior and an inner" face; an exterior useful, for instance, for the proper condition of human societies, and an inner useful for the knowledge of the truth.[101] An ambiguous speech in the second sense would, then, be a speech with one face toward the vulgar, and with another face toward the man who understands by himself. Not only speeches, or sentences, but also words with two faces were indispensable to Maimonides, when he attempted to reveal the truth to the latter while hiding it from the former. For a secret is much less perfectly concealed by a sentence than by a word, since a word is much smaller in extent, and consequently *ceteris paribus* a much better hiding place than a whole sentence.

[100] I, 56 (68b; 89, 18–20). Cf. H. A. Wolfson, "The Amphibolous Terms in Aristotle, Arabic Philosophy and Maimonides," *The Harvard Theological Review* XXXI (1938), 164.

[101] I, Introd. (6b-7a; 7, 15–8, 3). The fact that the whole passage (6a–8b; 6, 19–9, 25), which apparently deals with parables only, actually has still another meaning, is indicated by the seeming clumsiness with which the apparent subject is introduced.

This is especially true of common words, placed unobtrusively within an unobtrusive sentence. It is just such common words of hidden ambiguity which Maimonides has primarily in mind when he asks the reader to pay very close attention to every word which he happens (or rather seems to happen) to use; and when he emphatically entreats him not to explain anything in the *Guide*, not even a single word, unless it expressed something which had already been accepted and openly taught by earlier Jewish authorities.[102] Evidently the explanation of a single word cannot be so grave a matter unless that word is filled with high explosive which can destroy all beliefs not firmly grounded in reason; i.e., unless its actual and hidden meaning lends to some important statement a sense totally different from, or even diametrically opposed to the sense which it would have, if this particular word were to be accepted in its apparent or conventional meaning. Is such a word not to be called an ambiguous word, "a word fitly spoken"? Apart from all general considerations, one may cite a number of individual examples of ambiguous terms intentionally used by Maimonides. Such terms are: "the wise" or "the learned," "the men of speculation,"[103] "the virtuous," "the community of the believers in [God's] unity," "government," and "providence," "addition," "secret," "belief," "action," "possible."

Returning to Maimonides' use of contradictions, one may assume that all important contradictions in the *Guide* may be reduced to the single fundamental contradiction between the true teaching, based on reason, and the untrue teaching, emanating from imagination. But whether this be the case or not, we are certainly in need of a general answer to the general question: which of the two contradictory statements is in each instance considered by Maimonides as the true statement? That answer would be *the* guide for the understanding of Maimonides' work. It is provided by his identification of the true teaching with some secret teaching. Consequently, of two contradictory statements made by him that statement which is most secret must have been considered by him to be true. Secrecy is to a certain extent identical with rarity; what all people say all the time is the opposite of a secret. We may therefore establish the rule that of two contradictory state-

102 I, Introd. (9a; 10, 4–7).
103 Cf., for instance, I, Introd. (9b; 10, 21); III, 15 (28b; 331, 27–29).

ments in the *Guide* or in any other work of Maimonides that statement which occurs least frequently, or even which occurs only
once, was considered by him to be true. He himself alludes to this
rule in his *Treatise on Resurrection*, the most authentic commentary
on the *Guide*, when he stresses the fact that resurrection, though a
basic principle of the law, is contradicted by many scriptural passages, and asserted only in two verses of the Book of Daniel. He
almost pronounces that rule by declaring, in the treatise mentioned,
that the truth of a statement is not increased by repetition nor is
it diminished by the author's failure to repeat it: "you know that
the mention of the basic principle of unity, i.e., His word 'The Lord
is one,' is not repeated in the Torah."

To sum up: Maimonides teaches the truth not plainly, but
secretly; i.e., he reveals the truth to those learned men who are
able to understand by themselves and at the same time he hides it
from the vulgar. There probably is no better way of hiding the
truth than to contradict it. Consequently, Maimonides makes
contradictory statements about all important subjects; he reveals
the truth by stating it, and hides it by contradicting it. Now the
truth must be stated in a more hidden way than it is contradicted,
or else it would become accessible to the vulgar; and those who
are able to understand by themselves are in a position to find out
the concealed statement of the truth. That is why Maimonides
repeats as frequently as possible the conventional views which are
suitable to, or accepted by the vulgar, but pronounces as rarely as
possible contradictory unconventional views. Now a statement
contradictory to another statement is, in a sense, its repetition,
agreeing with it in almost every respect and differing only by some
addition or omission. Therefore we are able to recognize the contradiction only by a very close scrutiny of every single word, however
small, in the two statements.

Contradictions are the axis of the *Guide*. They show in the
most convincing manner that the actual teaching of that book is
sealed and at the same time reveal the way of unsealing it. While
the other devices used by Maimonides compel the reader to guess
the true teaching, the contradictions offer him the true teaching
quite openly in either of the two contradictory statements. Moreover, while the other devices do not by themselves force readers to
look beneath the surface — for instance, an inappropriate expression
or a clumsy transition, if noticed at all, may be considered to be

merely an inappropriate expression or a clumsy transition, and not a stumblingblock — the contradictions, once they are discovered, compel them to take pains to find out the actual teaching. To discover the contradictions or to find out which contradictory statement is considered by Maimonides to be true, we sometimes need the help of hints. Recognizing the meaning of hints requires a higher degree of understanding by oneself than does the recognition of an obvious contradiction. Hints are supplied by the application of the other Maimonidean devices.

To make our enumeration of those devices somewhat more complete, and not to mention intentional sophisms and ironical remarks, we shall first briefly clarify our foregoing remark on Maimonides' extensive use of words of certain kinds. We may call those words secret words. His secret terminology requires a special study, based upon a complete index of words which have, or may have, secret meaning. These words are partly ambiguous, as in the instances mentioned above, and partly unambiguous, such as *âdamiyyûn, fiqh, dunyâ*. In the second place we may mention various kinds of apostrophes to the reader and mottoes prefixed to the whole work or to individual parts. Another device consists in silence, i.e., the omission of something which only the learned, or the learned who are able to understand of themselves, would miss. Let us take the following example. Maimonides quotes in the *Guide* four times, if I am not mistaken, expressly as an utterance of Aristotle, and with express or tacit approval, the statement that the sense of touch is a disgrace to us.[104] Such fourfold repetition of an express quotation in a book so carefully worded as the *Guide* proves that the quotation is something like a *leitmotif*. Now, that quotation is incomplete. Maimonides omits two words which profoundly alter its meaning. Aristotle says: δόξειεν ἂν δικαίως (ἡ ἀφὴ) ἐπονείδιστος εἶναι.[105] Maimonides omits, then, those two words which characterize the utterance as an ἔνδοξον. Readers of the *Guide*, cognizant of the teachings of the "prince of philosophers," naturally noticed the omission and realized that the passages

---

[104] II, 36 (79a; 262, 11–12); 40 (86b; 272, 4–5); III, 8 (12b; 311, 9–10); 49 (117a; 447, 1–2). Cf. also III, 8 (14a; 313, 18–19).

[105] *Eth. Nic.* 1118b2. I am naturally following that interpretation of the passage cited, on which is based the Arabic translation as quoted by Maimonides. Cf. Averroes *ad loc.*: "et iustum est nos opinari a nobis [sic] quod sensus iste opprobriosus est nobis." Cf. *De anima*, 421a 19–26.

into which the quotation is inserted are of a merely popular, or exoteric character. If one examines the four quotations more closely, one notices that while in the second and third citation Maimonides mentions the name of Aristotle, but not the work from which it is taken, he expressly cites the *Ethics* in the first passage, thus intimating that its source is a book based mainly on ἔνδοξα. In the last quotation Maimonides adds the remark that the quotation is literal, but two or three lines further on, while speaking of the same subject, he refers to the *Ethics* and the *Rhetoric*, i.e., to books devoted to the analysis of ἔνδοξα. There can be no doubt that Maimonides was fully aware of the fact that his citation from Aristotle actually reflected popular rather than philosophic opinion. It is still less doubtful that Maimonides, while agreeing with the complete statement of Aristotle, viz., that the sense of touch is popularly considered disgraceful, by no means believed in the soundness of this popular judgment. As a matter of fact, he contradicted it quite openly by denying any difference in dignity between the senses and by ascribing to the imagination of the vulgar the distinction between senses which are supposed to be perfections and those believed to be imperfections.[106] The reader of the *Guide*, familiar with the main controversial topics of the Middle Ages, will at once realize the bearing of Maimonides' misquotation: the statement of Aristotle, as cited by Maimonides, would afford an excellent justification of ascetic morality — for what Maimonides would call "exaggeration"— and in particular for an ascetic attitude toward sexuality.[107] And the reader who looks up the passages in question in the *Guide* will notice that one of these misquotations is inserted into what Munk calls the "définition générale de la prophétie." Another characteristic omission is Maimonides' failure to mention the immortality of the soul or the resurrection of the body, when he attempts explicitly to answer the question of Divine Providence.[108] He begins his discussion (III, 16–24) by reproducing the philosophic argument against individual providence, mainly

---

[106] I, 47, 46 (51b–52a; 68, 16–21); 2 (14a; 16, 22–17, 3).

[107] Cf., in this connection, III, 8 (14a–b; 313, 22–314, 14).

[108] This is not to deny that Maimonides mentions here the "other world," in connection with such views of Providence as he rejects or the truth of which he neither discusses nor asserts. The phrase in III, 22 (46a; 354, 3–4), "the thing which remains of man after death," is naturally noncommittal with respect to the immortality of the individual soul. Cf. I, 74 (121b; 155, 9–10).

based on the observation that the virtuous are stricken with misery, while the wicked enjoy all forms of happiness. It is therefore all the more perplexing that he pays no attention to what Leibniz has called[109] "le remède [qui] est tout prêt dans l'autre vie." Neither does he mention that remedy in his express recapitulation of the view of Providence characteristic of the literal sense of the Torah.[110] On the other hand, he elsewhere explains in the same context the "good at thy latter end" alluded to in Deuteronomy 8:16 as the fortitude acquired by privations from which Israel had suffered while wandering through the desert.[111]

The fourth and last kind of hints to be indicated here are the *rashei perakim*. This expression, which we have hitherto rendered as "chapter headings," may also mean "beginnings of chapters." In some cases, indeed, Maimonides gives us important hints by the initial word or words of a chapter. The opening word of the section devoted to the rational explanation of biblical commandments (III, 25–49) is the noun, *al-af'âl* ("the actions"). The *af'âl*, synonymously used with *a'mâl*, constitute the second half of the law, the first half consisting of *ârâ'*[112] ("opinions"). Thus this opening gives us a hint that all the preceding chapters of the *Guide* (I–III, 24) are devoted to the "opinions," as distinguished from "actions," which are taught or prescribed by the law. The initial words in the first chapter (III, 8) devoted to theodicy, or the question of providence, is the expression "All bodies which come into existence and perish." These words indicate that this whole group of chapters (III, 8–24) deals exclusively with bodies which come into existence and perish, and not with bodies or souls which do not come into existence or perish. That this guess is correct is shown by other remarks of Maimonides.[113] From this opening, moreover, we must draw the inference that all preceding chapters (I, 1–III, 7) are devoted to things which do not come into existence and perish, and in particular to souls or intelligences which do not

[109] *Théodicée*, § 17.

[110] III, 17 (34b–37b; 338, 21–343, 5).

[111] III, 24 (52b–53a; 362, 10–363, 4). Cf. M.T. Teshubah 8, 1–2.

[112] Cf. in particular III, 52 (130b; 464, 26–465, 5) with Farabi, *'Ihṣâ al-'ulûm*, chap. 5 (or the Hebrew translation by Falakera, in *Reshit ḥokmah*, ed. by David, p. 59). For the two Arabic words for "actions," cf., for instance, III 25 (57a; 368, 8 and 10).

[113] III, 23 (50b–51a; 360, 1–14); 54 (135a; 470, 21–26). Cf. above, pp. 73 f.

come into existence and perish, i.e., to *ma'aseh merkabah*. This inference is confirmed by Maimonides' statement, made at the end of Book III, Chapter 7, that all the preceding chapters are indispensable for the right understanding of *ma'aseh merkabah*, whereas in the following chapters not a word will be said, either explicitly or allusively, about that most exalted topic. Equally important are the beginnings of Book III, Chapter 24, which opens with the ambiguous word *'amr*, which may mean "thing" as well as "command,"[114] and the beginning of the very first chapter of the whole work.

Necessity has led us to make such incoherent and fragmentary remarks about Maimonides' methods of presenting the truth that it will not be amiss if we conclude this chapter with a simile which may drive home its main content to those readers who are more interested in the literary than in the philosophic question. There are books the sentences of which resemble highways, or even motor roads. But there are also books the sentences of which resemble rather winding paths which lead along precipices concealed by thickets and sometimes even along well-hidden and spacious caves. These depths and caves are not noticed by the busy workmen hurrying to their fields, but they gradually become known and familiar to the leisured and attentive wayfarer. For is not every sentence rich in potential recesses? May not every noun be explained by a relative clause which may profoundly affect the meaning of the principal sentence and which, even if omitted by a careful writer, will be read by the careful reader?[115] Cannot miracles be wrought by such little words as "almost,"[116] "perhaps," "seemingly"? May not a statement assume a different shade of meaning by being cast in the form of a conditional sentence? And is it not possible to hide the conditional nature of such a sentence by turning it into a very long sentence and, in particular, by inserting into it a parenthesis of some length? It is to a conditional sentence of this kind that Maimonides confides his general definition of prophecy.[117]

[114] Cf. III, 24 (54a; 364, 16 and 20 f.).

[115] Cf. in this connection I, 21 (26a; 33, 11–17), 27 *vers. fin.*

[116] Cf. III, 19 (39a; 345, 6).

[117] II, 36 (78b–79b; 262, 2–263, 1). Cf. Munk, *Guide*, II, 284, n. 1. Other examples of the same method occur in III, 51 (127b; 460, 27–461, 1) [cf. Munk, *Guide*, III, 445, n. 2] and III, 18 (39a; 344, 22).

6. THE *Guide* AND THE CODE

As we have seen, the *Guide* is devoted to the true science of the law, as distinguished from the science of the law in the usual sense, the *fiqh*. It remains to be considered whether, according to Maimonides, the two kinds, or parts, of the science of the law are of equal dignity or whether one of them is superior to the other.

Several arguments tend to show that Maimonides attached a higher importance to the *fiqh*, or to use the Hebrew term, to the *talmud*,[118] than he did to the subject of the *Guide*: (1) He calls his codification "our great work," whereas he describes the *Guide* as "my treatise." (2) The former exercised a great influence on traditional Judaism, in which respect the *Guide*, already two or three centuries after its publication far surpassed by the *Zohar*[119] in deep and popular appeal, cannot possibly compete. (3) Even under the profoundly changed circumstances of the present time, the *Mishneh Torah* is able to elicit strong and deep emotions in modern readers, whereas the *Guide* is of hardly any interest to people who do not happen to be historians. (4) Whereas the subject matter of the *Mishneh Torah* is easily ascertainable, the question of the field to which the subjects of the *Guide* belong is highly perplexing; it is not a philosophic nor a theological work, nor a book of religion.[120] (5) The code is styled a "repetition of the Torah," whereas the "treatise" is a mere "guide for the perplexed." (6) The *fiqh's* precedence to the subject matter of the *Guide* (the *ma'aseh bereshit* and *ma'aseh merkabah*) is expressly stated by Maimonides when he says, as it were in defense of the *talmud* against the sages of the Talmud, that "although those things [the explanation of the precepts of the Torah] were called by the sages a small thing — for the sages have said 'a great thing is *ma'aseh merkabah*, and a small thing is the discussion of Abbaye and Raba'— yet they ought to have precedence."[121] (7) Having gone so far, one might be tempted to go even farther and assert that the subject of the *Guide* is subservient to and implied in the *talmud*. For Maimonides explicitly

---

[118] Cf. III, 54 (132b; 467, 19–22) with M.T. Talmud torah 1, 11.

[119] Cf. G. Scholem, *Die Geheimnisse der Schöpfung. Ein Kapitel aus dem Sohar* (Berlin, 1935), pp. 6 f.

[120] See above, p. 44.

[121] M. T. Yesodei ha-torah, 4, 13.

says that *pardes* (i.e., *ma'aseh merkabah* and *ma'aseh bereshit*) is included in the *talmud*.[122] This argument might be reinforced by (8) a hint which, as such, in a book such as the *Guide*, is incomparably more significant than an explicit statement. Maimonides explains the true science of the law at the very beginning of his work, whereas he explains the meaning of *fiqh* in the very last chapter. To understand this hint, we must make use of another hint contained in the "chapter headings" of the first and the last chapters. The first chapter begins with the word "Image," while the last chapter opens with the term "Wisdom." This indicates that readers of the *Guide* are to be led from "Image," the sphere of imagination, to "Wisdom," the realm of intelligence: the way which readers of the *Guide* go is an ascent from the lower to the higher, indeed, from the lowest to the highest knowledge. Now the last of the themes treated in the *Guide* is law proper, i.e., the commands and prohibitions of the Torah, and not *ma'aseh bereshit* and *ma'aseh merkabah*, which are dealt with in the preceding sections. Consequently, the precepts of the law, far from being "a small thing," are actually the highest subject, indeed, the end and purpose of the true science of the law. (9) This conclusion is confirmed by an express statement by Maimonides, which establishes the following ascending order of dignity: (a) knowledge of the truth, based on tradition only; (b) such knowledge, based on demonstration; (c) *fiqh*.[123] (10) This hierarchy is also in accordance with the saying of the sages that not study, but action is most important, and it is actions which are determined by the *fiqh*. That hierarchy is imitated by the whole plan of the *Guide*, inasmuch as Maimonides assigns the explanation of the laws to the last group of chapters of that work, and as he explains the meaning of *fiqh* in the last chapter of it: the end is the best.

We have marshaled here all the evidence in favor of the view that Maimonides attached greater importance to the *Mishneh Torah* than to the *Guide*, and hope not to have missed a single argument which has been or could reasonably be adduced in its support. Impressive as they may seem at first sight, however, these arguments possess no validity whatsoever. The second and third arguments are wholly immaterial, for they do not reflect Maimonides'

[122] M. T. Talmud torah, 1, 12.
[123] III, 54 (132b; 467, 18–25).

own conviction, but deal exclusively with what other people thought, or think of the matter. Neither can the fourth argument claim serious consideration, for it, too, is neither based on a Maimonidean statement, nor does, in itself, the perplexing nature of the subject matter of a book necessarily prove its lower rank; the example of Aristotle's *Metaphysics* might be to the point. We shall, then, turn to the remaining seven arguments which are at least apparently based on explicit or implicit statements of Maimonides.

The inference drawn from the description of the *Mishneh Torah* as "our great work" and of the *Guide* as "my treatise" is of little weight. For it is based on a hint, and no evidence has thus far been forthcoming to prove the fact that, or to show the reason why, Maimonides was prevented from stating quite openly that the halakah is of higher dignity than the subject of the *Guide*. The description of the *Mishneh Torah* as a "great" work may very well refer to its length rather than to its dignity, for it is quite natural that a code should be lengthier than the discussion of "roots." Or are we to believe that Maimonides attached a higher value to the "great book" of the Sabean Isḥâq "on the laws of the Sabeans and the details of their religion and their feasts and their sacrifices and their prayers and the other subjects of their religion" than he did to the "book" of the same unknown author "on the defence of the religion of the Sabeans?"[124] Moreover, it is doubtful whether Maimonides actually called the *Guide* a "treatise," rather than a "speech," and whether he called the *Mishneh Torah* a "work." "Work" would be a synonym for "book."[125] While Maimonides, for the most part, uses the two terms interchangeably, yet in one instance at least he hints at a distinction between *kitâb* (*sefer*, "book") and *ta'lîf* (*hibbur*, usually translated by "work"). He does this when speaking of the contradictions which are to be found "in any book or in any *ta'lîf*."[126] Abravanel, in his commentary on this passage, suggests that Maimonides means by "books" the books *par excellence*, i.e., the Bible, while he means by *tawâlîf* (or, rather, *hibburim*) the talmudic and philosophic literature. However grateful we ought to be to Abravanel for his indicating the problem, we certainly cannot accept his solution. For in the same section of the

---

[124] Cf. III, 29 (66b; 380, 13–15).

[125] See Louis Ginzberg's note s.v. *hibbur*, in his appendix to I. Efros's *Philosophical Terms in the Moreh Nebukim*, New York, 1924. Cf. above, p. 46.

[126] I, Introd. (9b; 11, 7–8).

Guide Maimonides mentions also the "books" of the philosophers.[127] On the other hand, two lines below this distinction, Maimonides applies the word *ta'lîf* to such works as the Mishnah, the Baraitot, and the Gemara.[128] We shall then suggest that by occasionally distinguishing between "books" and *tawâlîf*, Maimonides intended to point out once for all the distinction between such writings as the Bible and the works of philosophers on the one hand, and other literature, as exemplified by the talmudic compilation on the other hand. In fact, "compilation" would be a more literal translation of *ta'lîf* or *ḥibbur* than is "work" or "book." We know from the example of *maqâla* that Maimonides, when using a word emphatically, uses it in its original sense, which, as such, is often more hidden, rather than in its derivative and more conventional meaning. Thus we ought to render *ta'lîf* or *ḥibbur*, when emphatically used by Maimonides, by "compilation," rather than by "work." Since he doubtless uses it emphatically when he regularly calls the *Mishneh Torah* a *ta'lîf* or a *ḥibbur*, we ought to substitute the translation "our great compilation," for the usual translation "our great work."[129] Maimonides does not, then, distinguish between the *Guide* and the *Mishneh Torah* as between a treatise and a sublime work, but rather as between a confidential communication and an extensive compilation.

It is likewise but a popular fallacy to assume that Maimonides attributes a higher dignity to the *Mishneh Torah* than to the *Guide*, because he calls the former "*our* great composition," whereas he calls the latter "*my* treatise." For the plural is not necessarily

[127] I, Introd. (11b; 13, 8). Abravanel's comment may have been suggested by a mistake of Ibn Tibbon (or of a copyist or printer), since we find, in our editions of Ibn Tibbon's translation, the words "the books of the philosophers" rendered by "the words of the philosophers." But it is also possible that that suggestion was caused by I, 8 (18b; 22, 26–27), where a distinction is drawn between the "books" of the prophets and the *tawâlîf* (or *ḥibburim*) of the "men of science."

[128] Cf. I, Introd. (10a, 11, 10) with *ibid.* (10b–11a; 12, 12–19).

[129] The correctness of this translation becomes fully apparent when one examines the way in which Maimonides employs, in his introduction to M. T., the terms חבר and חבור as against כתב and ספר. The M. T. is a חבור, because he has composed it לחבר דברים המתפררים מכל אלו החבורין (i.e., from the talmudic and gaonic literatures). Cf. Teshubah. 4, 7 (86b 11 Hyamson). For the original meaning of חבור, see also Yesodei ha-torah, 1, 11; 3, 7. L. Blau's suggestion (in MbM, II, 339 f.) that חבור corresponds to *summa*, as distinguished from *commentatio*, is ruled out by the fact that both M. T. and C. M. are called by Maimonides *ḥibburim* (or *tawâlîf*). See, for example, I, 71 (93b; 121, 19).

a *pluralis majestatis*. The significance of the singular and the plural in Maimonidean usage comes out most clearly in the discussion of Providence. There, he distinguishes, with an unequivocalness which could hardly be surpassed, between *"our* opinion" and *"my* opinion." He introduces "what I believe" as one interpretation of "our opinion, i.e., the opinion of our law," and contrasts it with the interpretation accepted by "the general run of our scholars." Somewhat later he distinguishes the opinion of "our religious community" about divine knowledge from "my discourse" upon that subject.[130] Even more explicitly he demarcates "what we say, viz, we, the community of the adherents of the law" and "our belief" from the opinion of the philosophers and "what I say." Finally, he distinguishes between "the opinion of our law," which he had identified before with "our opinion," and the correct, or "my" opinion.[131] One may explain this distinction in the following way: "our opinion" is based on the literal sense of the Bible, whereas "my opinion" is in accordance with the intention of the Bible, i.e., with its hidden or secret meaning. For "my opinion" brings into harmony the intelligible view with the literal sense of the Bible.[132] "My opinion" is distinguished from "our opinion" by including some additional idea which reveals itself only after a careful examination and which alone really matters. "Our opinion," on the other hand, is the opinion to which all consent and which all repeat and which does not contain any idea peculiar to any individual, and especially not to "my opinion."[133] Although the identity of the correct opinion with "my opinion" is yet to be proved, and although in the present stage of research it would be rash to exclude the possibility that "my opinion," too, is an exoteric opinion, it is most important in the present connection to realize that the distinction between "our opinion" and "my opinion" is characteristic not only of Maimonides' discussion of Providence, but also of the whole *Guide*. This is, indeed, the considered view of a medieval commentator, who sees in the distinction here made between the opinion of "the general run of our scholars" and "my opinion" merely the application of a general principle which Maimonides pronounces at the beginning

[130] III, 17 (34b; 338, 21–24). Cf. *ibid.*, (35b; 340, 10 ff.). III, 18 *in fine.*
[131] III, 20 (41a–42a; 347, 21–348, 16); 23 (49b; 358, 26–359, 1).
[132] III, 17 (34b–35b; 338, 22; 339, 16; 340, 13 f.). Cf. *ibid.* (37b; 342, 26–27).
[133] Cf. III, 23 (50a; 359, 4–15).

of his book by quoting Proverbs 22:17.[134] He understands this verse to signify "Bow down thine ear, and hearken to the words of the sages,[135] but apply thine heart unto mine opinion." This verse, then, establishes from the outset the principle of the *Guide* to reveal "my opinion" as an "addition" to "our opinion." Therefore the work is called "my speech." This conclusion is confirmed, rather than refuted by Maimonides' immediately preceding quotatation from Proverbs 8:4, "Unto you, O men, I call; and my voice is to the sons of man," which, in Maimonides' interpretation, means to say that his call is addressed to the few elect individuals partaking of the angelic nature, while his articulate speech is addressed to the vulgar.[136] For, as has been shown, "my speech" is far from being identical with "my articulate speech"; "my speech" or perhaps "my opinion" is much more likely to be identical with "my call." Thus, we repeat, the *Guide* is "my speech" revealing "my opinion," as distinguished from "our opinion," expressed in "our compilation," the *Mishneh Torah*, where generally speaking, Maimonides appears as the mouthpiece of the Jewish community or of the Jewish tradition. Since Maimonides doubtless subordinated his own views to those of the Jewish tradition, one may object, his hint of calling the *Guide* "my" book and the *Mishneh Torah* "our" book would still prove that he attached a higher dignity to the latter work. We must therefore discuss the remaining six arguments.

The fifth argument is based on the hints supplied by the titles of the two books; a "repetition of the Torah" must be of a much higher order than a mere "guide for the perplexed." We shall not raise the objection that the former title ought not to be translated by "repetition of the Torah," but rather by "the second [book] after the Torah." It is true that the latter translation is based on the only explicit statement by which Maimonides justifies the title of his code.[137] But a book which is second to another book and

---

[134] Shem Tob on III, 17 (34b; 338, 21–24): ועל זה ועל כיוצא בו נאמר הט אזנך ושמע דברי חכמים ולבך תשית לדעתי. See also *idem* on III, 18 *in fine*. Cf. also W. Bacher, MbM, II, 180.

[135] Cf. II, 33 (76a; 257, 26–258, 1); M. T. Yesodei ha-torah 4, 13. See also C. M. on Sanhedrin X (Holzer, p. 9, or Pococke, p. 147).

[136] I, 14; M. T. Yesodei ha-torah, 2, 7.

[137] See Blau, MbM, II, 338. From this fact, pointed out by him, Blau draws the inference that "das Wesen des Buches ist im Worte חבור ausgedrückt," viz., it is not expressed by the words *Mishneh Torah*. And he adds in italics:

which restates its only authentic interpretation may also rightly be called a repetition thereof.[138] The *Mishneh Torah* certainly is a repetition of the oral law, which, according to Maimonides, is the only authentic interpretation of the (written) Torah. It is hardly necessary to add that the allusion to Deuteronomy, is anything but unintentional.   It should not be forgotten, however, that, some time before Maimonides, Abraham bar Hiyya had drawn the inference from the traditional designation of the fifth book of Moses as "Mishneh Torah" that a distinction is to be made between the Torah, i.e., the second, third, and fourth books of Moses, and the Mishneh Torah, i.e., the fifth book. According to Abraham, who, as it were, anticipated the most important result of modern biblical criticism, the Torah regulates the "order of service"(i.e., of worship) to be followed by the "holy congregation," which cares little for earthly things and in particular not for national defense. This "order of service" is the rule of life which Israel followed while wandering through the desert, when it was protected in a miraculous way against any external menace, and which is also to be followed by Israel whenever it lives in exile and, unable to defend itself against its enemies, must place its reliance exclusively upon God's mercy. The Mishneh Torah, on the other hand, adds to the "order of service," which it presupposes or repeats, "the order of service to the kingdom"; it is addressed to the "just kingdom," a community undetached from earthly things and concerned about national defense. Mainly devoted to matters of jurisdiction, especially in agricultural life, and to laws concerning kings and wars, it establishes a rule of life which Israel followed as long as it lived in its own land.[139] I venture to suggest that Maimonides remembered Abraham bar Hiyya's interpretation when he selected the name *Mishneh Torah* for his code, which contained not only the laws of exile but also those of the land; and that a certain reason, implied in Abraham's interpretation, led Maimonides to conclude his code so impressively with the laws regarding kings and their wars. In

---

"Der Name *Mischne Torah* findet sich tatsächlich kein zweitesmal bei Maimuni." If this remark were correct, it certainly would deserve to be italicized, since it would show that Maimonides attached an extremely high and secret importance to the name *Mishneh Torah*. But as a matter of fact, that name occurs, I believe, ten times in the *Guide*.

[138] Cf. S. Zeitlin, *Maimonides* (New York, 1935), p. 86.

[139] *Hegyon ha-nefesh*, ed. by Freimann, pp. 38a–39b.

translating the title by "repetition of the Torah," we are also mindful of the peculiar significance with which the word *repetition* is used by Maimonides. But does the fact that the *Mishneh Torah* is a repetition of the Torah entitle us to assume that Maimonides judged that work, or its subject, to be more important than the *Guide* or its subject? "Repetition of the Torah" is an ambiguous expression: it may mean a repetition, reproducing the Torah in accordance with its external proportions, or one reproducing it with regard to the hidden and true proportions of its various subjects. There can be no doubt that the code reproduces the Torah according to its external proportions only. For the Torah consists of true "opinions" and of "actions," and whereas the "actions" are determined by it in great detail and with extreme precision, the true "opinions" are indicated only in bare outline. This proportion was preserved intact by the Talmud, since the sages of the Talmud spoke for the most part of precepts and manners, and not of opinions and beliefs.[140] In exactly the same way, the *Mishneh Torah* deals in the most detailed fashion with "actions," but speaks of the basic truths only briefly and allusively (though by allusions approximating clear pronouncements) and by haphazard.[141] The *Guide*, on the other hand, is devoted mainly, if not exclusively, to "opinions," as distinguished from "actions." Now "opinions" are as much superior in dignity to "actions" as is the perfection of the soul to that of the body. Therefore, the highest aim of the Torah is the regulation of our opinions, to which the order, prescribed by the Torah, of our actions is subservient.[142] Thus the true proportions of the subjects of the Torah are imitated not by the *Mishneh Torah*, which is devoted to the science of the law in its usual sense, but by the *Guide*, which is devoted to the true science of the law. We conclude, then, that whereas the *Mishneh Torah* is the "repetition of the Torah" *simpliciter* the *Guide* is the "repetition of the Torah" *par excellence*.[143] Should the objection be raised that the title of the

[140] III, 27 (59b and 60a; 371, 29 f.; 372, 9 f.); 28 (60b–61a; 373, 7–17); I, Introd. (11a–b; 13, 2–5).

[141] I, Introd. (3b and 6a; 3, 7; 6, 8–9); I, 71 (97a; 125, 14).

[142] III, 27.

[143] An allusion to that relation may be found in the fact that the M. T. consists of 14 (=2 x 7) books, and that the precepts of the law are divided in the *Guide*, too, into 14 groups, whereas the explanation of the highest secret of the Torah, i.e., of *ma'aseh merkabah*, is given in 7 chapters of the *Guide*. Compare

Guide does not indicate its being a repetition of the Torah, we need only refer to the affinity between *guide* and *guidance* (*torah*).[144] The *Guide* is a repetition or imitation of the Torah particularly suitable to "perplexed" people, while the *Mishneh Torah* is such a repetition addressed primarily to people who are not "perplexed."

The sixth argument, referring to the explicit statement of Maimonides concerning the precedence of the *fiqh*, ignores his failure to contradict the talmudic saying that "the discussion of Abbaye and Raba is a small thing" as compared with *ma'aseh merkabah*. He merely explains that saying by adding to it the remark that knowledge of the precepts ought to precede concern with the secret topics. For knowledge of the precepts is indispensable for their execution, and their execution is indispensable for one's composure of mind, as well as for the establishment of peace and order; these, in turn, are indispensable for acquiring "the life of the coming world" or for acquiring true opinions.[145] That is to say, knowledge of the precepts is merely a means to an end, which, in its turn, is only a means to another, the ultimate end, i.e., to the understanding of *ma'aseh bereshit* and *ma'aseh merkabah*. Knowledge of the precepts precedes, then, knowledge of the secrets, as the means precedes the end. Maimonides adds yet another reason: the precepts can be known to everybody, to young and old, to unintelligent as well as intelligent, whereas the secret teaching, which is clear and manifest to the "men of speculation" only, was not fully grasped even by some of the greatest sages of the Talmud.[146] We conclude, therefore, that the precedence attributed by Maimoni-

---

also the 49 (= 7 x 7) chapters which lead up from "Image" to "Angels," i.e., to a subject which is second to one subject only; and the 70 (= 10 x 7) chapters which lead up from "Image" to *rakab*, i.e., to the grammatical root of *merkabah*. To understand the number 70, one has to bear in mind that the word *âdamiyyûn* occurs, if I am not mistaken, 10 times in the *Guide*, and that the Torah speaks according to the language of *benei adam*. The word *adam* is explained in the fourteenth chapter of the *Guide*; the number of the chapter explaining the various meanings of man is the same as the number of books of the M. T. or of parts of the law. See also above, n. 137.

[144] Compare the explanation of *torah* as *hidâya* in III, 13 (25a; 327, 10 f); I, 2 (13b; 16, 9) with the synonymous use of *hadâ* and *dalla* in II, 12 (26b; 195, 27). See also III, 45 (101a; 425, 17).

[145] M. T. Yesodei ha-torah, 4, 13. Cf. M. T. Teshubah 8, 5–6, 14; M. N. III, 27 (59b; 371, 25–28).

[146] III, Introd. (2a; 297, 6–8, 9–10). Cf. also I, 17. M. T. Yesodei ha-torah 4, 13.

des to knowledge of the precepts is merely a priority in time, and not at all a superior dignity.

The seventh argument is based on Maimonides' statement that *ma'aseh bereshit* and *ma'aseh merkabah* belong to the *talmud*. Maimonides makes this statement in connection with his division of the study of the Torah into three parts: the study of the written Torah, that of the oral Torah, and the Talmud. The study of the prophetic writings and hagiographa belongs to that of the written Torah; the study of explanations thereof is part of the oral Torah; and the study of secret subjects is included in the *talmud*.[147] In order to understand this statement correctly, we must first bear in mind that *talmud* may be used ambiguously for a certain group of writings (the Babylonian and Jerusalem Talmuds), as well as for a peculiar kind of study. In the former sense, the statement that secret topics belong to the *talmud*, and not to the written or oral Torah, would mean that they are to be found in the Talmud rather than in the Bible,[148] but it would have no bearing upon the subordination of the secret teaching to the *fiqh*. If we take *talmud*, as we probably should, in its second meaning, it would indeed seem at first sight that Maimonides subordinates the study of the secret topics to the *fiqh*, just as he certainly subordinates the study of the prophetic writings and the hagiographa to that of the Pentateuch. But what does he actually say? Starting from the implicit assumption that all studies which are of any value are comprised within the study of the Torah, he raises the question: to which part of that study does the study of that "great thing" (i.e., of the secret teaching) belong? And he answers: since the secret topics are the most difficult topics,[149] their study must belong to the most advanced part of the all-comprising study of the Torah, i.e., to the *talmud*. He does not preclude the possibility that this most advanced study be subdivided into two distinct parts, the *fiqh* and the true science of the law.[150] In fact, he alludes to this possibility when he says that men, after having reached a more advanced stage of wisdom, ought to devote their time almost exclusively to the *talmud*, according to the level of their intelligence.

[147] M. T. Talmud torah, 1, 12.
[148] Cf. I, 71 (93b and 94a; 121, 11 f., 25 f.) and the parallel passage in III, Introd. (2b; 297, 17 f.).
[149] M. T. Yesodei ha-torah 2, 12; 4, 11, 13.
[150] I, Introd. (3a; 2, 12–14); III, 54 (132a–b; 467, 2–22).

The tenth argument is based on the saying of R. Simeon ben Gamaliel that not study, but action is most important, and on the assumption that Maimonides must have accepted this saying in its apparent meaning. But, according to his explanation,[151] it merely refers to speeches about laws and virtues and merely demands that man's actions be in accordance with his speeches expressing obedient and virtuous thoughts. Otherwise, he expressly recognizes in the *Mishneh Torah* that study of the Torah is superior in dignity to all other actions.[152] Above all, in the last chapter of the *Guide* he asserts that most precepts of the law are merely a means for the acquisition of moral virtue, which, in turn, is merely a means subservient to the true end, namely, speculative virtue, or the true knowledge of things divine.[153]

In the light of this Maimonidean assertion and of the place where it is found, the eighth argument cannot possibly be sound. If, indeed, the first "chapter heading" of the *Guide*, "Image," were contrasted with a last "chapter heading," "Wisdom," we certainly would have to conclude that all readers of the *Guide* are meant to ascend from the lowest to the highest knowledge. But, as it happens, the last "chapter heading" is not "Wisdom," but "The word wisdom." Now "The word wisdom" is not necessarily superior to "Image," as is shown by the fact, constantly present in Maimonides' mind, that many learned people living in a world of imaginary and imaginative ideas call their possession and use of these ideas "wisdom" or "speculation." On the other hand, "wisdom," if rightly understood, indicates something absolutely superior to "image"; a man who understands the word wisdom according to its true meaning has overcome, or is on the way to overcoming, his imaginary views. The equivocal last "chapter heading," when contrasted with the unequivocal first "chapter heading," indicates the ambiguity inherent in the reading of the *Guide*. Its reader may ascend from imaginary views to true wisdom, but he also may not leave the world of imagination for a single moment, so that he finally arrives at the mere word "wisdom," which is but a shadow or image of wisdom itself. But let us apply to such readers the Maimonidean dictum that there is no reason for mentioning them in this place

[151] C. M. on Abot I, 17.
[152] M. T. Talmud torah, 1, 3; 3, 3–5.
[153] III, 54 (133b–134b; 468, 22–470, 11).

in this treatise.[154] Let us think of that reader only to whom the *Guide* is addressed and who, after having undergone training by the *Guide*, will certainly have substituted intelligent views for imaginary ones. For such a reader the study of the *Guide* is an ascent from the lowest to the highest knowledge. This is only tantamount to saying that by understanding the last chapter, or the last group of chapters, he will have attained to a knowledge more complete than that which he had acquired before reading these chapters. But it obviously does not of necessity indicate the superior dignity of the subjects treated in the last group of chapters.

In order to grasp the principle underlying the arrangement of the various subjects in the *Guide*, we must remind ourselves of its original purpose to repeat the Torah with regard to the hidden proportions of its subjects. The Torah having been given to man by an intermediary prophet, we may be permitted for a little while to replace Torah by prophecy. Maimonides asserts that the prophet's ascent to the highest knowledge is followed by his descent to the "people of the earth," i.e., to their government and instruction.[155] The prophet is, then, a man who not only has attained the greatest knowledge, indeed a degree of knowledge which is not attained by mere philosophers, but who is able also to perform the highest political functions.[156] A similar combination of theoretical and political excellence is required for the understanding of the secret

[154] I, Introd. (4b; 4, 11–12).

[155] I, 15 (22b; 28, 4–7). Cf. Plato, *Republic*, VII, 519c8–520a4 (also 514a, 517d5).

[156] That Maimonides conceived of the prophets as statesmen is shown also by the main division of the affirmative precepts in S. M. (or in the enumeration of the 613 commandments at the beginning of M. T.). There he lists first the precepts regulating the relations between man and God, and then those which order the relations among men. (See the remarks of Peritz in MbM, I, 445 ff.). The second class of these precepts (Nos. 172–248) opens with the commandments regarding the prophet, the king, and the high court; the prophet evidently is the head of the political organization. Cf. II, 40 (85b–86a; 270, 24–27). The question of the relation between king and priest is touched upon in III, 45 (98b; 422, 9–13). How far Maimonides accepted the teaching of the *Falâsifa*, according to which a "priestly city" is one of the bad constitutions, must here remain an open question. See Ibn Baǧǧa, *k. tadbîr al-mutawaḥḥid*, chap. 1, in the Hebrew extraction by Moses Narboni, ed. by D. Herzog, p. 8; and Averroes, *Paraphrasis in Rempubl. Plat.*, tr. 3., in *Opp. Aristotelis* (Venice 1550), III, 187c19–24.

teaching of the prophets.[157] Since the *Guide* is devoted to the interpretation of that secret teaching, Maimonides will also have imitated, in some manner or other, the way of the prophets. To be sure, the prophet is enabled to perform his political function of governing the "people of the earth" and of teaching them by the power of his imagination, i.e., by his capacity of representing the truth to the vulgar by means of images or parables, as Maimonides clearly intimates in the general definition of prophecy and in the chapter following it.[158] He himself, however, attempts to replace the parables by another method of representing the truth. Yet the fundamental similarity between the prophet, the bringer of the secret teaching, and the interpreter of the secret teaching remains unaltered by that change in the method. Therefore, we are from the outset entitled to expect that the sequence of topics in the *Guide* would imitate the way of the prophets, which is ascent, followed by descent. This expectation is proved to be correct by the actual structure of the *Guide*. Maimonides, or his reader, gradually and slowly climbs up from the depth of "image" to *ma'aseh merkabah*, the highest subject, which is fully treated in Book III, Chapters 1–7 only. At the end of this exposition, Maimonides declares that he will say no more about that subject. Accordingly, he begins the next chapter with the heading, "All bodies which come into existence and perish." Finally, he descends one more step, from "opinion" to "actions." The same prophetic way of ascent, followed by descent, is evidently used as a model in his recommended order of studies for unprophetic men, referred to in the ninth argument, namely, (1) knowledge of the truth, based on tradition only; (2) such knowledge based on demonstration; (3) *fiqh*. For the demonstrative knowledge of truth is the highest degree attainable to unprophetic men.[159]

To sum up, according to Maimonides the *Mishneh Torah* is devoted to *fiqh*, the essence of which is to deal with actions; while the *Guide* deals with the secrets of the Torah, i.e., primarily opinions or beliefs, which it treats demonstratively, or at least as demonstratively as possible. Demonstrated opinions or beliefs are, according to Maimonides, absolutely superior in dignity to good actions

---

[157] See above, p. 56.
[158] See also Falakera, *Reshit ḥokmah*, ed. David, p. 30.
[159] III, 54 (132b; 467, 18–27). Cf. I, 33 (36b; 47, 25–26).

or to their exact determination. In other words, the chief subject of the *Guide* is *ma'aseh merkabah*, which is "a great thing," while the chief subject of the *Mishneh Torah* is the precepts, which are "a small thing." Consequently, the subject of the *Guide* is, according to Maimonides, absolutely superior in dignity to the subject of the *Mishneh Torah*. Since the dignity of a book, *caeteris paribus*, corresponds to the dignity of its subject, and since, as is shown by a comparison of Maimonides' own introductory remarks to the two books, he wrote the *Guide* with no less skill and care than his code, we must conclude that he considered the *Guide* as absolutely superior in dignity.

This conclusion, based on the general principle underlying his entire work and nowhere contradicted by him, that knowledge of the truth is absolutely superior in dignity to any action, is reinforced by some further statements or hints. We have started from the distinction made by him at the very beginning of the *Guide* between the true science of the law and the *fiqh*: the former deals chiefly with the secrets of the Bible or, more generally, with opinions and beliefs both secret and public;[160] in other words, it demonstrates the beliefs taught by the law. Maimonides repeats this distinction in the last chapter, in a somewhat modified manner; he there distinguishes three sciences: the science of the Torah, wisdom, and *fiqh*.[161] The science of the law, or the science of the Torah, does not demonstrate the basic principles taught by the law, since the law itself does not demonstrate them.[162] The *fiqh*, which at the beginning of the *Guide* had been identified with the science of the law, is now clearly distinguished from it or from the science of the Torah, as well as from wisdom.[163] Wisdom is the demonstration of the opinions taught by the law. Now the *Guide* is devoted to such demonstration; hence the true science of the law, mentioned at the beginning as the subject of the work, is identical with wisdom, as distinguished from both the science of the law and from the *fiqh*. Maimonides repeats, then, the distinction between the true science of the law and the science of the law; yet he no longer calls the former a science of the law, but wisdom, and no longer identifies

---

[160] Cf., for example, I, 1 (12a; 14, 14), 18 (24a; 30, 7) with I, 35.

[161] III, 54 (132b; 467, 18–20).

[162] III, 54 (132a–b; 467, 2–9, 13–14).

[163] III, 54 (132a–b; 467, 18–23 and 7 and 13–14). Cf. III, 41 (88b; 409, 15–16); M. T. Talmud torah, 1, 11–12.

the (ordinary) science of the law (or of the Torah) with the *fiqh*. The relation of wisdom to the *fiqh* is explained by a simile: the students of the *fiqh*, arriving at the divine palace, merely walk around it, whereas only speculation on the "roots," i.e., demonstration of the basic truths taught by the law, leads one unto the presence of God.[164]

Though Maimonides discloses his view at the end of his work only, he does not fail to give hints of it on previous suitable occasions. When he tells the story of his abandoned plan to write two books on the parables of the prophets and the Midrashim, he states that he had intended those books for the vulgar, but later realized that such an explanation would neither be suitable for, nor fill a need felt by the vulgar. That is why he has limited himself to that brief and allusive discussion of the basic truths of the law, which is to be found in his code. In the *Guide*, however, he goes on to say, he addresses himself to a man who has studied philosophy and who, while believing in the teachings of the law, is perplexed in regard to them.[165] Those sentences, enigmatic and elusive as they are, show clearly that the *Guide* was not addressed to the vulgar, nor the *Mishneh Torah* to the perplexed. Are we, then, to believe that the latter was written for students of philosophy who had not become perplexed as regards the teachings of the law? Hardly, since Maimonides does not tire of repeating that the code is devoted to the *fiqh* and consequently is addressed to students of *fiqh*, who may or may not be familiar with philosophy. This is also shown by his failure to discuss in the *Mishneh Torah* the basic truths of the law, according to his primary and main intention and only, as it were, incidentally or haphazardly.[166] Evidently the *Mishneh Torah* was written also for people who had not studied philosophy at all and therefore were not perplexed; in other words, it was addressed to "all men."[167] This is quite clearly the meaning of the following passage in the *Guide*: "I have already explained to all men the four differences by which the prophecy of our teacher

[164] III, 51 (123b–124a; 455, 21–28). In his commentary on this chapter, Shem Tob relates that "many talmudic scholars have asserted that Maimonides had not written this chapter, and that, if he did write it, it ought to be suppressed, or rather, it would deserve to be burned."

[165] I, Introd. (5b–6a; 5, 18–6, 11).

[166] I, Introd. (3a; 2, 13–16); 71 (97a; 125, 23–24).

[167] Cf. M.T. Yesodei ha-torah, 4, 13.

Moses is distinguished from the prophecy of the other prophets, and I have proved it and made it manifest in the Commentary on the Mishna and in the *Mishneh Torah*." The meaning of "all men" (*al-nâs kâffa*) is incidentally explained in connection with a synonymous phrase (*ǧamî' al-nâs*): "all men, i.e., the vulgar."[168] This allusion to the exoteric character of the code and the commentary naturally has to be taken into account, not only in the interpretation of these two works but also for the adequate understanding of all quotations from them in the *Guide*.

We conclude: The *Mishneh Torah* is primarily addressed to the general run of men, while the *Guide* is addressed to the small number of people who are able to understand by themselves.

[168] II, 35 *in princ.*; III, 22 (45b; 357, 10). Cf. also M. T., Introd., 4b, 4–19 (Hyamson), and *Ḳobeṣ*, II, 15b.

CHAPTER FOUR

MAIMONIDES'
TREATISE ON RESURRECTION:
A COMPARATIVE STUDY

By JOSHUA FINKEL

To Professor Duncan B. Macdonald, Teacher and Friend

WHILE the Arabic original of Maimonides' *Maqala* has become
known only in recent times,[1] Samuel ibn Tibbon's (*c.* 1150–
c. 1230) Hebrew translation of it has come down to us in a considerable number of MSS and editions. An English rendering of
it was published in 1859 by Morais.[2] In spite of its frequent mention in many polemical epistles and theological treatises of the
Middle Ages, modern critics have not given it the full attention
it deserves. The writer is fully aware that the problems connected
with the *Maqala* are vaster and more complicated than are presented in this analysis. An examination of the long and bitter
controversy precipitated by it and a comparison of Maimonides'
doctrine with the various views on resurrection held by the Kalam
philosophers and the unclassified thinkers of Islam would require
a monograph in itself. But it is hoped that even within its limited
compass, the present essay will help to clear up some essential
points of this minor but important theological treatise of Maimonides.

[1] It is extant in several incomplete manuscripts in the possession of the
Library of the Jewish Theological Seminary of America and the British Museum.
Cf. the writer's critical edition of the Arabic and Hebrew texts in *Proceedings of
the American Academy for Jewish Research*, IX (1939), 87 ff.

[2] *The Jewish Messenger*, New York, VI (No. 11), 82–83; (No. 12), 90–91;
(No. 13), 98; (No. 14), 106; (No. 15), 114. For an old Latin translation and for
a report of another Hebrew version and a retranslation into Arabic, see Steinschneider, *Hebräische Übersetzungen des Mittelalters*, Berlin, 1893, p. 431 and his
Arabische Literatur der Juden, Frankfort, 1902, p. 210.

1. THEORETICAL DIFFICULTIES

The *Maqala* may be divided into three parts: the introduction, the main section, and the postscript. In his opening remarks the author discusses briefly the unity of God, resurrection, and the future world. To lend strength to his thesis of the ultimate incorporeal state of the individual, he suggests as a parallel the incorporeity of God. After reviewing his previous statements on this topic, he adds that what has prevented the multitude from grasping his stand on the nature of the future existence of the soul is their inability to conceive the reality of the spiritual, which is the reality *par excellence*. He then describes the events which had led to the composition of the *Maqala*. After the *Mishneh Torah*, his *magnum opus*, became known in many lands, one of the pupils of the Academy in Damascus openly voiced disbelief in the resurrection of the body, basing his denial on some statements in Maimonides' code. Maimonides ignored the incident, on the assumption that such a flagrant misunderstanding of his teaching was singular and unlikely to recur. However, in the year 1189 he received a letter from Yemen in which the writer, *inter alia*, also complained of a widespread denial of resurrection, among the Jews of southern Arabia, and asked him for the clarification of various mooted points. Maimonides complied with the request. He intimates that the gist of his reply was that resurrection of the dead is a basic creed, that scriptural references to it are in no wise to be allegorized, and that life in the world to come is to supersede the state of existence after resurrection. Nevertheless, two years later he was informed from Babylonia that Samuel ben Ali, the head of the Bagdad Academy, approached with a similar inquiry from Yemen, had composed an impromptu essay on the subject, in which some of Maimonides' eschatological views were sharply assailed. It was this essay, which, upon reaching Maimonides, gave him the final impetus for the composition of the present treatise. In a few general remarks he deprecates his opponent's uncritical use of edifying rabbinic utterances concerning the life beyond and proves the latter's incompetence and utter confusion in matters philosophical. Here his rejoinder virtually ends; it consists of a refutation of method, rather than specific arguments. Indeed, barring one more severe censure of the Bagdadian for having falsely accused him of denying the explicit mention of resurrection in the Bible, Maimonides does not again refer to him directly in the discourse.

He then launches into the exposition of his conception of resurrection and the future world, stressing the fact that essentially there is nothing here which he had not already discussed in his *Commentary* on the Mishnah and in the *Mishneh Torah*; the amplified presentation here is due only to repetition, the expanded phraseology being designed to aid popular understanding. Soon thereafter he injects, almost parenthetically, the gist of his peculiar and much quoted theory of resurrection: "And so it appears[3] to me from these verses that the individuals, whose souls will return to their bodies, will eat, drink, marry and procreate, and then die after enjoying that very long span of life characteristic of the Messianic era."

He next proceeds to prove the denuded state of the soul in the world to come on teleological grounds. Since God brings nothing to pass which is unprofitable, and since the earthly conditions, in adaptation to which the various organs have been formed, will not obtain there, repeated bodily existence is unthinkable in the hereafter. This argument is implied in the talmudic statement "There will be no eating, drinking, etc. in the world to come."[4] However, if *creatio utilitatis causa* is not contradicted, reincarnation is possible. Thus the quickening of the dead is not inconsistent with God's design as far as it is mundane. In contradistinction to the immortality of the soul, it is effected by means supernatural. However, the overwhelming subjective interest of humanity in it must not delude us into exaggerating its significance per se. It certainly will not bring with itself a cosmic cataclysm, nor will it outmiracle miracles, but it will be a miracle like all other miracles. Its denial, of course, leads inevitably to the denial of all miracles, and that in itself is enough to brand one as an unbeliever. Hence, *resurrectio carnis* must be accounted a principle of faith.

He further claims that his limiting the clear references to resurrection to only one or two instances in Scripture does not

---

[3] "Appears" = יבדו in the Arabic text. This does not imply that Maimonides did not intend to express himself positively on the subject. C. *Ḳobeṣ*, I, 26a: ‏ודבר שהוא מפלפולי אומר בפי' יראה לי שהדבר כך כך‎.

[4] Berakot 17a.

prove in the least his reluctance to accept it. Once admitting its unequivocal mention in a single verse, he has as stoutly committed himself on it as one who finds it repeated in a thousand verses. Moreover, he just as often discounts literal interpretation with regard to miracles in general. Would anyone be justified, or has anyone, indeed, ever accused him on this account of disinclination to allow them in principle? To be sure, he opposes the prevalent tendency among the masses to accept indiscriminately, at their face value, all wondrous stories, as if the Bible were an anthology of the weird and uncanny, and not a book with a rational world outlook. It must be borne in mind that the ancients often wrote of natural phenomena in terms defying ordinary experience. The uninitiated, carried away by the glamor of the miraculous, mistake form for content, while the discerning student fathoms the intended matter-of-fact meaning. However, no method of getting at the bottom of the biblical figures of speech is infallible. He has received no revelation, nor is there any authorized tradition as to which biblical statements are narrations of fact and which are hyperboles or metaphors. Some are of realistic purport, beyond question, and some are unmistakably allegorical. As for the doubtful ones, it is only by applying to them the canons of philosophical and literary analysis that we may hope to attain a degree of verisimilitude and an approach to the truth.

Many people, too, he goes on to say, were unduly perturbed by his remark in the *Mishneh Torah* that, among other things, the Messiah should not be expected to resurrect the dead. They thought that this was a flat contradiction to his statement in the *Commentary* on Ḥelek that resurrection is a principle of faith.[5] But if the Messiah is not to bring them back to life, it does not follow that neither will God. Indeed He may achieve that at any time, whether before, after, or during the lifetime of the Messiah. Similarly, the fact that in his previous writings he referred but briefly to the doctrine is by no means indicative of a disinclination on his part to avow it. In the first place, brevity is the spice of his style. And secondly, there is not really much that one can say on the subject. Unlike immortality of the soul, it is not a philosophical verity, to be arrived at by a series of proofs and propositions. It is a typical miracle, self-evident to the believer in the way it is

[5] M.T. Melakim, II, 3; C.M. on Sanh., ed. Holzer, p. 29, text.

foretold in the Bible, and there the matter ends. It goes without saying that the multitude would fain see him harp upon the colorful rabbinic dicta in connection with it, but this procedure would more befit those who are wont to exploit such dicta for their particular ends.

In conclusion he once more emphasizes the fact that the present discourse contains nothing that he had not already propounded elsewhere on the subject. Theoretically, he considers it a *useless piece of work*. He appends, therefore, two short *novellae*, dealing with special questions not touched upon previously. In the first, he attempts to show that II Samuel 14:14; Isaiah 38:18–19; Psalms 78:39; 88:11; Job 7:9; 10:21; 14:14 do not, as some suppose, disprove resurrection. These verses have in view the natural course of things. Thus the skepticism of "if a man die, may he live again?" (Job 14:14) is restricted to the same sphere of experience as that of "are we to bring you forth water out of this rock?" (Num. 20:10). In both phrases the fact is precluded as a natural event, but not as a miracle.

The latter part of the postscript takes up the question as to why resurrection is not mentioned in the Pentateuch. The Sabian religion, whose tenets were adopted by the Egyptians, taught that miracles were not of divine origin, but were magic and black art wrought by human contrivance. The Hebrews naturally became contaminated with this pernicious doctrine. Thus in spite of their having witnessed numerous wonders both in Egypt and in the wilderness, they remained unimpressed by their true cause and nature. Hence, at the end of their forty years' journey in the desert, Moses accosted them, saying: "And the Lord hath not given you a heart to know" (Deut. 29:3). Now, if they made so light of miracles they saw, how much less credence would they give to a miracle promised to them at the end of humanity's earthly existence? Moreover, only the prospect of more immediate reward or punishment could serve, with the people of that generation, as an efficacious deterrent from evil. The Torah therefore omitted the mention of resurrection and chose instead to requite them for their good or bad deeds during their days on earth. One might pertinently ask why, in the face of such circumstances, an act of resurrection was not demonstrated to them at the time, to encourage its expectancy in the happy era? To this there is only one answer. We cannot fathom God's wisdom. A stone might as well have turned into a lion as a staff into a snake, but it happened as it happened, and we know not wherefore or why. His ways are inscrutable.

In the light of this summary, we may understand why a critical analysis of the *Maqala* will have to deal first with the author's theory of resurrection, its contradictions, if any, to his other teachings, and next with the reasons for the composition of the treatise.

Prima facie, Maimonides' theory seems to be unique. Naḥman- ides, in touching upon it, declares that Maimonides alone has limited the era of resurrection and made it preparatory to a final eschatological stage.[6] However, Aaron ben Meshullam (*c.* 1210), in a letter to Meir ha-Levi Abulafia, contends that Saadia and Hai, too, believed that the quickened bodies would die again. The correspondent, completely taken aback, retorts that, on the contrary, both Saadia and Hai had consistently taught the eter- nality of the corporeal posthumous existence.[7] Aaron, all too eager to defend Maimonides, evidently overshot the mark and quoted Saadia out of context. According to the latter, only those revived in pre-Messianic times, such as the son of the widow of Zarephath (I Kings 17:22), the son of the Shunammite woman (II Kings 4:35), and the dead of the valley (Ezek. 37:10) have died again, but those that are to be revived in the Messianic era will die no more.[8] That Hai also shared Saadia's view as to those resurrected in the past may be gathered from a passage of Abraham ben Solomon's commentary on Samuel.[9]

On the other hand, Abraham ibn Ezra (1092–1167), Maimon- ides' older contemporary, speaks of a finite Messianic period. In his commentary on Daniel he says,

It seems to me that the righteous who died in the diaspora will be revived when the Redeemer comes. . . . . They will then partake

---

[6] *Torat ha-Adam*, near end of last chapter.

[7] *Rasa'il*, pp. 36, 53–54; *Ḳobeṣ*, III, 12c.

[8] *Al-imanat wal-i'tiqadat*, ed. by Landauer, p. 223; *Ha-Emunot veha-de'ot*, VII, 8.

[9] In the possession of the Library of the Jewish Theological Seminary of America, Enelow Memorial Collection, f. 130b–131a: וכד'לך רב שרירא ורב האיי ולדה יעתקדא אן אללה תעלי אחייא שמואל חין סאל שאול בעלת אוב ואנה כאן מענ לאן בעל אוב לא יקדר יחיי מייתא ואנמא יסמע קול מבין שחיו ונירה.

of the Leviathan, Ziz and Behemot and die a second death only to be again resurrected in the future world, in which they will neither eat nor drink, but will luxuriate in the splendor of the Shekina.

He repeats his theory in connection with the very verse (Dan. 12:2) cited by Maimonides. We know, too, that Maimonides was an admirer of Ibn Ezra to the extent of once recommending the study of his exegetical works to the exclusion of all other biblical commentaries. These facts, therefore, point to the influence of the latter on the former. However, Maimonides, who must have for a time tutored his son Abraham (1186–1237), in his testament voices regret over his failure to teach him the works of Ibn Ezra with which he had himself become acquainted only after he had "finished the *Guide.*"[10] By this phrase Maimonides could not possibly have alluded to a date immediately following the completion of the *Guide* in 1190,[11] for Abraham was then a mere child of four, unfit as yet for serious study, especially of the commentaries of Ibn Ezra. Consequently, the phrase implies a date well beyond 1190–91, during which our *Maqala* was written. Moreover, Maimonides, if not explicitly stating his belief in a temporary Messianic epoch, clearly implied it in a work written before 1168, i.e., about the time Ibn Ezra expressed his identical view.[12] Both writers must have drawn their information from earlier sources. And here Saadia looms up again. The second question of the ten

---

[10] *Ḳobeṣ*, II, 40a. Some scholars have doubted the authenticity of the latter passage (see Steinschneider, *Catalogus librorum hebraeorum in bibliotheca Bodleiana*, Berlin, 1852–60, p. 1899; Guttman's remarks in MbM, II, 229, n. 3), but their contention is by no means proved.

[11] Graetz, (*Geschichte*, 3d ed., VI, 306, n. 2) has so fixed the date on the basis of the explicit references to the *Guide* in the *Maqala*. Even the still earlier traditional date of 1185 has found a recent champion in Z. Diesendruck, the author of an exhaustive and ingenious study of the "Date of Completion of Moreh Nebukim," *Hebrew Union College Annual*, XII–XIII, (1937–38), 461–97.

[12] C.M. on Sanh., ed. Holzer, p. 14, text: כי הטובה והתכלית האחרון הוא להגיע. *Ibid.*, pp. 16–17, text: אל החברה העליונה. ודע כי האדם ... ותחית המתים לצדיקים בלבד. יש לו למות בהכרח ... אמנם ימות המשיח הוא זמן שתשוב המלכות לישראל ויחזרו לארץ ישראל ... . Maimonides completed his *Commentary* on the Mishnah in 1168 (Steinschneider, *Arabische Literatur*, p. 200), roughly a decade after the composition of Ibn Ezra's larger commentary on Daniel in 1155 (Samuel Ochs, *Ibn Esras Leben u. Werke* [Breslau, 1916], p. 37; *Monatschrift für Geschichte und Wissenschaft des Judentums*, LX, 196) or during 1156–57 (Ludwig Levy, *Reconstruction des Commentars Ibn Esras zu den ersten Propheten* [Berlin, 1903], pp. xviii–xix.

which Saadia mentions as having been asked of him by his pupils, and which he answers in the negative, is: "Will they die again [after having been resurrected]?"[13] Should we regard this question as the *locus in quo* that suggested to Ibn Ezra and Maimonides their common theory? Hardly so. The question, though pertaining to a transitory Messianic period, stops short of concerning itself with what is to follow this period, whereas Ibn Ezra and Maimonides deal with two stages of posthumous existence and apparently reach the same conclusion as to the nature of the second stage. Abraham bar Ḥiyya (1065–1136) in his *Megillat ha-megalleh* likewise contends that there will be two resurrections, one during the Messianic period for the righteous only, and one at its close, which he terms the resurrection of the Great Judgment Day, when both righteous and wicked will rise in the flesh.[14] Bar Ḥiyya's discussion implies that the view was not exclusively his, but was fairly widespread among his predecessors and contemporaries. The question to be asked then is: To what earlier source are all these kindred views to be traced?

Temporary Messianic periods of various duration are frequently spoken of in the Apocrypha and sporadically also in rabbinic literature, but a clear case of such periods inserted between two resurrections is found only in I Enoch 91–104 and II Baruch 49:2–51. In all probability Eleazar of Modin's "Davidic dynasty," "new world," and "future world" imply such an eschatological scheme, if we are to understand by the new world the final abode of the spirits, or rather *Lichtkörper*, and by the Davidic dynasty the Messianic dynasty.[15] Elsewhere in the rabbinic literature, however, the Messianic period glides imperceptibly into the future world. The soul does not appear to divest itself of its earthly body on its entry into the final stage of existence. Except for location, no other change seems to occur. In the writings of the later Middle Ages, the worlds of resurrection and immortality appear so completely merged that Naḥmanides could consider the Maimonidean

---

[13] *Ha-Emunot veha-de'ot*, VII, 8; מאמר תחיית המתים, ed. by Bacher, *Festschrift Steinschneider*, p. 110. The question is the third in the *Bet neḳot ha-halaḳot*, ed. by Horowitz (Frankfurt a. M.), 1881, p. 59.

[14] Ed. by Poznanski (Berlin, 1924), p. 49.

[15] *Mekilta, Beshallaḥ*, ed. by Weiss, p. 59. Cf. also the expressions, *zeman ha-zeh, yemot ha-mashiaḥ*, and *'atid la-bo* in *Pesiḳta rabbati*, ed. by Friedmann, fol. 98b–99a; Shabbat 113b; Zebaḥim 118b.

theory of two successive posthumous existence as altogether novel and unique.

Whether the apocalypses of I Enoch and II Baruch or quotations therefrom were utilized by Bar Ḥiyya, Ibn Ezra, Maimonides, and the pupils of Saadia is open to question, for there is no evidence of the accessibility of these sources to medieval Jewish writers. It is more likely that the statement of Eleazar of Modin gave rise to the heterodox opinion. Indeed, Maimonides, in describing the blissful era, speaks of the successive reigns of the Messiah, his son and grandson, which accords with another statement in the same source, in which the length of the Messianic period is limited to three generations.[16]

The possibility of Christian influence commends itself least to serious consideration. Thus Shahrastani informs us that the Jacobite Balyaris (?) believed that the righteous, upon reaching the Upper Kingdom, will eat, drink, and procreate for a thousand years and will thence be transported to the Paradise promised by Arius, in which these functions will cease, but the pious will be compensated therein by an all-permeating joy and exultation.[17] This temporary Messianic period of a thousand years should, of course, be traced to the $\chi i \lambda \iota a$ $\check{\epsilon} \tau \eta$ of Revelations 20:2. Its parallel in Pesikta rabbati[18] should also be noted. Moreover, the Paradise, with the souls of its denizens clothed in idealized bodies, closely resembles that of I Enoch and II Baruch, and is, in fact, identical with that of Berakot 17a, which Maimonides so eagerly misconstrued, either willfully or unwittingly, as presupposing a state of incorporeal existence. Furthermore, the shift from the Upper Kingdom to a yet higher celestial residence implies a second resurrection. Evidently Balyaris followed a lost apocalypse or else combined the features of I Enoch and II Baruch with those of Revelations and concocted from them a theory of his own. There is a remote possibility that this theory reached the Jews through their disputations with Christian sectarians, but it is more likely that the Jews were influenced by kindred views developed on

[16] C.M. ed. by Holzer, p. 17, text; *Mekilta, Beshallaḥ*, end. Eleazar of Modin, rather than Eliezer, seems to have been also the author of this statement as he is cited in the parallel passage with a variation in its drift in *Mekilta*, ed. by Hoffmann, *Beshallaḥ*, end. Cf. also Sanh. 99a.

[17] Ed. by Cureton, p. 178.

[18] Ed. by Friedmann, p. 4a; cf. also *Yalkut Tehillim*, 806 and Sanh. 99a.

Jewish soil. A Lower Paradise is also mentioned in the Talmud and Midrash, as well as in the mystical and philosophic writings of the Jews in the later Middle Ages. In fact, a passage in the *Ma'ani-al-nafs* closely resembles that of Shahrastani, to wit:

And God has bestowed upon this class of the righteous a place specified in Scripture, the *gan elohim*, i.e., the earthly paradise . . . . They will linger therein until they will brighten and become resplendent . . . . Afterwards they will ascend to the Upper Paradise to mingle therein with the angels.[19]

The fact that Balyaris' period of thousand years plays no part whatever in Ibn Ezra's and Maimonides' eschatology is also best accounted for by the absence of such Christian influence.

2. ARABIAN DOCTRINES OF RESURRECTION

Muslim scholastic theology, on the other hand, knows nothing of a double resurrection. In view of Sura 2:26; 22:65 and 30:39, *yuḥyikum* of Sura 45:25, cannot refer to the future. Consequently, the phrase in which it occurs cannot be translated "Allah will revive you, then cause you to die, then resurrect you, etc.," but, following the unanimous opinion of commentators, must be rendered by "Allah giveth you life, afterwards causeth you to die, and hereafter will resurrect you, etc." Nevertheless, if we are to probe Maimonides' belief in *resurrectio carnis* for inconsistencies, we must necessarily extend our investigation to include the views of the Mohammedan philosophers on the subject. Maimonides' debt to them was profound, and should similar inconsistencies also crop up in their views on resurrection, our inquiry may be greatly aided by that objectivity and fullness of perspective which only comparative data can afford. However, no more than three sources can be cited to this effect, for of all *philosophical* eschatologies only those of the "Brethren of Purity," Avicenna, and Averroes have come down to us. The following quotations will summarize their ideas on the subject.

The Brethren of Purity teach:

[19] *Kitab ma'ani al-nafs*, ed. by Goldziher (Berlin, 1907), pp. 60–62, Introduction, p. 67, text. See also *Tamid* 32b and *'Erubin* 19a.

Know, O brother, that those who believe that man is no more than a bundle of flesh and bones, etc., animated by *accidentiae*, regard resurrection not otherwise than the restoration of the decomposed body with its effaced *accidentiae* to its former integral state, in preparation for final judgment. This sort of doctrine befits women, children and the ignorant rabble, inasmuch as it can best spur them on to good and best deter them from evil. However, those possessed of a higher intelligence believe that the body is associated with a substance that is independent of it and nobler than itself, called "soul" or "spirit." According to them, this spirit, after death, may return to the original or to a substitute body. This opinion is loftier and comes nearer to the truth, and, at the same time, serves the moral ends within its respective sphere as adequately as the first within its own. But there is also a third group whose intellectual powers rank highest. These believe that the purpose of the soul's sojourn in this world is to set itself aright, perfect its form, pass from the state of potentiality and concealment into that of manifestation and activity, broaden its outlook through contact with the sense objects and images, and acquaint itself with the natural, political and theological sciences. Enriched by these multifarious experiences, the soul will awake from its slumber and remissness and will longingly look up to the spiritual world whence it came. It will then find itself immersed in an alien material cosmos, sunk in its whirlpool of passions . . . and beset by its plight and tribulations. Yet in spite of all these hardships, it will consider its sufferings evanescent and its imprisonment in this world as of temporary duration. And whosoever casts life into such shadow and disapprobation cannot conceive resurrection otherwise than the severance of the soul from the body in order to lead an autonomous existence in its pristine abode. Indeed the prophet has said: "By his very death one achieves his resurrection."[20]

. . . Know, O brother, that every thoughtful and provident craftsman knows that his shop is doomed to demolition, i.e., that some day the strength of his body will wane and his youth will disappear. He who has thus anticipated its destruction and accumulated resources for the fateful day will need no other "shop" to derive subsistence therefrom, but can thereafter afford to live in retirement and thrive on what he has saved.[21]

More reservedly, Avicenna asserts:

It is fitting to define at this juncture the transformed state of the human soul upon separating from the body. It is imperative that you know that the promise of resurrection is partly doctrinal in

---

[20] *Ikhwan al-ṣafa'*, Bombay ed., III, 88–90. Cf. also II, 336–42, 351–58.
[21] *Ibid.*, III, 81–82.

nature, and, as far as this aspect of it is concerned, there is no way to ascertain it except by referring to the Koran and by implicit belief in its authority. This promise pertains to the flesh. And since the ultimate bodily rewards and punishments are well known from the ample descriptions of them in Scripture, it is not necessary to expatiate here on the subject. As for the other aspect of it, it can be rationally made out and proved, and is also attested by prophecy. It relates to the ultimate spiritual rewards and punishments. These can be intellectually gauged, in spite of the fact that at present they cannot be grasped by our imaginative faculty for reasons that I shall make clear in the sequel. The philosophers of divinity are more concerned with the spiritual than with the bodily rewards, so much so as to appear not to care for the latter, even if they were offered to them as an immediate reality.[22]

One of the tasks of the science of theology is the analysis of the concept of resurrection. It proposes to expound the fact that were it to be assumed theoretically that the body would not be quickened after death, the surviving soul alone would then be subject to reward and punishment. The virtuous spirit, i.e., the tranquil soul that contemplates truth in sound judgment and performs the good deeds that are binding by Scripture and reason, would then attain a degree of happiness which is beyond all imaginable happiness, surpassing the one vouched for in Scripture. Reason, however, does not deny it that exceeding delectation may also be in store for the body. Indeed, by the words with which He inspired His apostles, God has graced His pious servants with the promise of a twofold bliss, both spiritual and material. He is mighty at any time to carry out this promise, if He only so wishes. The analysis goes on to show that reason alone is sufficient to ascertain the reality of the supreme spiritual bliss. On the other hand, the reality of the ultimate material prosperity can only be established by the authority of the Divine Law. In parallel manner, we infer that the future spiritual plight of the wicked is more intense and lasting than described in Scripture. Our analysis also endeavors to characterize those who will bear for ever those transcendent spiritual sufferings and those who will be afflicted with them for a time only. But it does not touch upon the physical sufferings to which the sinful creatures are doomed, for reason alone, without the aid of Scripture, is not sufficient to prescribe their reality. On the other hand, the reality of the mental woes can also be established by means of speculation, analogy, and logical proof. Now, the ultimate punishment of the body is attested by prophecy whose validity in turn is recognized by reason, and whose existence is cogent by proof. The prophetic pronouncements therefore com-

[22] *Kitab al-najat* (Rome, 1593), p. 80; *Al-shifa'*, Teheran ed., twelfth page from end.

plement the findings of reason. In other words, in the case of phenomena regarded by reason to be only possible, but not actual or cogent, should prophecy (which, as we said before is rationally sustained), confirm specifically their existence or non-existence, its verdict must be binding upon reason. Thus what was rationally a mere possibility and no more, has now with the aid of prophecy been raised to a more positive status of knowledge.[23]

Finally Averroes asserts:

Religions differ as to the posthumous condition of the blessed and wretched souls. Some do not represent in sensate terms what the virtuous soul will experience then of delight and the accursed one of sorrow, but explicitly state that conditions then will be spiritual and pleasures angelic. Others, on the other hand, have striven to depict them apperceptively, i.e., to illustrate the joy there by means of the pleasures of the flesh here, deducting of course the anguish with which they are inextricably bound in this world. In similar manner, they have described the distress there in terms of the bodily sufferings here, subtracting naturally the pleasures incidental to them in the present life. This happened either because the prophets of the latter religions by revelation learned of these conditions something which the pure abstractionalists did not learn, or else realized that sensate descriptions are best understood by the common people, and that they can best crave for them or shun them. Hence they told us that God will cause the return of the blessed soul to the body in which she will everlastingly enjoy the most sensate gratification, and that is its state in paradise; and that, on the other hand, God will restore the wretched soul to the body to suffer therein the greatest physical pain, and that is its condition in hell.

And this is the case with our religion, Islam, when describing the life beyond. We thus find in the Koran proofs comprehensible by all as to the possibility of these conditions, and this is the utmost that the mind can predicate about those matters. All these proofs either belong to the category of inferring the possibility of the existence of an object, or rather its coming into existence, from the fact of the existence of its equal, or to the category of deducing the possibility of the generation of the fewer and smaller from the fact of the existence of the many more so and greater of its kind.[24] Sura 36:37 ff. may serve as an example of the first proof:

[23] *Rasa'il* (Constantinople, A.H. 1298), pp. 78–79.

[24] I substitute here الأصغر for الأكثر and الأكثر for الأكبر. The need for these emendations is obvious. M. J. Müller's German translation (Munich, 1875) is accurate on the whole, but at times he failed to understand the text. Mohammed Jamil's English translation (Baroda, 1921) is altogether impossible.

"And he propoundeth unto Us a comparison [that we cannot resurrect the dead], and forgetteth that We have created him," etc. The proof in these verses is effected by means of the analogy drawn between the return and the first entry (of the soul into the body), these being phenomena of equal significance. Moreover, this proof, besides affirming the possibility of *resurrectio carnis*, removes by the words "He giveth you fire out of a (moist) green tree" all doubt as to the admissibility of the doctrine, even if one should regard the concepts of "entry" and "return" as not being of parallel purport. In other words, the claim of unparallelism, advanced on the ground that the "entry" was into the hot and moist and the supposed "return" will be into the dry and cold, is to be overriden by the consideration that God can evolve and create the contrary from the contrary as He can the like from the like. As for an example of the second proof, it is found in Sura 36:81 ff.: "Is not He who hath created the heaven and earth able to create [new creatures] like unto them? Yea, certainly, for He is the wise creator," etc. (To be exact), these verses contain two positive proofs of the possibility of resurrection with a refutation of a denial of it to boot. Indeed were we to exhaust all the verses in the Koran bearing on these proofs, our discussion would become unduly longdrawn, especially since they may all be classified under the (two) types of proof we have mentioned.

As we have said above, all faiths agree that the soul after death is subject to various states of happiness and misery, but they differ as to the description of these states and as to the manner of impressing the people with their existence. And it seems that such concrete presentation of them, as in our religion, makes for the greatest enlightenment of the greatest number and can best fascinate them with what there is in store for them in the hereafter. And, (mind you), it is with the multitude that all religions are primarily concerned. As for the abstract presentation, it seems that it is less likely to impress the masses with the need for contemplation on the things of the hereafter, and that they would crave and fear it less than they would the physical presentation. To resume, it appears that the concrete presentation would be more appealing to the average man than the abstract one, and that the latter would be more to the liking of the Kalamists, the controversialists among men, and these are in the minority.

And so we find the Moslems divided into three groups as to the interpretation of conditions in the life beyond. One group maintains that the pleasures and sufferings there are the very pleasures and sufferings we experience here, that is to say, they are qualitatively identical, but differ from each other only as to perpetuity and termination, i.e. the former are eternal and the latter of temporary duration. The second group believes that the existences are heterogeneous in nature, but this group is subdivided into two groups. One thinks that the yonder world, though described in terms of concrete experience, is really a world of spirits, and that it has been described so in order to bring it down to the level of popular understanding. In support of this claim they adduce many scriptural proofs, but since these are well known, it would serve no purpose to enumerate them here. The second of these groups believes that the yonder world is an abode for bodies, but that the quality of corporeality there must be fundamentally different from that of mundane corporeality, if only for the fact that the former is everlasting and the latter doomed to disintegration. These too ground their contention on many Scriptural proofs. It seems that Ibn 'Abbas shared this opinion, for there is a saying attributed to him "There is naught in this world of the hereafter except names." It further seems that this opinion is better suited for the enlightened minority, for its possibility rests upon propositions recognized by all (learned), first that the soul is immortal, and second that its return to a new body does not strike us as unthinkable as its return to the old one, for the substance of the bodies here passes through reproduction and otherwise from one body into another, i.e., the substance that once constituted part of a single body may be found at different times in different persons. To be sure, all these bodies could not exist *in actu*, for they have the selfsame substance in common. To offer an example: a man dies, and his body is transformed into dust, and the dust into a plant. Then another man eats that plant. This changes in his system into semen, and from it a new individual is born. However, the difficulty is obviated, if we assume the generation of a new body at resurrection. Indeed the truth about the doctrines is that one may adequately perform his religious duty of professing it no matter how he chooses to construe it, provided his speculation does not lead him to deny posthumous existence altogether. Such an opinion must needs stamp one who espouses it as an unbeliever, for we derive our knowledge of the future state from both religion and reason, on the basis that the soul is immortal.[25]

The text of the Brethren of Purity leaves no doubt as to the author's stand on *resurrectio carnis*. It is clear that he roundly denies it. This is part of the Ismailian teachings evolved by 'Abdallah ibn Maymun al-Qaddah (ninth century). The Ismailian missionary, or *da'i*, after exacting the oath of allegiance from the neophyte, would gradually introduce him to the further degrees of initiation, nine all told. In the eighth degree, the proselyte was taught among other things to understand allegorically the

[25] M. J. Müller, *Philosophie und Theologie von Averroes* (Arabic text, Munich, 1859), pp. 120–23.

resurrection and future reward and punishment.[26] But the sect, for obvious reasons, had to be very deft and cautious in insinuating its doctrines; hence we find the following statement in the same *Risala*:

Know, O brother, that the resurrection of the bodies from the obliterating graves and their quickening from the dust will take place when these souls and spirits that were temporarily attached to them in the former existence will have returned unto them. And these corpses will become sensate and reinvigorated, and will live and move after having lain inert. They will then be gathered, brought to account and recompensed, for recompense is the purpose of resurrection. And know, O brother, that the reëntry of the blessed soul into the perishing body might spell death for her in the sense that she reverts to ignorance and to being steeped in the benighted flesh ... on the other hand, the resurrection of the soul and the quickening of the spirit means the awakening from the sleep of remissness and the arousal from the slumber of ignorance ... and the return to her world of spirits.[27]

This passage, contradictory in itself as well as to that previously quoted, may have thoroughly perplexed the unwary reader, but this is exactly the state of mind into which the writer schemed to steer him. By bewildering him, he avoided the appearance of a downright skeptic, and, at the same time, succeeded in planting in his mind the first seeds of philosophic doubt. Moreover, his innocently conceived paradox that the soul reverts to ignorance as it enriches itself with this world's physiological and intellectual experiences must have made confusion worse confounded. Perhaps even the seasoned Kalamists might thus have come to wonder if any of his inconsistencies should be readily condemned as deliberate. But, be that as it may, orthodox perspicacity has penetrated the enigmatic veneer and rightly denounced the tenets as un-Muslim.

As for Avicenna, discreet as he too had to be with regard to the doctrine, he could no longer follow the antiquated tactics of the Brethren of Purity. By his time, only through subtleties of a higher order could one hope to shield himself effectively from accusations of unbelief. Thoughts abruptly suppressed and contradictory theories left in mid air would now be indicative of naught else than insidiousness. Hence Avicenna had to tax his

[26] Browne, *A Literary History of Persia*, I, 407, 415.
[27] *Ikhwan al-ṣafa'*, III, 86.

ingenuity to make the bitter pill as palatable as possible. This he tried to achieve by clearing the débris of his predecessors' dialectics and, as if to counteract the cause of their disrepute, advanced what might have passed as a well-knit and consistent, although involved, exposition of the subject. Not only are the pronouncements of prophecy equal in truth value to the findings of reason, but they are doubly important, for prophecy, besides drawing from its owns *fons veritatis*, indirectly partakes of the nature of the *veritas intellectualis*, since the very fact of its existences is cogent by reason. To reach for a truth surpassing itself is manifestly beyond human venture, but when a proposition is rationally deficient and revelation is capable of integrating it legitimately, can anything be more gratifying to the searching mind? Thus *resurrectio carnis*, which to begin with is rationally problematic, becomes, through the added prophetic certainty, rationally indubitable. This *tour de force* may have dispelled many misgivings about him among the theologians, but modern critics cannot regard it as sincere argumentation. Moreover, Avicenna, in speaking of a degree of ultimate spiritual happiness and distress not vouched for in Scripture, berates thereby, as it were, scriptural insight into those furthest limits of the soul's experience. While it is true that they defy detailed description, Scripture might at least have mentioned them. Besides, his assertion that "the philosophers of divinity are more concerned with the spiritual than with the bodily reward, so much so as to appear not to care for the latter, even if it were offered to them as an immediate reality" borders on the blasphemous. May Allah's gift to the righteous be spurned, though ever so material? Surely it is an artful hint on the part of our philosopher that the promise of bodily delight in paradise is either a naïve prognostication or a sop thrown to the fools.

As we have seen, the latter assumption is guardedly advanced by the Brethren of Purity, and more systematically and with yet greater caution by Averroes. Horten, in summarizing the above quotation, hastily concludes that a posthumous existence in *verklärte Leiber* was Averroes' personal doctrine and believes that the phrase "this opinion [Ibn 'Abbas'] is better suited for the enlightened minority" implies its acceptance by the philosopher.[28]

[28] *Texte zu dem Streite zwischen Glauben und Wissen im Islam*, Bonn, 1913, pp. 42–43.

Averroes' attitude toward theories reported by him with seeming approval is not so simple, however. His remark, for example, that the theory of pure spirituality in the world to come should be more to the liking of the Kalamists is as puzzling as it is intriguing. Were not the Kalamists the champions of mundane corporeality in the hereafter, and were not Averroes and his fellow philosophers the ones accused by them of upholding the diametrically opposed doctrine? Through this remark, therefore, he must have planned to evoke in the minds of his opponents a line of reasoning such as the following: "Certainly Averroes neither is, nor considers himself to be, a Kalamist; and since he states, whether true or not, that the Kalamists are most susceptible to the insidious doctrine, surely he, at least, must not be accused of it." In other words, it was a ruse on his part, designed to sidetrack suspicion of him; and since it bore all the earmarks of an indirect and unintentional defense, what deeper snare could there be laid for gullibility? Or was it perhaps not so much fear-ridden as it was tinged with playful sarcasm to gall his adversaries to the quick, as if to say, who could more appreciate a future world of abstract cerebration than people wholly given to casuistic squabbles? And with a bit of more serious reflection upon it, may we not discern in it an innuendo of the Kalamists' colossal hypocrisy in that, while overtly not disavowing a scintilla of popular religion, they harbor in their heart of hearts the full measure of unbelief of which they accuse the philosophers? In fact, Ibn Ṭufayl so turned the tables on Ghazali when he said that the latter advised keeping certain ideas to oneself, revealing them to none save to those disposed to think likewise.[29]

But to return to Averroes' "enlightened minority." As we have seen, the Brethren of Purity class the same enlightened minority together with those who believe in the return of the soul to the original body, considering the former's belief in the return of the soul to a new body as something approaching the truth, but not the truth itself, which is the belief in a future spirituality that is pure and incorporeal. Of course, Averroes could not be as outspoken as was the anonymous writer of the Brethren of Purity, who by pursuing the policy of unceremoniously eating his own words could hope to wriggle himself out of tight situations. Not

[29] Gauthier, *Ḥayy ibn Yaqdhan* (Alger, 1900), p. 13, text.

so Averroes. He bore the fullest responsibility for what he wrote, and besides he neither could nor would employ puerile methods for masking his personal, unconventional opinions. To conceal his verdict on the views he marshaled, he objectivized them to a greater degree than did his predecessors, and to make detection yet more difficult he lent to an innocuous, but not overly gross, opinion, such as that of Ibn 'Abbas, a semblance of approval. Many of his contemporaries must have succumbed to the artifice, judging from the fact that even a modern critic like Horten accepted it in good faith. Indeed it is a caution to be extended toward all Mohammedan philosophers; they often pose as sphinxes while expounding delicate matters of faith. Although often accused, they could escape the full legal consequences as long as they did not unequivocally state their subversive doctrines.

It may not be amiss, for the clearer understanding of the genre of rationalism applied by Averroes to the doctrine of resurrection, to comment briefly on his general attitude toward religion and philosophy. Renan, in his *Averoës et l'averroisme*, successfully disproved the medieval legend of Averroes' militant atheism and insolent impiety, but still held him to be an unalloyed rationalist and avowed freethinker. Munk, De Boer, and Gauthier cling to the same opinion, while Mehren, Asín Palacios, and Horten consider him an antirationalist, a revelationist, who subordinates reason to faith and philosophy to religion.[30] While some of these critics based their findings on inaccurate translations of Averroes and strained inferences of Arabic theologians concerning him,[31] others utilized his original works in part or in full. This is especially true of Gauthier, Asín Palacios, and Horten. If the former has reached an opposite conclusion to the latter two scholars, we may safely ascribe it not to objective factors but to a difference in interpretation and to the varying degree of trust in the sincerity

[30] Munk, *Mélanges*; Munk, "Averroes," *Dictionnaire des sciences philosophiques*; De Boer, *Die Wiedersprüche der Philosophie nach al-Ghazzali und ihr Ausgleich durch Ibn Rošd*, Strassburg, 1894; De Boer, *Geschichte der Philosophie im Islam*, Stuttgart, 1901; Gauthier, *La Théorie d'ibn Rochd*, Paris, 1909; Mehren, "Études sur la philosophie d'Averroes . . . ," *Muséon*, VII–VIII (1888–89); Asín Palacios, "El averroismo teologico de Santo Thomás de Aquino," *Jubilee Volume in Honor of Francisco Codera* (Zaragoza, 1904), pp. 271–331; Horten, *op. cit.*

[31] For similar misrepresentations in Jewish literature, see Wolfson's *Crescas' Critique of Aristotle* (Cambridge, 1929), pp. 487–88.

of our philosopher's professions. It would take us far afield to compare and analyze all the passages in the *Tahafut* or *Faṣl al-maqala* which have been the subject of divergent interpretation, but it is feasible to comment briefly on the second point of difference. Perhaps a middle ground may thus be found to determine Averroes' stand.

Horten maintains that in the Middle Ages the Koranic revelation was recognized by the Mohammedan world as an incontrovertible fact. Hence Averroes' acceptance of it was not a proffer of sham conciliation but an honest delusion on his part.[32] This is undoubtedly a truism, but it has its limitations. There existed a Dahriyya movement, enduring through the ages, whose teachings ranged from agnosticism to downright atheism. It denied divine revelation and the immortality of the soul. It resulted from the infiltration of Greek ideas as well as from a spontaneous, unphilosophical, common-sense materialism. Whatever its actual strength in numbers, it stands to reason that it could emerge from cover only faintly and sporadically. Yet all Muslim theologians and philosophers took definite cognizance of it and fought it not as a phantom but as a palpable danger. The executioner's axe cut off the heads of many of its avowed adherents, but many, however outspoken, undoubtedly managed to die a natural death. Not every neighbor denounced them to the Qaḍi, and not every Qaḍi to the Caliph, and not every Caliph condemned them to the block. After all, society is on its unofficial side quite human, and so the mills of the ungodly might have ground slow but fine. And what a lowly latitudinarian seldom or never dared to say, a potentate so minded might have freely uttered. Thus Birdi quotes Iṣbahan ibn Qara as having said to 'Ali Bey, who refused to eat with him on a Ramadan morning:

You torment yourself for nothing. Man is like a seed of grain that sprouts and grows up and is then mowed down to perish forever, and that's all there is to it. So snap out of it, and eat and drink.[33]

The quotation is undoubtedly authentic, for part of it is recorded in that trenchant vernacular which I aimed to reproduce in the translation; and apparently Iṣbahan suffered nothing in con-

[32] *Op. cit.*, p. 23; *Orientalistische Literaturzeitung* (1910, No. 12), pp. 539 f.
[33] Birdi's *Annals*, ed. by Popper, VI, 720.

sequence except the disapprobation of the chronicler. In the realm of the *amthal*, too, we find the Dahriyya represented; oriental atheistic proverbs are by no means a rarity.[34]

In the face of such untrammeled opinions regarding the principles of faith, it can hardly be said that revelation was universally considered an incontrovertible fact. When the Muslim philosophers upheld it as a supernatural source of knowledge, they could hardly regard it as a self-evident rational truth, but rather as one syllogistically arrived at. With Averroës it was even less than that. After rejecting and scoffing at the specious and abstract arguments of the Kalamists in proof of divine revelation, he develops his own proofs, the proof of general history and the proof of the Koran. It is difficult to say how serious Averroes was about these proofs, but the sentence with which he introduces his lengthy discussion is vital for the understanding of his standpoint, to wit: "With the exception of the Dahriyya, whose opinion is to be ignored, all philosophers, in fact all mankind, are agreed that there existed a class of people who received divine revelation."[35] Thus the nearest to a rational argument that Averroes can offer is a universally indulged-in hearsay argument, and with a qualification at that. Evidently the whole excursus is an attempt on his part to find a basis for this *praeambulum fidei* that would least compromise his intellectual integrity. Here lurks the admission that in the last analysis the doctrine must rest on one's inner religiosity and not merely on a religiosity that is prescribed, i.e., it must ultimately rest on one's sense of responsibility before God. And faith in God he had! So the gulf that separates the modern from the medieval mind, especially from that of its leading thinkers, is after all not abysmal. And the sooner this legend of medieval out-and-out differentness is dispelled, the less medieval will we appear to a critic a thousand years hence.

But that which the *falasifa* could not rationally substantiate and in which they had no faith, they more or less denied, albeit under a layer of protective contradictoriness which varied in thickness with the individual writer. The doctrine of *resurrectio carnis* is a case in point. Plotinus had flatly denied it,[36] and the

---

[34] Horten, *Die Philosophie des Islam* (Munich, 1924), p. 367.

[35] Müller, *Philosophie* (Arabic text), pp. 92 ff., 98.

[36] Resurrection is an awakening from the body, not with the body (*Ennead*, III, 6, 6).

Muslim philosophers followed suit, but the Koran was too out-spoken about it; consequently the Brethren of Purity had to blow hot and cold in the same breath. Then came Avicenna and com-promised what could not be compromised, but not without an *arrière pensée*. And finally Averroes, although daring to state openly that a Muslim who denies it is still a good Muslim, yet avoided personal commitment and, still further to becloud the issue, employed the devices stated above. It may also be noted that his admission that prophets of other religions may have received revelations purporting a material hereafter was another inconsistency calculated to complicate the enigmatic exterior of his teaching.

3. ENFORCED CIRCUMSPECTION

In the light of these comparative data, it should be a foregone conclusion that Maimonides, in his denial of a material hereafter, would likewise resort to ambiguities to lessen its impact. The problem confronting him, although on the whole less acute, was even more complicated. While the doctrine of resurrection is an integral part of Judaism, its psychological implications are not so all-pervading as are those of its Islamic counterpart. According to one of the writers of the Brethren of Purity, resurrection is either referred to or alluded to in the Koran no less than 1,700 times.[37] It is a peculiar gift of the Muslim to attach himself with the most intimate ties to the invisible reality and to cultivate this close touch with it by the monotonous reiteration of pious ejacu-lations. The intense reality of the Hell and Paradise is next only to that of Allah, and how vivid that is even a casual observation of Muslim life will suffice to ascertain. And to crown it all, the Future Bliss is lavishly sensuous.

There is only one *Akhira*, however, while in Judaism the future state is subdivided into the preparatory Messianic Kingdom and the blissful state proper. Resurrection precedes the former, and the new life thus initiated is perpetuated in the latter. *Ergo*, post-humous physical existence is, as it were, doubly affirmed. More-over, the inception of the eternal life takes place in mundane sur-roundings. Indeed so close and interwoven are its connections

[37] *Ikhwan al-safa'*, III, 84.

with things earthly that it is thought to institute a new political order among men. Thus in denying resurrection, Maimonides would have had to modify two doctrines, the doctrine of the messianic period and the doctrine of the future world, while the Mohammedan philosophers would have had to grapple with only one, the doctrine of the *Akhira*. And although by the time of Maimonides the *consensus gentis* had already thoroughly fused the double aspect of posthumous existence, the two doctrines remained distinct, if in name only. Such a double-edged doctrinal sword allowed no quarter to a compromise formula. Maimonides was therefore constrained to develop such notions about the messianic days as would fit in with his eschatological ideas. The old concept of a temporary Messianic period suited his purport best. At its close, he could again disembody the individual and let him enjoy thereafter a purely spiritual existence. By using this subterfuge, he escaped the necessity of insinuating ambiguities concerning the nature of the life to come, such as were employed by all Muslim philosophers. In fact, he now felt so much superior to them in this respect that he did not hesitate to berate the philosophic value of Avicenna's arguments concerning resurrection.[38] On the other hand, his scheme resulted in a resurrection shorn of its glory and deprived of its deeper meaning. "Rather than suffer the pangs of death again I had better not be resurrected," poignantly remarked Abulafia, apropos Maimonides' theory.[39] Less poetical but even more to the point was Ḥasdai ha-Levi's question, "What is in this case resurrection for?"[40] Maimonides' only reply, "Know that we cannot fathom the ways of the Lord," is manifestly a confession of weakness, for he can no longer apply to it his teleological axiom that "God does not create things in vain." At this point he appears to have abandoned rationalism for a doctrine. But the doctrine, being so singular and contrary to popular belief, could not impress the people as one subordinating reason to faith, but rather as one making a false show of it. No wonder that he had to hide the *Maqala* from the public, revealing it only to those who shared his view.[41]

[38] *Ḳobeṣ* II, 9a: וכן יזכור דברים שנלקחו ממאמר הנמול לאבן ציני וחשבם מאמרים פילוסופים.

[39] *Ibid.*, III, 12c; *Rasa'il*, p. 53.   [40] *Ḳobeṣ*, II, 24d.

[41] Ibn al-Qifṭi, *Ta'rikh al-ḥukama'*, ed. by Lippert (Leipzig, 1903), p. 319; Bar Hebraeus, *Ta'rikh mukhtaṣar al-duwal*, ed. by Salhani (Beirut, 1890), p. 418.

We may now more clearly perceive the reasons for its composition. In the *Mishneh Torah*, Maimonides, affirming at length the incorporeity of life in the future world, does not even so much as touch upon resurrection, but mentions it perfunctorily among the twenty-four items through the denial of which one loses the future bliss. However, in his introduction to Ḥeleḳ, besides expounding in detail the pure spirituality of the life to come, he also refers briefly to *resurrectio carnis* and posits it as one of the articles of faith.[42] But he makes no attempt in either case to reconcile the flagrant discrepancy. Evidently he is thus following the Muslim philosophers in leaving the reader in a quandary as to what really was his personal view on the nature of ultimate existence. His statement that the Messiah is not to be expected to resurrect the dead could merely strengthen the suspicion. The inference was now doubly clear: There is no general resurrection of the righteous during the pre-messianic, the Messianic, and the post-messianic periods. The interval between the first two periods is also ruled out by the expectation, here denied, of its occurrence during the second period. What significance is thus left to the Maimonidean postulate of resurrection as an article of faith?[43]

The leaders of the Yemenite community, perhaps more so than those of any other Jewish community at the time, realized the

[42] M.T. Teshubah, 3, 6, 8; C.M., on Sanh. ed. by Holzer, p. 16 and p. 29, text.

[43] M.T. Melakim 11, 3; 12, 1–2. By citing Samuel's statement אין בין העולם הזה לימות המשיח אלא שעבוד מלכיות בלבד (Berakot 34b) Maimonides clearly implies an outright denial of the universal resurrection of the righteous. If he thought that the company of the illustrious Samuel would save him embarrassment, he decidedly underestimated the wary reader's reluctance to suspect the Amora of heresy. After all Samuel may have believed in universal resurrection at the close of the messianic period, while Maimonides, who postulated the incorporeity of the ultimate existence, could not possibly share this view. What is more, Samuel's statement probably was but typical of other אין בין formulae in rabbinic literature. Cf., for instance, אין בין יו״ט לשבת אלא אוכל נפש בלבד ... אין בין שבת ליום הכפורים אלא שזה זדונו בידי אדם וזה זדונו בכרת ... אין בין ספרים לתפילין ומזוזות אלא שהספרים נכתבין בכל לשון ותפילין ומזוזות אינן נכתבות אלא אשורית. (M. Megillah, I, 5, 8). Certainly more than one difference obtains between the members of each group, but, applying a restricted scheme of comparison, the author stresses only a single difference. In our case Samuel cared to differentiate only the political status of the two periods. It should also be noted that he based his statement on Deut. 15:11, which evidently offered proof that poverty will also exist in the messianic era, but not that poverty is incompatible with resurrection.

danger inherent in such a policy. The epistles of the Brethren of Purity were so much in vogue among the Yemenite Jews that Nathanel ibn al-Fayyumi (incidentally, father of the inquirer to whom Maimonides addressed his *Iggeret Teman*) composed for his coreligionists the *Bustan al-'Uqul* (*The Garden of Wisdom*) in which he followed the Epistles in both style and content. In fact, when he speaks of the future world he makes an unmistakable allusion to the incorporeity of its denizens.[44] Many other Yemenites must have shared this view long before they ever read the works of Maimonides. Little wonder that when these finally reached them, they eagerly invoked the philosopher's authority to fortify their own recalcitrant stand; hence the bitter complaint of the conservative Yemenite leader in his letter to Samuel ben Ali:

This has caused great confusion. Many people despair of the Redemption, and many have taken to the reading of heretical books. This is grievous to us. Our waters have failed, and there is none to show the nation the way of truth. And know, Sir, that revolt is rife among the Jews in the cities of Yemen.[45]

Maimonides' reply to the Yemenite community has not come down to us, except for a brief summation of it in the present *Maqala*, which puts his theory in a nutshell. It is to be inferred that it did not produce the desired effect, for the Yemenites, subsequent[46] to its receipt, sent another inquiry on the same topic to Samuel ben Ali, the head of the Bagdad Academy. The latter in his answer openly accused Maimonides of denying resurrection.[47] Upon becoming directly acquainted with the contents of the reply, Maimonides resolved to make clear once and for all his stand in an essay especially devoted to the subject. This happened in the year 1191.

Now Maimonides, at least as early as 1168,[48] had half committed himself to a disembodied existence in the hereafter, but during nearly a quarter of a century thereafter he did not earnestly seek to allay the suspicions of his literary opponents by the

[44] Ed. by D. Levine (New York, 1908), pp. 87–88, text; 136–38, translation.

[45] Cf. the quotation in a fragment discovered by Harkavy and published by him in *Zeitschrift für hebräische Bibliographie*, II (1897), 125 ff.

[46] The lapse of two years between the replies of Maimonides and Samuel ben Ali to the Yemenites strongly suggests that the former antedated the Yemenite inquiry in Bagdad.

[47] Harkavy, *op. cit.*, p. 125: וֹפִי is a misprint for נפִי.   [48] See note 12.

publication of a detailed apologia. This does not exactly mean that he ignored them, but, like the rest of the *falasifa*, he very likely thought that cryptic methods served practical ends best and that, for that matter, the ambiguity in his *Commentary on the Mishnah* could hardly be improved upon. But Samuel ben Ali, because of his official position, was undoubtedly a most formidable antagonist. The latter's weighty attack, coupled with widespread minor protests,[49] must have finally convinced Maimonides that he could no longer leave matters in suspense but had to state his case unequivocally and consistently. He risked, to be sure, the forcing of his unpopular idea into the open, but he was now generally accused of it anyway. Even his favorite and loyal pupil, Joseph ibn 'Aknin, understood him as favoring an allegorical interpretation of all biblical references to resurrection, an implication which he highly deplored.[50] The old device having thus definitely failed, Maimonides now resolved to embark on a new line of defense, which somehow vindicated him as upholding at least a semblance of the doctrine of resurrection.

Other circumstances, to which Maimonides could not well refer, might also have prompted him to write the *Maqala*. The Fatimid caliphs, for the most part quite content with political power, evinced no interest in the religious convictions of their subjects, while the theologians, to return the compliment, shunned *ex animo* their courts and festivities.[51] Exposed to Ismailian influence, moreover, the caliphs themselves very likely were inclined to deny the *resurrectio carnis*. Saladin, on the other hand, after the suppression of the Fatimid dynasty in 1171, became the redoubtable champion of orthodox Islam. His secretary, Baha' al-Din al-Asadi, thus describes him, by way of contrast:

He showed the greatest zeal in his observance of the precepts of religion, *openly maintaining his belief in the resurrection of the bodies* of the just in Paradise and of the wicked in Hell. He believed steadfastly in all the teachings of the Divine Law, accepting its doctrines with an open heart. He detested philosophers, heretics, materialists, and all adversaries of orthodox religion.[52]

[49] Cf. Poznanski, *Babylonische Geonim* (Berlin, 1914), pp. 24, 30, 34.

[50] Munk, *Notice sur Joseph ben Iehouda* (Paris, 1842), p. 23.

[51] O'Leary, *A Short History of the Fatimid Khalifate* (London, 1923), pp. 245,259.

[52] Schultens, *Vita et res gestae ... Saladini* (Leiden, 1732), p. 7; *The Life of Saladin* by Beha ed Din (London, 1897), p. 10 (Palestine Pilgrims' Text Society Library, Vol. XIII).

There is reason to believe that the year 1189–90 was even more
ominous for Maimonides. During that time 'Abd al-Laṭif al-
Baghdadi arrived in Egypt.[53] One of the three persons he was
most desirous to see there was Maimonides. Himself a student of
medicine, he would naturally be eager to become personally
acquainted with a physician of Maimonides' rank. But, unfortunately for Maimonides, our visitor's interests extended also to
philosophy and he took special delight in vituperating the Muslim
rationalists, notably Avicenna. No wonder that in Cairo he hastened to glance through Maimonides' *Guide* and to denounce it as
"a pernicious book that undermines the principles of *all* faiths by
the very means with which it appears to buttress them." To round
out his invective, he attacked Maimonides' alleged vanity, flattered
by the latter's connections with the world's puissant figures.
Although obviously inspired by professional jealousy, his ill-will
must have been keenly felt by the philosopher. 'Abd al-Laṭif was
a friend of Saladin, a recipient of his largess, and had access to his
headquarters in Syria and Palestine. Even during his most strenuous campaigns Saladin would not neglect his religious lucubrations
and would often invite theologians to his tent to engage in learned
conversations on law and tradition.[54] It goes without saying that
these meetings had far-reaching repercussions. The theologians,
knowing full well Saladin's grim determination to rid Islam of
heresies, found in them an excellent opportunity to libel opponents
who espoused independent opinions. As a result of such denun-
ciations, Saladin ordered the execution of the mystic philosopher,
Suhrawardi. The accepted date of his martyrdom is the fifth of
Rajab 587 A.H. (July 30, 1191).[55] The completion of the *Maqala*
before June 25 — July 23 of that year[56] definitely precludes any
direct connection between its composition and the death of Suhrawardi. But it evidently was written during Suhrawardi's pro-
longed imprisonment, probably owing to the efforts of Saladin's
son to secure a pardon for him. It is needless to say how depressing
this event must have been to Maimonides, and how apprehensive

[53] 'Abd al-Laṭif, on his way to Egypt, met Saladin who was then engaged in
war operations before Acre, which terminated before the winter of 1190–91.
Cf. Lane-Poole, *Saladin* (New York, 1898), p. 276.

[54] Uṣaybi'a, II, 205–6; *Vita . . . Saladini*, p. 7.

[55] Ibn Khallikan (Cairo, 1310), II, 261, 263; Uṣaybi'a, II, 169.

[56] Resp., p. 367: תמוז אתק״ב לשטרות.

he must now have grown of 'Abd al-Laṭif and others of his kind.

Whether or not Suhrawardi's arrest appreciably hastened the appearance of the *Maqala*, the air was charged with the persecution of philosophers whom Saladin hated with a holy horror. Islam fought the battles of its life against the Crusaders. Could philosophers think of nothing better than to undermine its foundations? Maimonides was a philosopher and was accused of denying a principle of faith which with Islam was even more basic than with Judaism. Although not a Muslim, he was a writer of great influence and the leader of his community. The least he could suffer for his subversive teachings would be banishment and the burning of his book, a horrible enough prospect to contemplate. Such punishment of literati was not rare in Islamic countries. Indeed, only a few years later it was meted out to Averroes.[57]

It was imperative, therefore, for Maimonides to revise or restate his doctrine of resurrection in such a way as to lessen its vulnerability. While he could hardly have regarded the *Maqala* as impervious to the attacks of his coreligionists, he may well have thought that it would forestall successful denunciation to Muslim authorities. After all, the Muslims would not quibble over the secondary aspects of the doctrine. He may have expected them to reason as follows: Since the *Taurat* in the hands of the confounded *Yahud* has become corrupted by and large, some of them may have given the idea of resurrection just that twist which Maimonides advocates. Thus, in their case, it would be not a philosopher's malevolent innovation, but a trick that Satan played on a misguided people. The controversy, thus being a purely Jewish affair, could have no repercussions on the Muslim faith.

But however circumspect Maimonides had to be in postulating his theory, the present inquiry has clearly shown that, as far as we know, he was the only medieval philosopher who dared to commit himself openly and unequivocally on the incorporeity of ultimate existence. It is true that Maimonides had a tactical advantage over the Muslim philosophers inasmuch as he could shift resurrection from the threshold of the eternal future state to

---

[57] Ruth Stellhorn Mackensen, "Moslem Libraries and Sectarian Propaganda," *American Journal of Semitic Languages*, LI (1935) 111–12; D. B. Macdonald, *Development of Muslim Theology, Jurisprudence, and Constitutional Theory* (New York, 1903), pp. 245 f., 255; Macdonald, *Encyclopaedia of Islam*, II, 410b.

that of a temporary messianic period; yet this does not detract in the least from his relative courage in upholding his convictions. The fact remains that even among Jewish medieval writers we find none voicing Maimonides' opinion in explicit fashion, unless they were influenced by him and took refuge in his authority. The views of the author of the *Ma'ani al-nafs* and Ibn Ezra may be technically identical with that of Maimonides, but an absolute affirmation on their part of a pure spiritual existence in the hereafter is significantly lacking. Similarly those Rabbanites and Karaites[58] who went beyond Maimonides in their allegorical interpretation of Daniel must not be understood as denying *resurrectio carnis* in principle. Indeed they impair the doctrine even less vitally than does Maimonides, as may be learned from an interesting statement of Bar Ḥiyya. In his *Megillat ha-megalleh*, Bar Ḥiyya avers that many of his contemporaries in Spain and in France, while firmly believing in *resurrectio carnis* preparatory to the ultimate future state, deny its occurrence during the temporary messianic period. This compels them to allegorize all the biblical references to resurrection, for these, bespeaking earthly conditions, would, if taken literally, affirm mundane resurrection, which is with them an impossibility.[59] This, indeed, is a theory diametrically opposed to that of Maimonides.

Thus Maimonides' theory may after all be considered unique.

[58] See Ibn Ezra's commentary on Dan. 12:2: ‏ורבי ישועה אמר כי ישני עפר משל על‎ ‏ישראל שהם בגלות כמו מתים‎. For Yeshuah ben Yehudah (middle of the eleventh century), cf. Schreiner, *Studien über Jeschua ben Jehuda*, p. 1. See also Yephet ibn Ali's *Commentary on Daniel*, ed. by Margoliouth (Oxford, 1889), p. 139, text.

[59] *Megillat ha-megalleh*, pp. 48–49.

CHAPTER FIVE

A RESPONSUM OF MAIMONIDES

By RICHARD GOTTHEIL

WHILE working in the library of the University of Cambridge, England, during the Summer of 1935, I came across a number of fragments from the Genizah of Cairo, which referred to Maimonides. Some of these had been bound into a thin volume; others had been placed between thin glass. I was interested in the Arabic "Questions and Answers," especially as most of the answers were written, or at least signed by Maimonides himself. Professor Schechter and the authorities of the Library had recognized their worth, even though most of them related to trivial matters of law.

I give one, merely as a specimen. It is between glass and is marked T-S. 12.200 and is 8 x 4½ inches in size. It is on paper. The beginning is not wholly preserved. Evidently it contained the address to Maimonides. The answer is entirely in Maimonides' handwriting. After line 20, the page was turned around and the writing began at the top of that which previously was the bottom.[1]

TEXT

1. ‏ימיו שהוא בחיר י׳ י׃‏
2. ‏פי ראובן ושמעון משתרכין פני???‏
3. ‏וסאכנין פיהא פקאל ראובן לשמעון‏
4. ‏מא אסאכנך מן אגֹל אן כאן בינהם‏
5. ‏הזק ראיה אמא תאגֹרני או תסתאגֹר‏

---

[1] I cannot find that this has been published, either in its Arabic original or in a Hebrew translation. I have looked through Lichtenberger's *Kōbeṣ Teshubōth ha-Rambam* (Leipzig, 1859) and Abraham Hayyim Freiman's *Moses ben Maimon. Responsa* (Jerusalem, 1934). The latter is probably a complete collection in Hebrew of the *Responsa* of Maimonides.

‫מני פקאל לה שמעון מא אנרך ולא‬ .6

‫אסתאנר מנך לאנך אכרבת אלמלך‬ .7

‫אעמרה כמה כאן ואסתאנר מנך‬ .8

‫או תסתאנר מני פאנכר ראובן דלך‬ .9

‫יורינו רבינו מא ילזם אן יחכם‬ .10

‫בינהם ושכרו כפול מן השמים‬ .11

‫אלגואב‬ .12

‫ילזם אן יתאמל מא דכר‬ .13

‫שמעון אן אכרבה ראובן בל‬ .14

‫ילזם ראובן אמארתה או‬ .15

‫גראמה מא אפסד פאן אנכר‬ .16

‫ראובן דלך יחלף שבועת‬ .17

‫הסת ובעד דלך יסכנאן סנה‬ .18

‫סנה אלמלך בנמלֹתֹך אן כאן‬ .19

‫אלמלך בינהמא נצפין‬ .20

‫באלסויה או יכרי אחד המא‬ .21

‫מן אלאכר גזאת סנה ואחדה‬ .22

‫ובעד דֹלך יכרי אל אכֹר‬ .23

‫גזאת לצאחבה סנה תֹאניה‬ .24

‫וכתב משה‬ .25

TRANSLATION

1. his days; for he is the chosen one of the Lord.
2. Regarding the case of Reuben and Simeon who are partners to [a house],
3. and are dwelling in it. Now, Reuben said to Simeon:
4. "I will not dwell with you, for
5. lack of privacy;[2] either rent to me or rent
6. from me. "Said Simeon to him: "I will not rent to you nor
7. rent from you, for you have damaged the property.
8. Restore it as it was, and I will rent from you,
9. or you will rent from me. "But Reuben would not agree to this.
10. May our Master teach us how we should decide
11. between them, and his reward will be doubled by Heaven.
12.   The Answer
13. It is necessary to pay due regard to Simeon's

---

[2] ‫מן אגֹל אן כאן בינהם הזק ראיה‬ is parenthetic and literally means "Because theirs was a case of damage resulting from being exposed to each other's view." For the phrase ‫הזק ראיה‬, see Baba batra 1b.

14. claim as to the damage caused by Reuben. Indeed
15. Reuben must put it (the property) in good order[3] or
16. pay for the damage. If Reuben is
17. unwilling to do either, he shall take "an equitable
18. oath." After that each should occupy
19. the entire property in alternate years, if
20. they are equal partners
21. to the property; or (in case not) A during (his) year (of residence)
22. should be responsible for the rental of B's share,
23. and vice versa
24. in the following year.
25. Moses has written [this].

---

[3] עמארתה=אמארתה. Cf. 1.8: אעמרה. It is either the copyist's misspelling or that of Maimonides' secretary.

CHAPTER SIX

THE ECONOMIC VIEWS OF MAIMONIDES

By SALO W. BARON

1. ECONOMIC SCIENCE AND JEWISH LAW

MAIMONIDES was not an economist. This is true not only in the sense of modern economic science, as it has developed since the days of the mercantilist theoreticians, but also as compared with the theories of some of the leading thinkers of medieval Islam and Christendom. We shall search in vain in his writings for a program such as that given by Ibn Khaldun to his "new science," which was to investigate, among other matters, "the occupations to which men devote their work and their effort, the lucrative professions, the crafts which supply a livelihood, the sciences and the arts."[1] Nor did he ever evince direct interest in economic problems, as did Thomas Aquinas, who devoted to them several special treatises as well as extensive passages in his major works. It is truly remarkable that the Jewish people, whose transformation into a predominantly mercantile group had made rapid progress during those very centuries in which Jewish scholasticism and jurisprudence reached their highest degree of fruition, never produced an economic thinker to lend theoretical formulation to the existing reality.

Maimonides himself, in his early treatise on *Logical Terms*, clearly suggests the reason for this failure. Partly following the Aristotelian classification, he places the sciences under the two

---

[1] Ibn Khaldun, *Prolegomena to History*, ed. in Arabic with a French trans. in *Notices et extraits des manuscrits de la Bibliothèque Imperiale* in Paris, XVI/1, 56 (Arabic); XIX/1, 71 (French). Cf. also, in general, M. Kamil Ayad, *Die Geschichts- und Gesellschaftslehre Ibn Ḥalduns*, Berlin, 1930; and Sobhi Mahmassani, *Les Idées économiques d'Ibn Khaldoun*, Lyons, 1932, with a brief sketch of the preceding history of economic doctrines under Islam.

main headings of theoretical and practical philosophy. The latter, also called human science or political science, consists of four sub-divisions, for the second of which he uses the term domestic economy, or rather the government of the household (הנהגת הבית), which is a literal translation of the Greek οἰκονομία. This science of economics he defines rather narrowly as "the science by which [the head of the household] knows how the members are to help one another and how they are to be provided for in the best possible way in accordance with the requirements of a given time and place."[2] However, after briefly discussing also the two types of "politics," he concludes the discussion by stating:

On all these matters philosophers have written many books which have been translated into Arabic, and perhaps those that have

[2] *Treatise on Logic* (*Millot ha-higgayon*), Chap. XIV. Cf. also Harry A. Wolfson, "The Classification of Sciences in Medieval Jewish Philosophy," *Hebrew Union College Jubilee Vol.* (1925), p. 309. Although the Arabic original of this passage is not available in any of the extant manuscripts (cf. M. Ventura's and Israel Efros's recent editions of the manuscript fragments of the original, entitled *Maḳālah fi-ṣinā'at al-manṭiḳ*, Paris, 1935 and New York, 1939), this passage, upon which there is practically no disagreement in the numerous Hebrew manu-scripts and editions, seems fully to render the meaning of the original. It does not enable us, however, to answer definitely the intriguing question as to Mai-monides' familiarity with the rather meager economic literature of the Arabs, and especially with the Arabic translation of the Hellenistic treatise, the *Oikono-mikos*, by Bryson. Since the writings of Aristotle and his school on this subject apparently were never translated into Arabic, this rather platitudinous booklet was the only fairly comprehensive Greek work which had exercised some influ-ence on economic thinking under medieval Islam. Cf. its recent edition with a Hebrew translation of the fourteenth century and an incomplete Latin translation of about 1300 A.D., in M. Plessner's *Der Oikonomikos des Neupythagoräers "Bryson" und sein Einfluss auf die islamische Wissenschaft*, Heidelberg, 1928 (*Orient und Antike*, Vol. V). Cf. also R. Gottheil, "A Genizah Fragment of a Treatise on the Sciences in General," JQR, n.s. XXIII (1932–33), 171, 178, where Bryson's work is characterized as "the most renowned book" on the subject of domestic economy, while Avicenna's (the Head Sheikh's) similar treatise gives but "the quintessence of the book" by Bryson. Shem Tob ibn Falakera, in his *Reshit ḥokmah* (p. 58), mentions economics as the second of the three practical sciences (next to ethics and politics) and describes it by saying that "it acquaints man with the way he is to govern his household which is common to him, his wife, children and servants, so that it be arranged in such order as to achieve success. All this is found in Bryson's work on Economics and I have referred to it in my *Epistle on Ethics*." Cf. Israel Efros, "Palquera's Reshit Ḥokmah and Alfarabi's Iḥsa al'Ulum," JQR, n.s. XXV (1935), 227–35, and Leo Strauss, "Eine vermisste Schrift Farabis," *Monatsschrift für Geschichte und Wissenschaft des Judentums*, LXXX (1936), 96–106.

not been translated are even more numerous. But nowadays we no longer require all this, namely the statutes and laws, since man's conduct is [determined] by the divine regulations.[3]

Many years later Maimuni reiterated in his *Guide* that it is exclusively "the true law, which as we said is one, beside which there is no other law, viz. the Law of our teacher, Moses," which can direct the Jew toward the attainment of his physical as well as spiritual perfection.[4]

This belief in the exclusiveness of the Torah's guidance in social philosophy is shared not only by such an outspoken "nationalist" thinker as Yehudah Halevi,[5] but also by Abraham ibn Daud, Maimonides' immediate and highly influential Aristotelian predecessor. In the third chapter of his *Exalted Faith*, entitled "Mental Therapy,"[6] he explains that

the goal towards which practical philosophy is striving is the attainment of happiness. This can be achieved first, by ethics;

[3] The meaning of this passage, which has led to many disputes, becomes clear when we insert, with most manuscripts, the word היא before בענינים אלהיים (cf. Ventura's edition, p. 120) or, with one manuscript the word אלא before הנהגת האנשים. Cf. Efros's introduction to his edition, pp. 18 f. It has been correctly interpreted, also with reference to Alfarabi, by Leo Strauss in his "Quelques remarques sur la science politique de Maimonide et de Farabi," *Revue des études juives*, C[bis] (1936), 8 ff. For the meaning of the complex term נמוסים, cf. Wolfson, *op. cit.*, pp. 311 f., supplemented in *Hebrew Union College Annual*, III (1926), 374 f. Cf. also Falakera's statement, directly connected with economic matters and incidentally rather obviously dependent on Bryson, והיה שם הנימוס נדר אצל היונים מההנהגה, in his *Sefer ha-Mebakkesh*, ed. Hague, 1772, p. 47. This work, being a poetic elaboration of *Reshit ḥokmah*, is also greatly dependent on Alfarabi.

[4] M.N. III, 27–28.

[5] Cf. especially *Kuzari* IV, 19; V, 14.

[6] This expression, fairly common in contemporary Muslim letters (cf. Ibn Al-Jauhar's works under this title, the reference thereto in the afore-mentioned Muslim classification of sciences, ed. by Gottheil, *loc. cit.*, and other references in Chaim Neuburger's *Das Wesen des Gesetzes in der Philosophie des Maimonides* [Danzig, 1933], p. 114, nn. 304–5) is used by Maimonides to characterize ethics rather than the entire field of practical philosophy, in C.M. on Abot Introd (=Eight Chapters), III–IV. Here, too, he invokes the supreme authority of the Mosaic Law in all fundamentals of ethical conduct, including such ethical aspects of economic behavior as excessive liberality. There is no reason, consequently, to exclude ethical science from Maimonides' negation in his logical treatise, as suggested by Strauss in the *Revue*, C[bis], 11 f. Like Alfarabi and Ibn Daud, Maimuni sees the whole "practical philosophy" adequately covered by the religious law.

secondly through domestic economy; thirdly, through political laws. But we shall show that this is found in our Law in the fullest possible way.[7]

The repudiation of an independent economic science thus conceived, of course, has nothing to do with an ascetic denial of the importance of economic endeavor. The realities of Jewish life, the constant process of the adjustment of the Jews to the changing economic trends, and their increasing dependence on the fiscal interests of the governments in their revenue-producing activities were too tangible and inescapable even for their most idealistically minded leaders. The jurists, especially, were forced to acknowledge the vital importance of economic transactions in the life of their people. Enjoying a large measure of judicial self-government, the Jews had to regulate many phases of their industrial and commercial life by a process of continuous legal adaptation. Maimonides himself devotes three entire books (XI–XIII) of his great legal code to matters predominantly economic, while numerous references of economic interest are included in the remaining eleven sections. In his philosophical *magnum opus* he consciously avoids discussing problems other than metaphysical and physical,[8] but in his remarkable attempt to detect the rational basis of the biblical-talmudic commandments he emphasizes the fact that the aim of the Torah is twofold: "the well-being of the soul and the well-being of the body," the latter being established "by proper management of the relations in which we live one to another." He is even ready to concede that measures concerning the well-being of the body are "anterior in nature and time, although inferior in rank," to those aimed at the promotion of the well-being of the soul. In enumerating the fourteen classes of biblical legislation, he assigns the fourth

[7] *Emunah ramah*, p. 98. Ibn Daud repeats (*ibid.*, p. 101), with special reference to domestic economy which he defines as "the government of wife, children, and slaves" (see above, n. 2), that "this, too, is found in the Torah." He proceeds to explain it with the biblical laws concerning wives and children, but fails to mention slaves, except in connection with the political law governing the discharge of Hebrew slaves after six years. See below.

[8] Cf., for instance, M.N., Introd., end, where in explaining the general similarity in his exegetical method and that of the talmudic sages, he also stresses the difference between the rabbis' attempt to reconcile prophetic utterances concerning laws and moral behavior and his endeavor to eliminate apparent disagreement in scriptural passages referring to opinions and beliefs. Cf. also M.N. III, 8, end.

to commandments relative to charities, loans, and gifts; the fifth to responsibility for damages; the sixth to crimes, particularly those committed against property; and the seventh altogether to civil law (*dinei memonot*).[9] His son, Abraham Maimuni, otherwise far more otherworldly and mystical, comes quite close to economic determinism when he states that the extent of a person's reliance on God and the firmness of his faith is largely determined by the nature of his calling. Men entirely dependent on human beings for their sustenance will, in his opinion, be found generally weak in their faith, whereas tillers of the soil and hunters, whose livelihood so greatly depends on chance, will usually appear among the staunchest believers. Midway between these two extremes come merchants and traders.[10]

Thus it was not lack of recognition of the economic springs of human conduct, but the conscious attempt to prevent the Graeco-Arabic social philosophy from modeling the economic relations among Jews, which determined the relative aloofness of medieval Jewish thinkers. This attitude is doubly remarkable in the case of Maimonides, for whom the "theoretical philosophy" of the ancients was wholly on a par with the Jewish sources of divine revelation and for whom Aristotelian metaphysics became far more than a mere *ancilla theologiae*.[11] Nothing but a firm conviction of the inadequacy of Aristotelian economics, politics, and even ethics for the realities of Jewish life can explain this consistent negation. What benefit could a minority people in Exile, whose political and economic life was determined by a complex variety of external and internal forces, derive from a social philosophy reflecting conditions in a more or less normal, autochthonous society? While medieval Arabs and Christians could proceed to a profitable reinterpretation

[9] M.N. III, 27, 35, 39–42; M.T. Yesodei ha-torah 4, 13.

[10] Samuel Rosenblatt, *The High Ways to Perfection of Abraham Maimonides*, (New York, 1927), I, 91. Cf. the equally sweeping statement of Ibn Khaldun in his *Prolegomena*, XVI, 220 (Arabic); XIX, 254 (French).

[11] Cf. Thomas Aquinas's comment: sed quia hoc videtur repugnare documentis S. Scripturae, Rabbi Moyses Judaeus volens utrumque concordare posuit quod . . . secundum Aristotelem . . . ad salvandam Scripturam . . . (*Summa theologiae*, I, 50, 3). Cf. also Outlook, pp. 105 f. That the phrase of philosophy as a "maidservant of theology" is exaggerated to a large extent also in the case of the Christian scholastics has been rightly pointed out by Martin Grabmann in *Der Gegenwartswert der geschichtlichen Erforschung der mittelalterlichen Philosophie* (Vienna, 1913), p. 28.

of Greek social teachings in terms of their religiously oriented but still mainly political realities, the Jews turned for enlightenment exclusively to their own largely nonpolitical literature. For more than a millennium, prophets, priests, and scribes had striven hard to build the new and unique structure of Judaism in Exile and had achieved in the talmudic law and doctrine a synthesis of the conflicting forces, which was to remain essentially intact until the new era of Emancipation.[12]

The all-powerful principle of talmudic social legislation, to counteract the innate economic appetites and to subjugate them to the dictates of morality, added force to Maimonides' and his confreres' denial of autonomy to economic thinking as well as to economic behavior. Saadia, while unable to repudiate the truth of the assertions — which he presents with dramatic clarity — concerning the all-pervading power of money, points out the psychological and moral insecurity attached to its possession and concludes with the advice that everybody should appreciate it to the extent of trying to keep what God has bestowed upon him, but should not take special pains in order to acquire it. Bahya, discussing three major psychological aspects of controlling a large fortune, demands from its owner inner humility and recognition of the

---

[12] The conflict between the powerful political realities of medieval Christendom and its essentially nonpolitical biblical heritage left a permanent imprint upon the social teachings of the church. "From the first century of the Christian era until the later years of the eighteenth century, political theory presents itself to us as dominated in form by the conception that the great institutions of society, and especially the institution of government, were artifical or conventional not 'natural' or primitive." Not even the adoption of the basic political teachings of Aristotle by Thomas Aquinas could prevail against this evasive compromise. Cf. R. W. Carlyle and A. J. Carlyle, *A History of Medieval Political Theory in the West* (Edinburgh, 1928), V, 441. Islam, starting from basically political Scriptures, had less difficulty in squaring the political institutions of the caliphate with both the Koran and Greek politics. Although the superiority of the divine teachings over the philosopher's writings on economics, political science as well as ethics is intimated also by the Muslim author of the above-mentioned Genizah fragment (cf. n. 2), his pious endings of the three series of descriptions are rather vague in regard to the practical superfluity of this type of scientific literature. The deep affinities, on the other hand, between medieval metaphysics and the psychology and social structure of the medieval man, so convincingly demonstrated by Wilhelm Dilthey (*Einleitung in die Geisteswissenschaften* [Leipzig, 1883], I, 453) were much less obvious. Maimonides, for one, could readily believe in the universal validity of metaphysical doctrines and their intrinsic roots in human reason as such.

divine grace which alone had given it to him.[13] Maimonides, too, realizes that some of the strongest human fears are centered around the loss of money and that men usually value their money on a par with, or even above their lives, but emphasizes the insecurity of its tenure and man's relative independence of earthly possessions. Accepting the classification of "ancient and modern" philosophers, he declares "the perfection as regards property," in the acquisition of which people spend most of their days, to be the lowest of the four degrees of human perfection, inferior not only to those of intellectual achievement and ethical conduct, but even to that of physical beauty, because at best it means the attainment of "perfectly imaginary and transient things."[14]

Thus regarding excessive economic appetites not only as prejudicial to the higher morality but also as disturbing "the order of the people of the city and the government of the household," Maimonides contends that it is "among the objectives of the perfect Law to remove the desires, to disparage them and to reduce them to the absolutely indispensable minimum."[15] The Torah (which naturally includes for Maimuni the entire structure of Oral Law) alone can furnish both elucidation in fundamentals and regulation in all detailed economic matters. That is why the juridical works of Maimonides and his confreres reflect their economic teachings, as well as the modifications forced upon them by changing economic realities, much better than do their strictly philosophic writings. To be sure many legal adjustments were due to the inner workings of a juristic technique, which, in Judaism as in Islam,[16] frequently pursued its own independent course. The intensive study of legal minutiae in the great academies of learning followed its own peculiar logic and methodology and led to many new formulations, which can neither be explained by the original tradition nor by evident new social needs. Once established, moreover, such new formulations colored not only the economic theory, but also influenced, through the force of judicial precedent, economic practice in both application and evasion.

[13] Saadia, *Beliefs and Opinions*, X, 8; Bahya, *Duties of the Heart*, VI, 4, in the Hebrew edition of Zifroni (Jerusalem, 1928), p. 179.

[14] M.N. III, 37, 40, 54; M.T. De'ot 1, 4. For a similar contention of Abraham Maimuni, cf. Rosenblatt, *op. cit.*, p. 90.

[15] M.N. III, 33.

[16] Cf. also Max Weber, *Wirtschaft und Gesellschaft* (Tübingen, 1922), pp. 395, 424.

Bearing all this in mind, the economic doctrines incorporated by Maimonides in his juristic as well as philosophic works may serve both as a truly representative summary of the general rabbinic attitude toward economic life and as a reflection of the numerous adjustments made by the vast and prosperous Jewish community under medieval Islam. The compass of the present analysis need not be limited to subjects which Maimuni himself would have included in the field of domestic economy. Did not Alfarabi put agronomy and navigation in a class with "physical" sciences? Whether or not Maimuni accepted this classification, he certainly placed all matters of national economy, apparently even the problems affecting slaves, largely in the field of political science in its narrower sense. Nevertheless, for our purpose a comprehensive discussion only of Maimonides' most significant economic teachings, in the contemporary meaning of this term, may yield a more or less satisfactory result.[17]

2. ECONOMICS AND SOCIAL JUSTICE

The corner stone of all of Maimuni's socio-economic views is the old Aristotelian doctrine of the innate social propensities of man. Like many Arabic thinkers — whose prevalent deductive method evoked the scorn of the social empiricist, Ibn Khaldun — and Thomas, he invokes the well-known Aristotelian statements concerning the origin of organized society. "It has already been fully explained that man is naturally a social being and that, by virtue of his nature, he seeks to form communities." And it is "the domestic order which is the principal base of the polity."[18] Among

[17] Cf. Alfrarabi, *Ueber den Ursprung der Wissenschaften (De ortu scientiarum)*, ed. by Clemens Bäumker (Münster i.W., 1916), pp. 12, 20. Mahmassani (*op. cit.*, p. 61) rightly emphasizes the main preoccupation of Arabian economists before Dimashki and Ibn Khaldun with domestic rather than national economy. Cf. also, in general, S. W. Baron, *A Social and Religious History of the Jews* (New York, 1937), I, 307 ff.; III, 75 ff.

[18] M.N. II, 40; III, 41; Aristotle, *Nicomachean Ethics* 1097[b]; Ibn Khaldun, *op. cit.*, XVI, 62, 66, 68 ff., 72 ff. (Arabic); XIX, 78, 83, 86 ff., 89 ff. (French). Ibn Khaldun himself, however, could not refrain from using the Aristotelian ζῷον πολιτικόν as a starting point. Cf. also Ayad, *op. cit.*, pp. 165 ff., 175. Of course, for Maimuni the נטאם אלמנזל, domestic order, is the object of study for the תדביר אלמנזל, the science of domestic economy which, as we have seen, is included in the teachings of the Torah.

the main psychological springs of social coöperation appears the force of imitation, since it is "the innate way of man to follow his friends and associates in his opinions as well as in his deeds"[19] and, more, the yearning for love by one's fellow men. With special reference to Aristotle's *Nicomachean Ethics*, Maimuni emphasizes the fact that "it is well known that man throughout his life requires persons who love him" and he sees a great advantage in the religious festivals and the consumption of the "second tithe" in Jerusalem, which fostered love among members of various social groups. Such love is naturally strongest among close relatives and greatly cements the unity of the household.[20] But the ultimate motive for the creation and the maintenance of political forms is man's realization of the great differences in character as well as economic disparity among individuals and groups. Although Maimuni nowhere mentions the alternative of *bellum omnium contra omnes*, as he does not recognize even in theory any discrepancy between a natural and a civilized state, he clearly implies that it is fear of the ensuing anarchy which leads men to agree to submission to a leader, "so that the natural variety be submerged in the great conventional harmony and the community be well organized."[21]

[19] M.T. De'ot 6, 1. While the postulate that a Jew associate only with pious and learned men is based upon talmudic injunctions (e.g., M. Abot I, 6–7; IV, 14; Ket. 13a, 111b, and so forth, cf. also C.M. on the passages in Abot), the general formulation of the motive of imitation is Maimonidean, under the influence of Alfarabi. So is the extreme demand that "if all the cities he knows, or has heard of, follow a bad course as in our day, or if he is prevented through the insecurity of the roads, or through illness, to emigrate to a city where good customs prevail, he ought to live a lonely life . . . , but if evildoers and sinners make it impossible for him to stay in the city without mixing with them and adopting their wicked customs he ought to withdraw into a cave, an abandoned field, or a desert" (M.T., *ibid.*). To be sure, this demand, emphasized by the sweeping denunciation of all contemporary civilization, is purely theoretical. But Maimonides was undoubtedly in earnest when in another connection he argued that a Jew, threatened in the free exercise of his religion, should instantly repair to more hospitable regions. Cf. *Iggeret Teiman*, ed. by Holub, p. 27 (*Ḳobeṣ* II, 3c). Cf. also M.N. III, 33, discussing the desirability of man's accomodation to his fellows' wishes.

[20] M.N. III, 39, 43, 49. The various types of "love" are further defined by Maimuni, again with special reference to Aristotle, in C.M. on Abot I, 6. For the influence of the *Nicomachean Ethics* upon Maimonides, cf. David Rosin, *Die Ethik des Maimonides* (Breslau, 1876), pp. 6 ff.

[21] M.N. II, 40. Maimuni evidently does not think in this connection about the various economic needs of humanity and the necessity of a variety of callings

Such social coëxistence imposes, of course, many obligations upon the individual. The ultimate goal of the chosen few may, and should, be lonely intellectual achievement, the living in the realm of otherworldly contemplation, where not only their own earthly desires and the demands of the flesh become meaningless, but where in their meditative aloofness they need have no consideration for their fellow men. However, even these chosen few, Maimuni emphasizes, must not withdraw mentally into the realm of the superlunary world, which, as was claimed by some philosophers, is the sole domain of Providence. Taking a clue from Jeremiah 9:22–23, he insists

that the perfection in which man can truly glory is attained by him, when he acquires, to the extent of his ability, the knowledge of God and the recognition of His Providence over His creatures as it manifests itself in His creating and continually governing them. Having acquired such knowledge, he will be determined always to seek loving-kindness, judgment and righteousness and thus to imitate the ways of God, as has frequently been explained in this treatise.

---

to satisfy them as the main motive for the rise of organized society, as suggested by the two leading commentators, Falakera and Efodi, *ad locum*, but much rather of the psychological disparity among individuals, for which Crescas, *ad locum*, tries to supply mainly physiological reasons. Nevertheless, Maimuni himself describes elsewhere (M.N. I, 46), how the peaceful coëxistence of a physically weak, but wealthy, banker and a powerfully built beggar presupposes the existence of an organized state. Discussing the needs of man for food, dwelling, bath, and so forth, he states "one man alone cannot procure all this; it is impossible for an individual to reach this goal except within a social group, since man, as is well known, is by nature a social being" (M.N. III, 27. The expression כן may mean dwelling, but it may also mean clothing, cf. Munk, III, 212, n. 2. Both were regarded, next to food, as the most vital needs of man. Cf., for instance, Plato's *Republic* 369d and Al-Ghazali's *Ihya 'ulum ed-din*, III, 155 ff. It is notable that Maimonides, the physician, places the need for a bath in the same category.) We shall see that Maimuni, in other aspects, too, fully recognized the social import of the division of labor. It is not impossible that, like Plato, he regarded division of labor as largely derived from different human aptitudes — hence, from the basic characterological differences. Cf. *Republic*, 370b and Zevi Diesendruck's note 59 to his Hebrew translation thereof. It is also remarkable that in contrasting the social propensities of man with the unsociability of animals, Maimonides pays no attention whatever to the gregariousness of ants, bees, and flocks of birds, such as were emphasized by both Aristotle and Alfarabi. Cf. F. Dieterici and Paul Brönnle, *Die Staatsleitung von Alfarabi* (Leiden, 1904), p. 50, and the Hebrew trans. by Samuel ibn Tibbon, ed. by Filipowski in *He-Asif* (Leipzig, 1849), p. 32.

The wisest of men thus must share with the common mass of humanity the responsibilities imposed upon all by the existing conditions of human society.[22]

In their economic endeavors, too, men must remain mindful of the ultimate social aim. "Men engaged in such transactions must not refrain from mutual assistance in order to promote their common interest; neither of the parties must strive to increase only his own profit, and that he alone should enjoy the whole benefit of the transaction." It is therefore the duty of every Jew not only to love his coreligionists like himself, but "to have compassion over the other fellow's property as much as over that belonging to himself." Conversely, "most of the damage done to people in the various states arises from the lust for money and its accumulation and the excessive desire to increase possessions and honors."[23]

The prevention of social injustice and oppression is thus one of the major aims of political as well as religious legislation. To achieve the well-being of the body one must first "remove violence from among men; that is to say, that everyone shall not be guided in his actions by his likes and dislikes or by his power to act, but that everyone shall constantly do what is good for the common

[22] M.N. III, 54. It is precisely this last chapter of the volume, ending in the intense hope: "may He grant us and *all* Israel with us to attain what He promised us . . . ," which, if read in its full context, shows how greatly overstressed is the alleged "asocial" ultimate goal, set up by Maimonides. Cf. Isaac Husik's *History of Medieval Jewish Philosophy* (2d ed., New York, 1930), pp. 299 f., and Neuburger, *op. cit.*, pp. 13 ff., 86 f. Like almost all of his philosophic predecessors from the mystic Philo to the rationalist Ibn Daud, Maimonides, in all his works, and no less in his *Guide*, remained the exponent of the preëminently social orientation of biblical and rabbinic Judaism. His chief philosophic teachers, Aristotle, Avicenna, and Alfarabi likewise being socially minded, Maimonides, with his profound distrust of sufistic asceticism, would have been led to the strong affirmation of social action and responsibility, even if he had not simultaneously been the distinguished jurist and the semipolitical leader of his people.

[23] M.N. III, 39, 42 (cf. also Munk's note in his translation, III, 336, n. 2); M.T. De'ot 6, 3. The latter passage is a typical Maimonidean amplification of Hillel's negative golden rule (Shabbat 31a) and other talmudic statements. In C.M. on Abot II, 11 (13) Maimuni renders עין הרע by "greed," which, together with excessive desire and misanthropy stemming from the pathological "melancholia," leads to man's self-destruction. This type of greed, however, consists primarily in the mere negativistic envy of other man's possessions, which drives the person so obsessed into solitude. While this interpretation is not at all certain in the Arabic original of C.M. ed. by E. Baneth, it was so understood by the Hebrew translator. Cf. also *ibid.*, II, 9 (11).

welfare."[24] Following the rabbinic doctrine, Maimuni includes the prohibition of "robbery" among the universal laws common to all mankind and consequently obligatory also for all "sons of Noah." These six or seven Noahidic commandments have all the attributes of "natural" laws in medieval scholasticism, although Maimonides and his Jewish confreres could not, of course, claim for them any superiority over the "positive" laws of Judaism, all of which were supposed to be derived from the same *ius divinum* and to have retained their binding force in the post-Mosaic age only through their inclusion in the divine revelation to Moses. "He who robs from his fellow-man," says Maimuni, "an object of the value of one *perutah* [the smallest coin] acts as if he took his life." The appropriation of money which came into one's temporary possession with the consent of the owner is equal to robbery, and both are strictly prohibited, even with respect to the property of pagans. Neither is the right of capturing booty in war wholly consonant with the idea that Israel's camp is like God's temple.[25]

[24] M.N. I, 46; III, 27 (cf. Munk's notes, *ibid.*, III, 211), 35–40.

[25] M.T. Melakim 9, 1 based on Sanh. 56–57; *ibid.* 8, 11; Gezelah, 1, 2, 4, 13, based on B.Ḳ. 113a; B.M. 111a, and so forth; M.N., III, 41. For Maimonides' attitude to "booty," see below. Cf. also Outlook, pp. 13 ff., and George Foot Moore, *Judaism*, I, 274 f.; III, 86. The emphasis: אע׳׳פ שכולן הן קבלה בידינו ממשה רבינו, והדעת נוטה להן, מכלל דברי תורה יראה שעל אלו נצטווה is significant for Maimuni's realization that there is no plain scriptural authority behind these laws (cf. Karo's comments *ad loc.*), but that, while in agreement with the general tenor of Scripture, they are based upon a combination of Mosaic tradition and human reason. In this sense it is possible for him, on the basis of talmudic statements, to include in the term "robbery" by Gentiles a variety of violations of property rights which, in the case of Jews, constitute different, mostly lesser crimes, and to demand for all of them much harsher punishment and a greatly simplified prosecution. M.T. Melakim 9, 9, 14. The omission of a part of 9, 14 in certain manuscripts, such as Codex Trivulzio, is evidently due to a copyist's regard for Gentile sensitivities. Cf. J. Feigenbaum, שנויי נוסחאות (Frankfort, 1889), p. 147. Cf. also Nahmanides' citation in his *Commentary* on Gen. 34:13. It is clear that, side by side with tradition, reason is mainly responsible for this vast extension of the two Noahidic commandments concerning "robbery" and "laws." In "idolatry," on the other hand, the position of a Gentile in a Jewish country is roughly similar to that of a Jew. With respect to "blasphemy," "murder" and consumption of "living flesh," too, there are but minor aggravations due to removal of talmudic minima, and so forth, whereas in "incest," as a result of the rabbinic low estimate of pagan family life, the prohibition for Gentiles is less severe. While in general this old, universal human law appears crude and Draconian, because it lacks the fine nuances of the more highly developed Mosaic legislation, the distinction is nowhere drawn by Maimonides as sharply as in the endless variety of crimes against property and in the legal procedure designed to safeguard society against them. His extreme stand in

The objective of both civil and criminal law is to regulate economic life and to prevent injustice, not so much for the sake of the individual as for that of society as a whole. Although "mercy" is undoubtedly one of the paramount principles of ethics and of Jewish law, failure to punish the criminal would but perpetuate a class of persons of evil designs. "They are feeble-minded who contend that the abolition of all penalties would be an act of mercy towards men; on the contrary, it would be perfect cruelty to them and injury to the social order."[26] The same argument is advanced by Maimuni to justify the extreme measures to be taken against instigators to heresy, "because cruelty against those who mislead the people to seek vanity, is real clemency to the world."[27] That is also why one of the major prerequisites for a judge in Israel should be "a strong heart to save the oppressed from the oppressor."[28] Thus in Maimuni's opinion the major purpose of the criminal law is the safeguarding of the interests of society, i.e., primarily the

---

interpreting stray talmudic passages referring to these Noahidic commandments has aroused widespread objections. Cf. Nahmanides, *loc. cit.* But it is precisely this extremism which reveals the decisive role ascribed by Maimuni to criminal legislation in economic matters within the framework of organized society, however primitive. For the general kinship of the "Noahidic commandments" with "natural law," cf. the remarks of Nathan Isaacs in "The Influence of Judaism on Western Law," *The Legacy of Israel* (Oxford, 1928), pp. 383 ff.; and of M. Laserson in his *Ha-Pilosofiah ha-mishpaṭit shel ha-Rambam* (*The Maimonidean Philosophy of Law*) (Tel-Aviv, 1939), pp. 11 f.

[26] M.N. III, 35. Maimuni repeats (*ibid.*, 39) the idea that "mercy on sinners is cruelty to all creatures," and rejects the opposed principle of indiscriminate hospitality toward visitors which had found frequent expression in Arabian poetry, especially of the pre-Islamic era. Cf. Munk, *op. cit.*, III, 304 f. Cf. also Abraham Maimuni's objections to the protection of criminals in Rosenblatt, *op. cit.*, p. 95, and Th. W. Juynboll, *Handbuch des islamischen Gesetzes nach der Lehre der schafiʿitischen Schule* (Leiden, 1910), p. 285.

[27] M.T. Sanh. 11, 5. It is characteristic that instead of quoting Deut. 13:9, the original injunction concerning the heresiarch, cited also in Maimuni's direct talmudic source, Sanh. 37a, he prefers verse 18, which, although referring rather to a condemned town, expresses better the idea that the punishment of sinners is not refusal of mercy, but its truer application.

[28] M.T. Sanh. 2, 7. While in general agreement with the opinions expressed in various connections by the ancient sages, this interpretation of Exod. 18:21 is largely Maimuni's own contribution. If Abraham de Boton finds a source for it in the Palestinian Talmud, this is due to his mistaken reading of Moses of Coucy's *Sefer miṣvot ha-gadol*, Positive Commandment 97, where this citation from Maimonides (without mention of the name) is preceded by another passage from j. Sanh. II, 1, 19d. Cf. *Leḥem mishneh ad loc.*, and *Sefer miṣvot*, ed. Venice, 1547, fol. 286c.

prevention of crime. To be sure, he neither wholly deprecates the element of correcting the criminal through various psychological modifications of the prescribed penalties nor that of retaliation, the primitive expression of direct retribution. Although recognizing the talmudic sages' departure from the rigid biblical *ius talionis*, he nevertheless concedes it to be the basic, divine law of biblical revelation. His own preference, however, is decidedly for meting out only such punishment as would supply the most effective deterrent to the repetition of the crime by the original perpetrator or his would-be emulators.[29]

Social solidarity includes, in the Maimonidean theory, the extreme obligation for each individual actively to interfere whenever he is in a position to prevent a wrong. "He who can protest and does not do so, is himself guilty of the transgression for which he had failed to reprimand the transgressor." In the case of murder and incest, failure to prevent the crime is equivalent to the breaking of one positive and two negative commandments; in all other cases, to that of one prohibition. Although forced to admit that mere failure to act cannot be punished by the usual single or double flagellation, Maimonides insists that it is one of the gravest offenses, particularly, if the preventable crime consists in incitation to heresy. He who fails to participate in the suppression of any form of heresy by fearing the false prophet, failing to advance an accusation against him, or merely hesitating to assasinate him because of his high station in life, commits a grievous sin. While this requirement bears all the earmarks of sheer theory, it reveals the extent of the individual's responsibility towards society as visualized by the philosopher.[30]

[29] A brief reference to the penetrating analysis of the biblical-rabbinic criminal law by Maimonides in M.N. III, 40, must suffice here. Cf. also *ibid.*, III, 35, and the entire section "Nezikin" in M.T. For the idea of "correction," cf., for instance, *ibid.*, Gezelah 1, 13, where, on the basis of B.Ḳ. 94b, the advice is given that, if a repentant robber, after the loss of the original object of the robbery, wishes to indemnify the owner, such restoration be refused and the sinner fully rehabilitated, without any financial liability to himself. Of course this advice went beyond the bounds of strict law, and is given by both the Talmud and Maimonides in very cautious terms. Cf. also Saadia, *Beliefs*, X, 13. The Maimonidean theories of criminal law would deserve special investigation; the apologetical essay of Solomon Funk, *Das Grundprinzip des biblischen Strafrechts nach Maimonides und Hofrat Müller*, Berlin, 1910 has not even scratched the surface. Cf. also Chaim Neuburger, *op. cit.*

[30] M.T. De'ot 6, 7; Roṣeaḥ 1, 14–16; and 'Akum 5, 9, based on Shab. 54b, Sanh. 73–74, and so forth. Cf. also C.M. on Sanh. VIII, 7; S.M. Commandment, 247; Prohib. No. 297 (quoting Sifre; cf. also Ch. Heller's introd. to his ed., p. 12, and p. 68, n. 3); M.N. III, 40.

This extreme social solidarity is for Maimuni also the guiding
principle which ought to govern economic relationships. Economic
enterprise is in itself neither an evil nor a good. Its value is meas-
ured by its effects upon both the individual and society. Although
nowhere stating it in so many words, the tenor of the Maimonidean
utterances is fully in agreement with the definition of Thomas that
the ultimate aim of economy is "totum bene vivere."[31] Maimonides
in various connections stresses the importance of a healthy body
and of the possession of such material goods as are necessary for
the maintenance of a good physique. "It is one of the principles of
the Torah that a man should engage in this world in either of two
things: either in the study of the Law, so that his soul be perfected
in its wisdom, or in work (also crafts or commerce) which should
help him to maintain his livelihood." Maimuni stresses in particular
the obligation of every Jew to earn a livelihood rather than become
a public charge. Even the highly desirable devotion to intellectual
pursuits is no excuse for economic inactivity, and "he who makes
up his mind to engage in study exclusively, to have no other occupation and to live on charity, has desecrated the name of the Lord,
depreciated the Torah, extinguished the light of the law, caused
misfortune unto himself and shut himself out from the world to
come." On the other hand, economic pursuit should merely be
secondary, and, if at all possible, man should devote most of his
time to study. Assuming a twelve-hour working day, Maimuni
prefers the assignment of three hours to earning a living and of
the remainder to the study of the Torah. But unlike the early

[31] Maimonides speaks of the pursuit of happiness as essential especially in
connection with political science in the stricter sense. In his *Treatise on Logic*,
Chap. XIV, he describes it as "a science which imparts to its adepts the knowl-
edge of true happiness . . . and . . . the relinquishing of illusory happiness."
He follows therein Alfarabi. Cf. Harry A. Wolfson, "Note on Maimonides'
Classification of Sciences," JQR, n.s. XXVI (1935–36), 374; and Strauss in the
Revue, C*bis*, 10 ff. The same Tibbonian term הצלחה (Ahitub's trans., ed. by M.
Chamizer in the *Hermann Cohen Festschrift Judaica* [Berlin, 1912], p. 449, and
by Efros, *op. cit.*, p. 99, hás the colorless טובה) is used by both Ibn Tibbon and
Alharizi in their translation of the idea of "felicity," which may be obtained,
according to Maimonides, by purely human, political legislation (M.N. II, 40).
We have seen that he regarded at least national economy as part of "politics."
Maimonides himself incidentally uses הצלחה in his Hebrew writings more in the
prevalent sense of success, especially economic success. Cf. M.T. De'ot 5, 10:
. . . והצלחתו ממונו כפי ביתו אנשי את וזן ושותה אוכל חכם תלמיד; Teshubah 9, 1: והצלחת
מעשה והפסדו, and so forth. Cf. also his use of the Hebrew phrase הצלחת יוסף בבית
המצרי in the Arabic context of M.N. II, 45 (ed. Munk, fol. 94a).

Christians and some ascetic teachers of medieval Islam and Christendom, Maimuni finds no words of praise for poverty as such.[32] In exceptional cases, such as candidacy to the office of high priest, Maimuni accepts the talmudic requirement of wealth, together with physical strength, wisdom, and good looks. If the candidate is poor, his fellow priests ought to make proportionate contributions in his favor, so that he becomes the wealthiest of them all. Neither may men become high priests or kings if they have been engaged, be it only for one day, in the menial occupation of a butcher, barber, bathing master, or tanner, "because people will always hold them in low esteem." Moreover, as soon as a man is appointed to a leading position in the community, he must refrain from performing manual labor in the presence of three persons, "lest he become humiliated before them." In fact, no manual laborers, including master craftsmen, must be allotted places of honor ahead of scholars. Finding in the Mishnah the picturesque description of how the bearers of the first fruits arriving in Jerusalem were first welcomed there by the artisan groups, he states that this was a specific exception in honor of the visitors.[33] At the same time he harshly

[32] Cf. especially C.M. on Sanh. III, 3; Abot *passim*; and M.T. De'ot *passim*. Cf. also *Iggeret shemad*, 1a, and M.T. Talmud torah 1, 12; 3, 10. Maimonides becomes here rhetorical and quotes a number of equally exaggerating talmudic utterances, because he thereby tries to stem the tide of the growing commercialization of learning under the semicapitalistic conditions of early Islam. Cf. also his sharp denunciation of professional learning written, on second thought, in C.M. on Abot IV, 5, and his overoptimistic assurance that God rather than men will take care of the pious in time of need. M.T. Matenot 'aniyim 10, 19; Zekiyah u-mattanah 12, 17.

[33] M.T. Klei ha-mikdash 5, 1, based on Yoma 18a, and so forth; Melakim 1, 6, based on Kidd. 82a; Sanh. 25, 4 based on Kidd. 70a; C.M. on Bikkurim III, 3. It is to be noted that in the second passage Maimuni ignores the talmudic motivation of possible sexual licentiousness and selects, among all the occupations there listed, only those four which seem to have had a low socio-economic status in his time. Cf. also Karo's comments *ad loc.*, and Yom Tob Lippman Heller's *Tosefo Yom Tob* on 'Eduyot I, 3. Cf. also M.N. III, 8; and, for similar views of Abraham Maimuni, Rosenblatt, *op. cit.*, I, 82–106. The importance of ornate and even expensive attire for any person of standing in the Orient is well known. It is also stressed by Abraham Maimuni, *ibid.*, p. 94, and by Judah ibn Tibbon, who urgently advised his son, "take off from your belly and put it on your back." Cf. his Ṣavaah, in Israel Abrahams, *Hebrew Ethical Wills* (Philadelphia, 1926), I, 66. Maimonides, too, stresses cleanliness and beauty in one's dress, but demands that it be worn with moderation. M.T. De'ot 5, 9. For the frequent deprecation of the working classes among the Arabs, cf., for instance, the violent tirade of an Abbasid courtier, Al-Fadl ibn Yahya, who, after stating that only the four upper

condemns the exaggerated quest for fortunes, and finds sharp words of condemnation for the prevalent human greed. He even heatedly objects to those "foolish sensuous Arabs" who depict the glories of the world to come in terms of enjoyment of physical pleasures."[34]

When economic interest conflicts with religious duty, the former has to yield. If a Gentile army besieges a Jewish city and is exclusively bent upon pillage, the threatenting financial ruin is not a legitimate excuse for breaking the Sabbath. If money used for idolatrous purposes gets mixed up with money belonging to a Jew, the owner must abandon his share. Should anyone drop a coin in front of an idol, he must not bend down to pick it up, because he might give the appearance of bowing before the idol.[35] Discussing the problem of Jews forced to adopt another religion by royal decree, such as occurred under the Almohades, Maimuni commends voluntary exile and argues that if people emigrate for purposes of earning a living, how much more is voluntary exile necessary when

---

and middle classes count at all, dismissed all others: "The remainder are filthy refuse, a torrent of scum, base cattle, none of whom thinks of anything but his food and sleep." Quoted from *Kitab al-Buldan* by Reuben Levy, in *An Introduction to the Sociology of Islam* (London, 1929–31), I, 96. Cf. also Al-Ghazali and Abul Fadl, quoted by Mahmassani, *op. cit.*, p. 83; At-Tusi, quoted by Plessner, *op. cit.*, pp. 65, 131. The antiquity of this deprecation, which may be pursued in a straight line from Panaetius and Cicero to the medieval scholastics, is stressed by Otto Schilling in his *Die Staats- und Soziallehre des heiligen Augustinus* (Freiburg i.B., 1910), pp. 227 f. Had not Aristotle already declared that artisans and wage earners could not possibly devote themselves to a life of virtue? Cf. his *Politics*, III, 5. Cf. also E. Troeltsch, *The Social Teaching of the Christian Churches* (New York, 1931), I, 317. As to Jews in the menial crafts, mentioned by Maimonides, cf. the statement of an Arab writer, Abû Nu'aim, concerning the Jews of medieval Isfahan in Persia, quoted by A. Mez in *Die Renaissance des Islams* (Heidelberg, 1923), p. 36, n. 3. For the general attitude of Maimonides to labor, see below.

[34] Cf. especially C.M. on Abot Introd. (Eight Chapters), V; M.T. Teshubah 8, 6; 9, 1; M.N. III, 39–40.

[35] M.T. Shabbat 2, 23, based on 'Erubin 45a; 'Akum 3, 7 and 7, 10 (cf. also RABD and Karo, *ad loc.*), based on 'A.Z. 12a, Zeb. 74a; M.N. III, 37. Similarly decency in matters of sex and in speaking thereof should be maintained, even when one faces financial losses on this score (M.N. III, 49). On the other hand, Maimuni, following B.B. 9a, relaxes the general prohibition of emigrating from Palestine except in case of absolute need, although he believes that a really pious man would hold out to the end (M.T. Melakim 5, 9). Evidently this was sheer theory in Maimuni's time, whereas his tannaitic source reflected sincere, but futile, endeavors of the Palestinian leaders to stem the rising tide of emigration, especially after the fall of Jerusalem.

it offers better opportunities for learning or for the observance of the Torah.[36] The primacy of religion comes clearly to the fore also in his interpretation of the Sabbath idea, in which the social element of rest appears wholly subordinated to those of religious sanctification and historical commemoration. On the other hand, along with the geonim and Alfasi, he repudiates the extreme observance of the Sabbath even in the face of serious danger to life or limb, as was then advocated by some Karaite leaders. "The laws of the Torah are not for vengeance in the world, but for compassion and peace in the world."[37]

The social foundation of economics serves Maimuni also as a justification for the principle of economic leadership. Although nowhere discussing the problem of management versus labor in detail, Maimuni acknowledges the necessity of a leader and entrepreneur because of the great diversity of individual functions.

For the food which man requires for his subsistence demands much work and preparation, which can only be accomplished by reflection and planning, by the utilization of many utensils, and by the employment of numerous individuals, each performing a particular function. That is why they need one person who should guide and unite them, so that their group be properly organized and endure, and that they should coöperate with one another.

Such division of labor is also necessary for the provision of shelter and of all other human needs. If, on the other hand, "in services and functions entrusted to many people, each were not assigned to a particular task, this would result in general neglect and laziness." Division of labor thus necessarily leads to combined efforts under

---

[36] *Iggeret Teiman*, ed. by Holub, p. 27 (*Ḳobeṣ*, II, 3c). Bahya goes further and objects to emigration on purely economic grounds, because it implies lack of reliance upon God. Cf. *Duties of the Heart*, IV, Introd., p. 119.

[37] M.N. II, 31; III, 32. Cf. also Ibn Ezra's comments on Deut. 5:14. In the long section on Sabbath in M.T., climaxed by an enthusiastic finale on the great significance of the Sabbath observance, Maimuni discusses many detailed regulations governing compulsory rest, but refrains from explaining the underlying social reasons. The accent here, too, is evidently upon sanctification rather than recreation. However, when confronted by an important economic problem, such as navigation on rivers, Maimuni leans toward the milder interpretation and advocates the application of the less stringent rules governing the operations of the merchant marine on salt-water seas. Cf. the extended correspondence in Resp. Nos. 67–69, supplemented *ibid.*, pp. 361–67. For the controversy over the permissible breaking of the commandment, cf. M.T. Shabbat, 2, 3, based on Yoma 84b; B. M. Lewin, *Otzar ha-Geonim*, VI (Jerusalem, 1934), pp. 30 ff.; Baron, *History*, I, 348.

some sort of authority.[38] Such statements clearly reflect those "aristocratic" leanings which Maimuni had taken over from the Muslim schools of philosophy,[39] but they do not offer any intrinsic justification for existing economic inequalities. Maimuni, taking such inequalities for granted, sees in them primarily the expression of divine grace or reward. In a remarkable passage he contends that one who is rich today may be poor tomorrow and vice versa — a phenomenon particularly frequent in the semicapitalistic and autocratically governed Muslim states. While by no means advocating the abolition of class differences, Maimuni finds in them the reflection of a higher purpose, viz., the stimulation of efforts aimed at their righting through charity and loving-kindness. Confronted by a Jewish society which, apart from its traditional egalitarian theory, had no permanent class distinctions and certainly no "estates" in the European sense, Maimuni could thus disregard the obvious differences in income and social status.[40]

3. PRIVATE OWNERSHIP

The institution of private ownership is likewise taken for granted rather than justified by Maimonides. The Christian scholastics, writing against a background of early Christian communism (in consumption, if not in production) and Franciscan glorification of poverty, had to put up a staunch defense for the individual's right

[38] M.N. I, 72; III, 45. Cf. also III, 40, and above, n. 21. The enormous significance of the division of labor was a commonplace in ancient and medieval philosophy from Plato's *Republic* (369–70) on. Bryson had derived therefrom an interesting theory concerning the rise of the city and the necessity of money. Cf. Plessner's ed., pp. 148–49 (Arabic and Hebrew; not extant in Latin). For a specific religious motivation of the role of the entrepreneur, cf. Bahya, *Duties*, IV, 133. Cf. also the rather biased discussion of Fr. M. Robert in his "Hierarchie nécessaire des fonctions économiques d'après St. Thomas d'Aquin," *Revue thomiste*, XXI (1913), 419–31.

[39] M.N. Introd. and M.T. Talmud torah 6, 10, where the motivation כדי שלא יתבזו בפני עמי הארץ is a typically Maimonidean rationalization of the existing privileges liberating Jewish scholars from the public *corvée* which had been demanded, and largely attained, in B.B. 8a. Cf. also Eppenstein in MbM, II, 29 f., and above, n. 33.

[40] M.N. III, 35. Cf. also n. 14. For the conflict between theory and practice in medieval Islam and Christendom, cf. R. Levy, *op. cit.*, I, 80 ff.; Ayad, *op. cit.*, p. 190; Carlyle, *op. cit.*, I, 6 ff.; V, 443 ff. and Edmund Schreiber, *Die volkswirtschaftlichen Anschauungen seit Thomas von Aquin* (Jena, 1913), pp. 8 f.

to own property. While Gratian in his Code had to admit that "according to natural law all things belong to all men; . . . only by virtue of custom or positive law this thing belongs to me and that to another person," Thomas Aquinas advanced mainly practical arguments for private ownership in production. Without such ownership, he contended, people would lack an incentive to efficient effort, there would be confusion rather than rational division of labor, and social peace would be threatened by constant feuds among collectivist owners.[41] Maimonides, as well as the other Jewish and Arab thinkers, was less troubled. Starting with the Old Testament or the Koran, Judaism and Islam had accepted private property as an eternal and God-given institution under certain specific limitations. These limitations, rather than the basic institution, are hence the major subject of discussion. Of course, both believed that God is the ultimate master of all things and that his individual Providence determines their ultimate distribution. But once acquired by an individual, such property is entirely his own and, subject to stated limitations, may be freely disposed of by him. Not even those who cherished poverty as an ideal, such as the Sufists and Al-Ghazali (and their Jewish followers), departed from this accepted pattern. They merely emphasized the inner virtue and, to a certain extent, the personal bliss of the man without property, as against the absorption in constant worry over his possessions by the moneyed individual. Preference for public as opposed to private ownership, as a matter of principle, was not even characteristic of some semi-communistic, heretical trends within Islam and found still less articulate expression among the heterodox groups in medieval Jewry. The prevalent maladministration by the Muslim bureaucracy; the abuses of that sort of state-socialism which existed, for instance, in the Egypt of Maimonides; the self-interest of Jewry as a whole, which prospered mainly in the domain of free enterprise, all operated against the rise of collectivist trends such as had existed among the ancient Rekhabites and Essenians.[42]

[41] Gratian, *Decretum*, VIII, 1, in Migne's *Patrologia latina*, CLXXXVII, 43–46; Thomas, *Summa theol.* II, 2, 66, 2. Cf. also J. B. Kraus, *Scholastik, Puritanismus und Kapitalismus* (Munich, 1930), pp. 24 ff.; R. H. Tawney, *Religion and the Rise of Capitalism* (London, 1926), pp. 3 ff.; and Richard McKeon, "The Development of the Concept of Property in Political Philosophy," *Ethics*, XLVIII (1938), 297–366.

[42] For medieval Egypt, cf. especially, C. H. Becker's *Islamstudien* (Leipzig, 1924), I, 146–233. It may be true that Ibn al-Rawendi, the leading exponent of Arab heterodox collectivism, was the son of a heretical Jew, as is claimed by one

The principle of private ownership remains unimpaired by the various types of public property. Following the talmudic doctrine, Maimuni recognizes, in the first place, the existence of the related groups of *hefker* and *reshut ha-rabbim*. The former belongs to no one in particular, until such time as somebody seizes it through one of the accepted methods of appropriation. It includes objects freely available in nature, such as fish in rivers and lakes, or birds in deserts. Maimuni does not acknowledge the riparian rights of the neighboring landowners, and expressly states that all river fronts to the extent of a four-ell strip are public. In contrast to RABD, he also denies the preferential rights of a tribe living in the neighborhood of the river or the desert.[43] *Res derelictae* likewise become *hefker*. It matters little whether the owner decides to relinquish his rights forever or merely for a limited period, except that in the former case he can retract only during the first three days, in

---

of his opponents, Ibn al-Ğauzi. Cf. H. Ritter, "Philologica, VI," *Der Islam*, XIX (1930–31), 9. But there is no evidence for the penetration of these ideas into the Jewish sects of that time, which, as in the case of most Karaite groups, were, on the contrary, more radical exponents of individualism than the traditionalist Rabbanites. Even the ascetic groups of "Mourners for Zion," Karaite as well as Rabbanite, show little predilection for communal ownership. This individualistic coloring of the Karaite schism is by no means controverted by Raphael Mahler's recent attempt to demonstrate its "national-social character." See his Yiddish essays in *Jiwobleter*, Vols. VIII–IX (1935–36).

[43] M.T. Zekiyah u-mattanah 1, 1: הפקר כל המחזיק בו זכה, וכן המדברות והנהרות והנחלים כל שבהן הפקר ... where Maimonides clearly distinguishes between the *res ommium communes*, which never belonged to anyone in particular and cannot be appropriated, and the objects which potentially belong to everybody and frequently had had a former owner. Only such he classifies as *hefker*. This legal clarity is the more remarkable as we find the talmudic sources frequently applying a looser terminology. Cf., for instance, Sanh. 49a: מה מדבר מופקר לכל אף ביתו של יואב מופקר לכל. Cf. also *Shulḥan ʿaruk*, H.M. 273, 12, where Karo gives preference to this exact Maimonidean formulation over the looser phraseology of Jacob b. Asher; Asher Gulak's *Yesodei ha-mishpaṭ ha-ibri* (*The Principles of Jewish Law*) (Berlin, 1923), I, 97; RABD's objections and Ibn Gaon's and Don Vidal's comments on M.T., *ibid*. Don Vidal correctly points out that Maimuni in this connection accepts certain limitations of the rights of the Palestinian landowners, imposed upon them by a specific ten-point agreement among the original Israelitic settlers under Joshua. For these fairly comprehensive limitations, cf. Outlook, pp. 41 f. Unlike Isserles in his note on H.M. 274, Karo evidently shares Maimuni's view that this agreement affected only Palestinian land and not such as was owned by Jews outside that country. That is why, considering the agreement obsolete in his day, Karo fails to mention it in his Code. Cf. also M.T. Genebah 8, 2 and, further on, n. 46, for further clarification of the difference between the terms *hefker* and *res nullius*. For Islam, cf. *Koran* II, 27, and Von

the latter case through the entire period.[44] The decease of a proselyte leaving behind no legitimate Jewish heirs — Gentile heirs are
not recognized — places all his possessions in the same category,
and enables anyone who comes first to seize as much as he can.
There is one interesting exception, inasmuch as the restoration of
property, robbed from the proselyte in his lifetime, and of the
additional legal fine of one-fifth of its value is to be made, if
previously denied, not to the ownerless estate, but to the priests
of that division to which the proselyte had belonged.[45] In all these
aspects the state has no superior claim on account of its supposed
"eminent domain." Of course, Maimuni is ready in this, as in all
other branches of civil law, to respect divergent legislation of the

Tornauw, "Das Eigentumsrecht nach moslimischem Recht," *Zeitschrift der
Deutschen Morgenländischen Gesellschaft*, XXXVI (1882), 291. It may not be
redundant to state that for the purposes of our present discussion the purely
juridical aspects of private ownership enter only insofar as they color the economic views of the writers.

[44] M.T. Nedarim 2, 14–19, based on Ned. 43–44 and j. Ned. IV, 10, 38d. Cf.
also C.M. on Pe'ah VI, 1, and Ned. IV, 8. Gulak (*op. cit.*, I, 138 ff.) stresses the
difference between the Roman *res derelicta* and relinquished property in Jewish
law: while the Romans demanded an act of overt abandonment, the Jews were
satisfied with the mere expression of a wish on the part of the owner. To be sure,
Gulak somewhat exaggerates the Maimonidean repudiation of the validity of
such acts. Maimuni rejects only inconclusive acts, but where they take place
under circumstances which clearly indicate the owner's desire to relinquish his
property or merely his conscious abandonment of hope to recover it (יאוש), it has
all the effects of an expressed wish. Cf. M.T. Gezelah va-abedah 11, 9–11, and
H.M. 261, 4, where Karo once more gives preference to the Maimonidean terminology, even though the Talmud (B.M. 21a, and so on) clearly discusses such
"conscious losses" under *hefker*. Cf. also Judah Ashkenazi's comments on the
controversy between Karo and Isserles, *ibid.*, and 260, 11. Although from the
economic point of view the effects of the Roman action and the Jewish wish are
practically the same, this distinction further illustrates the importance attached
by the Jewish jurists, including Maimonides, to the psychological assertion of
property rights.

[45] M.T. Zekiyah u-mattanah 1, 6; 2, 1; Gezelah va-abedah 8, 5, 14, based on
M.B.B. III, 3 (cf. also C.M. thereon), B.Ḳ. 109ab, and so forth. No mention is
made here or elsewhere of heirless estates of native Jews, because Maimonides
assumes that by tracing back his genealogy far enough a Jew will always detect
some lawful heirs. Cf. M.T. Naḥlot 1, 3. In the somewhat analogous situation
of land acquired by a Jew from a Gentile, before the purchaser takes regular
possession, the occupant must indemnify the purchaser with the full amount of
the purchase money. M.T. Zekiyah u-mattanah 1, 14; 2, 1, based on B.B. 54b.
Cf., however, Samuel b. Meir's comments thereon and H.M. 194. Cf. also
below.

Gentile state. He can do it here with fuller complacency, however, as the Muslim state had often (for instance, through a decree of 923) recognized the right of the respective religious communities to inherit the estates of their deceased heirless members. From the standpoint of Jewish law, in any case, for Maimuni the only divine and eternal law, any accidental passer-by has the full right of appropriation.[46]

The *reshut ha-rabbim* (public ground), on the other hand, is permanently open to common use, but can never be appropriated by the individual. Maimonides defines such common property especially in connection with the observance of Sabbath laws, since the carrying of any object from private to public grounds is forbidden. Deserts, forests, and roads (sixteen ells wide or over) are examples of "public grounds," while a city surrounded by walls whose gates may be closed at night is classified as "private ground." In between is the intermediate type of *karmelit*. Economically, however, these distinctions are less significant. An open city, for example, may become at once "private" by erecting a wall. Although Maimuni nowhere mentions it, there certainly existed in his day a public authority charged with the creation of new, and the maintenance of old roads. Such authority could naturally regulate the width of the road at will, except perhaps for the limitations imposed by custom. Newly founded fortified cities would also naturally occupy

[46] M.T., *ibid.* 1, 15. For the edict of 923, cf. Mez, *op. cit.*, p. 106. Safra (pseud.) in his brilliant Hebrew essay on "Private Property in Jewish Law," *Ha-Mishpaṭ ha-'ibri*, II (1927), 25–73, emphasizes the importance of the idea of *hefḳer* for the relativity of private ownership in the biblical and talmudic law. Starting with the idea of the common use of the agricultural produce during the Sabbatical year (cf. the dominant opinion of the school of Hillel in M. Pe'ah, VI, 1; C.M., *ibid.*), *hefḳer* was not altogether ownerless, but was merely open to everybody's use. This theory, to be sure, accounts mainly for the various types of *hefḳer* resulting from dereliction, the estate of proselyte or Gentile land already sold to a Jew, all of which had original owners; it does not, and need not explain the real *res nullius*, such as deserts, which never had belonged to any individual. Although, with the majority of the rabbis, Maimonides rejects the opinion of R. Jose that relinquished objects remain the property of their original owners until their definite acquisition by somebody else (for the connection of this controversy with that in M. Ned. IV, 8, cf. the Palestinian Talmud and C.M. on that Mishnah), he still retains the three-day period for reconsideration. This is not a period of grace, but is mainly intended to serve as a check on fraudulent dereliction followed by immediate reappropriation, which would enable the owner to get rid of all legal obligations resting on the "relinquished" object.

an area which might formerly have been deserted or which in some other way belonged to public grounds.[47]

In short, there is, according to Maimuni, a complex variety of objects either under direct public ownership or open to permanent public use, which roughly come under the following six headings: (1) public property belonging to no one and accessible to everybody for free use, e.g., deserts; (2) public property belonging to a corporate group, but open to general use, e.g., highways; (3) potentially private property belonging to no one, but available for free appropriation, namely all relinquished and some lost objects; (4) private grounds belonging to the ownerless estate of a deceased proselyte, equally open to free appropriation; (5) private grounds not yet taken over by a Jew from a Gentile, open to appropriation against compensation; (6) private grounds in a walled city, open to everybody's use but not to appropriation. A seventh group, although not mentioned by Maimuni, is clearly implied by him: public property which at one time or another was taken over by a "private" body of men, such as a city, or even by individuals, but which has retained some

[47] The main Maimonidean discussions on the subject of רשות הרבים are to be found in C.M. on Shabbat I, 1, and M.T. Shabbat 14, 1. Both texts agree that deserts and highways "running through" (מפולשים) are public grounds, but the emphasis מפולשים להן is evidently intended to exclude the extreme opinion of R. Simon b. Lakish לעולם אין רשות הרבים עד שתהא מפולש מסוף העולם עד סופה (j. 'Erubin VIII, 8, 25a) which, if consistent, would lead to the direct negation of such public grounds. For the different types of roads, ranging from the private road 2½ ells wide through the country road between two cities 8 ells in width, to the regular highway of at least 16 ells, cf. M.T. Mekirah 21, 9, based on B.B. 100ab. The paving and maintenance of roads and the provision of other facilities for travel and transportation are regarded by Maimuni as the foremost duties of municipal government. Cf. M.N. III, 40. Cf. also M.T. Nizkei mamon 13, 26, based on B.M. 107b for the facilities to be extended to boatmen on rivers. The markets (שוקים) in M.T. Shabbat 14, 1, are perhaps in the same class with highways, provided they are situated in "open" cities. The reading עיירות (towns) in certain editions of M.T. is undoubtedly a corruption of יערות or יערים (forests) as stated in C.M. loc. cit., the Amsterdam edition of 1702, and the main commentaries. In M.T. 'Erubin 1, 1–5, Maimuni takes great pains to assert that a township, with its streets and markets, if surrounded by a wall ten handbreadths high, is "private ground," and that King Solomon instituted 'erubin in such cities only in order to counteract popular misapprehensions. Cf. Outlook, pp. 51 f. In contrast to Maimonides, Solomon ibn Adret, quoted also by Don Vidal. placed deserts and forests in the intermediate class of karmelit. Cf. also M.T. Bet ha-beḥirah 7, 14; Biat ha-miḳdash 3, 8, and so forth, on the differences between Jerusalem and other walled cities.

of its public character. All these categories, which evidently do not fit into the Roman classes of *res nullius* and *res omnium communes*, have in common (except for the extralegal seventh group) that they are applicable for either free appropriation or free use on the part of any person, or at least any Jew.

There exists, however, a different type of property owned by a king, municipality, or Jewish community, which can neither be freely appropriated nor used. This type of ownership does not differ in any essential from that of an individual. In general Maimonides distinguishes but little between the private estates of the king, acquired through the usual channels of civil law, and the funds received through the exercise of the royal prerogatives of taxation and (legally delimited) expropriation. The same applies to municipal or communal property. The public aspects of both royal and communal property will be considered by the present author in another connection.

Thirdly, there exists the "sacred" property (*hekdesh*) of the Temple in Jerusalem. This type of property, similar to the Muslim *waqf*, has many peculiar characteristics, favorable as well as unfavorable. On the one hand, sacrilegious theft, committed on such property, is not to be prosecuted by earthly courts. Besides divine wrath, the criminal has to fear only punishment by the enraged populace, whose spontaneous reaction in this respect is encouraged by both the Talmud and Maimonides.[48] On the other hand, the accumulation of wealth by the *mortmain* is facilitated by the curtailment of its civil responsibility for damages and the greater freedom in making pledges in its favor.[49] Of course, for Maimuni, as

[48] M.T. Sanh. 18, 6, based on Sanh. 91b–92a. While in C.M. on Sanh. IX, 6, Maimuni states, at least with respect to the analogous case of sex relations with Gentiles, that "we do not advise" lynching, in M.T. he refers to all these cases of popular violence as to meritorious deeds: וכל שהורגן זכה. Cf. also *ibid.*, Issurei biah 12, 4, and Outlook, p. 34. In Muslim law, too, most crimes against religion, as such, were not punished by earthly courts, but left to divine judgment. Cf. Josef Schacht, "Zur soziologischen Betrachtung des islamischen Rechts," *Der Islam*, XXII (1935), 209.

[49] M.T. Nizkei mamon 8, 1, 4, based on various passages in B.K. The reciprocal liberation of civil offenders for damages to sacred objects was mitigated by the strong incentive for every owner of a damaging animal to donate it to the Temple and thus escape all further responsibility. M.T. Mekirah 22, 15: *hekdesh* acquires rights from a donation of an as-yet-nonexistent object because man ought to keep his sacred pledges, even if they are considered void in commercial

for most of his rabbinic predecessors since the destruction of the Temple, this entire form of sacred ownership was a purely theoretical matter. Medieval Jewry had little to fear from the effects of such accumulation upon public welfare, while such fears, combined with greed, inspired many Muslim rulers to lay hands upon the estates of the Mosque. The property of the medieval synagogue had none of that "sacred" character, and was but part and parcel of the usual private or communal property.[50] But even the Temple *hekdesh*, in its technical sense, was essentially subject to the usual laws governing private property and its modes of acquisition.

A fourth type of property consists in the negative group of objects placed *extra commercium* by the religious prohibition of their use under any form (*asurim behana'ah*). Maimonides, frequently at a loss to furnish adequate rational grounds for each prohibition, mentions a large number of objects outlawed by biblical-talmudic legislation. To a lesser extent are excluded from commerce also those numerous foodstuffs which, while usable in various ways, may not be consumed by Jews (*asurim ba'akilah*). Maimonides enumerates, for example, meat of dead or otherwise ritualistically unfit animals, insects, priestly portions in the first-born animals and agricultural crops, and the produce during the Sabbatical year. But he specifically allows the trade in various prohibited fats and also of such articles as are outlawed for consumption not by biblical, but by rabbinic law.[51]

---

transactions. The rabbis extended special legal protection to "sacred" institutions in their character of depositors. M.T. Sekirut 2, 1–2. For the encouragement of both vows and pledges to "sacred" causes, cf. especially M.T. Maaseh korbanot 14. Cf. also Gulak, *op. cit.*, I, 98 f.

[50] The use of *hekdesh* to designate contemporary charities was fairly prevalent in Maimuni's time, however. Cf., for instance, *Sha'arei teshubah*, No. 145; Alfasi, *Responsa*, No. 6; Joseph ibn Megas, *Responsa*, No. 207. Maimonides, too, at least in reply to an inquiry using that term, makes use of it in its new meaning, cf. Resp. No. 80; but in M.T. Mekirah, 15–17, he uses it in contradistinction to charity. In any case, he deals with objects of philanthropy, here and elsewhere, as with usual civil property, except for certain legal peculiarities which will be discussed by the present author in another connection. For the Muslim *waqf*, cf. Becker, *op. cit.*, I, 62 f., and Levy, *op. cit.*, II, 84 f.

[51] Cf. especially M.T. Ishshut 5, 1; Ma'akalot asurot 8, 15–18; Sheluhin ve-shutefin 5, 10, based on Pes. 24b, Kidd. 56b, and so forth. In this connection Maimuni demands that Jews should generally refrain from raising animals, such as pigs, whose consumption had been prohibited by biblical law. C.M. on B.K. VII, 8. Curiously in M.T. Nizkei mamon 5, 8, he prefers to advance the original tannaitic reason that pigs are likely to become obnoxious to neighbors. He may

A fifth type of property, of an entirely different order, consisted for Maimuni in the ideal claim of every Jew to four ells of land in Palestine. Assuming that God alone is the true lord of Palestine and generally teaching that forcible deprivation of land never despoils the rights of the real owner, Maimuni could not repudiate the geonic doctrine that the Jews still have an inherent claim to the Palestinian soil. From the practical point of view, this legal fiction served as an important vehicle in facilitating transactions frequently required under the more advanced economy of the Muslim empires. Maimuni, not arguing against the principle as such, rejects its practical application, because no contemporary Jew could prove his personal share in his claim (as Karo explains it, he might be a descendant of a proselyte or a liberated slave), nor was the property in his possession, possession being for Maimuni a necessary prerequisite for those particular transactions.[52] Even he insisted, however, upon the continued validity, under the necessary modifications imposed by the Exile and the seizure of Palestinian land by Gentiles, of the numerous commandments associated with Palestinian agriculture, notably those governing the observance of the Sabbatical year and the payment of tithes.[53]

Since the third and fifth of these classes of ownership were purely theoretical in Maimuni's time and the fourth reflected but

have been influenced here by the consideration that through such reasoning, one could outlaw the raising of, and trade in these undesirable creatures not only by Jews, but by Gentiles as well. For Islam, cf. G. Bergsträsser and J. Schacht, *Grundzüge des islamischen Rechts* (Berlin, 1935), p. 44. Cf. also C.M. on Ḳidd. II, 9; M.T. Ma'akalot asurot 10, 6, 9; 14, 10–13, and so forth, and M.N. III, 46, 48.

[52] M.T. Sheluḥin ve-shutefin 3, 7, in conjunction with *ibid.*, Gezelah va-abedah 8, 14. Cf. also *Haggahot Maimuniot*, Karo's and Abraham de Boton's comments on the former passage, and Adolf Schwarz's article in MbM, I, 382 ff. For the geonic sources and especially the conflicting opinions of the academies of Sura and Pumbedita in regard to this claim, cf. Simha Assaf, *Teshubot ha-geonim min ha-genizah* (Jerusalem, 1929), p. 31 and n. 3; Louis Ginzberg, *Genizah Studies*, II (New York, 1929), pp. 11, 38, 632; and H. Tykocinski, *Die gaonäischen Verordnungen* (Berlin, 1929), pp. 117 ff. This controversy may originally have been actuated by the Palestinophilism of the academy of Sura and the more "Babylonian" self-assertion postulated by the academy of Pumbedita, but Maimuni, despite his own devotion to the Palestinian ideal, does not hesitate to follow in this respect the lead of Pumbedita.

[53] Maimuni devotes not only entire sections in his *Code* and long passages in M.N. to a discussion of these commandments, but also writes several responsa to explain certain details in their contemporary operation. Cf. Resp. Nos. 133, 136, and so forth. Cf. also Outlook, pp. 60 f.

a religious postulate that owners abstain from the exercise of their otherwise undeniable right, Maimuni thus recognized essentially only two types of ownership: the private ownership of individuals or public bodies, and the various forms of either *hefker* or *reshut ha-rabbim*. The objects belonging to the latter were, in part, permanently ownerless, not transferable, and merely open to public use. In part, however, they could be appropriated by somebody and then instantly subjected to the usual private ownership. Most objects of *hefker*, moreover, originated from property privately owned and were expected soon to be privately owned again. Their status was, so to speak, one of actual, though unidentifiable private ownership. They were, indeed, less ownerless than, for instance, the Roman *hereditas jacens*.[54]

Under these circumstances one might regard Maimonides and the other exponents of Jewish law as champions of private ownership. One might also consider them as indentifying such ownership with the "plenary control over an object," were it not for some very stringent limitations of the exercise of private ownership upon which they vigorously insisted.

In a general way ownership includes complete mastery over the object, with all its appurtenances. If people write into their contracts such specifications as that they will sell an orchard with its trees, fruits, and fences — which Maimuni encourages them to do — this is merely a formality which at best may serve to obviate judicial controversies.[55] Through the acquisition of an object, however temporary, one obtains the transfer of ownership of that object *quoad usum*, not the transfer of a right. A tenant, and even a borrower, become, for or without a consideration, temporary owners, just as a purchaser or a recipient of a gift becomes its permanent owner. Like their Muslim confreres, the Jewish jurists had no term for the Roman institution of *servitus*.[56] Mere possession is of slight importance. An object unlawfully withdrawn from its owner

54 Cf. Safra, *op. cit.*, p. 70.

55 M.T. Mekirah 24, 14, a translation of R. Judah's statement B.B. 96b, with an additional motivation.

56 Cf. especially *ibid.*, 22, 14; 23, 1; She'elah u-piḳḳadon 1, 5. This is not contradicted by the statement in M.T. Terumot 1, 17, concerning the liberation of the Jewish coloni and tenants of Gentile land in Syria from the tithes לפי שאין לו בגוף הקרקע כלום, which is merely a reference to the peculiar situation of Syria. Cf. the more precise explanation given in C.M. on Ḥallah IV, 7. Cf. also Safra, *op. cit.*, p. 44; and Von Tornauw, *op. cit.*, p. 329.

remains his, as long as it lasts unaltered. Despite the importance generally attached to the psychological assertion of ownership, the abandonment of all hope of restitution in this case does not involve loss of ownership. According to law, in its strict sense, if someone forcibly appropriates a beam and puts it into a newly erected structure, the owner may insist upon the destruction of the whole building so that he get back his beam. However, in order to encourage repentance, says Maimuni, the sages have allowed the substitution of monetary compensation for the beam itself.[57] On the other hand, possession is significant, inasmuch as no one can sell an object which is not in his possession; this would be the transfer of a mere right. For the same reason one may not dispose of a future, as yet nonexistent property, such as one's prospective inheritance or other expected acquisitions. The rabbis themselves had to grant dispensations in favor of the children of persons on their deathbeds when the children tried to obtain money for funeral expenses on the security of their prospective estates, or to needy fishermen who tried to sell their prospective catch.[58]

All these regulations, emanating from a predominantly agricultural economy of the biblical-talmudic period, would have proved a serious handicap for the growing Jewish commerce in the Muslim caliphates, were it not for the extensive use made of deeds and various legal-commercial instruments. To be sure, Maimonides takes a rather conservative stand in interpreting the talmudic regulations concerning the transfer of deeds, which dispensed with many of the formalities usually required for the transfer of movable property. By declaring the transfer of commercial instruments to be but a rabbinic innovation, Maimuni reaches the extreme conclusion that if the original owner of the deed renounces his rights, the purchaser may not force a third person, such as the original debtor, to execute its provisions; he may only try to recover his damages from the man who had transferred the deed to him. This interpretation is not only sharply rejected by Abraham b. David — who, like many contemporary scholars, wished to facilitate the transfer of deeds by the insertion of a clause in the deed itself, reading, "I am obligated to you and to your legal successors"—

[57] M.T. Gezelah va-abedah 1, 5; 2, 1, based on B.Ḳ. 94b, and so forth.
[58] M.T. Mekirah 22, 1, 5–6, based upon several rather controversial talmudic passages. Cf. also Don Vidal's comments *ad loc*. For Muslim parallels, cf. Levy, *op. cit.*, II, 85.

but Maimonides himself is forced to admit that a deed written in favor of an anonymous bearer may be utilized by any person possessing it. This is the more remarkable as the meaning of the talmudic passage referred to is rather equivocal. A mere perusal of the Maimonidean code reveals the tremendous significance attached by the author to transactions in all sorts of deeds, even though he may theoretically claim that "according to biblical law, it is the thing itself, rather than its proof, that is being acquired."[59]

More important are the following direct limitations of property rights: Ownership of a parcel of land does not in itself include that of the space underground or in the air above. In each case of transfer, these extensions have to be explicitly stipulated and the property disposed of as "from the bottom of the deep to the height of the sky."[60] In the detection of treasure trove, Maimuni decidedly favors the finder as against the owner of the ground or building in which it was found. This preference was very important in the Muslim countries, where treasures were frequently hidden away in order to withdraw them from the grasp of oppressive governors and where caliphs themselves often professed to have unearthed ancient hoards, in order to explain to the public the large monetary stocks accumulated through excessive taxation.[61]

[59] M.T. Mekirah 6, 11–12; Malveh ve-loveh 24, 9 based on Ket. 86a; B.B. 76b–77a, 172b; RABD, and Abraham de Boton's comments on the first and Judah Rosanes's comments on the second passage. The latter rightly points out the inconsistency in Maimuni's view, which evidently arose from his attempt to reconcile his conservative interpretation of ancient sources with his recognition of widespread contemporary practice. Cf. also the related controversy among post-talmudic authors in Ginzberg's, *Genizah Studies*, II, 109 ff. For the economically significant question as to whether or not such easily negotiable instruments were to be found in the talmudic period, cf. L. Auerbach, *Das jüdische Obligationsrecht* (Berlin, 1871), I, §13, answering the question in the affirmative; and Gulak, *op. cit.*, pp. 140 f., giving a negative answer. In any case, however, there was enough talmudic material for Maimuni to derive therefrom his moderately liberal interpretation, and for his perennial opponent, RABD, to go several steps further. For the relatively inferior position of deeds in Muslim law, on the other hand, where they were accepted merely as subsidiary to the testimony of witnesses, cf. Schacht, *op. cit.*, p. 213

[60] M.T. Mekirah 24, 15, based on B.B. 63b. Cf. also Don Vidal's comments thereon and the formulas for a deed of sale in the *Sefer ha-Sheṭarot* (*Book of Deeds*) of Hai Gaon, ed. by S. Assaf (Jerusalem, 1930), pp. 26 f.; and in that of Judah al-Barceloni, ed. by S. J. Halberstam (Berlin, 1898), pp. 45 f.

[61] M.T. Gezelah va-abedah 16, 7–11; C.M. on B.M. II, 3, based upon B.M. 25b–26a. The stronger emphasis upon: שאני אומר של עכו"ם הקדמונים הן is probably due to the provisions of Muslim law, which recognized the finder's right only

Other limitations arise from considerations of public welfare, which transcend individual property rights. A city may remove outside its boundaries members of certain trades, such as tanners, because of the odors emanating from the exercise of their calling. Characteristically, it may also remove all trees in a radius of twenty-five to fifty ells giving upon open squares; it has to compensate the owners only, if such trees indubitably grew there before the ordinance was issued.[62] One must also consider the

---

with respect to treasures dating from pre-Islamic days. Cf. Bergsträsser-Schacht, *op. cit.*, p. 51. While Maimuni generally tries to protect owners, even beyond the talmudic requirements, and cautions finders not to touch treasures which might belong to the house owner, he draws no distinction, such as suggested by RABD, between houses guarded by their owners and such as are not watched, in which latter alone the finder has presumptive rights. To justify this infringement upon the rights of ownership, Maimuni construes a rather unconvincing conclusion *a fortiori* from objects lost in the sea. Cf. also Ibn Gaon's, Don Vidal's comments, and *Haggahot Maimuniot, ad loc.* Despite the obvious precariousness of such hiding places, C.M. on B.M. III, 10; M.T. She'elah u-piḳḳadon 4, 4 mechanically repeats the injunctions of B.M. 42a that a depository ought to conceal all money entrusted to him one handbreadth below the surface of the soil or in the wall below the ceiling. Cf. also M.T. *ibid.*, 7, 8. Neither does Maimuni pay any attention to the fact that, if such advice, prompted by certain specific conditions in third-century Babylonia, were to be generally followed, it would merely facilitate the search by thieves. He adopts, moreover, a suggested extension of these injunctions to include all valuable objects which would not be damaged by preservation in the soil and does not seem to exonerate a paid depository from responsibility for theft, even after he has taken all these precautions. Cf. Don Vidal's comments and *Tosafot* on B.M. 62a s. v. אמר. He adheres to these stringent postulates also in the actual case recorded in his Resp. No. 290, relaxing them slightly only in the case of gold and silver objects other than money (and possibly gold or silver bars), which, he admits, according to custom could be kept in a tower or hidden chest. This literal acceptance of practical advice given in the Talmud is the more remarkable, as Judah al-Barceloni, one of Maimuni's Spanish predecessors, had stated in terms of an old tradition that the talmudic injunctions were conditioned by the prevalence of thieves in the ancient period, but that subsequently one was entitled to hide deposited money in any normal receptacle used for the safekeeping of one's own funds. Cf. *Ṭur* H.M., 291, and *Haggahot Maimuniot* on M.T., *loc. cit.* For the prevalence of "treasures" under medieval Islam, cf. W. Björkmann, "Kapitalentstehung und Anlage in Islam," *Mitteilungen des Seminars für Oriental. Sprachen ...* *Berlin*, XXXII (1929), 91, 95; D. S. Margoliouth, *Lectures on Arabic Historians* (Calcutta, 1930), p. 135; Walter J. Fischel, *Jews in the Economic and Political Life of Mediaeval Islam* (London, 1937), pp. 13 f.

[62] M.T. Shekenim 10, 1–4 based on B.B. 24b–25a. More explicit is C.M. on B.B. II, 7–9, where Maimuni advances two, rather than one, reasons for the removal of tanners, as well as of brush, to a distance of fifty ells from the city. In

interests of one's neighbors. Nuisances, such as noises and smells, and undue infringements on privacy (insofar as they are resented by gregarious Orientals) must be avoided. The neighbors may invoke the assistance of the authorities to check them.[63] Moreover, every neighbor has an inherent right to interfere in the case of a contemplated sale of property; he may exercise the right of preemption, under the same conditions as those offered by a strange purchaser. Maimuni, to be sure, in the interest of greater liquidity, so necessary in the semicapitalist economy of his period, hedges around this right of the neighbor (בן המצר) with severe limitations, such as the immediate exercise of the option and the deposit of ready cash. He incidentally favors thereby the wealthy neighbor, whose credit is good, as against one whose word carries less weight. He also tries to restrict the rights of the neighbors, whenever these are in conflict with a still higher social aim, as by assistance to owners forced to dispose of their property by liquidation, encour-

---

his *Code* he has evidently reconsidered both statements, undoubtedly because in the meantime he realized that east winds were not so uncommon in Palestine as he had first thought; and that thorny brushes should really be counted among trees. It is uncertain, however, whether he likewise dropped the intimation in C.M. on B.B. II, 9, that these laws, essentially militating against all city parks, applied also to those Babylonian and other non-Palestinian cities where the Jews formed the majority of the population. Rashi and Solomon ibn Adret clearly decided that they were valid only in Palestine. Cf. Don Vidal's comments on M.T. *loc. cit.* With respect to the exclusion of the parks from Jerusalem, cf. also M.T. Beit ha-beḥirah 7, 14, based on B.Ḳ. 82b, both strangely contrasting with Ḳohelet 2, 5. Perhaps it was this Hellenistic character of the Palestinian gardens which aroused rabbinic antagonism with respect to the Holy City, but Maimuni is conspicuously silent also about the removal of truck gardens to a distance of 1,000 ells, this being logically derived from the talmudic discussion by the Tosafists on B.B. 24b s. v. מרחיקין. This deduction would also have been in full agreement with Maimuni's own acceptance of the idea underlying that discussion in M.T. Shemiṭṭah ve-yobel 13, 2. Cf. Abraham de Boton's comments on M.T. Shekenim 10, 1. As a physician he certainly realized that walking in beautiful parks is one of the most effective remedies for men stricken with melancholy. C.M. on Abot, Introd., Chap. V. One cannot escape the conclusion that through his silence Maimuni modified the stringent talmudic regulations, in order to meet contemporary needs in the Muslim environment, where flourishing parks, suburban orchards, and truck gardens were very common.

[63] Maimuni discusses an endless variety of mutual rights of neighbors in his M.T. Shekenim, 3 ff., culminating in the general principle that in "all matters, where one person benefits without any loss to another the latter is forced" to comply with the former's request. *Ibid.* 7, 8. The opposite behavior is stigmatized as that of Sodom.

agement to the study of the Law, and protection for women or orphans.[64]

Another illustration for the supremacy of public over private interests may be found in those rabbinic regulations concerning trade in stolen articles which, because of their divergence from both the Roman and the Teuton laws, have aroused such widespread comment. It is needless to state that Maimonides and the other rabbis tried to discourage theft and its mercantile extensions with all means at their disposal. Although deciding that one does not technically become a thief until one acquires the stolen object by one of the methods legally prescribed for the acquisition of movable property, Maimuni demands that even minors who commit this crime should not escape unpunished. Both minors and slaves, he declares, although free from the usual fines, should be severely beaten so as to discourage repetition of the offense.[65] He also emphasizes the great sin involved in trading in stolen articles, because, by furnishing a market for his exploits, it encourages the thief and induces him to continue his criminal pursuits. It is in the higher interest of society, however, that a bona fide buyer, and especially a professional merchant who cannot possibly check the origin of all his wares, be protected to the full extent of his investment. This law of the Talmud, which indirectly seems to have influenced various privileges granted to Jews in medieval Europe and, through them, the development of a significant legal institution

[64] M.T., *ibid.* 12, 4–5, 9, 13–14; 14, 1–3, based on B.M. 107; C.M. on B.B. II, 4. Maimonides frequently goes beyond the literal meaning of his talmudic sources in trying to reduce the burden of this law. For example, he excludes from its operation all leases (*ibid.* 12, 8), and explains the equivocal passage הני ציירי והני שרי as referring to ממהרים לצאת יותר מזויו, thus enabling the purchaser by depositing especially good currency to spring a surprise upon the hapless neighbor. There is also a slight shade in the meaning of Maimonides' אמור שיש לו against the talmudic: אי נברא דאמיד הוא דאזיל ומייתי זוזי. Like Alfasi and Rashi, however, he refuses to go all the way toward the liberalization of these laws in favor of the owner's free disposal of his property, where no superior social interest is involved. That is why he evidently would have repudiated the decision of Jacob Tam that no right of preëmption may be exercised with respect to urban real estate. Cf. *Tosafot* on B.M. 108b s. v. ארעא. Cf. also the extensive geonic responsum in *Teshubot geonim ḳadmonim*, ed. by David Cassel, No. 9; and, with respect to land sales to Gentiles, *Sha'arei ṣedeḳ*, IV, 8, 1; 21–22 (fol. 30a, 33b); and further on, n. 88.

[65] C.M. on B.Ḳ. VII, 7; M.T. Genebah 1, 10. The commentators are here at a total loss to find a talmudic source or precedent.

in Western lands, appears in Maimuni's *Code* with important reservations. On the one hand, the person of the criminal is to be considered. If he happens to be a notorious thief, no legitimate excuse of good faith can be advanced, and the purchaser must return the stolen object to its owner without compensation. He may merely seek whatever redress he can obtain directly from the thief. On the other hand, should the owner have given up all hope of restoration — usually after a considerable lapse of time — he has no claim upon the object itself and may demand only monetary compensation in the case of a notorious thief or none at all in other cases. Such is the consequence of the loss, by the owner, of his psychological hold on the property, this, as we have seen, being an integral part of the rabbinic doctrine of private ownership. Maimuni stresses in all these connections that these laws, although somewhat in conflict with absolute ethics, have been enacted "for the benefit of the market." Indeed RABD and others find many a flaw in the Maimonidean interpretation, which, on the whole, favors the merchant against the original owner. It is evident, however, that Maimonides was prompted not by the consideration of the interests of the individual merchants, but of those of the "market" as a whole, i.e., of society. Similar considerations, based upon equally or even more complex trade relations in the large modern urban areas, induced almost all Western legislators gradually to adopt many of these rabbinic regulations.[66]

[66] M.T. Genebah 5, 1–7, based on B.Ḳ. 114b ff. RABD'S objection, if it refers to 5, 2 (so in the printed editions; Ibn Gaon and Don Vidal take it to be aimed at a misreading of 5, 3), is evidently based upon an inclusion of Raba's statement in the concluding passage in the Talmud: והלכתא בכולהו, and so forth. Maimuni, like the Tosafists, *ad loc.*, excludes it, thus further obstructing fraudulent trade. For divergent views of Hananel and Hai Gaon, cf. *Haggahot Maimuniot, ad loc.* Cf. also Resp. No. 148 and, for a similar treatment of articles forcibly taken away from their owner, M.T. Gezelah va-abedah 5, 7. For other geonic material, cf. Jacob Mann, "The Responsa of the Babylonian Geonim as a Source of Jewish History," *JQR*, n.s. X (1919–20), 131 ff.; and, for the so-called *Hehlerrecht* in medieval Jewish privileges, Moses Hoffmann, *Der Geldhandel der deutschen Juden während des Mittelalters* (Leipzig, 1910), pp. 64 ff.; G. Kisch, "Research in Medieval Legal History of the Jews," *Proceedings of the American Academy for Jewish Research*, VI (1934–35), 244; Kisch, "The 'Jewish Law of Concealment,'" *Historia Judaica*, I (1938), 3–30. The objections raised by I. F. Baer (in his review of Raphael Straus's *Die Judengemeinde Regensburg im ausgehenden Mittelalter* in *Kirjath Sepher*, XII [1935–36], 463 f.) against the alleged nexus between the tannaitic law and medieval legislation are very inconclusive. The nexus here postulated is not between "two laws which had been

Custom, that all-pervading force in medieval civilization, likewise plays a great role in limiting free ownership. Anybody may help himself, for instance, to dates strewn on the ground by the wind, unless the owner puts up a fence around his orchard, indicating his desire to keep out strangers.[67] Gifts sent to a man on the occasion of his wedding are based upon reciprocity; if he refuses to return a present when the donor's wedding takes place under exactly the same circumstances, the latter may lawfully take back his own gift. Expenses incurred in the preparation of a wedding feast, including payments to clerical assistants, must be repaid by the bride, if she suddenly changes her mind and renounces her marriage.[68]

While a man's right to give away his possessions, while alive or *mortis causa*, to whomever he wishes, cannot be limited except for the advice not to be ruinously charitable, his dispositions concerning the inheritance of his estate are under strict surveillance. In general "a man must not bequeath his possessions to one not called upon to inherit, nor disinherit a legitimate heir." Moreover, a pious person will refrain from witnessing a will which discriminates, through any of the admissible linguistic subterfuges, against a misbehaving son in favor of a learned and decent brother.

---

enacted under totally different social conditions and from totally different juristic considerations," but between a talmudic law vigorously restated by Maimonides and other medieval rabbis and fully practiced in commercial transactions among Jews, and a privilege, repeatedly granted to Jews by medieval rulers. Prompted by an existing economic need, the Jews, in their negotiations with the authorities, were in a position the more readily to insist upon such a privilege, as they could stress its actual operation in the Jewish quarter over a period of many generations.

[67] M.T. Gezelah va-abedah 15, 16, based on B.M. 22b. For the special rights of a worker to help himself to the fruits of his employer, to which the original Deuteronomic injunction (23:25–26) had been reduced by the Talmud B.M. 87b, cf. below. For the significance attached to custom by Maimuni's predecessors, cf. the material assembled by J. L. Fishman in his " 'Custom' in Geonic Literature" (Hebrew), *The B. M. Lewin Jubilee Volume* (Jerusalem, 1939), pp. 132–59.

[68] M.T. Zekiyah u-mattanah 7, 1 ff., based on B.B. 145; *ibid.* 6, 24, in the name of his teachers. Cf. also RABD's objections and the commentaries. Maimuni also accepts (*ibid.* 6, 21–23) his predecessors' opinion concerning the customary return of gifts exchanged between fiancé and fiancée, if the engagement is broken. Even the food consumed in the meantime in each other's houses is to be paid for. For a practical application, cf. the interesting Resp. No. 225. Cf. also *ibid.*, Gezelah va-abedah 12, 11, 14; Sheluḥin ve-shutefin 5, 1, and so forth.

The Law has shown us to what extremes one is to go in the practice of this virtue of favoring one's relatives and of treating kindly those with whom one is bound by family ties, even if they happen to be offensive and hostile. A relative may prove to be extremely wicked, but nevertheless one ought to treat him with due compassion.[69]

In fact, all offices and appointments in Israel ought to be hereditary, provided that the son "can take the place of his ancestors by virtue of his wisdom and piety."[70] On the other hand, the heir must not enter into any agreements to refuse an inheritance legally due him. A husband, for example, may arrange to forego the inheritance from his deceased wife only before he marries her, i.e., before he becomes her legitimate heir. The reason for this limitation is the wish of the Torah that "no condition be valid in matters of inheritance regulated by biblical law, and the sages have strengthened their own regulations so as to place them on a par with the biblical law."[71] The heir is obliged to provide an appropriate funeral for the deceased; the court may forcibly collect the amount needed for hiring professional mourners, male as well as female.[72] All this is the more remarkable, as the heir is by no means a continuator of the deceased man's legal personality. He is responsible for debts only up to the amount of the inheritance. All partnerships of the deceased, overt or silent, even if entered into for a specific period, are immediately terminated; the heir must, if he desires to continue them, make a fresh start.[73] This compromise between the rigid

---

[69] M.T. Naḥlot 6, 1 ff., 11; M.N. III, 42, based on M.B.B. VIII, 5, and so forth. For the ramified Jewish inheritance laws in general, cf. Gulak, *op. cit.*, II, 71 ff.; and M. Mielziner, *The Rabbinical Law of Hereditary Succession*, Cincinnati, 1900. We are here, of course, concerned only with those phases of the law which throw light on the economic aspects of private ownership.

[70] M.T. Melakim 1, 7, based on Sifre, and so forth. Cf. *Haggahot Maimuniot*, *ad loc.*

[71] M.T. Ishshut 12, 9; 23, 5–7, based on M. Ket. IX, 1 in conjunction with b. 83a and B.B. 49ab (cf. also C.M. on Ket., *ibid.*); Resp. No. 319, where he combats an attempted distinction by Alfasi. Maimuni seems to believe, however, that the heir may refuse the inheritance after it falls due, against his teacher, Joseph ibn Megas's contrary opinion. Both agree, however, that the heir may relinquish his rights by making them *hefḳer*. Cf. also Freimann's notes on Resp., *ibid.*

[72] M.T. Ebel 12, 1, based on Sanh. 46–47b. Cf. also M.T. Zekiyah u-mattanah 11, 24 and Ket. 48a.

[73] M.T. Sheluḥin ve-shutefin 5, 11: "so did the geonim teach." Cf. also Schwarz, *op. cit.*, p. 385.

laws of inheritance and the full liberty to give away one's property was necessitated by the conflict between the ancient residua of communal ownership and the considerable economic individualism in the semicapitalistic society of the early talmudic or the geonic period. Maimuni adhered to this compromise, even where a revered predecessor, Alfasi, was ready to pursue a more individualistic line of reasoning. Moreover, he emphasized the fact that "the sages have enjoined us that no one [even] in his lifetime should discriminate among his children to the slightest extent so that there should not arise among them rivalry and envy as among Joseph and his brethren."[74]

Most significant are the limitations upon free spending. Ethically, a man should spend only such moderate amounts as are necessary for the upkeep of his body and mind, because "the main design in the acquisition of wealth should be to expend it for noble purposes and to employ it for the maintenance of the body and the preservation of life, so that its owner may obtain the knowledge of God insofar as that is vouchsafed unto man."[75] Luxury of any kind and especially, to use a modern term, conspicuous consumption for the display of one's wealth are to be curtailed. To be sure, the advice that a Jew, no matter how wealthy, should not marry more than four wives — this was also the prevalent law under Islam — is prompted mainly by the consideration that he thus might cohabit with each at least once a month.[76] But even a king ought not to marry more than eighteen wives, to have more horses than are absolutely needed for his carriage, and to accumulate money beyond his usual expenses, except for certain necessary reserves for public expenditure in emergencies.[77] Reflecting the prevalent economy of scarcity,

[74] M.T. Naḥlot 6, 13, somewhat stronger than Shab. 10b. For Alfasi, cf. n. 71.

[75] C.M. on Abot, Introd. (=Eight Chapters) Chap. V, trans. by Joseph I. Gorfinkle (New York, 1912) p. 70. Cf. also M.T. De'ot 2, 7; M.N. III, 39, and so forth.

[76] M.T. Ishshut 14, 4, based on Yeb. 44a. Cf. also C.M. on Yeb. IV, 11.

[77] M.T. Melakim 3, 12–14, based on Sanh. 21ab. Cf. also C.M. on Sanh. II, 4, and S.M. Prohib. 363–64. In all of these Maimuni goes beyond his talmudic sources in emphasizing the right of the king to use cavalry and to accumulate financial reserves for future emergencies. As to the contrast between the limitation to eighteen "wives" in S.M., which allows for an additional unlimited number of concubines, and the total of eighteen wives and concubines of M.T., to which RABD objected, cf. the variants in the latter text reported by Ibn Gaon, ad loc., and Heller's comments in his edition of S.M., p. 135, n. 5.

moreover, Maimuni strictly prohibits the waste of commodities of any kind. "He who unnecessarily burns a suit of cloth or breaks a vessel," as well as one who cuts down healthy trees, is subject to flagellation. Neither must one cause damage directly or indirectly to a neighbor, even though one is willing to pay for it. Indeed mere compensation does not absolve from the sin so committed, but the guilty person must, first repenting, confess and abstain from ever doing it again.[78] Fear of scarcity was undoubtedly also coresponsible for the great consideration given by Maimuni and the other Jewish leaders to all matters involving considerable monetary losses, to obviate which they were ready to interpret many older laws in a milder vein.[79]

All these limitations imposed upon private ownership merely stem from the far-reaching principle, adopted and even expanded by Maimonides, of the right of Jewish leadership to disregard private property rights when these conflict with common welfare. The Talmud had already made use of the legal maxim that "the court may declare anybody's property as belonging to none" (hefker beit din hefker), to justify certain departures from biblical law.[80] Maimonides asserts even more sweepingly: "A judge may always expropriate money belonging to whomsoever, destroy it and give it

[78] S.M. Prohib. 57; M.T. Nizḳei mamon 5, 1; Teshubah 1, 1. Maimonides' more radical interpretation of B.Ḳ. 23b called forth a sharp rebuke by RABD and caused embarassment to his friendly commentators on Nizḳei mamon, loc. cit. The Talmud evidently had in mind only legal protection against (possibly unrecoverable) future damages; Maimuni thinks of the ethico-economic implications of waste. He also finds the same motives underlying the prohibition of raising small cattle in Palestine, B.Ḳ. 79b. Cf. M.T., ibid., 5, 2, and C.M. on B.Ḳ. VII, 7. For different interpretations, cf. Baron, History, I, 279 f.; III, 69. Through the psychology of scarcity we may also explain Maimuni's rhetorical denunciation of those who put precious silk or gold-woven garments as shrouds upon the corpses of wealthy personages before interment. "They should be given to the poor rather than thrown to the worms." M.T. Ebel 4, 2; 14, 24, going beyond the ancient sources listed by Michael Higger in his edition of the Treatise Semaḥot (New York, 1931), pp. 81, 178, n. 87.

[79] Cf. M.T. Sheḥitah, 11, 15, and so forth.

[80] For the ramifications of this principle, cf. Sheḳalim 3a, Yeb. 89b and 90b, Giṭṭin 33a, 36b, B.B. 48b, and so forth. These cases include the juristic fiction of a retroactive annulment of marriage by the court's expropriation of the money originally used for the betrothal. This fiction sometimes appears without the psychological motivation of the supposed implicit consent of the bridegroom that his betrothal be valid only with the rabbis' approval. Cf. especially Rashi and Tosafot on Giṭṭin 33a and B.B. 48b.

away, if, in his judgment, this would serve to prevent the breaking down of the fences of the law, to strengthen its structure and to punish a mighty offender." He applies this principle particularly to salvaging as much as possible of the property (or the rights thereto) of an apostate for his Jewish heirs. While acknowledging the basic right of a renegade Jew to inherit his father's estate, he insists that in practice the court should transfer the inheritance to the grandchildren, if they remain Jewish, or to other close Jewish relatives. The wife of an apostate may demand immediate payment of her marriage settlement, although, according to strict law, she is entitled to it only when she becomes a widow or divorcee.[81] Such "daily" practice was, indeed, but a necessary safeguard for a people whose very survival was threatened by recurrent waves of conversion under Islam. But it also revealed the inherent precariousness of "the plenary control over an object" by its private owner, in the face of the overwhelming social control of the medieval Jewish community.

Finally, there are certain peculiar legal-economic features attached to the ownership of land. In many ways characteristic of Maimuni's economic views is his high evaluation of land as against movable property. In his *Code* he gives the curious advice that a man

should not sell a field and purchase a house, or sell a house and acquire a movable object, or use the purchase money to engage in business, but should rather convert movables into landed property. In general he should aim to acquire wealth by converting the transitory into the permanent.

[81] M.T. Sanh. 24, 6; Naḥlot 6, 12; Resp. Nos. 202, 302. For certain geonic rather than talmudic antecedents of these decisions of Maimonides, cf. the sources quoted by Freimann on Resp. No. 202; Lewin, *Otzar ha-Geonim*, IX, 30 ff. Characteristically, Maimuni is once more careful in the use of the term *hefḳer*. In the first of the above passages he uses it correctly, as the judge's action to declare any man's property as *hefḳer*; in the second, where he deals merely with the transfer of the inheritance from one heir to another, he says but לאבד את ממונו; in the third he uses the term merely in quoting the talmudic formula; in the fourth he subscribes to a decision of others based upon a similar quotation. Cf. above, n. 42. Such interference by Jewish judges with the inheritance of a Jew converted to Islam was by no means hampered by state legislation. On the contrary, it was a fairly accepted principle that no Muslim, Christian, or Jew should inherit the estate of a member of another creed. Cf. Mez, *op. cit.*, pp. 30, 106; Juynboll, *op. cit.*, p. 243; Bergsträsser-Schacht, *op. cit.*, p. 45. Cf. also Juster, *Les Juifs dans l'empire romain* (Paris, 1914), I, 259 ff.; II, 90 f.

This sweeping statement, for which the commentators are at a loss to find a talmudic source or parallel, has a decidedly personal ring. It certainly goes far beyond R. Isaac's well-known advice that a man should divide his fortune so as to invest one-third in land, another third in commerce, and keep the last third ready at hand. While its tenor undoubtedly is in consonance with the conservative attitude of agricultural Jewry in talmudic Babylonia and echoes certain parallel teachings in Arabian letters, this sharp emphasis upon sound rather than profitable investments may well have been due to the serious business reverses sustained by Maimuni and his family during the first years of their settlement in Egypt. These reverses caused him to accept as the lesser evil both the heavy land taxes resting upon Jewish and other non-Muslin landowners and the bureaucratic chicaneries of the state-capitalist government in Egypt.[82] Contending with the Talmud that inexperienced minors are likely to prefer the glitter of ready cash to the steadiness of landed estates, Maimuni demands for land sales not only the normal age of maturity in Jewish law (thirteen for boys, and twelve for girls), but also full understanding of the financial transactions involved. In the case of inherited lands, the age limit is raised to twenty. At the same time, the sale of movables may be perfected by a child of six or more, if, not having a guardian, he must take care of his own resources and is economically mature for his age. Maimuni controverts, however, those of his teachers who wished to annul all land sales by boys under twenty, even if, upon reaching that age, they failed to protest the sales. To safeguard the rights of the purchasers, Maimuni considers such tacit approval as legal reaffirmation of the original transfer. On the other hand, land acquired by a child through regular channels, without the intervention

---

[82] M.T. De'ot 5, 12; Letter to Yefet b. Elijah in Ḳobeṣ II, 37d. Cf. also M.T. Naḥlot 11, 6; Eppenstein in MbM, II, 36. R. Isaac's advice (B.M. 42a) was evidently prompted by his opposite predilection for cash, quite understandable in the light of the economic precariousness and the fiscal burdens of land tenure in both Palestine and Babylonia at the end of the third century. For the opinions of Arab economists, cf. Bryson's advice to a man to sell movable property quickly, but to delay the sale of land, "even though the profit may be slight in the disposal of merchandise and substantial in that of land," echoed as elsewhere almost verbatim by Maimonides' contemporary, Abul-Fadl al-Dimashki. Cf. Plessner, *op. cit.*, pp. 158–59 (Arabic and Hebrew; not in Latin); and Mahmassani, *op. cit.*, p. 87 n. 82.

of his guardian, is to be retained as its property, "since we acquire rights in the absence" of the beneficiary.[83] Similarly, hired workers may contractually renounce their rights to consume some of the agricultural produce which they happen to be raising. They may also renounce their rights, in the name of their coworking adult family members or slaves, who, having full knowledge of the facts, are entitled to forego anything they please. However, one must not give up any such rights of minors, "because they consume something that comes neither from their father nor from their master, but from Heaven." In many other respects, too, land differs from other articles of commerce. Along with slaves and deeds and sometimes also "sacred" property and that belonging to Gentiles, land is subject to specific administrative regulations. Neither can man ever be forcibly deprived of his land, even if he relinquishes all hope of regaining its possession; at a favorable moment he may simply take it back, without any compensation, from the last possessor who may have obtained it after a series of a thousand bona fide transactions.[84]

In short, land is not a simple commodity. Speaking in religious terms, it is, even more than any other object, under the direct overlordship of God. That is why, in Maimuni's opinion, the biblical lawgiver, by introducing through the Jubilee year a periodic *restitutio in integrum*, tried to forestall the permanent alienation of Palestinian land from the original owners. An irredeemable sale of Palestinian land constitutes a serious crime, although, because of its legal ineffectiveness, it is not punishable by flagellation. The seller may evade the law only by selling his land for a specified period of time, such as sixty years, but Maimonides urgently counsels Palestinian Jewish property holders, even should the Jubilee year be in operation, not to rely upon its subsequent restitution and to sell their houses or fields only in extreme emergency.

[83] M.T. Mekirah 29, 1, 6, 11-16, based on Giṭṭin 59a, B.B. 195-96, and so forth. For a practical illustration, cf. Resp. No. 220. Maimonides' opinion that legal obstacles be placed in the way of squandering any of a youth's inherited land, and not only his direct patrimony, is shared by Maimuni's teacher Ibn Megas, but contradicted by others. Cf. Don Vidal's comments on 29, 13.

[84] M.T. Sekirut 12, 14, based on B.M. 92b-93a; Gezelah va-abedah 8, 14, based on the implication of B.Ḳ. 116b-117b (cf. also C.M. on B.Ḳ. X, 5). For partly divergent opinions of scholars, cf. Rosanes's comments thereon; and *Teshubot geonim ḳadmonim*, ed. by Cassel, No. 41. Cf. also M.T. Sekirut 2, 1; Genebah 2, 2; Zekiyah u-mattanah 1, 14, and so forth.

Although these teachings evidently have no bearing upon the realities of the Maimonidean age, they illustrate the philosopher's basic idea of what the Torah intended to achieve through the institution of a Jubilee year, besides "arousing sympathy with our fellow men and promoting liberality toward all men." Just as the Sabbatical year has the additional economic function of "the land increasing its produce and improving when it remains fallow for some time," so it is the Jubilee year's objective to maintain permanent social equilibrium. It is

to provide stability in securing for the people a permanent source of supply of the necessaries of life by converting the land into the inalienable property of its owners, so that it could not be sold in an irredeemable manner .... In this fashion the property of a person remains intact for him and his heirs and he can enjoy only the produce thereof.

Usufructus of rather than plenary control over Palestinian land was thus the ultimate aim of the lawgiver.[85]

This high estimate of land by Maimonides — largely a restatement of traditional views with a strong personal note — should not mislead us into assuming that he tried to emphasize rural as against urban economy. In fact, land is for him urban real estate just as much as tillable soil. In his own day the role of the Jews in urban occupations undoubtedly far exceeded their activity in agriculture. Although the forces which effectively operated for the elimination of the Jews from the soil in the West were largely absent in the countries of Islam, the discrimination in taxation against the "infidels," especially the burdensome land tax of some 20–50 percent of the crops, combined with the vast industrial and commercial opportunies offered by the speedily expanding metropolitan economy under the Caliphate, led to the progressive urbanization of Jewry.[86] There still were a great many Jews who owned and

[85] M.T. Shemiṭṭah ve-yobel 11, 1–3; M.N. III, 39. Cf. Munk's translation and notes, III, 301 f. Cf. also S.M. Prohib. 227; Rosanes's comments on M.T. *loc. cit.*; and Rosenblatt, *op. cit.*, I, 112. It goes without saying that Maimuni did not attach practical significance to the Jubilee year. S.M. Comm. 136 states that it is observed only "under the condition that every one of the tribes be settled in its place, i.e., in its portion of Palestine, and that they should not be mixed up with one another." This seems to indicate that he did not expect the revival of the Jubilee year even in the Messianic age. Cf. also Outlook, pp. 94 ff.

[86] For the early land flight of the non-Muslim peasants, cf. Edgar Probster, "Privateigentum und Kollektivismus im mohammedanischen Liegenschaftsrecht, insbesondere des Maghrib," *Islamica*, IV (1931), 431; Ben Zion Dinaburg, *Israel*

tilled the soil, but for the majority the city opened much vaster
fields of endeavor. No wonder that for both the Muslim and the
Jewish jurists of the day, notwithstanding their heritage from a
nomadically and agriculturally oriented scriptural law, the city
appears as the focal point of all civilized life. Maimuni, who incidentally uses the expression *medinah* not only in his Arabic but
also in his Hebrew writings to designate a city rather than a country
or a province,[87] regards city life as the prevailing form of civilization. In his opinion the lawgiver has no need to enumerate, for
instance, all the kinds of "forewarned animals," because they are
rarely found in civilized regions and still less often in cities. Trying
to explain the remarkable difference between the severe penalties
imposed upon a thief in biblical law (two to fivefold restoration)
and the much milder treatment of the robber (only single restoration, plus one-fifth of the value for the forgiveness of the sin) —
a fairly widespread distinction in primitive law, which frequently
deprecates stealthy cowardice more than open attack — Maimuni
stresses particularly the greater frequency of stealing. "Theft is
possible everywhere, while robbery can be comitted in a city only
with some difficulty." Little wonder that, following the Talmud,
Maimonides asserts his preference for a city neighbor over a country
neighbor, if both wish to acquire property without having the
statutory privilege of preëmption. Moreover, such privilege is
lost altogether, if the neighbor intends to place the parcel under
cultivation while the alien purchaser wants to use it as a building
plot. The latter is to be preferred because of society's interest in
human settlement.[88] This predominantly urban orientation, shared

---

ba-Golah (Tel-Aviv, 1926), I, 58. One may hear an echo of the contemporary
situation in Saadia's disparagement of landed property because it gives its owner
constant worries. The farmer is not only dependent on God's will with respect
to the weather, and the like, but also on "the fiscal burdens of the kings and the
imposts of their servants, so that the entire yield goes to them and the owners
receive nothing at all." *Beliefs and Opinions*, X, 10. In the Egypt of Maimonides, particularly, the position of the peasantry, which had sunk into a state of
villeinage, was anything but enviable. Cf. Becker, *op. cit.*, I, 209 ff.

[87] C.M. on Shabbat I, 1; B.Ḳ. I, 5, etc.; M.T. 'Akum 7, 6; Shabbat 5, 18;
12, 3; Niẓḳei mamon 5, 3; Malveh ve-loveh 9, 4; etc.; M.N. *passim*. The Christian
scholastics, too, speak of the *civitas*, the city. Thomas thus renders the original
Aristotelian *polis*, which helps us to understand some of his teachings. Cf.
Schreiber, *op. cit.*, p. 24.

[88] M.N. III, 41; M.T. Shekenim 14, 1, 5, based on B.M. 108b, in general following Alfasi's (and Rashi's) interpretation. Maimuni generally champions
these social measures in favor of neighbors, scholars, and relatives, against the

also by the majority of Muslim jurists and philosophers, naturally colored the Maimonidean views in all domains of economic endeavor.

4. THE JUST PRICE

This urban orientation naturally renders trade and trade morals of primary significance in the economic outlook of Maimonides. As the son and leader of a people for whom the exchange of goods increasingly became the main basis of subsistence and living in Egypt, which in his day had become one of the main arteries of the world's commerce, he could not help acknowledging the socioeconomic function of mercantile enterprise. He could but try to stem its excesses and to subordinate it to the dictates of law and ethics. Once more he was not burdened by an anticommercial tradition, such as found expression in the exclamation ascribed to St. Chrysostomus: "No Christian ought to be a merchant, or if he should wish to be one, he ought to be ejected from the Church of God." Nor did he have to contend with a genuine *hadith* of Umar I, which, directed against the excessive speculation in grain in the Mecca of that day, assumed a tone of hostility to commerce in general. He seems to have had few, if any, compunctions such as those voiced by Augustine about the merchant's opportunities to live the life of virtue, or about his excessive mental absorption in his occupation. Maimonides, confronted by daily realities, saw clearly that apart from the inescapable necessity for most of his coreligionists to engage in trade, commerce offered better opportunities for carrying out his program of devoting a large part of the day to the study of the Law than did farming and industry, with their prevalent long working hours. It also extended considerable facilities for that silent partnership of scholars in business, which alone could stem the tide of the commercialization of scholarship which

---

more "liberal" view taken, for instance, by the Tosafists on B.M. 108b s. v. שכירי. Cf. above, n. 64. Cf. also M.N. III, 46, concerning magic in urban centers. For the dominant Arab opinion, cf., for example, Alfarabi's statement that "the villages exist only for the service of the city." Cf. his *Staatsleitung*, p. 51. Ibn Khaldun made the distinction between the urban and the nomadic civilizations one of the corner stones of his sociological interpretation of history. Cf. also Becker, *op. cit.*, I, 55. Thomas, following Aristotle, claims that, by nature, man lives in cities (*civitates*; cf. n. 87); the rural economy is for him but the effect of misfortune and want. Cf. Troeltsch, *op. cit.*, I, 298, 318.

he so vigorously denounced. That is why he never made the reservation, expressed by Thomas, "that the perfect city ought but moderately to employ merchants," a reservation, incidentally, partly
determined by the scholastics' deprecation of the merchant-
patricians' military prowess. Rather, like most Arabian writers
living under the more advanced economy of the caliphate — for
instance the ninth-century philosopher Ğahiz of Basra, who wrote
a treatise *On the Praise of Merchants and the Blame of Officials* —
Maimuni accepts commerce as a necessary and unobjectionable
human institution.[89]

To be sure, he realizes that in ancient times agriculture was
far more important; he even discusses the original conflict between
paganism and the patriarchal monotheism in terms of their relative
significance for the success of the agricultural harvest. He also
knows that the much-revered patriarchs were shepherds and cattle
breeders — a none-too-honorable calling in the later talmudic law,
as restated by himself. But for his own day he chooses his examples
largely from the domain of business, as when he discusses the effects
of the accidental success of a business venture upon superstitious
minds.[90] Without writing an apology for commerce, he merely
tries to restate or refashion the traditional ethical standards so as
to make them govern also all trade relationships. Here, too, the
interest of society is paramount, and the individual Jew, while
seeking to obtain a livelihood, must take into account the interests
of his fellow tradesmen, of his customers, and of society at large.

Such balance between opposing interests is unavoidable also from
the purely economic point of view. "Since financial coöperation

[89] Pseudo-Chrysostomus, *Opus imperfectum in Matteum*, hom. 38 (Migne,
Patrologia graeca, LVI, 839 f.); Plato, *Laws*, 743 D, 918 DE; Augustine, *De
opere monachorum* 15 (Migne, *Patrologia latina*, XL, 561); Thomas, *De regimine
principum*, II, 3; Björkmann, *op. cit.*, pp. 85 f., 89; [O. Rescher], *Exzerpte und
Uebersetzungen aus den Schriften des Philosophen und Dogmatikers Ğahiz aus
Basra (150–250 H.)* (Stuttgart, 1931), I, 186–88. Cf. also Mez, *op. cit.*, pp.
442 ff.; Becker, *op. cit.*, I, 186, 213 f.; *Encyclopaedia of Islam* s. v. Egypt; Mahmassani, *op. cit.*, pp. 82, 184; Schreiber, *op. cit.*, pp. 4 ff.; Kraus, *op. cit.*, pp. 45 ff.;
H. Coutzen, *Geschichte der volkswirtschaftlichen Literatur im Mittelalter* (2d ed.,
Berlin, 1872) p. 63; Schilling, *Augustinus*, pp. 249 ff. The occasional anticommercial statements of M. Ḳidd. IV, 14, and so forth, had been so thoroughly
disposed of in the talmudic and geonic periods that Maimuni had no compunc-
tion about leaving that Mishnah without comment.

[90] Cf. M.N. III, 30, 37, 39, as against M.T. 'Edut 10, 4, and so forth. Cf.
also below.

is necessary for the people of every city, it is impossible to
have these transactions without a proper standard of equity and
without useful regulation."[91] That is why laws introducing order
into the relations among men and judges to administer these laws
are such universal features. Beside being one of the Noahidic
commandments, the appointment of judges was also, next to the
Sabbath, one of the first divine ordinances imposed upon the Israelites after their Exodus from Egypt. When a legal problem is
involved, it makes little difference, according to Maimuni, whether
the subject of controversy amounts to a thousand denars or to one
perutah. Not even the ethically important consideration of the
relative economic positions of the litigants is to be taken into account. Maimuni reiterates the biblical admonition to the judge
not to lean backward to extend even the slightest favor to a poor
litigant, only because he happens to be poor. The specific protection to be granted by society to its disinherited is a matter of charity
and social work, but is outside the confines of the administration
of justice. Even in the Exile, where the courts are devoid of the
power of imposing the ancient Palestinian "fines," they are called
upon to interfere in all matters involving financial losses "so that
the rights of the people, such as those arising from loans, sales,
transfers, legal disputes and damages should not be lost."[92]

It falls under the jurisdiction of both the civil and the judicial
administrators carefully to supervise the weights and measures
used in business transactions. Maimuni insists upon the rigid
control of scales, weights, and measures at the very moment when
these implements are manufactured. "The same applies to the
measuring of land where one ought to establish the figures relating
to the survey of the land with full exactitude in accordance with the
principles elucidated in the geometric works, since even a finger's
width of land is to be treated as if it were a field full of crocus."

[91] M.N. III, 3, 35.

[92] Ibid. III, 32; M.T. Sanh. 20, 4, 10; Malveh ve-loveh 1, 4; Melakim 9, 1, 14;
S.M. Comm. 177; Prohib. 277; C.M. on B.Ḳ. VIII, 2. Cf. also above, n. 24.
Personally, Maimuni would have liked to see class distinctions between scholars
and illiterate persons carried into the court room to the extent of seating the
former and merely perfunctorily inviting the latter, too, to be seated. But he
must admit that since the close of the Talmud, all courts of justice have indiscriminately invited all parties and even witnesses to be seated, "in order to
obviate controversy." This is because, he adds with a sigh, "we have no power
to carry the requirements of the Law into full effect." M.T Sanh. 21, 3–5. Cf.
also C.M. on B.Ḳ. VIII, 6 and Tykocinski, op. cit., pp. 167 f.

It is also the duty of the Jewish administration to appoint supervisors in every city and county to visit the shops, check the scales and measures, and, upon finding anyone in possession of faulty weights, to subject him to flagellation and to a fine in the discretion of the court. In another connection Maimuni declares that the use of measures below the standard agreed upon by the population of a particular city constitutes the breaking of a negative commandment, although it is not punished by flagellation, the transgressor being obliged to pay damages. Even an unintentional miscalculation makes the transaction null and void, and the injured party may demand the restoration of the precontractual status. The mere possession of a defective measure or scale in a private dwelling is a serious crime. Maimonides becomes rhetorical when, using a hyperbolical exclamation of R. Levi as a motto, he writes:

The punishment for [incorrect] measures is more drastic than the sanction on incest, because the latter is an offense against God, while the former affects a fellow man. He who denies the law concerning measures is like one who denies the Exodus from Egypt which was the beginning of this commandment.[93]

Society is also obliged to prevent excessive profits. Maimuni enumerates in the same breath the duty of the courts to appoint supervisors over weights and measures and their obligation to fix prices. It is really in this field of economic regimentation that we may find a major criterion for the extent of his advocacy of active social control. Evidently at this point he comes very close to the doctrine of the just price, which played such an enormous part in the economic views of the Christian scholastics. Under the more advanced semicapitalistic economy of Muslim lands, the limitation of mercantile profits was less important. Nevertheless Maimuni insists that

[93] M.T. Genebah 7, 1–3, 12; 8, 1, 20; Mekirah 15, 1; S.M. Comm. 176; Prohib. 271, where mathematical surveying is contrasted with the "illusory proceedings possessing no truth whatsoever in which most people indulge." In many of these passages Maimuni goes beyond his talmudic sources, as when he gives a scientific turn to B.B. 89b or when in M.T. Genebah 7, 12 he contrasts a statement of R. Levi (*ibid.* 88b) with one in Sifra Ḳedoshim 8, 12, giving both a personal metaphysico-social motivation. Cf. Don Vidal's comment, and Outlook, p. 28, n. 51. For כרכום, cf. j. Sanh. II, 5, 20c. The distinction between שפט (judge) and שוטר (police supervisor) corresponds to that of the Arab functionaries *kadi* and *muḥtasib*. Cf. also *Koran*, Sura 7, and Björkmann, *op. cit.*, p. 93.

no overcharge is permitted in sales; only the known and customary rate of profit [must suffice]. The law has fixed the conditions under which a sale should be valid; and, as is well known, warned us even of verbal cheatings.[94]

He refers here to those sections of his *Code* in which he had reiterated the talmudic regulations to safeguard the application of the *justum pretium* for both the merchant and the customer. He realizes, however, as may be seen in several significant points, the necessity of adjusting the law to the novel economic conditions.

What is the just price? We shall search in vain for a full definition by Maimuni. He undoubtedly was familiar with Aristotle's penetrating analysis of the elements of value in the *Nicomachean Ethics*, a work quoted by him on several occasions. None the less we shall find in his presentation neither a clean-cut decision for the more objective criteria of the costs of production and the element of work as emphasized, from the standpoint of the producer, by Augustine and Thomas, respectively, nor one for the more subjective element of the need and utility on the part of the consumer, as seen by Aristotle himself or by Duns Scotus.[95] Like the Talmud, Maimonides merely insists that no one should obtain a profit, or incur a loss, exceeding one-sixth of the due price. While he thus seems to be leaning toward the element of cost, he qualifies this immediately by excluding from the operation of this law all transactions based upon the frank admission by the seller of his original cost and the intended profit. In this case, the profit may far exceed

[94] M.N. III, 42. For the general rabbinic legislation concerning the just price, and numerous ancient and modern parallels, but with practically no reference to Jewish, Muslim, or Christian scholasticism, cf. P. Dickstein, "The Just Price and Misrepresentation" (Hebrew), *Ha-Mishpaṭ ha-'ibri*, I (1926), 15–55. The author makes it appear quite plausible that the rabbinic law had exercised considerable influence upon these phases of Western legislation ever since the days of Diocletian. (Cf., however, the opposing view of H. F. Jolowicz, in "The Origin of Laesio Enormis," *Juridical Review*, XLIX [1937], 53 ff.) Heinz Grünwald, in *Die Uebervorteilung im jüdischen Recht* (Göttingen, 1933), offers a careful analysis of the juridical aspects of the law of *ona'ah*, but cites little comparative material except in occasional brief remarks on Roman and Canon Law. Neither author pays any attention to that law's economic causes and effects, nor to its operation within the entire framework of Jewish economy.

[95] For Aristotles's views, cf. the careful analysis of W. Gelesnoff in "Die ökonomische Gedankenwelt des Aristoteles," *Archiv für Sozialwissenschaft und Sozialpolitik*, L (1922–23), 1–33. The Christian scholastics are treated especially in Kraus, *op. cit.*, pp. 45 ff. where it is shown that they, too, were oscillating between the objective and the subjective criteria of value.

one-sixth. The only requirement is that in his calculations of the original cost the merchant should include only overhead, such as transportation and hotel expenses, but not, without express indication of so doing, the expected remuneration for his own time and efforts.[96] The law of "misrepresentation" (ona'ah) thus applies only to the usual transactions, in which the purchaser is not taken into the seller's confidence or vice versa. It is evident that for Maimuni, as for the rabbis generally, the prevailing price is based upon some sort of profit added to the merchant's own cost. To determine it he accepts two legitimate criteria: the market price and that fixed by the authorities. True to his urban orientation, he decides, on the basis of a rather incidental discussion in the Talmud, that it is the market price of the city rather than that established in a small town or village which really counts. He thereby assumes that the price, at least of agricultural produce, would be higher in the city than in the countryside, nearer the actual place of production, although this was not always the case in the Muslim cities. He also recognizes seasonal fluctuations.[97]

The acceptance of a freely established market price, however, would lead to the recognition of the uncontrolled operation of the law of supply and demand. This, of course, is repudiated by Maimuni, as by all other medieval thinkers. That is why, besides the barriers of custom, he expects communal regulation to establish the prices of all important articles, in fairness to the producer, the distributor, and the consumer. Only in necessities of life, such as wine, oil, and flour, however, does Maimuni insist upon price fixing

[96] M.T. Mekirah 13, 5–6; 14, 1, based upon Maimuni's interpretation of B.M. 51b, which agrees in the main with that of Alfasi, Hananel, and Tosafot against that of Rashi. However, his explanation אלא מפרש ואומר לו כך וכך אני משתכר is hardly borne out by the text of the Talmud. Cf. Don Vidal's and De Boton's comments. Maimonides' intention thus to withdraw numerous commercial transactions from the operation of the law of one-sixth appears undeniable. Rashi, on the other hand, frequently more typically "medieval," tries to shift the impact of the more liberalistic Baraita to the different sphere of a merchant and his agent, which would leave the main law intact.

[97] M.T. Malveh ve-loveh 9, 4, 7, amplifying the discussion of B.M. 72b, notwithstanding the considerable difficulties of such interpretation. Cf. Don Vidal's comments and Haggahot Maimuniot, ad loc. The contrary phenomenon of lower prices of grain in large cities, as the result of a larger supply, is mentioned by Ibn Khaldun, Prolegomena, ed. Paris, XVII/1, 239 ff. (Arabic); XX/1, 282 ff. (French). Cf. also M.T. Mekirah 21, 4; Ma'aser sheni ve-neta reba'i 4, 22, and so forth, and below.

to allow a margin of profit of but one-sixth for the merchant. With respect to all other merchandise, he leaves price regulation, if any, entirely to the discretion of the Jewish communal authorities, and especially the distinguished leader of a city, clearly assuming that they would take cognizance of these conflicting interests and adopt a middle-of-the-road policy in accordance with the demands of justice. In other words, one might accept for Maimonides the definition soon after formulated by Albertus Magnus: "Justum autem pretium est, quod secundum aestimationem fori illius temporis potest valere res vendita."[98] Such governmental "estimation" really corresponded to the prevalent practice of Egyptian state capitalism in Maimuni's day, which failed, however, to check all abuses arising from the excessive speculation in grain. Thus the subjective criterion of the court's opinion is substituted for the other subjective element of the merchants themselves fixing the price in accordance with supply and demand. Maimuni is ready, however, to accept the latter, in case of the absence of authoritative regulation, which, under the conditions of his time, he hardly expected to serve as universal standards even with respect to basic commodities.

These subjective criteria of value evidently are in full consonance with the subjective character of the entire system of private ownership, as analyzed above. Even the overcharging or underselling by one-sixth is discussed in the subjective term of "cheating" the other party. We have seen that as soon as the injured party is informed of this excessive raise or fall in the price, the transaction is valid. The very fixing of one-sixth as the standard measure is due to the likewise "subjective" assumption that people are ready to forego their rights to that extent, and that the injured party would voluntarily renounce its due. That is also why "verbal cheating," consisting in willful misrepresentation entailing no

[98] M.T. Mekirah 14, 1–2, 9, 11, based upon a peculiar interpretation of B.B. 8b, 90a, and so forth. On the one hand, Maimuni fails to mention the price fluctuations between the acquisition of the merchandise by the merchant and its sale, such as were stressed by Samuel b. Meir on B.B 90a s. v. המשתכר. It may be assumed that Maimuni left this decision to the court at the time of its price fixing. On the other hand, by placing it in connection with a subsequent unrelated discussion, he reduces the requirement of one-sixth to life's utmost necessaries, namely wine, oil, and flour. Meat and bread, for instance, are no longer in this category. Cf. also Don Vidal's comments and *Haggahot Maimuniot*, *ad loc.* For Albertus Magnus, cf. Kraus, *op. cit.*, p. 52; and, more generally, Wilhelm Endemann, *Studien in der romanisch-kanonistischen Wirtschafts- und Rechtslehre* (Berlin, 1883), II, 36 ff.

financial loss whatsoever, is regarded as equally injurious. Indeed, since it affects personal integrity rather than property and since it does not lend itself to financial compensation, Maimuni denounces it with even greater vigor.[99]

In his elaboration of these principles Maimuni tries to meet the requirements of justice, but it evidently is justice in the psychological and judicial rather than the economic sense. In the case of the one-sixth overcharge, he is concerned principally with the prevention of willful or unconscious misrepresentation. As long as the case is correctly and clearly stated and no party can complain of having misunderstood the other, there is no legal redress, even though the injured party may have been compelled by urgent economic reasons consciously to concede to the other an undue advantage. In clarifying the case of "honest" trading, Maimonides states that the seller may either mention his own purchase price and the desired profit, or else clearly indicate that the deal shall not be annulled on account of the stipulated overcharge. A condition phrased in general terms or stating the overcharge in obviously exaggerating terms (e.g., "this object sold to you for 100 denars is worth only 1 denar"), is not valid, because it does not give the purchaser full information. But Maimuni would not accept — as did some Franco-German scholars — the purchaser's frank admission that he had realized the extent to which he had been overcharged, but, being in need of the purchased object, he gladly overpaid by more than one-sixth, so as to assure the subsequent annulment of the contract. Such cynicism, even if dictated by economic stress, could perhaps be tolerated in feudal northern Europe; it would play havoc with the widespread mercantile relations of the Jews under Islam.[100]

[99] C.M. on B.M. IV, 10; M.T. Mekirah 12, 3; 14, 12–18, based on B.M. 49b, 58b–59 slightly expanding here the talmudic homily on Lev. 25:17, rather than repeating that on Amos 7:7. Cf. also S.M. Prohib. 250–51; M.T. De'ot, 1, 6, and so forth. Maimuni admits, however, that verbal cheating is not subject to prosecution by earthly courts. It is needless to say that if the legitimate profit from the sale of the most important commodities amounts to no more than 16.66 percent, the assumption that people gladly renounce a slightly smaller difference is hardly realistic. But this merely adds emphasis to the "subjectivity" of the motivation and of the underlying general outlook.

[100] M.T. Mekirah, 13, 4–5; 15, 11. The latter is a Maimonidean extension of B.M. 51b. The extreme Franco-German opinion was expressed by Eliezer b. Joel ha-Levi, as quoted by Mordecai b. Hillel on B.M. 51b and by Isserles on H.M. 227, 7.

In other respects, too, this insistence upon merely psychological "honesty" often favors the merchant rather than the customer. In the first place, the very standard of one-sixth enables the former to demand restoration if he sells the merchandise anywhere between 14.3 and 16.66 percent below the just price, while the purchaser can claim credit only if he pays from 16.66 to 20 percent over the just price. Above these percentages the entire transaction becomes null and void, at the request of the injured party. It has been estimated that any object worth, say, 210 denars can fetch up to 244 denars before the purchaser is entitled to raise the issue, or down to 181 denars before the seller may do so. Actual annulment comes only if the price goes either beyond 252 or below 175 denars. In other words, the seller overcharging by 34 to 42 denars is in the same position as the purchaser underpaying by 29 to 35 denars. At the same time a simple mistake in weight does not annul the transaction, but is to be adjusted by either the merchant placing at the disposal of the purchaser the additional weight or receiving back from him the excess.[101] More important is the fact that

---

[101] M.T. Mekirah 12, 1–4; 15, 1–2, based on Maimuni's interpretation of B.M. 51ab, B.B. 83b–84a, Ḳidd. 42b, and so forth. For the computation of the actual range of possible misrepresentation, cf. Dickstein, *op. cit.*, pp. 52 f. This list shows the paradoxical result that the sale of an object worth 210 denars for 175, 180, 245, or 252 denars would be valid and would merely require indemnification of the injured party in the amount of 35, 30, 35, or 42 denars, respectively; whereas its sale for 176–79 or 246–51 denars would completely nullify the transaction. Don Vidal and De Boton, who wish to explain Maimuni's opinion in a less casuistic way, must ultimately resort to textual emendation — a desperate expedient, indeed. This is but another illustration of Maimonides' main concern with the formal judicial, rather than the economic effects of these laws. The same formal psychological slant may be seen also in his exclusion of a conspicuous discrepancy between price and value, which far exceeds one-sixth of the latter. Like Nahmanides and Ibn Adret, he believes that "if the discrepancy is very large, there is neither misrepresentation nor annulment; because of the large discrepancy one is not likely to err in such matters. This is a basic principle and remember it, since we may assume that he [the purchaser] consciously gave him [the seller] a present." C.M. on B.B. V, 2. Similarly in M.T. Mekirah 27, 3, Maimonides disregards the price difference as long as the term used is, according to usage, clearly indicative of the range of the sale. That is why "he who sells a yoke, sells the cow" along with it. We have here once more the precedence of the formal psychological over the economic factor. Cf. also Don Vidal's and Rosanes's comments on 12, 4. In all discrepancies exceeding one-sixth, moreover, the injured party alone has the choice of either retaining the object, *without* compensation, or annuling the contract. Against the opinion of other jurists, Maimuni does not concede the right of annulment to the misrepresenting per-

according to rabbinic law the purchaser has the right to withdraw from the transaction only during a limited period of time, namely, until he has a reasonable chance to show the merchandise to an expert or to one of his relatives, who might turn his attention to the excessive price. The merchant, however, can claim annulment (or restoration) at any future date, because it is assumed that, not being any more in possession of the sold object, he is in no position to ascertain its real value. To be sure, Maimonides tries somewhat to qualify this indefinite right. Although echoing R. Nahman's evidently impulsive exclamation, "forever," he states that if the seller happens to come across an identical object, he must immediately raise his claim. In the case of objects of unchanging quality, such as pepper, his claim expires as soon as he may obtain information in the market. Maimuni pays no attention, however, to the special need of protection for the usually ignorant customer as against the more experienced merchant, which undoubtedly had inspired the original legislators to enact this entire body of protective laws.[102]

Following the Talmud, moreover, Maimuni stipulates so many exemptions from the operation of the principle of just price that its effectiveness is highly curtailed in an advanced economic system. While refusing to follow a gaon's opinion that the principle, as such, applies only to the sale of foodstuffs, he admits that such significant branches of economy as transactions in land, slaves, and commercial paper (apart from the more or less obsolete *hekdesh*) are generally exempt.[103] Since "land" included all types of rural

---

son, because he does not regard the contract as intrinsically void, but merely as one which may become void through the psychological decision of the injured party. He wholly disregards the economic reality that annulment might either be impossible, if the object had been disposed of in the meantime, or more injurious than the overcharge. Restoration of the difference can, nevertheless, be demanded only in the exceptional case that the discrepancy amounted to exactly one-sixth of the price, neither more nor less. On the other hand, following his teacher, Ibn Megas, but against the opinion of RABD and others, Maimuni demands payment of the difference rather than annulment, in the case of a mistake in the weight or measure. This realistic view merely puts into bolder relief the sheer casuistry of most of his discussions on "misrepresentation."

[102] C.M. on B.M. IV, 3; M.T. Mekirah 12, 5–8, based on an interpretation of B.M. 50b which is not shared by all rabbis. Cf. Don Vidal's comments.

[103] C.M. on B.M. IV, 9; M.T. Mekirah 13, 8, based on B.M. 56b–57b. By emphasizing אפילו מכר שוה אלף בדינר ושוה דינר באלף, Maimuni, like Alfasi, rejects the recurrent attempts in the talmudic and geonic periods, as well as in some modern legislations, to limit the permissible overcharge (as opposed to the *laesio*

and urban real estate, since a large number of Jews in Maimuni's age were still engaged in the slave trade, and since many important business transactions consisted in the transfer of sale and loan contracts or other deeds, one can easily visualize that the ability to sell or purchase all these significant articles of commerce at the best price obtainable facilitated its unhampered development. To be sure, here too Maimonides introduces a number of qualifications, beyond those stated in the Talmud. Sales perfected on either side by plenipotentiaries, guardians of minors, and to a certain extent by courts acting in behalf of minors (or of charitable funds) are subject to the laws affecting "misrepresentation." While contractual labor for wages, like slavery, is exempt, Maimuni is apparently the first jurist to demand the application of these laws to contractors and artisans undertaking a specific job.[104] But he

---

enormis) on land to 100 percent. Cf. Don Vidal's comments, Hilai Gaon's responsum in *Sha'arei ṣedeḳ*, IV, 6, 24, 28, fol. 83ab; *Teshubot ha-geonim*, ed. by Harkavy, Nos. 77, 435; Lewin, *Otzar*, IX, 116. On the other hand, again following Alfasi, Maimuni includes in C.M. on B.M. IV, 9; M.T. Mekirah 13, 13, all movable objects, such as cattle, jewels, swords, and scrolls of law, which some sages had tried to exempt from the operation of the law. Cf. also Dickstein, *op. cit.*, pp. 45 ff.

[104] M.T. Mekirah 13, 9–18, based upon various talmudic passages. In Resp. No. 144 Maimuni applies these regulations in favor of a court acting in behalf of an estate bequeathed for charitable purposes. He goes to the extreme of allowing the court to revoke the sale of a house simply because it had been "unnecessarily" (ללא הכרח) sold, and even to deduct the amount of rent, collected in the meantime by the purchaser, from the price to be returned. In the case of mistakes involving the loss of one-sixth or more, Maimuni insists that sales perfected by guardians or courts should be annuled only in their favor, not in that of the purchasers, thus establishing another unusual disparity between the contracting parties. This disparity is justified by the purely formalistic consideration that the purchaser's status as such remains the same, whether he buys directly from an adult owner or from the local representative of a minor. Maimonides refuses, however, to extend this privilege to a plenipotentiary acting in behalf of an adult; it would, he realizes, merely have the undesirable effect of encouraging land sales through substitutes. RABD, more consistently, objects to any disparity. With respect to the courts, Maimuni himself qualifies their right of retraction to cases where they did not regularly estimate the property and duly advertise it or where no such public announcement is legally required. M.T. Malveh ve-loveh 12, 11. Since in the case of slaves and deeds no announcement is needed at all, and in that of land it is required only in an emergency, this qualification has little practical value, except in land sales effected by the court for the satisfaction of creditors. Only in the case of movables the court seems to be placed on a par with ordinary sellers. In extending all these one-sided privileges Maimuni, undoubtedly guided by the humanitarian motive of

could not repudiate those basic exemptions which had been granted by the talmudic authorities evidently because they did not consider them as vitally affecting the rule itself. They became immeasurably more important, however, in the days of Maimonides.

Another important talmudic exemption was granted to the nonprofessional seller of household articles, who was allowed to dispose of his property at the best possible price. Maimuni, like many other commentators, seems to have expanded this privilege to include the one-sided right of such a seller to claim restitution or annulment, if he sold below the market price. This is motivated by his usual personal attachment to the sold objects, which, again psychologically rather than economically, modifies their value.[105] On similar grounds Maimuni, taking a clue from an inconclusive talmudic analogy, postulates a general exemption for barter of specific objects. Barter between two kinds of fruit, he admits, is subject to "misrepresentation," because they possess an objective value. But "he who exchanges vessels for vessels or an animal for another, even if he exchanges a needle for a coat of mail or a lamb for a horse, has no claim of misrepresentation, because such a man may wish to have the needle rather than the coat of mail."[106] Whatever

---

furthering the protection of minors, readily overlooks the economic effects of the ensuing legal uncertainty for the purchasers. If, in acquiring slaves, commercial papers, or many parcels of land belonging to minors, they could not rely upon the court's official estimate and advertisement, but had to accept the price as final for themselves but not for the court and frequently not even for the guardian, one can hardly see any incentive for them to negotiate such dubious purchases. That, with price concessions beyond 14.3 percent being equally precarious, this discriminatory treatment might greatly curtail the demand and ultimately entail hardships for the orphans themselves, does not seem to trouble Maimonides and most of his fellow jurists. But he realizes that he is not voicing an accepted opinion when in both crucial points (M.T. 13, 9, 11) he inserts the personal נראה לי. The same remark precedes his statement in 13, 18, removing the contracting artisans from the class of workingmen and placing them on a par with merchants. For Maimonides' views on the general relationship between the contractor and the laborer, as well as for his equation here of free labor with temporary slavery, cf. below. Cf. also H.M. 109; 247, 30, 48–49, and the commentaries thereon.

[105] M.T. Mekirah 13, 2. Cf. Don Vidal's comment, and Joseph ibn Megas, *Responsa*, No. 104.

[106] M.T. 13, 1. For the difficulties of reconciling these views of Maimonides (as well as of his teacher, Ibn Megas) with the talmudic sources and the opposing interpretation of RABD, cf. Ibn Megas, *Responsa*, No. 107, and the ingenious, though not altogether satisfactory explanations of Ibn Gaon, Don Vidal, and De Boton, *ad loc.* For Muslim law, cf. Bergsträsser-Schacht, *op. cit.*, pp. 62 f.

influence the endless Muslim casuistry concerning the unlawful increment — which was classified as "usury," whether obtained by a credit transaction or otherwise — may have exercised upon Maimonides, he remains true to his constant psychological interpretation of this law, with little, if any, regard for the economic realities.

Equally far-reaching qualifications are attached by Maimonides to his demand for authoritative price fixing and related measures against unbridled speculation. Indeed, it was through a juxtaposition of these two lines of reasoning that he limited price fixing to the necessaries of life. The Talmud has really postulated the suppression of all commerce in wine, oil, and flour, in order that the consumer be able to obtain his food directly from the producer without paying for the middleman's services. Maimuni, literally applying some statements of the ancient Palestinian sages, limits this prohibition to Palestine. Even there he admits the exception, stated previously in the tannaitic period, that when oil is plentiful a legitimate trade may draw profits from mediating between the producer and the consumer.[107] Maimuni seems to disregard geographic boundaries only in the case of eggs, when he demands that the first purchaser alone be entitled to sell them with profit, whereas all subsequent buyers should resell them at cost.[108] To prevent an undue rise in prices, the Talmud had discouraged grain speculation through the storing up of grain and other necessaries for resale at a higher market price. Maimuni limits that prohibition to Palestine

[107] M.T. Mekirah 14, 1, 2, 4, based on a combination of passages in B.B. 90b–91a. Cf. Don Vidal's and Karo's comments.

[108] M.T. ibid., 14, 3, based on B.B. 91a by evidently ascribing it to Samuel, against Don Vidal's opinion. However, Karo is hardly right in regarding eggs as merely an example of food in general. Maimuni adheres strictly to the talmudic classification; eggs in ancient Palestine were certainly much less of a necessity than oil, which Karo evidently misunderstands. He also overlooks the fact that both meat and bread appear in 14, 9, outside the realm of life's necessaries. Under "bread" Maimuni very likely understands here the bread of barley, the unleavened bread, or that baked in oil, as against the white bread which he probably includes in the term סלת. The former types of bread, indeed, as well as many meats are regarded by him as bad for digestion. Cf. M.T. De'ot 4, 9–10. The denial of any profit to the second merchant undoubtedly has the same practical effect as the prohibition for the first merchant to sell eggs for purposes of resale, as it appears in the more literal interpretation of Samuel b. Meir on B.B. 91a s. v. תגר.

and to all other places where the Jews constitute the majority, "because from such practices suffering arises for Israel." The agricultural producer, however, may store up his own produce and sell it at a time most convenient to him. Before a Sabbatical year, everybody may accumulate the yield of harvests to provide for the needs of three years, namely the year of fallowness and the year preceding and following it. In emergency periods, however, when there is famine in Palestine, one must not store away even a measure of the cheapest food, such as St. John's bread, "because one thereby brings a scourge into the market prices." Another safeguard was the prohibition of exportation of such necessaries from Palestine, or even from one suzerainty to another in Palestine. In general, "he who raises prices [through speculation] or stores up produce in Palestine or in any other place where the majority consists of Israelites, is like a usurious money lender." There is no evidence that Maimuni contemplated the practical application of most of these laws to his own time.[109]

Maimonides' indecisive views on competition are equally illuminating. He allows arrangements between members of an artisan group mutually to divide up the working days, so that they should not compete with one another. Any breach of the arrangement, subject at most to the approval of an outstanding communal leader wherever one exists, may be punished by a stipulated fine. A group of shipowners or members of a caravan may also agree upon a sort of mutual insurance for losses in ships or donkeys, sustained by individual members. But this is far from regimentation along the lines of a medieval guild, or even of such guilds as had existed in Sassanian Persia and in the declining Roman Empire. That is perhaps why Maimuni nowhere mentions that the general arrangements concerning working days must be agreed upon by all artisans

[109] M.T. Mekirah 14, 5–8, based upon B.B., *loc. cit.* Contrast these moderate limitations with the sweeping condemnation of contemporary storing of wheat and barley as well as wine and oil, for speculative purposes, by Natronai Gaon in Ginzberg's *Geonica*, II, 117 f. (despite poor preservation, this is clearly the meaning of the responsum). There was no need of generally legislating against the purchase of agricultural futures for speculative purposes, since no transaction was valid if it involved as yet nonexistent crops. Cf. M.T. Mekirah 22, 1, and n. 58 above. The acquisition of future crops in orchards, where this argument would not hold true, is prohibited on the ground that it leads to usurious gains, in M.T. Malveh ve-loveh 8, 5.

in a city, as demanded, for instance, by the Spaniards, Judah b. Barzillai and Nahmanides.[110] On the other hand, he does not object to underselling one's competitors or using other "fair" methods of competition. It is once more the psychological element of frankness and clarity, rather than the economic consideration of a neighbor's rights, that offers the criterion for fairness. Paraphrasing the liberal view of a majority in the Mishnah, he writes:

A merchant may distribute cakes and nuts among children and servant girls so as to induce them to frequent his shop. He may undersell the market price, so as to attract more customers, and the members of the market may not prevent him from so doing. There is nothing underhanded in that.[111]

To be sure, he wishes to protect individuals well established in a certain craft against unfair competition. At least ethically he regards it as one of the essentials "not to infringe upon the calling of a fellow Jew." In a notable case which was brought to his attention he harshly condemned the revengeful proceedings of a wealthy citizen, who, to spite the *mohel* of the community, circumcised all newborn boys in the region and spent the fees on charity. "This is the fulfillment of a commandment arrived at through sin . . . because he interfered with the established livelihood of a poor and learned person." He used here metaphorically — as did many other rabbis — the ancient phrase of "the removal of a neighbor's boundaries," even though he himself had taught that, in the strict legal sense, this biblical prohibition (superimposed upon the general prohibitions of theft and robbery) referred only to concrete land boundaries in Palestine. It was merely for the promotion of Jewish

[110] M.T. Mekirah 14, 10 (also Don Vidal's comments); Gezelah va-abedah 12, 12–15. Characteristically, there is no mention here of price fixing by such interested groups. Only the community at large is entitled to do this. Of course Maimuni also acknowledged governmental price regulation, but there was little opportunity for monopolistic practices of individuals or corporations. Both Muslim and Jewish law failed to develop legal facilities for large mercantile companies, so that we possess but occasional references to a sort of monopolistic control over a certain branch of economy by a large and wealthy family. There also were, under medieval Islam, associations of artisans, but notwithstanding their strong Persian and Byzantine antecedents, they possessed few of the extreme price-fixing powers of the medieval European guilds. For the medieval Jewish professional associations and their relation to early Muslim guilds, cf. the present author's forthcoming volume on the "History of the Jewish Community."

[111] M.T. Mekirah 18, 4, based on M.B.M. IV, 12.

education that he welcomed competition among elementary teachers even when it interfered with such acquired rights. Nevertheless in another practical case he insisted that a newcomer in a community be excommunicated, unless he desisted from engaging in elementary instruction without first obtaining the permission of the local teacher, who happened to be his superior in learning.[112] But apart from such general moral injunctions, the allowance of certain discretionary powers to Jewish courts and public opinion, and the recognition of customs wherever they existed, Maimuni nowhere consistently denies the legitimacy of competition in the furtherance of one's strictly commercial interests.

Similarly there is full contractual freedom, according to Maimuni, with respect to leases of houses and shops. Legally a lease is but a sale for a specified or unspecified period. That this interpretation favors, from the economic point of view, the landlord rather than the tenant is of less concern to Maimuni than that there be full legal clarity. In fact, in every dubious case he is inclined to side with the landlord, since "the land is in the landlord's possession and we may not withdraw from him any rights without clear evidence."[113] No one is entitled to live in an unoccupied, but habitable dwelling without paying rent. Such failure to pay rent, even if the landlord knows nothing about it, has some of the earmarks of robbery.[114] At the expiration of the contractual

[112] M.T. De'ot 5, 13; Talmud torah 2, 7; Genebah 7, 11; Resp. Nos. 103, 386; S.M. Prohib. 246. Similarly in M.T. Ma'aser 6, 15, he restates the law of M. Pe'ah I, 6 (cf. also C.M. thereon) and j. Pe'ah I, 6, 16c, that a *kohen*, or Levite, who acquires produce from an Israelite after the ingathering must himself pay the tithe and the heave-offering to another priest and Levite. In restating this regulation, intended as a deterrent against sharp practices by unscrupulous Levites, who otherwise would buy up all such untithed crops to the detriment of their slower or more conscientious colleagues, Maimuni denies its application to produce, the harvesting of which is not completed, because at that time the grains or fruits are not yet legally subjected to a tithe. Once more the criterion for the unfairness of the competition is the formalistic date of the obligation to pay tithes, rather than the economic power of the richer Levite and his ability to invest money in the early acquisition of grain.

[113] M.T. Mekirah 13, 14, 17; Sekirut 7, 1-2; C.M. on B.M. VIII, 8, based on B.M. 56b, 102b. The first source is incidental, the second controversial.

[114] M.T. Gezelah va-abedah 3, 9, based upon Alfasi's rather arbitrary distinction with reference to B.Ḳ. 21a. Cf. the difficulties of this interpretation, as pointed out by the commentators, *ad loc.* This is the more remarkable, as Maimonides rejects the opinion of R. Judah in M.B.M. X, 3. Cf. C.M. thereon and Resp. No. 361.

term of the lease, the tenant may be evicted "without an hour's delay." However, in indefinite leases in summer either party must give thirty days' notice in the case of shops, and twelve months' notice in that of metropolitan dwellings, while no eviction can take place in winter between the Feast of Tabernacles and Passover.[115] However, the landlord may raise the rent, just as the tenant may reduce it, without warning, if the market fluctuates. If the landlord suddenly becomes homeless, or requires a new home on account of his son's unexpected marriage, he may evict the tenant without due notice. Maimonides, largely restating here traditional law, advocates only minor modifications in favor of the tenant, as when he insists upon the latter's right to sublease his place to the same number of occupants without the landlord's consent. The owner may still choose, however, the abrupt termination of the lease.[116] In any case, in a crowded civilization, such as is here envisaged, where urban rents — otherwise usually the first target for authoritative regulation — are allowed to fluctuate freely and where the landlord is generally favored, provided his behavior is psychologically correct, regimented economy could hardly be much more than an occasional pious wish.

The upshot of these Maimonidean norms governing the price structure is that (1) every community, if necessary with the coöperation of a great leader, may in its discretion fix the prices of all articles; (2) every community should fix the prices of necessaries, allowing for a total profit of but one-sixth; (3) wherever there are no communally fixed prices, the seller is wholly free to set his own price on land, slaves, free labor, and commercial paper; (4) a merchant may do the same with respect to movables, if he gives com-

[115] M.T. Sekirut 6, 6–8, based upon Alfasi's interpretation of B.M. 101b and j. VIII, 8, 11d. It is notable that Maimuni withdraws here his decision in C.M. on B.M. VIII, 6, which had favored the professional bakers and dyers with an extended notice of three years. Cf. also Don Vidal's comments on M.T. and Bertinoro's exposition of that Mishnah. Some rabbis have also contended that the tenant need not give an equally long notice. Cf. *Haggahot Maimuniot, ad loc.*

[116] M.T. Sekirut 6, 9–10, based upon B.M. 101b. The vital point of fluctuating prices is stated in the Talmud merely as an escape from an embarrassing question of R. Nahman, whose opinion is usually accepted as authoritative. Maimuni is in general satisfied with the formal equality between landlord and tenant, even though the former has precedence in the case of unavoidable conflict. He does not mention even the tenant's safeguard against eviction on account of the landlord's sudden need, if the term of the lease had been stated and had not yet expired. Cf. Don Vidal's comment.

plete and candid information to the other party; (5) however, in case of failure to do so, he runs the risk that the injured party may choose to demand restitution of the balance of precisely one-sixth, or complete annulment of the contract if the difference exceeds one-sixth of the market price; (6) an error in weight or measure merely calls for the restitution of the difference; (7) the merchant is entitled freely to sell below the prevailing market price and employ other "fair" methods of competition.

Under these circumstances, one can see that economic regimentation, as visualized by Maimonides, was left entirely to the discretion of the local authorities. In finding his way through a chaos of contradictory and frequently purely theoretical talmudic utterances, voiced in various periods by various individuals living under changing economic systems in both Palestine and Babylonia, he accepted from his immediate predecessors and further elaborated certain compromise formulas which left the way open to either comprehensive regulation or to great legal latitude. We have practically no evidence of the actual operation of these talmudic requirements in the ancient period. We have still less convincing proof of their practical application in the more capitalistically oriented Jewish economy under medieval Islam. It is notable that the several hundred extant inquiries addressed to Maimuni himself — for many years the recognized leader of Egyptian Jewry — do not refer to a single instance of communal price fixing or to a complaint of "misrepresentation."[117] There must have occurred innumerable cases not only of undue profiteering, but of normal mercantile profits exceeding 16.66 percent, but no one seems ever to have raised a legal issue on this score. Much of what Maimuni restates here as a binding legal norm appears unreal and bears the earmarks of an accepted legal fiction.

Nevertheless, in his reformulation, adaptation, and modification of the traditional law we may perceive what he regarded as desirable and, to a certain extent, as feasible under the conditions known to him. Two elements clearly stand out in his theory: the communal will is supreme; it *may* regulate all prices, and *should* regulate those prices which vitally affect the consumer. On the other hand, there should be as little interference as possible in those big fields of land transfer, the acquisition of slaves, the hiring of labor, and the trade in commercial papers, which are of direct

[117] Cf. Resp., *passim.*

concern only to landowners, merchants, and other entrepreneurs.
Whatever protection is to be extended to slaves and free workers
shall be afforded to them, as we shall see, through a specific set of
labor laws, not through the operation of the law of just price. In
other words, a proper balance between regimentation and freedom—
this is another of those happy mediums which are the core of all
Maimonidean ethics. The basic aim of the Maimonidean, indeed
of the entire rabbinic economic legislation, is to extend a well-
balanced protection to the consumer, the producer, and the middleman, each acting within his legitimate sphere. In Christian scholasticism the doctrine of the just price had to become the corner
stone of all economic thought, because, through the elements of
labor and cost, it offered a much-needed justification for mercantile
profits and indirectly for private ownership as a whole. In Judaism,
as well as in Islam, where no such justification was urgently needed,
this doctrine plays but a relatively minor role in the economic
thinking of the leaders, and is easily overshadowed by the complex
doctrine of "usury" and its extensive ramifications.

5. MONEY

Problems of money, and especially currency, are frequently
discussed in Maimonides' writings. To be sure, he does not seem
to have given much thought to the essence and function of money,
and followed rather closely the talmudic doctrine. But he realized
that since the currency of his day was in many ways different from
that of the talmudic period, it called for considerable modification
of the talmudic law.

He frequently goes to great lengths in explaining the talmudic
references to the Roman and Persian currencies, and reiterates on
several occasions that a *sela'* was the equivalent of four *denars*,
a *denar* amounted to six silver *ma'ahs*, a *ma'ah* to two *pondions*,
a *pondion* to two *issars* (asses), an *issar* to eight *perutahs*! There
also existed at one time a *dareikon*, worth two *sela's*. In another
connection he states that a Palestinian *sela'* was an alloy containing
only one-eighth of a pure silver *sela'* and amounting to one-half
of a silver *denar*, or three and one half copper *denars*, and that consequently a fine of one hundred *sela's* was really the equivalent of
only 12½ original silver *sela's*. Even in this Jerusalem currency,
however, the *ma'ah* was still computed on the old silver basis as

the equivalent of pure silver in the weight of 16 grains of barley. He warmly defends this computation against that of his teachers, whose method, he feels, he can prove to have been erroneous. He informs us elsewhere of the source of his statement that the ancient Palestinian currency was weighed in grains of barley. "It is a tradition with us from my father, blessed be his memory, who received it from his father and grandfather . . . and I do not know any reason for it." He then proceeds to explain that the ancient shekel, consisting of 24 drachmas of 16 grains each, amounted to 384 grains. Since the Egyptian dirhem weighs 61 barley grains, the shekel is equivalent to approximately 6⅓ dirhems. The 50 shekels referred to in the Bible, for example, thus amount to approximately 314¾ Egyptian dirhems. There were also other monetary changes after biblical times. He insists that the biblical half-shekel· was the minimum paid by the Jews at any time, while sometimes the payment rose with the introduction of a more highly valued unit of currency. For instance, when the unit was a *dareikon*, the payment amounted to a *sela'*; when it consisted of a *sela'* it declined to one-half of a *sela'*, the exact equivalent of a biblical half-shekel; but it was never allowed to fall below this amount.[118]

[118] C.M. on B.M. IV, 5; Bekorot VIII, 10, and so forth; M.T. Ḥobel u-mazzik 3, 10, based on Ḳidd. 11a; B.Ḳ. 36b; Sheḳalim 1, 3–6, based on M. Sheḳalim II, 4; j. *ibid.*, 46d; Ṭo'en ve-niṭ'an 3, 1–2, based on Shebuot 39b (cf. also Karo's and De Boton's comments, and C.M. on Shebuot VIII, 1), Bekorot 50ab. In C.M. on Ḳidd. I, 2, he likewise identifies a denar with 24 issars and 192 peruṭahs by stating that a denar equals 96 grains; an issar, 4 grains; a peruṭah, ½ grain. He adds here the significant identification of a drachma, equal to 4 issar (and consequently also to one ma'ah), with the Arabian dirhem. In C.M. on Ma'aser sheni II, 9, he pleads ignorance as to the value of an *asper*, although he believes that it is a *ma'ah* in Greek. In M.T. Ishshut 10, 8, he uses this computation for an estimate of the minimum amounts stated in M. Ket. I, 2 as indispensable in each marriage settlement. Allowing only one-eighth of the silver content for the 200 and 100 denars, respectively, he figures with an equivalent of 25 and 12½ pure silver *zuzim*, containing each 96 grains (=6 ma'ahs of 16 grains each). One can easily perceive the importance of this computation for contemporary practice. Cf. Irving A. Agus, "The Development of the Money Clause in the Ashkenazic Ketubah," *JQR*, n.s., XXX (1939–40), 221–56. Cf. also M.T. 'Erubin 1, 12, and Don Vidal's comments on both passages. In C.M. on Bekorot VIII, 10, he cites in the name of his father a responsum of a Babylonian gaon, from which it appeared that 5 biblical shekels amounted to 33⅓ dirhems, or about 2 dirhems more than according to his own computation. But he explains this discrepancy by the likely difference between the former Babylonian and the contemporary Egyptian dirhem. The existing differences between the coins circulating in Egypt, Babylonia, and Persia are, indeed, emphasized in the

In this interpretation of the rabbinic sources, to which Abraham b. David seriously objects, we find an adumbration of the Maimonidean view on the nature of money. Money, for him, is evidently a medium of exchange, the value of which is determined by the two independent criteria of its metallic content and its legal value. The former is important insofar as the payment of the Temple tax can never amount to less than the content of one-half of the biblical silver shekel; if, however, the nominal value of the existing unit of currency is higher than that of the shekel, payment must be made in one-half of the higher unit. Abraham b. David accepts the former, but denies the latter requirement, explaining the particular talmudic source as reporting merely a historic occurrence without permanent legal obligations. Israelites may, he thinks, under some circumstances be asked to pay more as a voluntary contribution, but they cannot be forced to do so. While one may sympathise with RABD's distrust of the nominal value of coins in a country such as France, where in his day no less than eighty-odd feudal lords had unrestricted minting powers, Maimuni, living under the somewhat better stabilized currency system of the Muslim lands, could express much more truthfully the spirit of the ancient rabbis. His combination of monetary nominalism, or *etatism*, with

interesting responsum in *Teshubot ha-geonim*, ed. by Harkavy, No. 386, discussing the views of Saadia, Sherira, and Hai on the conversion of talmudic coins into contemporary currency. For another, rather obscure, geonic responsum, cf. Ginzberg, *Genizah Studies*, II, 156 ff. Cf. also Lewin, *Otzar*, IX (Part 2), 66 ff.; *Tosafot* on Bek. 49b. s. v. רבי אמי and רבי יוחנן. That he was generally very exact in computing the ancient weights and measures is stressed by Maimuni himself in C.M. on Menahot Introd.: "and I have scrutinized it as carefully as I possibly could," referring also to other passages in C.M. Cf. also Immanuel Löw, *Die Flora der Juden*, IV (Vienna, 1934), 202, 204. For his generally successful attempts at exactness in calculating the data with respect to the related field of historical chronology, cf. Outlook, pp. 93 ff. In Resp. Nos. 213, 217, 277, 285, 287, 289, 293, 379 the coin in circulation is called פרחים. From the last two responsa, particularly, it appears that Maimuni had in mind the silver dirhem rather than the usual gold coin (denar or "florin"). Perhaps the later oriental translators or copyists of these responsa (all except No. 397 come from MS Oxford) confused this coin with one subsequently circulating in Turkey. For modern estimates of the value of the talmudic coins, cf. also Samuel Krauss, *Talmudische Archäologie* (Leipzig, 1911), II, 404 ff., 712 ff. The rabbinic theories on money and banking in general have been treated by Eliezer Lambert in "Les Changeurs et la monnaie en Palestine du Ier au IIIe siècle de l'ère chrétienne," *Revue des études juives*, LI (1906), 217–44; and by Simcha Ejges in *Das Geld im Talmud*, Giessen, 1930.

metallism underlies, indeed, all the numerous discussions in the Talmud. Both elements are also clearly discernible in the main Aristotelian discussion of money in the *Nicomachean Ethics*, with which undoubtedly Maimuni was also familiar:

Money has become by convention a sort of representative of demand; and this is why it has the name "money" [νόμισμα], because it exists not by nature but by law [νόμος] and it is in our power to change it and make it useless . . . . Now the same thing happens to money itself as to goods — it is not always worth the same; yet it tends to be steadier.[119]

The nominalist view becomes particularly significant in connection with the purchase of movable objects. Starting from barter, as the basic form of exchange, Maimuni, following the Talmud, regards the deal as completed, if one of the parties takes possession through lifting or drawing the other party's merchandise. Money, however, being but the standard medium of exchange and the common denominator of value — one may perceive both these elements in the rabbinic doctrine — but not ordinary merchandise dependent on its intrinsic value, cannot serve as such object of barter. The acceptance of the purchase price by the seller constitutes a moral obligation for both parties to consummate the sale, but legally each party may still withdraw. The only sanction upon such unethical withdrawal was the invocation, in open court, of divine wrath upon the malefactor, but the cancellation of the sale remained unaffected. Although this regulation was originally enacted by the rabbis for the protection of the purchaser, so that the seller, having received the money, should continue to take proper care of the sold object until it came into the purchaser's possession, it nevertheless emphasized the nominal value of money.[120]

[119] *Eth. Nic.* V, 5, 1133ab (trans. by Ross); cf. also *Politics* I, 8–11, 1256a–59a, and so forth. For a discussion of the complicated problems of the Aristotelian theory, cf. Giuseppe Majorana, "Le teorie della moneta e del valore in Aristotele," *Giornale degli economisti*, LXVI (1926), 49–61; Gelesnoff, *op. cit.*; and, in general, René Gonnard, *Histoire des doctrines monétaires dans ses rapports avec l'histoire de monnaies*, Vol. I, Paris, 1935. As usual the oriental theories, ancient as well as medieval, are passed over here in silence. For the Talmud, cf. Ejges, *op. cit.* Bryson and the Arab theorists following him assigned the entire first section of their treatises to a discussion of money and its functions.

[120] C.M. on B.M. IV, 2; M.T. Mekirah 5, 6; 6, 1; 7, 1–2, based on the extensive discussions in B.M. 44–49. There seems to be a slight difference between C.M. and M.T. with regard to the invocation of the divine wrath. C.M., more in accordance with the talmudic text, does not specify where the curse should

What is "money" in this legal sense? In the first place, it consists of silver coins, in the second place of gold and copper coins which are made legal tender by the inscription and enjoy general acceptibility in a certain region or period. "Bad moneys which the state or the city declares unfit, or coins which do not circulate in a particular city and are not being traded in until exchanged into other coins, are like fruits in every respect." Similarly gold and silver bars are not money, but merchandise. Maimonides gives a similar definition of money in connection with the "redemption" of the second tithe, which the owner was allowed to convert into "money" before proceeding to Jerusalem. Besides stressing the importance of the silver coin, he reiterates the significant statement of the Tosefta (in the interpretation of the Palestinian Talmud) that coins of ancient kings, if still readily acceptable, could be used for such redemption.[121]

While with respect to other objects all valid coins in circulation are "money," it is the silver coin which serves as the main "unit of accounts." In comparison with it even gold and copper coins sink to the position of merchandise, rather than medium of

---

be uttered, and leaves it to the injured party to pronounce it anywhere in the presence of the offender. M.T. demands its proclamation by the court in open session. The latter naturally offers better protection to the party withdrawing on account of newly arisen unforeseen circumstances. Cf. also C.M. on Ḳidd. I, 7; *Sha'arei ṣedeḳ*, IV, 2, 26–27, fol. 40b–41a; Lewin, *Otzar*, IX, 75 ff.; H.M. 204, 1, and the commentaries thereon. For a somewhat related opinion of the Roman jurist, Javolenus, that the value of merchandise may be estimated in money, but the value of money cannot be estimated in merchandise, cf. *Corpus juris civilis* L. 42, D. 46, 1. That this is at variance with the views expressed by modern economists, such as Adam Smith, at least with respect to the value of precious metals, has rightly been pointed out by Gonnard, *op. cit.*, p. 53, n. 6. For some Arab views, cf. Plessner, *op. cit.*, pp. 63, 152 f., 277 f.

[121] C.M. on B.M. IV, 1; Ma'aser sheni I, 2; M.T. Mekirah 6, 2, 6; Ma'aser sheni 4, 9–10, based upon B.M., *ibid.*, and Alfasi's interpretation thereof; j. Ma'aser sheni I, 2, 52cd; Tosefta, *ibid.*, I, 6, 86. Maimuni's interpretation of אסימון evidently agrees with that of Rashi and not that of Jacob Tam. It is etymologically more correct. Cf. also Ginzberg, *Geonica*, II, 2 ff. In M.T. Ma'aser sheni 4, 14, Maimuni adds that the redemption must be performed in local currency, regardless of its acceptibility in the place where the money happens to be. For instance, a man redeeming the second tithe may use Tiberian currency which he possesses in Babylonia, but not Babylonian currency at his disposal in Tiberias. This statement is at variance not only with B.Ḳ. 97b, but apparently also with j. Ma'aser sheni I, 2, 52d. It called forth a sharp objection from RABD and caused difficulties to the commentators. Cf. Karo's comments, *ad loc.*, and Moses Margolis's lengthy discussion on j., *loc. cit.*

exchange. That is why an exchange of coins of different metallic content is completed when the gold or copper coin is given and accepted, although the equivalent amount in silver has not yet been returned. But if silver coins alone are transferred, both the seller and the purchaser may legally withdraw, because the "merchandise," namely the gold or copper coins, has not yet been appropriated. These assumptions, derived from the Talmud, were fairly justified in the Roman Empire. Although Roman currency was essentially bimetallic, the gold coin apparently was subjected to more frequent variations in weight than was the silver coin. In the predominantly agricultural Jewish settlements of Palestine, moreover, the relatively precious gold coins had a much smaller circulation than the silver coins. After a period of hesitation, the last Tannaim decided for the preferential treatment of silver. Once proclaimed as a general principle in the Mishnah and accepted by the Talmud and the early geonim, it had to be maintained even in the face of the transition from a preponderant silver standard, or the bimetallism of the early caliphate, to the predominant gold standard of the tenth and eleventh centuries. Maimonides seems at first timidly to suggest that in his day gold coins were fully equal to those of silver. But in his *Code* he simply restates the explicit talmudic law. He fails, however, to draw from the talmudic discussion the evidently justified conclusion that copper coins, although inferior to silver, should likewise be considered preferred currency with respect to gold. This conclusion, drawn by other rabbis such as Ibn Adret, undoubtedly reflected experience in ancient Palestine, where copper coins were widely circulated. It would have sounded starkly unreal under the advanced money economy of the Muslim lands.[122]

[122] M.T. Mekirah 6, 3–5, based on B.M., *ibid.* C.M. on B.M. IV, 1 somewhat equivocally states that "there is no difference" between gold and silver coins, which may be but a pointed repudiation of Hai Gaon's statement that gold coins are always in the class of merchandise. Cf. *Teshubot ha-geonim,* ed. by Harkavy, No. 78; Ginzberg, *Geonica* II, 229, 231. In view of the prevalent gold standard in Hai's day (cf. the sources quoted by Fischel, *op. cit.,* pp. 3 f.), one may perhaps see in this decision of Hai without talmudic backing only the gaon's attempt to free the commercial transactions from the shackles of the Talmud's "protective" laws for the purchaser. For the relation between gold and copper, cf. H.M. 204, 6, and the commentaries thereon. The Maimonidean view of the redemption of the second tithe in gold, which he permits, because it facilitates transportation to Jerusalem, and in copper which he tries to restrict to the minimum necessary for spending, are in consonance with this general sequence of (1) silver,

The same prevalence of the silver standard may be seen also in the rules governing "misrepresentation," as applied to money exchange. A simple mistake in counting, as in other transactions, does not nullify the exchange, but merely imposes restitution of the difference, even after the lapse of many years.[123] However, if the difference arose out of the rate of exchange agreed upon by the parties, it is considered a normal commercial transaction and subjected to the limitations of the just price. Maimuni gives the following example: "If at the time a gold denar was worth 24 silver denars and it was exchanged for either 20 or 28 silver denars, the difference is to be returned; if the difference was larger, the exchange is null and void; if smaller, we assume [the injured party's] acquiescence." Like Alfasi and others, he thus accepts R. Simon's opinion that there is no difference between coins and other movable objects with respect to the principle underlying the laws of misrepresentation, that an overcharge of less than one-sixth is not resented. R. Meir and R. Judah undoubtedly were more realistic when they tried to reduce the possible overcharge to one-twenty-fourth and one-twelfth, respectively. They clearly realized that people, relying upon the nominal value of coins, expect fairly exact rates of exchange. Indeed, Naḥmanides and Asher b. Yehiel accept at least the reduction to one-twelfth. The general principle applies, according to Maimuni, also to damaged coins, the metallic weight of which is below normal by one-sixth or more, but which had not been withdrawn from circulation. Of course, if such coins are exchanged expressly on the basis of their weight, the slightest mistake calls for restitution. But so long as their nominal value alone is considered, a deficiency up to 16.66 percent may be disregarded. To diminish the injurious effects upon the recipient, Maimonides somewhat extends the talmudic time limit for claims. While generally repeating the talmudic statement that claims

---

(2) gold, (3) copper. Cf. M.T. Ma'aser sheni 5, 13–14; C.M. on Ma'aser sheni II, 7–8. In contrast, for instance, to the explanation of Samson of Sens, he selects here from the discussion in B.M. 44b–45a only that which involves no denial of the character of currency to either gold or silver, and translates הפורט סלע by the exchange of silver into copper rather than the opposite, as was done by Rashi and others. Cf. also Moses Margolis's comments on j. Ma'aser sheni II, 7–8, 53c.

[123] M.T. Mekirah 8, 6; 15, 1–2, following Ibn Megas' interpretation. Cf. also RABD's objection and the comments of Ibn Gaon, Don Vidal, and Rosanes, *ad loc.*

expire in villages on Fridays, when everybody is supposed to have a chance to exchange his money, and in cities as soon as one reasonably may consult a banker, "because the banker alone knows the coin, its deficiency and its monetary value," he qualifies it in the case of books, jewelry, or coins. If no expert is available and the recipient must either bring the book or the piece of jewelry to another district or await the arrival of an expert in his own locality, he may raise the issue at such later date. Similarly, if a coin cannot be put back into circulation, the claim for restitution remains valid at any time; if it can be disposed of with some difficulty, the matter depends on the nature of the transaction and the question of whether or not it was expected to be scrupulously exact.[124]

[124] C.M. on B.M. IV, 6; M.T. Mekirah 12, 8–12. Cf. Don Vidal's comments. For divergent opinions of other rabbis, cf. H.M. 227, 16–17, and the commentaries thereon. To illustrate the operation of the law of one-sixth, Maimuni places here the value of a gold denar as equal to 24 silver denars, although elsewhere he usually assumes a relation of 1:25. Cf., for instance, M.T. Mekirah 6, 4. But this is merely another illustration for the variations in the value of other coins with respect to the basic silver currency. Cf. also the next note. The regulation concerning books and jewelry, in 12, 11, is apparently influenced by Muslim economic thought. That it is not a mere denial of R. Judah's statement in M.B.M. IV, 9, as explained by some commentators, ad loc., and on H.M. 227, 15, may be deduced from Maimuni's previous rejection of R. Judah's view as a matter of course in 12, 8; his failure to reject also R. Judah b. Batira's opinion concerning the exemption of war implements in B.M. 58b, and his emphasis here upon the rarity and the need of expert knowledge in these articles, which is nowhere discussed in the Talmud. On the contrary, he seems to agree with R. Judah that scrolls of law and jewels attract certain individuals more than others, but denies their having, for this reason, no market value at all. One is reminded of Bryson's advice to investors not to put their money into merchandise for which there is no widespread demand, "such as precious stones which are needed only by kings and scholarly books which are only sought for by scholars." Plessner, op. cit., p. 158. Curiously the Hebrew translator (p. 159) adds another example; "such as weapons which are needed only for a limited time." It is not likely that he had found it in any Arabic version (although it might have been part of the Greek original), since in the Arab world implements of war evidently were easily marketable. Perhaps it is not altogether venturesome to assume that the translator was influenced here by the above-mentioned juxtaposition of B.M. 58b. Bryson's advice, in any case, was reëchoed by many Arab writers, among them Abul Fadl. Cf. Mahmassani, op. cit., p. 87. In M.T. Ṭo'en ve-niṭ'an 8, 10; Resp. 336, Maimuni places great emphasis upon the legal presumption that books as a rule are neither lent nor leased to anybody else. This interpretation, shared by Rashi on Shebuot 46b s. v. מיתמי, is contradicted by Hananel and the Tosafists on Shebuot, ibid., s. v. וספרא, B.B. 52b s. v., דברים, and so forth. Judah ibn Tibbon, in his "Ethical Will" (Abrahams, op. cit., I, 82),

Once more we find here the prevailing nominalist approach, but with due consideration of the metallistic element. It is evident that Maimonides does have in mind a bimetallic currency, where the relationship between gold and silver is fixed by law and where a difference in exchange would naturally be more in the nature of an error in counting. The price of gold coins is here allowed to fluctuate around some sort of market price, with a slight difference between the price paid and received by the banker, which constitutes his legitimate profit. It is not included in the one-sixth differential, which might vitiate the transaction. As in other merchandise, consequently, the market price, rather than the merchant's cost, is taken as a basis.[125]

Modified monetary nominalism comes to the fore also in the following Maimonidean regulations: One may redeem the second tithe in coins which are known to be deficient, as long as the deficiency does not exceed one-sixth of the metallic content and the coins are circulating, certain difficulties in their transferability notwithstanding. The usual requirement of a purifying oath by the defendant who admits part of the depositor's claim (*modeh be-miḳṣat*) applies only to admissions referring to the same type of currency. If the plaintiff, however, claims that he had deposited a gold denar and the defendant confesses only to the deposit of a silver denar, or if the claim is for ten Egyptian denars and the

---

merely advised his son to register every book lent out of the house and properly to enter its return. For the trade in both books and jewelry in Maimuni's time, cf. also the two interesting Resp. Nos. 287, 293.

[125] Cf. M.T. Ma'aser sheni 4, 18: ונותן המעות כמות שהשולחני פורט לא כמות שהוא מצרף, based on M. Ma'aser sheni IV, 2 (cf. also j., *ibid.*, 54d). In C.M. thereon we find, indeed, the illustration of 24 denars bid and 25 denars as the asking price. One may perhaps see in the figure, 24, in M.T. (cf. n. 124) not only a convenient amount divisible by six, but also the influence of the prevalent custom among bankers to charge one silver dirhem for the exchange of one gold denar. Cf. Fischel, *op. cit.*, pp. 21, n. 2; 25, n. 2. It must be borne in mind, however, that the dirhem amounted to more than 4 percent of the gold denar. Cf. also *Tosafot* on Bek. 50 s. v. דמזדבנא end, where the differentia of one silver denar is suggested as the fee of the mint master to coin 24 silver denars out of 25 denars worth of bullion. If there really was such a disparity between a 24-silver-denar bid and a 25-denar asking price, the result, according to the above example, would be that the banker could claim nullification of the transaction if he paid more than 28 denars, i.e., more than 3 denars above his purchasing price. His customer's claim would be valid only if the latter received less than 20 denars, which is more than 5 below the banker's purchasing price. Cf. also *Teshubot ha-geonim*, ed. by Harkavy, No. 73; and n. 101 above.

admission refers to ten Tyrian denars, the parties speak of different objects altogether, and no biblical oath is required. A robber, who appropriates a good coin which subsequently disintegrates or is declared unfit by the government, must return to the owner its full value at the time of the robbery. But if the coin, although declared unfit in one city, still circulates in another city, he may return it to the owner, regardless of the inconvenience accruing therefrom to the latter.[126] In all these respects the decisive feature is the character of the coin as a circulating medium, whether or not it serves as universal legal tender and hence possesses easy transferability. The metallic content and the intrinsic value of the respective metals are of but secondary importance.

Special modifications of the nominalist doctrine became necessary in connection with loan contracts, on account of the lingering suspicion that the lender might derive therefrom some profit, which would be tantamount to usury. Maimuni joins the geonim in declaring that if the loan is stipulated in a currency subsequently declared unfit, the lender is obliged to accept payment in that currency only if it still possesses ready acceptability in a region within his reach. Otherwise he may insist upon payment in the new currency.[127] On the other hand, if the metallic weight of the

---

[126] M.T. Ma'aser sheni 4, 19, based on B.M. 52ab; To'en ve-niṭ'an 3, 8, based on Sheb. 39b–40a; Gezelah va-abedah 3, 4, based on B.Ḳ. 96b–97a. Cf. also C.M. on Ḳidd. I, 5; Ket. XIII, 4; B.Ḳ. IX, 2; and the next note.

[127] M.T. Malveh ve-loveh 4, 12, based on B.Ḳ. 97ab. Although Maimuni repeats here the equivocal talmudic phrase המלוה את חברו על המטבע, which has given rise to endless discussions, by specifying later נותן לו ממטבע שהלוה, he clearly refers to a loan of money. Rashi, ibid., explains it as referring exclusively to an obligation arising from an ordinary commercial transaction with the price computed in money. There is no evidence that Maimuni would wish to exclude such a transaction from this regulation. More likely, like the Tosafists, ibid., he had in mind both types of credit; so, indeed, Don Vidal, ad loc, understands the passage. The difficulty raised by the Tosafists as to why a robber and not a debtor should be entitled to return the original coins is obviated by Maimuni's afore-mentioned decision that the robber's privilege applies only to money still circulating in another locality. This decision seems to have been overlooked by the author of Haggahot Maimuniot, ad loc. The additional qualification here, ויש לו דרך לאותה מדינה, is not of far-reaching significance. In this generic term Maimuni seems to include the difficulties placed by different states in the way of transfer of depreciated coins from one country to another. This problem undoubtedly loomed large under the frequent commercial conflicts between ancient Rome and Persia and then again in medieval Europe. That is why the Talmud and, still more, Jacob b. Asher and his satellites in H.M. 74, 7 attach greater significance to this issue than do Maimuni and the other rabbis under

coins borrowed is specified and subsequently the government increases their metallic content, the return of the same number of coins would yield a "usurious" profit to the lender. That is why a metallic increase of one-fifth or more unconditionally calls for a corresponding reduction in the amount due. A lesser increase may be disregarded, however, if there is no proportionate decrease in the cost of commodities. In other words, a fall in the prices of commodities resulting from metallistic appreciation, as well as any appreciation of 20 percent or more, even if commodity prices remain stationary, calls for a readjustment of the loan to its original intrinsic value. This provision, adds Maimuni, operates also in favor of the lender, if the currency is debased with respect to its metallic content in the period between the contracting of the loan and its repayment.[128] The significance of this Maimonidean

---

Islam. For the views of the geonim, cf. the statement of Semah Gaon, quoted by Eliezer b. Joel ha-levi and published by V. Aptowitzer in his "Fragments from Geonic Literature" (Hebrew) in the *Samuel Krauss Jubilee Volume* (Jerusalem, 1937), p. 103, as well as the geonic responsa cited there. Cf. also the sources cited by Freimann in his ed. of Resp. p. 218, line 25.

[128] M.T. Malveh-ve-loveh 4, 11, based on B.Ḳ. 97b–98a. Cf. also Ibn Megas, *Responsa*, No. 195. By adding here, and not in 4, 12, the significant qualification ופירש משקלו (apparently referring to both the loan and the marriage contracts), Maimuni considerably reduces the range of that talmudic discussion. It means that failure to specify the weight in the original contract makes the subsequent increase or decrease of the metallic content wholly irrelevant, since the nominal value of the currency is the same. Evidently this qualification likewise favors the lender, who is usually in a position to lay down the terms of the loan so as to include such specifications, if he fears devaluation of the currency, or to omit it, if an appreciation should be in sight. Cf. Karo in Y.D. 165, repeating verbatim Maimuni's statement, but eliminating this qualification, which he may have interpreted as referring only to the *ketubah*. Maimuni evidently accepts the statement of R. Semah Gaon that a fall in the prices of commodities, without change in the metallic content, does not diminish the nominal indebtedness, even though the creditor is thereby allowed to receive more than he had lent in terms of goods. Such "real" increment could not be regarded as usury, since the creditor might legitimately contend that the money would also have appreciated in value, if it had remained in his possession. Cf. Aptowitzer, *loc. cit.* This is, indeed, the burden of R. Ashi's distinction in B.Ḳ. 97b–98a. Cf. also *Teshubot ha-geonim*, ed. by Harkavy, Nos. 424, 518. We have a further illustration in the characteristic Resp. of Maimonides (No. 230) concerning a loan in a currency withdrawn from circulation. In the locality of the inquirers, the main circulating medium consisted originally in a standardized paper bag of a certain foodstuff; it was then successively replaced by two different units of silver dirhems. Nevertheless, after the introduction of the last dirhem the two older units did not disappear, but on the contrary appreciated in value. Maimuni,

extension may easily be gauged when one realizes that, throughout history, the metallic depreciation of currencies was so much more frequent and gradual than their appreciation or revaluation.

6. BANKING

These discussions on the essence of money and its legal status as currency had considerable practical significance under later medieval Islam, where the circulation of a variety of coins was stimulated by the political dissolution of the Caliphate into many mutually hostile states and by the frequent inner upheavals. This monetary instability must have deeply affected the Jews, an increasing number of whom derived their livelihood from one or another form of the money trade. While far less one-sided in its economic exploits than the Jewries of contemporary Europe north of the Alps, with their growing concentration on money lending, the Jewish population of western Asia and northern Africa, too, embraced a large number of bankers and their business associates. Indeed, after the tenth century the wealthiest and most influential leaders of the Jewish communities, next to the exilarchs and the rabbinic judges, belonged to this class of bankers and tax farmers, upon whose connections with the caliphs, sultans, and provincial governors frequently depended the welfare of their coreligionists.

The direct and indirect references scattered in Maimonides' writings to various phases of the money trade may conveniently be arranged under the following main divisions: (1) production of money, or minting; (2) money exchange; (3) money transfer or remittance; (4) deposits; (5) money lending. We shall see that the latter overshadowed in importance in the Maimonidean treatment

citing Ket. 110b, decided that the borrower should "pay back in the same currency, if it still exists, or in its equivalent in the new currency, if the former no longer exists." It goes without saying that the same principle operates to the creditor's disadvantage in the case of currency inflation and rise of commodity prices. The geonim and Maimuni failed to discuss this aspect, chiefly because it had no bearing upon any likely usurious gain for the lender. It may be of incidental interest to note that Maimuni, in repeating in M.T. Roṣeaḥ u-shemirat nafesh 12, 4 the prohibition of j. Terumot VIII, 4, 45d to place coins in one's mouth, amplifies the hygienic motivations as to the ensuing dangers to health. But he also reiterates verbatim the talmudic distinction between perspiration of the face, which is innocuous, and that of the rest of the human body which is "mortal poison."

all the other activities, not only in economic reality, but also largely on account of the problems of "usury." However, precisely because of this prohibition, the extension of credit as such was, at least in theory, not considered to be the essential business of the banker. In the Maimonidean terminology, the *shulḥani* is still essentially the *trapezites* of antiquity, whose main dealings consisted in exchanging over the counter one coin for another.[129]

Jewish contractors for by-products of coins produced by the official mint masters are often mentioned in the Maimonidean responsa and in other contemporary sources. Maimonides nowhere discusses the import of this activity upon the value of the currency. Evidently he regards such pursuits as purely commercial and sees nothing objectionable in the private sale of gold or silver "dust" remaining after the coinage, apparently transacted with the tacit approval of state or city. Such dust was, indeed, utilized for commercial rather than minting purposes. The regulation of the value of currency and the modalities under which it was to be put into circulation, however, undoubtedly were governmental prerogatives, although in some instances the actual production may have been delegated to private citizens. To what extent Jews were employed in such official "mints" is of less concern to our subject of inquiry. As a matter of fact, the disputes mentioned in the Maimonidean *Responsa* arose from certain legal aspects of partnership, rather than from those involving minting by-products as such.[130]

Maimonides' views on the exchange of money have in part already been treated. We have seen that, like his talmudic predecessors, he believed the banker to be an expert in coins circulating not only in his own locality, but in many other states and cities, and to possess more than ordinary knowledge of their metallic content. His services are remunerated by a fee, usually included

---

[129] Cf., for instance, the definition given in C.M. on B.M. II, 5.

[130] Resp. Nos. 269, 274, 277. Cf. also S. Assaf's note, *ibid.*, p. 377. The fact of governmental approval becomes evident when one considers the refusal of the defendant in No. 277 to divulge the name of the person to whom he was supposed to have given the amount due to the plaintiff, "because the matter depends on the state, and by making it public, we shall sustain a loss." The fact that two of these three cases had some connection with partnerships, if more than accidental, may perhaps sustain the conclusion that this was a large-scale business which required greater resources than could be marshaled by a single entrepreneur. For geonic sources referring to Jews trading in bullion, supplying it to mints, and grinding the gold and silver dust, cf. Mann in JQR, n.s. X, 331. Cf. also Ginzberg, *Genizah Studies*, II, 49 ff.

in the margin between his bidding and his asking price. Maimonides evidently permits such margin to be freely established by the usual fluctuations in supply and demand; he does not include money among the necessaries of life, the price of which ought to be fixed by the community. An error in counting calls for restoration of the difference, but a conscious overcharge in the rate of exchange is subject to restitution or nullification of the transaction only if it equals or exceeds 16.66 percent of the market price. Even then, it appears, the money changer still has an opportunity to forestall either effect by "honestly" informing the recipient of the discrepancy between his asking price and the prevalent market price. Since gold and copper coins, in relation to silver, were legally treated as merchandise, the banker obviously enjoyed a wide range of profit, even with respect to these essential parts of the currency circulating in his own country. We can see that, except for cases of fraud, his exchange business was subject to but few legal restrictions.

Connected with money changing was also the expert appraisal of coins. On a banker's expert judgment, as we have seen, depended the claim of an injured party after the exchange of coins. Money changers must have been consulted by laymen, particularly whenever new or unusual coins appeared in the market. It is only natural that bankers should charge a fee for such appraisals, in turn assuming responsibility for probable mistakes, and also that they should try to reserve this service to members of their profession. The rabbis lent them legal support in both endeavors, but also safeguarded the rights of their clients. Maimonides, amplifying the talmudic regulations in many significant points, states that an expert banker is responsible for damages arising from a mistaken appraisal only if he is paid for that service; a nonexpert is responsible even for freely offered advice provided that its recipient directly or indirectly intimates that he is relying upon it. The burden of proof of his competence rests with the banker. We are nowhere told how large the fee was, but it may be assumed that it rose in proportion with the banker's risks, arising from a larger variety of coins in circulation or the prevalence of coin clipping, and sank with the increase in the number of competing experts.[131]

[131] M.T. Sekirut 10, 5 largely based upon Alfasi's interpretation of B.Ḳ. 99b–100a. Other medieval rabbis wished to strengthen the banker's monopoly either by extending the responsibility of the nonexpert to cases where the inquirer failed to indicate his reliance upon the judgment of the appraiser, as suggested by the Tosafists (*ibid.*, s. v. אחוי; cf. also SeMaG, Comm. 89), or by wholly

Money transfer over long distances became an urgent necessity through the vast expansion of Islam. A legal instrument was soon developed in the so-called *suftaja*, a sort of letter of credit, or draft, which enabled bankers to remit considerable funds without the inconvenience and danger of shipping coins. Notwithstanding certain legal scruples arising from the banker's fee for what might be termed a credit transaction, both Muslims and Jews made extensive use of this significant invention.[132] Maimonides did not directly discuss this new type of business, probably because, in his general conservatism, he shared the talmudic distrust of all business dealings of an impersonal nature. Nevertheless, he admitted that if A sends an autograph letter to B, asking him to pay an amount due him to C, B may do so and acquit himself of his obligation. Although B is also free to refuse payment,[133] Maimonides' comprehensive

---

relieving even the paid expert from responsibility for errors, as taught by Ibn Adret, Luria, and so forth. Cf. Don Vidal's comment, *ad loc.*; H.M. 306, 6, and the commentaries thereon. For a different type of controversy between the money changer and his client, arising from contradictory claims as to whether the other party had fulfilled his part of the contract, cf. C.M. on Shebu'ot VII, 6; M.T. Mekirah 20, 9. Maimuni reduced the tannaitic regulation to the unlikely case that the money in dispute is placed on public ground, i.e., is in neither party's possession. He was forced to do so, because of his general theory that all the oaths mentioned in the Mishnah are of biblical origin. Cf. C.M. on Shebu'ot VI, 1; M.T. Shebu'ot 11, 7, and so forth, and the commentaries on M.T. Mekirah, *ad loc.* Very likely, however, Maimuni accepted Hananel's suggestion that the regulation of the Mishnah should also be applied to cases in which both the banker and the client held the coin in their hands. For an interesting record of a partnership in profits from money exchange, cf. *Teshubot ha-geonim*, ed. by Harkavy, No. 592 (Hebrew trans. and notes, pp. 340 f.).

[132] Cf. the numerous Muslim and Jewish sources quoted by Fischel, *op. cit.*, pp. 17 ff. While the author is right in stating that the *suftaja*, as used by Jews, is mentioned only in some Arabic responsa of the rabbis, one must bear in mind that the Jews could obtain somewhat similar effects by expanding their long-established legal instrument, the *harsha'ah*.

[133] M.T. Sheluḥin ve-shutefin 1, 8, largely following Alfasi's interpretation of B.Ḳ. 104b. According to one version, Alfasi went even further and accepted the "contemporary practice among merchants" to the extent of regarding such a note as legal, even if the recipient (or messenger) was not named therein. This would make it altogether a negotiable instrument issued to the bearer. Maimonides insists upon the recipient's name being included in this type of draft. Cf. Don Vidal's comments; *Tosafot* on B.Ḳ. 104b s. v. ורבי; and numerous sources quoted in the commentaries on H.M. 121, 4–5. It is the difficulty of forcing B to pay, and the risk for the latter involved in the intervening decease of A, that made the rabbis turn to the power of attorney for remedy. Cf. H.M. 122, 1.

treatment of the talmudic laws concerning the power of attorney left enough loopholes for a fairly effective utilization of the new remittance.

On the whole, the rabbis disliked the power of attorney as a part of legal proceedings before the courts of justice. In order to prevent excessive legal technicalities and constant delay, Maimonides urges that the parties should always appear in court and personally state the case, without the intervention of tricky or influential intermediaries. Only in the case of a party's excusable inability to attend does he allow the use of substitutes. He is especially outspoken in denouncing this system in his *Responsa*. Like the Talmud, he also construes such power of attorney to be an actual transfer of rights, in full or in part, to the representative, who is then supposed to act in his own name. This theory operates against the defendant, who cannot appoint a substitute, since he has no rights to be transferred; neither can the plaintiff do so after his claim has been denied by the defendant. This legal theory is immediately abandoned by Maimonides, however, in the case of a representative exceeding his instructions or otherwise failing to take the proper steps to safeguard the plaintiff's interests. Even if the latter writes into the authorization in express terms, as demanded by Maimuni, "institute proceedings, obtain a judgment and collect it for your own benefit," all proceeds go to the real plaintiff, just as all expenses are charged to his account.[134]

With all these limitations, the power of attorney could be utilised to transfer to a third person funds available in a distant locality. By inserting a specific clause one could also authorize the recipient to transfer this power to another person and the latter to still other persons, and thus make it, to all intents and purposes, a negotiable instrument. The difficulty of assigning money, which,

---

This is also the meaning of the conservative distinction in M.T., *ibid.*, 3, 5. For drafts on a local banker to pay certain regular wages to the client's employees, see below.

[134] M.T. Sheluḥin ve-shutefin 3, 1–2, 5; Resp. Nos. 300 and 301, based on B.Ḳ. 70a; Shebu'ot 33b, and so forth. The contemporary formulas of the writ of authorization quoted in M.T. are very likely similar to those contained in the *Sefer ha-harsha'ot* of Samuel b. Hofni, cited by the inquirers of No. 300. Cf. also *Teshubot ha-geonim*, ed. by Harkavy, No. 467 (Hebrew trans., p. 327). For the general problem of substitution in court, cf. the notes to Resp. *loc. cit.*, and S. Assaf, *Batei ha-din ve-sidreihem* (*The Courts and Their Organization after the Conclusion of the Talmud*) (Jerusalem, 1924), pp. 95 f.

as we have seen, was not considered a proper object of barter, was evaded by the simultaneous grant of a parcel of land. It was in connection with such assignments that the geonim had devised the remarkable legal fiction of every Jew being able to use for such purposes his ideal claim upon four ells of land in Palestine. Maimuni, to be sure, frowns upon this legal fiction. But even he admits that it may be utilized as a psychological threat to bring a reluctant debtor or depository before the court. Neither does he contradict the geonic departure from talmudic law, which permitted the assignment of loans, confirmed by deed or witnesses, even after their denial by the defendant.[135]

[135] M.T., *ibid.*, 3, 7–8. This section has given rise to many opposing interpretations. For our purposes the most crucial question is whether Maimonides accepted the innovation of the geonim concerning the assignment of loans. It is evidently to be answered in the affirmative. Cf. Karo's, De Boton's, and Rosanes's comments. The latter correctly cites in confirmation M.T. Malveh ve-loveh 20, 7. Maimonides still tries to salvage from the sweeping geonic reversal of talmudic law at least the invalidation, by speedy denial, of the assignment of debts, orally contracted, or of deposits. He disregards thereby the well-established custom, reported by Hananel, to rule out the debtor's denial from the consideration of the validity of a *harsha'ah*. While this eleventh-century Kairowan scholar is still puzzled about the reason of such deviation from a clear talmudic statement, Jacob Tam supplies one through a long casuistic discussion. Cf. *Tosafot* on B.Ḳ. 70a s. v. אמטלטלין and on Shebu'ot 336 s. v. היכא. Even Maimonides' sweeping condemnation of this practice on moral grounds, which, although quoted from Shebu'ot 31a, evoked a sharp attack by RABD (cf. also M.T. De'ot 5, 13), was toned down in Resp. Nos. 300–1, where he appears to be in agreement with his opponent (and probably also with *Tosafot* on Sheb., *ibid.*, s. v. זו). His qualification that such an assignment is justifiable in the case of debtors or depositories living in other cities was all that was needed to make the remittance of funds truly operative. All these Maimonidean scruples were increasingly swept away by the commercial needs of the people, and four centuries later both Karo and Isserles mentioned assignments of all claims, whatever their provenience and whether or not denied, as a prevalent usage in their time. Cf. H.M. 123, 1. Cf. also Ginzberg, *Geonica*, II, 290 f.; Schwarz in MbM, I, 382 ff.; B. Z. Halper's notes to his ed. of Resp. No. 300, in JQR, n.s. VI (1915–16), 225 ff.; H. Tykocinski, *op. cit.*, pp. 117 ff. One must also bear in mind that there was another, somewhat more clumsy method of assigning money, which consisted in endorsing, in the presence of two witnesses, the writ of indebtedness itself in favor of a third person and handing it to the beneficiary. Even the *suftaja* in the technical sense apparently was never forbidden. The geonic responsum which deals with it, although unable to offer any support from Jewish law, approves it, because it had become a widespread mercantile usage. Cf. *Teshubot ha-geonim*, ed. by Harkavy, No. 423 (Hebrew trans., p. 316). One wonders whether this timid recognition did not pave the way for those sweeping modifications in the talmudic laws governing "authorization," which, apparently

These discussions reveal merely a certain precariousness in the use of the *suftaja*, if the person or firm on which it was drawn wanted to raise legal difficulties; they did not prevent the smooth operation in the majority of dealings between more or less honest bankers in different cities. Maimonides may indulge in moral condemnation of those appearing with a power of attorney without valid excuse, but he cannot definitely outlaw it. Neither can he condemn it on the ground of supposedly usurious gains, since it is the purchaser of the letter of credit who may be regarded as the lender and it is he who pays the fee. The saving to him of transportation charges and insurance against the risk of shipping coins can hardly be considered a usurious gain, in terms of Jewish law. Even the Muslim jurists, who did object to it on these grounds, were unable to prevent the triumphant march of this new commercial paper through all the lands of Islam. From there, evidently not without the assistance of Jewish intermediaries, it penetrated Italy and the other European countries, contributing a significant element to the rise of modern capitalism.

The deposit of funds with a banker not only for safe-keeping, but also with a view to their gainful employment was likewise widespread under medieval Islam. Neither the mosque nor the synagogue seem ever to have held a position similar to that of the ancient Babylonian or Greek temples, or the medieval churches, which served as the main depositories under the sanction of religion. It is evident that the ability to employ the deposited funds in their own business made it unnecessary for the bankers to charge a fee to the depositors. But there is no evidence that they paid any interest on such deposits. If they did, both Muslim and Jewish jurists would have qualified such interest as violating the prohibition of usury, unless paid to a member of another creed.[136] In Maimonides' *Code* we find the simple regulation:

---

unknown to the early geonim, are here willy-nilly accepted by Maimuni. Cf. *ibid.*, Nos. 181, 200, 279 (the authorization may also be given to a Gentile), 467; Schwarz, *op. cit.*, p. 384, n. 1. Unfortunately the paucity of the available source material offers but little substantiation either for or against such a hypothesis. For the Muslim *suftaja* and the related *hawala*, as well as for the juristic objections to it, cf. Bergsträsser-Schacht, *op. cit.*, pp. 66 f. Cf. also Björkmann, *op. cit.*, pp. 89 f.

[136] Fischel (*op. cit.*, pp. 14 ff.) has shown that the important position of the banker in the field of deposits under Islam was largely due to the possibility thus given of withdrawing possessions from the immediate reach of rapacious govern-

A shopkeeper or money changer who receives a deposit in cash must not make use of it, if it is handed to him bound up and sealed or tied in an unusual knot . . . . But if there is neither a seal nor an unusual knot he may employ these funds.

In other words, unless the depositor signifies his contrary will, deposits of this kind, which the Romans styled *deposita irregularia*, are freely disposable in the hands of business men, whereas other citizens have to obtain specific authorization by the depositors. Professional depositories, on the other hand, are immediately responsible for all preventable theft and loss, but after employing the funds entrusted to them they become simple debtors, responsible even for enforced losses. In another connection Maimonides prohibits deposits in Gentile firms with the understanding that the latter might lend the money at interest to another Jew. This would be but a clear evasion of the prohibition of usury, but evidently there is no objection to either a Gentile or a Jewish depository using deposits for lending money to Gentiles.[137] To what extent the Jewish depositor may participate in the ensuing profit will be seen later.

The most important branch of banking, the supply of funds on credit, is treated by Maimonides in terms of charity rather than business. Money lending among Jews should yield no profits whatsoever to the lender, and be transacted merely as a matter of courtesy and assistance to a needy coreligionist. We shall see, however, that enough loopholes were left, largely against Maimonides' will, to allow for extended and profitable credit transactions between Jews, and still more between Jews and Gentiles. Only so

---

ment officials. That is why bankers were not only preferred to sanctuaries, but also were able to obtain funds without paying for them, the usual risks of business failure notwithstanding. The frequency of deposits among Jews seems also to be attested by the fact that Saadia Gaon felt prompted to write a special monograph on the laws governing them. Cf. *Teshubot ha-geonim*, ed. Harkavy, No. 454 (Hebrew trans. and notes, p. 322). Even assuming that this קצור הפקדון was but an excerpt from Saadia's more comprehensive monograph *On Pledges* (cf. Henry Malter, *Saadia Gaon, His Life and Works* [Philadelphia, 1921] pp. 163, 345), the evident interest of jurists in such a brief compilation can be explained only as the reflection of an existing social need.

[137] C.M. on B.M. III, 11; M.T. She'elah u-piḳḳadon 7, 6–7, largely based on Alfasi's interpretation of B.M. 43a; Malveh ve-loveh 5, 5, based on Tos. B.M. V, 19; b. 61b. Like Alfasi, Maimuni reads rather than interprets בנכרי as ביד נכרי, making the Gentile the immediate creditor. Cf. Rosanes's comment. For the actual reading, cf. Rabbinowicz's *Diḳduḳei Soferim*, XIII, 175, n. 10.

could Jewish law maintain a semblance of realism in a society in which numerous Jewish bankers were found among the outstanding citizens of their community.

In principle, Jewish law agreed with both Islam and Christendom that usury or, indeed, interest of any kind must not be charged to a coreligionist. Maimonides, summarizing talmudic regulations, declares that he who lends money on interest breaks six negative commandments; the borrower is guilty of two transgressions; the endorser, the witness, or any other accomplice in the transaction violates at least one biblical prohibition. Both the lender and the borrower, moreover, are guilty of moral turpitude and by implication place themselves on a par with those who deny the God of Israel and, more specifically, his deliverance of the Jews from Egyptian bondage.[138] The ostracism of a usurious money lender is pushed to the extreme of the treatment meted out to robbers. To be sure, to facilitate his repentance Maimuni demands that his offer to restore the unlawful gain, like that of a robber, be refused. But to show sincere repentance he ought, on his own initiative, to tear up all the writs of indebtedness in his possession and to abstain in the future from extending usurious loans even to Gentiles.[139] Both the usurious creditor and the debtor, being recognized as persons

[138] S.M. Prohib. 235–37; M.T. Malveh ve-loveh 4, 2, and 7, based on B.M. 61b, 71a, 75b. Cf. also C.M. on B.M. V, 13. For Maimuni's reading of B.M. 75b referring to two rather than three prohibitions of borrowing money on interest, cf. Alfasi's and Asheri's version, cited in the note to Don Vidal's comment. Rabbinowicz, *op. cit.*, XIII, 210, mentions no variants. Cf. also David ibn Zimri's *Responsa*, II, 313. The reason, according to Maimuni, why only a private transaction without witnesses implies a denial of the Exodus is clearly based upon the nexus between such secret money lending and the negation of individual divine Providence, as had manifested itself in the Exodus. Cf. Rosanes's comments, *ad loc.*; Outlook, pp. 27 f., and n. 93 above.

[139] M.T., *ibid.*, 4, 5, based on B.Ḳ. 94b, B.M. 61a; 'Edut 12, 5, based on Sanh. 25b. Cf. also C.M. on Sanh. III, 3. In the first passage Maimuni limits the refusal to accept restoration to usury paid in money and other replaceable articles, but permits the return of a specified object still in the creditor's possession. He seems, on the other hand, to include all usurious money lenders or robbers, however casual, in the same category — many other rabbis applied it only to professional usurers and robbers — and hence the restoration presupposed in 'Edut 12, 5 evidently refers only to specified objects, to money accepted by the debtor in defiance of the rabbis' displeasure, or else to usurious income spent on charity. For the divergent interpretations of the other rabbis, cf. *Tosafot* on B.Ḳ. 94b s. v. בימי, which also refer to Jacob Tam's opinion that the talmudic refusal to accept restoration was but an emergency measure enacted by R. Judah the Patriarch and applicable only to his generation. Cf. also H.M. 34, 29; 366, 1.

of inferior character, are disqualified from testifying in court. In any subsequent lawsuit against them, they lose the defendant's privilege in certain cases to take an oath denying the charges, and the oath devolves upon the plaintiff. They are still worse off if the plaintiff happens to be equally disreputable, because the oath legally reverts to the defendant, who, not being in a position to take it, must pay the entire claim which he cannot otherwise disprove.[140]

On the other hand, gratuitous loans to needy coreligionists are to be highly encouraged. Following the Bible and the Talmud, Maimuni declares it to be a positive legal commandment to extend such disinterested loans, if one is in a position to do so. Indeed "this is a pious act greater than charity." In his well-known classification of the ten degrees of charity, Maimonides actually mentions financial support toward the rehabilitation of the productive capacities of the recipient as by far the highest form of philanthropy. Even after extending the loan, the creditor must consider the debtor's capacity to pay. If he knows of the latter's inability to pay, his continued demand of repayment is a violation of a strict biblical prohibition.

It is forbidden for a man to appear before, or even to pass by, his debtor at a time when he knows that the latter cannot pay. He may frighten him or shame him, even if he does not ask for repayment.

Under these circumstances, Maimuni is undoubtedly right when, in referring in his *Guide* to his recodification of the laws governing loans, he states that "on examination of these laws one by one you will find them all to be filled with leniency, mercy and kindness toward the needy; that no one be deprived of the use of anything indispensable for his subsistence."[141]

[140] C.M. on Sanh. III, 3; Shebu'ot VII, 4; M.T. 'Edut 10, 4; To'en ve-nit'an 2, 2, 4 based on Sanh. 24b–25a; Sheb. 47a. For Maimuni's version (following that of Ibn Megas and some MSS) of the controversy between R. Meir and R. Jose in M. Sheb. VII, 4, cf. Rabbinowicz, *op. cit.*, X (Part 3), 100, n. 9. This Maimonidean interpretation of the controversy, in which he follows Alfasi against Hai Gaon and others, goes so far in punishing the usurer as to make him an easy target for another usurer's law-suit. It disregards thereby the encouragement it lends to the latter, to counteract which the other rabbis demanded a division of the claim into two halves.

[141] M.T. Malveh ve-loveh 1, 1–3; Matenot 'aniyim 10, 7; De'ot 5, 3; S.M. Comm. 197; Prohib. 234, quoting Mekilta 22, 24 ed. by Hoffmann, p. 151; Shab. 63a; B.M. 61a, 75b, etc.; M.N. III, 39.

What constitutes usury? Maimonides gives but a partial definition. However, he elaborates the principle in so many details that a general theory may be abstracted therefrom.

Usury in the biblical sense is any kind of increment obtained from any extension of credit. Its repayment may be obtained through the courts . . . . Every other thing prohibited as usurious is forbidden by the sages, lest one be led thereby to charging the type of usury prohibited by the Bible. This group is styled "a shade of usury" and cannot be reclaimed through the courts.

Even considerations of a purely personal nature sometimes fall under the term of usurious gain. A debtor, for instance, must not first greet his creditor, if he was not wont to do so before; he must not praise him or be among his early callers; he must not teach him Bible or Talmud, unless he used to do it before. There are, finally, contracts which, while permissible in themselves, are forbidden, because they appear as an "evasion of the laws of usury" (ha'aramat ribbit). Despite this prohibition, such contracts, if concluded, are valid and may even be enforced with the assistance of the courts. In this terminology, presented in his *Code*, Maimonides seems to have abandoned the distinction which he himself had suggested in his *Commentary* on the Mishnah between the biblical terms *neshek*, being the type of usury prohibited by biblical law, and *tarbit*, referring to usurious practices outlawed by talmudic law only. These practices are treated in the *Code* in the class of "shade of usury," which, as we have seen, constitutes a sort of *obligatio naturalis* the fulfillment of which cannot be demanded by the creditor, but which if fulfilled, cannot be reclaimed by the debtor.[142]

[142] C.M. on B.M. V, 1; M.T. Malveh ve-loveh 4, 1, 6; 5, 12–13, 15; 6, 1, supported by numerous illustrations mostly based on B.M., Chap. V. The difference between M.T. 4, 1 and C.M. may perhaps be explained by the difficulties of interpreting B.M. 62b, such as pointed out by De Boton, *ad loc.*, which induced Maimuni in C.M. to declare *tarbit* to be usury prohibited by the rabbis only. On second thought, he placed all such rabbinical prohibitions in the class of "shades of usury" which, having different legal effects, could not be identified with the definitive biblical prohibition of *tarbit* or, the later Hebrew equivalent, *marbit*. For the original meaning of these two terms, cf. the biblical dictionaries and Meyer Lambert's note in *Revue des études juives*, XXXVI (1898), 294. The expression ויוצאה בדיינין in the Maimonidean decision, in favor of R. Eleazar's view as against that of R. Johanan in B.M. 61b, evidently means the forcible collection by the court of any amount paid in excess of the original loan. Several of Maimonides' Spanish successors limited the court's intervention to the application of personal sanctions to force the recalcitrant creditor to return the usurious gain, but eliminated direct seizure of his property. Cf. Y.D. 161, 5. It is

In further substantiation of this fourfold division into (1) bibli-
cally prohibited usury, (2) shade of usury, (3) verbal usury, (4) evasion of the laws of usury, Maimonides furnishes numerous detailed
illustrations. The rabbinic term *ribbit* is clearly used in a much
more comprehensive sense than the English term "usury," which
as a rule applies only to excessive profits in money lending. Besides
including all interest and even noneconomic gratuities in the form
of "verbal usury," it embraces profits derived from a variety of
transactions which may juridically appear as sales, leases, wages,
and the like. None the less, a certain element of credit extended
to a borrower is concealed in every one of these transactions. Maimonides, to be sure, does not mention the drastic talmudic exception
allowing a man to borrow a denar to meet an instantaneous obligation — without going home, where he possesses the equivalent
amount in cash — and to pay a certain gratuity for this courtesy.
According to the Talmud, this is not a "usurious" loan, but the
exchange of a stipulated amount of money at home for a denar on
the spot. But Maimuni expressly permits the analogous temporary
borrowing of grain, if the borrower has some at home, regardless
of the possible subsequent rise in prices. He regards such a transaction as a sale rather than a loan. On the other hand, the rabbinic
ribbit is evidently less comprehensive than the Muslim *ribah*, which,
although undoubtedly influenced by it, drew the line still wider to
include almost every unlawful gain. Profit obtained through "misrepresentation," for instance, constitutes a separate talmudic transgression of *ona'ah*, but is part of the Muslim crime of *ribah*. The
modern German term *Wucher* goes even further in including all
forms of profiteering, wage exploitation, and so forth, but falls
short of the rabbinic and Muslim "usury" by excluding "legitimate
interest" and of course all forms of "verbal usury." The medieval
references to *usura* oscillate between the exclusive emphasis upon
income from money lending and one approaching the Jewish use
of the term.[143]

---

notable, on the other hand, that Maimonides does not seem to approve of the
sanction, proposed by Sar Shalom Gaon, for the lender on a "shade of usury."
The gaon demanded that such a creditor be forewarned not to negotiate a similar
loan for a second time, under the penalty of a fine and the forcible return of the
unlawful profit. Cf. *Sha'arei ṣedeḳ*, IV, 2, 3, fol. 34a.

[143] C.M. on B.M. V, 10; M.T. Malveh ve-loveh 10, 3–4, based on B.M. 75a.
Cf. Y.D. 173, 6, with reference to B.M. 46a. Thomas Aquinas deals with *usura*
principally in some connection with *mutuum*. But we find a close resemblance

Maimonides evinces little concern about the theoretical justification of the prohibition of usury. For him it is a simple case of exploitation of another Jew's plight. "Why is it [usury] called *neshek*? Because he [the lender] bites [*noshek*] and afflicts his neighbor and eats his flesh."[144] One senses in the Maimonidean and all other rabbinic discussions of the problem of usury the underlying feeling that it conflicts with the principle of equivalence between what is given by the creditor and what is repaid by the debtor. But nowhere does Maimuni attempt an analysis of this aspect of the question, which occupies such a prominent place in the lucubrations of the Christian scholastics. Neither does he refer in any way to the well-known Aristotelian doctrine concerning the supposed "sterility" of money. At most he restates in his own fashion the talmudic law that

it is forbidden to lease denars, since this is not like leasing a vessel which is being actually returned, whereas these denars are spent and others are returned. That is why there is a "shade of usury" in the payment of rent for them.[145]

to the rabbinic doctrine in the definition given in a medieval manual and quoted by Du Cange in his *Glossarium*, s. v. *usurarii* (Paris, 1846, VI, 892): "Et note quod usura non solum se extendit ad pecuniam mutuandam, sed ad quicquid ultra sortem accipitur, sive honoris, vel gagerii, vel comestione equorum, vel de illicitis venditionibus, et hujus modi." Cf. in general the two keen analyses of Jewish and Muslim law by Emil Cohn in his "Der Wucher im Talmud, seine Theorien und ihre Entwicklung," *Zeitschrift für vergleich. Rechtswissenschaft*, XVIII (1905), 37–72; and "Der Wucher im Qoran, Chadith und Fiqh," *Berliner juristische Beiträge*, Part 2 (1902); as well as Robert Salomon's recent monograph *Le Prêt à intérêt en la législation juive*, Paris, 1932. These investigations are concerned only with the juridical cohesiveness of the theoretical prohibition, and pay no attention to its effects upon economic practice.

[144] M.T., *ibid.* 4, 1.

[145] *Ibid.*, 5, 15, based on B.M. 69b. Maimonides emphasizes the fact that by merely calling the transaction a "lease," the responsibility of the borrower is not diminished in the case of money, which, being usually intended for spending, makes the recipient responsible also for forcible losses. Cf. n. 137 above and Rashi on B.M. 96b s. v. יתר. Nevertheless, this simple formal expedient eliminates for the creditor the danger of subsequent reclamation of the fee paid by the debtor. If the same money is physically returned, moreover, Maimuni would evidently accept the term "lease" at its face value and regard the fee as permissible. Cf. Don Vidal's comments and *Haggahot Maimuniot, ad loc.*, with reference to Tos. B.M. IV, 2. It is worthy of mention that, in contrast to the other Church Fathers, Augustine, too, objects to usury on grounds of humanity, but not because of the "sterility" of money. Cf. Schilling, *op. cit.*, pp. 246 f.

This emphasis upon the consumptibility of money — the Christian scholastics styled it *fungibilis* — is well in keeping with the prevailing monetary nominalism of the rabbinic doctrine. But it would have been sheer blindness toward reality or conscious opposition to it, such as had animated both Plato and Aristotle against the Attic banks of the fourth century B.C., for Maimonides and his confreres to invoke this principle of sterility in the face of the evident productive employment of capital in many branches of the semicapitalistic economy under medieval Islam. On principle they admitted, as we shall see, the productivity of money lent to Gentiles. It was precisely because money would normally "breed," i.e., be productive of income, that, according to Maimuni, the biblical lawgiver insisted that the money lender forego this income and offer gratuitous loans as a matter of charity. Unlike most Christian Church Fathers and scholastics having no compunctions about the principle of the return of the capital itself, and unlike Aristotle feeling no hostility toward commerce and mercantile profits, Maimuni was not impelled to search for deeper reasons in the prohibition of usury than the latter's obviously adverse effects upon the needy borrower.

This emphasis upon the charitable aspects of money lending had two vital effects. It facilitated a more lenient interpretation of the prohibition in cases where the borrower did not really require charitable credit, as in productive loans, or where the lender belonged to a class of persons requiring special protection. It also led to a series of protective regulations in favor of creditors, so "that you may not shut the gate before the borrowers." In either case it proved of great importance to the development of medieval Jewish banking.

In the first place rabbinic law grants considerable exemptions to orphaned minors. If they become heirs to an estate which includes income derived from usury, they are obliged to make restoration only if their father voices regrets before his death, and if the usurious gain consists in an extant specific object. The usual monetary gain is never subject to repayment. In managing a minor's estate, the court is also free to disregard the vast class of "shades of usury." What is more, even if the court happens to collect for the benefit of orphans regular usury in the biblical sense of the term, the debtor is urged not to reclaim it.[146] Another class of per-

---

[146] M.T. Malveh ve-loveh 4, 4, 14; Naḥlot 11, 1; Resp. No. 113, partly based on B.M. 62a, 70a. Maimuni accepts here the talmudic modifications of Mar

sons close to the heart of the rabbis were the scholars. Maimonides, in particular, sharply condemning the professional use of rabbinic learning, necessarily had to favor provisions for their obtaining some sort of unearned income. Next to that from silent partnership in business, which, as we shall see, likewise had its legal difficulties, revenue from money lending offered the best livelihood for persons devoting their undivided attention to study. Interpreting more broadly than most other medieval rabbis a dubious talmudic passage, Maimuni denied the usurious character of credit transactions among scholars, followed by the repayment of higher amounts than originally borrowed. "Since the parties know the seriousness of the prohibition of usury, it is obvious that the debtor merely extended a gift" to his creditor.[147] As a matter of fact, Maimuni generally took a more lenient stand with respect to the "renunciation of his rights" (*meḥilah*) by the debtor. Many geonim had declared the renunciation of usurious payments "made or to be made" by the debtor as null and void. They correctly argued that "every type of usury consists in the renunciation of the debtor's rights, but the Torah has not renounced these rights and forbidden any such renunciation." Maimonides, however, repudiated this interpretation and insisted that even when the creditor is told to restore his usurious gain, the debtor is still at liberty voluntarily to forego its

---

Samuel's sweeping statement that "one may lend on interest money belonging to orphans." By מותר ליתן he undoubtedly wishes to express that a court or its representative may do so. He disregards, however, the numerous detailed difficulties arising from the comparison of B.M. 62a with B.Ḳ. 94b, as pointed out by *Tosafot* on the latter passage s. v. אי. Neither does he amplify the complicated minutiae of this important exception in favor of orphans, for which see the material assembled in Rosanes's comments, *ad loc.* In Resp. No. 112 he merely restates his opinion that the court may try to collect for orphans various kinds of income ordinarily prohibited by the rabbis, against the view of those medieval jurists who wished to open to minors only the otherwise prohibited partnership, with a full share in profits and but slight responsibility for losses. There is no evidence, however, that he also placed communal funds in the same privileged position, a view expounded by many medieval rabbis. Cf. *Or Zarua*, I, 30; Menahem Recanati, *Piskei halakot*, No. 65; Y.D. 160, 17, and the commentaries thereon.

[147] M.T. Malveh ve-loveh 4, 9, based on B.M. 75a. While Maimuni excludes here only advance arrangements for such extra payments, other rabbis, ever since Amram Gaon, proposed more far-reaching qualifications. Many applied the fiction of a gift only if the creditor's profit was negligible; others, ready to concede fully 20 percent of the original amount, limited it to loans consisting of articles of food. Cf. Don Vidal's comments; *Tosafot* on B.M. 75a s. v. מתנה; Y.D., *loc. cit.* Maimuni's desire to favor the scholarly creditor appears undeniable.

acceptance.[148] From the economic, not the juridical point of view this opinion clearly enabled a creditor, personally acquainted with his debtor and relying upon his adherence to a sort of gentleman's agreement, to cash in all extra payments with practically no financial risks to himself. Even if neither of them was a scholar, and if the transaction was ultimately condemned by a court as usurious, the debtor, whose personal honor as well as future credit was involved, usually refrained from demanding restitution.

Much more important than these cases where the payment of interest is clearly identified as such are the various types of business transactions where such payment is concealed behind the screen of otherwise legitimate agreements. It is in these methods of circumventing the prohibition of usury, which was felt to be oppressive under the changed economic conditions, that the ingenuity of business men and jurists found ample means of fitting a vast and profitable credit system into the traditional legal structure. To be sure, following the Tosefta and the Talmud, Maimuni declares many such agreements, though in themselves permissible, forbidden because of their intrinsic purpose to evade the prohibition of usury (ha'aramat ribbit). But his illustrations refer only to such crude methods of evasion as few of his self-respecting contemporaries would have cared to apply. He mentions, for instance, the loan of merchandise and its subsequent repurchase for a smaller amount, which ultimately leaves the lender in possession of the entire merchandise and of an additional claim to the differential. Even such a clumsy contract, as we have seen, if properly executed, could not be legally annulled, but bankers in Maimuni's time could make much better use of the related *contractus mohatrae*, which, originating from an evasion of the Muslim prohibition of usury, was subsequently to play such a significant role in European money lending. To be sure, the bankers would first have to overcome certain technical obstacles in Jewish law. They could not sell a fictitious object at one price and instantly buy it back at a higher price *for future delivery*, because such sales of nonexistent (or as yet nonexistent) objects were generally invalidated by Jewish law. Neither

---

[148] M.T., *ibid.*, 4, 13. Asher b. Yehiel on B.M. 61a states the source for this difference of opinion, finally agreeing with Maimonides. Cf. also *Haggahot Maimuniot* and De Boton's comments, *ad loc.*; Y.D. 160, 5. Cf. also Aquinas, *Summa theologiae*, II, 2, 78, 2: "Si vero accipiat aliquid hujus modi [money or money's worth] non quasi exigens, nec quasi ex aliqua obligatione tacita vel expressa, sed sicut gratuitum donum, non peccat."

could they sell a particular object at a price higher than its actual value in the market without running the risk of recovering at the due date only the original market price. But what could prevent them from arranging for a sale below the market price of the moment, with immediate delivery, and for an instantaneous resale at the market price with future delivery? The original owner evidently was free to dispose of his holdings below the market price and thus obtain the needed cash, under the promise of returning a higher amount at the stipulated future date. Such a twofold contract would in the interim also place in the hands of the creditor a pawn or mortgage in the form of the "sold" object.

Maimonides cites another illustration of the prohibited but none the less legally valid evasion, viz., the leasing to the debtor of a field taken over by the creditor as security for his loan, the rental securing the stipulated income. This method, closely related to the "purchase of rents," which came to play such an important role in medieval Europe, was reluctantly legalized by the canonists and, with further hedging, by the European rabbis. Maimonides himself tries to modify the laws directed against the creditor deriving income from property mortgaged to him. In opposition to some geonim, he draws a distinction between income from a house, a shop, and so forth, which, being more or less certain, is straight usury, and one coming from a field which, dependent on a good or bad harvest, constitutes but a "shade of usury." Income from a field, moreover, is altogether permissible, if in return for it the lender discounts a stipulated amount, however small, from the debt. Neither does Maimuni apparently object to the lender leasing such a field to a third person for a higher rent than the discount. In the first example, too, there is nothing to prevent a merchant from extending to his neighbor a loan of a given sum of money in the form of merchandise according to its supposed market value and acquiring elsewhere the same amount of merchandise at wholesale prices. The usual span between the merchant's purchasing and selling price, which Maimuni wished to see authoritatively fixed at 16.66 percent but which, he admitted, could go much higher wherever there were no publicly fixed prices, would in this case clearly be mercantile profit in name, but substantial interest on a loan in its economic essence.[149]

[149] M.T., *ibid.*, 5, 15; 6, 7–8; 8, 1–2, based on B.M. 62b, 67b–68a. Cf. nn. 59, 109 above. For the operation of the *contractus mohatrae* in Muslim law, cf. Joseph

Another important means of evasion was given by the permission to acquire deeds with a discount. Since the bulk of business in Maimuni's time was transacted through the use of some commercial instrument, the flow of credit was greatly facilitated. For example, a merchant could sell merchandise on credit, at a price yielding him substantial profit, and obtain cash from the banker by discounting the bill given him by the purchaser. The underlying theory was that interest was prohibited only in direct relationships between lender and borrower. For the same reason one could pay a fee to an agent for his services in securing a loan. Since the law, according to Maimuni, did not object, if a third person, here the agent, paid a gratuity to the banker for the extension of credit to the agent's client, one can see how money could readily be diverted into profitable channels without exposing the lender and the borrower to public condemnation.[150]

Kohler's remarks in Cohn's *Der Wucher im Qoran*, pp. 32 ff.; Björkmann, *op. cit.*, p. 85. According to Don Vidal's interpretation of M.T. 8, 1–2, such evasion was greatly facilitated, if the object so sold and resold was a parcel of land, since land is not subject to the limitations of the market value. Don Vidal's concluding sentence (8, 1) well characterizes his intention: "Every contract under the form of sale is permissible so long as it does not look like usury." In both illustrations of "the evasion of usury" in 5, 15, Maimuni runs counter the opinion of many other rabbis. Nahmanides regards all profits through the loan of merchandise as actually noncollectible, while the leasing back of the field to the debtor is declared by Rashi (on B.M. 68a s. v. ולא) to be straight usury. Nevertheless, the main trend in medieval Jewish law was in the direction of further liberalization of the law, as evidenced by the sources assembled in the commentaries on Y.D. 163, 3; 164, 1; 172, 1. That Maimuni is right in saying (6, 8) that only some of the geonim opposed his view is evidenced by those quoted in Isaac b. Aba Mari's *Sefer ha-'Iṭṭur* under letter פ No. 1, who were, in part, even more liberal. Indeed, we learn therefrom that there existed an early and widely prevalent practice of allowing the creditor to collect all revenue from the field after granting a nominal discount to the debtor. Only Jacob Gaon demanded the fixing of the discount at 25 percent or more of the loan. Cf. also Schwarz in MbM, II, 389 f. In M.T. 7, 1–5, Maimuni is ready to respect even fartherreaching infractions of the prohibition, if sanctioned by local usage. For the merchant's profit, cf. nn. 97, 154; and Resp. No. 118, where the sale of merchandise on credit with 25 percent profit on the merchant's purchasing price is declared as "the usual run of business without which the source of livelihood would be destroyed."

[150] M.T., *ibid.*, 5, 14, based upon Tos. B.M. V, 16, 382; b. 69b. There is no indication that, like Nahmanides, Maimuni legalized the sale of deeds with a discount, only if the seller declined all responsibility. Cf. Don Vidal's comment. On the contrary, it appears that in accordance with M.T. Mekirah 6, 11–12; Ḥobel u-mazziḳ 7, 9, he wished to retain the precariousness of such a sale by

The most important method of evasion under many anti-usurious regimes was some sort of alleged silent partnership, in which capital was made to yield profit without work. While the rabbis strained their ingenuity to draw sharp juridical lines between real partnerships, going under the name 'iska, and concealed loan contracts, they could not entirely eliminate this means of securing income for money employed by others in a productive capacity. To be sure, the name "credit" was to be avoided. Even the early modern rabbis continued frowning upon the so-called *contractus trinus*, which came to be accepted by the later medieval canonists. This combination of contractual partnership with a sort of insurance for both capital and interest — hence the name — was regarded as admissible at best if the capitalist accepted the entire risk, which of course made it closely akin to the *commenda*, so widely accepted in the ancient and medieval Mediterranean world. The Arabs, too, recognized this institution under the name of *modarabat* and elaborated it in great detail in their great schools of jurisprudence.[151]

Maimonides, however, refers only casually to the usual *commenda*[152] and knows nothing of the *contractus trinus*. In restating

maintaining the right of the seller to renounce his claim. Under these circumstances, the seller, after having properly endorsed the deed, became responsible for the full face value of the deed, and not merely for the amount he had received. Neither do we find in Maimuni's formulation any of the restrictions upon the payment of a fee to the intermediary, or by the latter to the lender, such as were postulated by other medieval rabbis. On the other hand, he does not countenance the flagrant evasion of the law through allowing a "messenger" to contract a loan and pay interest for it, since such interest does not come directly from the borrower. This subterfuge, suggested by Rashi, found powerful support among the European rabbis confronted with the overwhelming reality of medieval Jewish money lending. Cf. *Haggahot Maimuniot*, Don Vidal's and Rosanes's comments, *ad loc.*; Y.D. 160, 13, and the commentaries. Cf. also n. 59 above.

[151] For the complicated rabbinic laws of 'iska, cf. E. E. Hildesheimer, "Das Recht der 'iska," *Jahrbuch der jüdisch-literarischen Gesellschaft in Frankfurt*, XX (1929), 337–77, reprinted in the same author's *Das jüdische Gesellschaftsrecht* (Leipzig, 1930), pp. 87 ff. The *contractus trinus*, evidently discussed in Y.D. 177, 6, is briefly compared with the Jewish שטר עסקא by Moses Hoffmann in *Festschrift . . . David Hoffmann* (Berlin, 1914), pp. 383–86.

[152] Resp. Nos. 267, 275, and 276 reflect a rather widespread use among Jews of the Muslim type of *commenda*, in which all the risks of the enterprise rested with the capitalist, in return for which the manager received but one-third of the profit. Cf. also the sources quoted by Hildesheimer, *op. cit.*, pp. 366, n. 157; 369, n. 165 (pp. 122, 124); and Bergsträsser-Schacht, *op. cit.*, pp. 75 f.

the complicated talmudic regulations and cutting through a maze of controversial opinion accumulated in the centuries of juridical evolution, he clearly reveals his personal bent in two directions: he wishes to safeguard as far as possible the interests of the active partner. At the same time he insists upon great latitude in contractual dispositions. As a matter of principle, he forbids partnerships without active participation, unless the active partner receives a special compensation for his services. If he devotes himself exclusively to serving the company, he may legitimately expect an added remuneration in the amount of wages which one normally would have to pay to an unemployed worker for doing the type of work which he (the active partner) had done before entering the partnership. As an alternative, he may be given a certain preference in the apportioning of gains or losses resulting from his business management. As a rule, he may be expected to participate in profits to the extent of two-thirds and in losses only to that of one-third. The parties are free, however, to make any other contractual arrangements, as long as the principle is maintained that the active partner be given some special remuneration for his labors. The parties may agree, for instance, that he share in the profits to the extent of one-ninth and in losses only to that of one-tenth. Maimonides argues specifically against his teachers who recognized such agreements only if the active partner pursues another occupation on the side. If the latter, moreover, contributes a part of the capital, however small, the contract still is, in Maimonides' opinion, one of 'iska, rather than of ordinary partnership. By thus making the active worker an entrepreneur in his own right, even if his capital share be only one-tenth of one percent, the special compensation for his services may be reduced, without previous contractual agreement, to a nominal amount, e.g., one denar for the entire period of partnership.[153]

[153] C.M. on B.M. V, 5; B.B. X, 4; M.T. Sheluḥin ve-shutefin 6–7; Malveh ve-loveh 5, 8–9; Resp. Nos. 214, 265–76, 294, and so forth. It may be noted that the presumptive share of the active partner, where there is no special agreement, is given, in M.T. Sheluḥin 6, 3–4, as two-thirds in profit and one-third in losses. Maimuni expressly rejects as erroneous the opinion that such share may be lowered to one-half of the profits. In C.M. and Resp. No. 268 Maimuni himself voices just that opinion, which, like that of RABD concerning the two-third share in profits and one-half in losses, seems more in agreement with the talmudic source in B.M. 68b. The proportion of one-half and one-third is also the prevalent doctrine of the geonim. Cf. Hildesheimer, op. cit., p. 348, n. 65 (p. 101). The geonic responsa offer, however, a number of illustrations of different special

There is no doubt that most of the 'iska contracts entered into by Jews in the Maimonidean age were legitimate business agreements. They became of vital importance with the growth of international Jewish commerce, because they enabled merchants to entrust consignments of merchandise to fellow Jews traveling to foreign lands. After the disposal of these goods abroad, the merchants got back the invested capital and a stipulated share in the profits. We learn, for instance, from the Maimonidean *Responsa* that both India and the Mediterranean countries offered ample opportunities for this type of trading. However, one cannot deny that, notwithstanding all the obstacles erected by Maimuni and the other rabbis, such silent partnerships could be utilized also as means of evading the prohibition of usury. By letting the borrower participate with a farthing in the capital of the supposed partnership, one could arrange that most of the profits from the latter's employment of the borrowed money should go to the creditor. The only two deterrents, which Maimuni tries to fortify, were the uncertainty of the profit and the risk for the lender in the loss of one-half of the capital, which, according to the rabbinic theory,

---

agreements. For example, one silent partner, contributing 60 percent of the capital, agreed to share in the profits only to the extent of seven-twelfths. Cf. *Sha'arei ṣedeḳ*, IV, 8, fol. 93a ff. (especially Nos. 6 and 12); and other sources quoted by Mann in JQR, n.s., X, 332 f. Maimonides' interpretation of Abbaye's statement in B.M. 68ab concerning the compensation כפועל בטל של אותה מלאכה דבטל מינה offering a sort of *lucrum cessans* to the active partner for work which he otherwise would normally have done, is contradicted by Maimuni's distinguished predecessors, Hai Gaon, Hananel, Alfasi, and Rashi, who offer different explanations. Cf. the commentaries on M.T. 6, 2; *Tosafot* on B.M. 68a s. v. ונותן and Hildesheimer pp. 345 f. (p. 98). Cf. also n. 189. While Maimuni in 6, 1 emphasizes the fact that the criterion for 'iska is the exclusive work done by one partner, with or without capital investment on his own part, Alfasi and others insist that the contribution of even the slightest amount by the active associate converts the arrangement into a straight partnership not subjected to the limitations of the 'iska contract. Cf. however, C.M. on B.B. X, 4, where Maimuni apparently accepts Alfasi's view. Such discrepancies between C.M. and M.T. are not altogether unusual, in particular when Maimuni decides, after more mature consideration, to repudiate the opinion of a revered predecessor. Cf. his own remarks in another instance, Resp. No. 240, and the literature cited there by the editor. To what extent Maimuni may also have been influenced, in the two instances cited here, by the growing trend toward restrictive state capitalism in Egypt to abandon views held by himself and his predecessors under the somewhat more "liberalistic" regimes of the earlier caliphates cannot be fully ascertained on the basis of the available evidence. Cf. also Y.D. 177, 3, and the commentaries thereon.

was to be treated as a deposit and for which the borrower's responsibility was rather slight. The subsequent development of rabbinic law substantially weakened even these deterrents.[154]

The protective legislation for the creditor arising from the principle of not shutting the gates to needy borrowers likewise has many aspects. Apart from the general principle of formal justice that one must not favor the poor debtor against the rich creditor, even if the collection of the debt entails serious hardships for the debtor and his family, Maimonides, as we have seen, recognizes certain types of usury as forbidden, but collectible; and others as nonreclaimable if paid. In a talmudic controversy he also endorses the opinion that a deed containing usurious provisions remains valid as to principal and becomes void only with respect to interest. Other rabbis wished to condemn the entire deed as a penalty for the inherent transgression. Maimonides also ethically advises all

[154] All medieval rabbis agreed with the talmudic principle that half of the money invested in 'iska should be treated as a gratuitous loan and the other half as a deposit from which the depositor might draw an income. But opinions differed on the extent of the "depository's" responsibility. Maimuni believed that he was responsible only for willful mismanagement, since he was receiving no direct remuneration for safe-guarding the deposit. RABD and others, viewing his income more realistically, made him responsible for robbery and theft, if not for enforced losses. The trend to facilitate profitable employment of capital became ever stronger, and the latter opinion prevailed. Cf. Y.D. 177, 2, 5. M.T. Malveh ve-loveh 5, 17, affirming the right of any third person to pay a coreligionist's defaulted head tax and to place him in bondage, although his work may yield the creditor a higher income than the original outlay, is but an antiquarian reminiscence of conditions prevailing in Sassanian Persia, as reflected in B.M. 73b. It illustrates, nevertheless, the extent to which Maimuni is ready to respect the law of the kingdom, even in matters of usury. One must bear in mind, however, that he had little choice, since the talmudic source is altogether unequivocal. The variant eliminating the word טפי, and thereby all excess income, is suggested by Tosafot ibid. s. v. משתעבדי, but apparently has no support in talmudic manuscripts. In Resp. No. 114, on the other hand, Maimuni is forced to deal with a contemporary problem arising from the equally drastic penalties imposed by the Muslim administration upon taxpayers in arrears. The dread of these penalties in the Great Caliphate had led many subjects to incur loans at the enormous interest rate of 1000 percent per annum. Cf. Mez, op. cit. p. 454 (Islamic Culture, VII, 322). A similar case was brought to Maimonides' attention, when a Jew, unable to secure an ordinary loan for the payment of his overdue head tax, had to "purchase" on credit three garments worth thirty-nine dirhem for sixty dirhem. Maimonides simply decided that the "purchaser" should pay only the equivalent of the market price of the garments and not the face value of the deed. Of course, as elsewhere, he did not object to the usual mercantile profit already included in the normal market price. Cf. n. 149 above.

debtors to pay their bills promptly.[155] More important were the far-reaching departures from talmudic law which enabled creditors to collect outstanding debts from persons or properties which the Talmud had declared immune. According to the ancient law, only land could be seized for the satisfaction of creditors; the talmudic sages themselves, going beyond what they regarded as biblical law, enabled the creditors to seize land of medium quality, even where inferior land was available. The geonim, confronted by an increasingly landless Jewish population with a growing need of credit, extended the law to allow the seizure of movable property as well. Indeed, movables were to be disposed of first, and only if they were found insufficient was the land to be seized. The geonim made heirs of an estate, including orphans, fully responsible for the indebtedness of its previous owner. Creditors able to prove only a claim derived from an oral agreement were now entitled to execute it from the movable property included in the estate. Maimonides fully accepts these far-reaching modifications of talmudic law, merely expressing a personal preference for the insertion of a specific clause to this effect in the original contract, such as had become customary in Morocco.[156]

Maimuni takes a similar stand with respect to the Sabbatical cancellation of debts and prevention of this through the so-called *prosbol*. Hillel had already motivated this abrogation of an ancient law by the need to stimulate charitable money lending. Maimuni is somewhat in a dilemma. Personally he would have liked to see the cancellation of debts by the Sabbatical year operative without restrictions. He becomes rhetorical in denouncing the judge who nowadays fails to apply the law as one who "does not fear God and robs the poor." Nevertheless, he admits the validity of the *prosbol*

[155] M.T. Malveh ve-loveh 1, 4; 4, 6; 5, 14; Yesodei ha-torah 5, 11. For the underlying reasons as well as the various qualifications of 4, 6 cf. *Tosafot* on B.M. 72a s. v. קונסין and Y.D. 161, 11–12.

[156] C.M. on B.Ḳ. X, 2; Giṭṭin V, 1; M.T. Ishshut 16, 7; 17, 6; 19, 17–18; Nizḳei mamon 8, 10–12; Gezelah va-abedah 5, 6; Malveh ve-loveh 11, 11; 19, 1. The innovation of the geonim was introduced about 787 because of the structural changes in Jewish landownership, and was solemnly proclaimed to the world at large. Cf. Sherira Gaon's *Iggeret* ed. by Lewin (Haifa, 1921), pp. 105, 108; *'Iṭṭur*, fol. 77d. While an early gaon tried to limit the new law to countries in which the Jews had few landholdings, Amram Gaon, and after him Sherira Gaon and Maimonides, emphasized the fact that it was applied in the courts throughout the world. Cf. also Schwarz, *op. cit.*, pp. 345 f., 372 ff., 391 f.; Mann in JQR, n.s. X, 310; and Tykocinski, *op. cit.*, pp. 34 ff.

because, since the discontinuation of the observance of the Jubilee year, the Sabbatical year has become a rabbinic rather than a biblical institution. While trying to discourage the indiscriminate use of the new instrument and insisting that only a court of very learned judges be given the right to issue it, he nevertheless accepts other protective measures for the creditor enacted long after the time of Hillel. In his opinion, the creditor need not produce evidence that he obtained the *prosbol* before the Sabbatical year. A simple declaration that he had such a writ and lost it is to be accepted as true. That is why not only minor heirs of a deceased creditor, whose interests are always safeguarded by the courts, but all heirs have the legal presumption on their side that their ancestor had secured a *prosbol* for the debt due him, even if such a transaction is nowhere recorded. Under these circumstances, the Sabbatical cancellation of debts might occasionally have affected the uninstructed private citizen extending a charitable loan to a fellow Jew, but had practically no effect upon the professional money lender who took the necessary precautions.[157]

Other alleviations were extended to the creditor in matters of judicial procedure. The creditor may force the debtor, says Maimuni, to follow him to a court of superior learning in another city, regardless of the old adage *actio sequitur forum rei*.[158] In order not to discourage prospective money lenders, the witnesses in monetary transactions are not to be subjected to the usual rigorous cross examination, and certain allowances are to be made for deeds the

[157] C.M. on Shebiit X, 3; S.M. Comm. 141; M.T. Shemiṭṭah ve-yobel 9, 2–3, 15–18, 24; Resp. Nos. 233–41, primarily based on Giṭṭin 36–37. M.T., *ibid.*, 9, 14: debts contracted on the security of land or pawn are not canceled by the Sabbatical year; 9, 27: scholars need not go to court, but may simply declare in the presence of their pupils their intention that their claims should not be canceled. No wonder that with so much hedging the entire institution of debt cancellation gradually died down, causing no little embarrassment to the later medieval rabbis. Cf. H.M. 67, 1, and the commentaries thereon. For Maimuni's computation of the Sabbatical cycles, brought down to his own day, cf. Outlook, pp. 94 ff. Cf. also n. 85 above.

[158] M.T. Sanh. 6, 7–9, based on Maimuni's interpretation of Sanh. 23a, 31b and the contemporary "daily" practice in Spain. Other rabbis interpreted the respective passages differently, Jacob Tam, for instance, extending the same privilege to the defendant. This procedural chicanery had to be altogether abandoned in the subsequent generations because of the growing independence of the local community, as opposed to the more centralized regional bodies such as the *negidut* of Muslim Egypt. Cf. H.M. 14, 1–2, and the commentaries thereon.

witnesses of which are not available for examination in court. For the same reason the sages have accelerated the proceedings in favor of creditors appearing in court with a deed. If the debtor can be speedily summoned to present his case, this should be done. Otherwise the plaintiff is allowed to take oath and immediately seize any of the debtor's possessions.[159] Moreover, Maimonides accepts the doctrine of his "teachers," against that of some geonim, that a creditor presenting a properly attested deed is obliged to take oath only if the debtor contends that he had paid the loan, whereas other contentions, such as that the deed is forged or based upon a usurious claim, have to be proved by the debtor. To obviate controversies, Maimuni demands that all loans, even to scholars, be given in the presence of witnesses or else on a pawn or other security and that preferably the transaction be recorded in a deed signed by witnesses.[160]

Maimonides rigidly objects to a Jew bringing a lawsuit against a fellow Jew before a Gentile court; even if a Jewish court happens to commit this grievous error and sends the litigants to a Gentile court, the sentence of the latter is to be disregarded. But he allows the creditor and other plaintiffs who cannot force their opponents to repair to Jewish judges or where the Jewish court is powerless to carry out its sentence to invoke the help of Gentile authorities. Considering the changed conditions of his age, he tersely informs an inquirer that

he who is indebted to somebody according to Jewish law, may be forced by the creditor to sign a deed to this effect according to Gentile law. This deed may then be deposited with a trustworthy

[159] M.T. 'Edut 3, 1, 4 based upon various talmudic passages (cf. Karo's and De Boton's comments, *ad loc.*); C.M. on Ket. IX, 6; M.T. Malveh ve-loveh 13, 1–2, based on Ket. 88a. Maimonides does not specify the time limit of במהרה, leaving it to the judge's discretion to choose a reasonable period. Alfasi seems to have demanded that, if the court's messenger could reach the defendant and report back within thirty days the hearing should be postponed. Cf. Karo's and De Boton's comments, *ad loc.*, and the sources quoted by the commentaries on H.M. 106, 1. Maimuni, however, apparently refuses to encumber this protective measure in favor of the creditor by any hard and fast rule. In Resp. No. 311 he does not inquire at all into the defendant's place of residence, but favors immediate action.

[160] M.T. Malveh ve-loveh 14, 3; Resp. No. 117. Cf. also RABD and commentaries, *ad loc.*, and Schwarz, *op. cit.* pp. 393 ff. Maimonides' decision was accepted by the majority of the later rabbis. Cf. H.M. 82, 10. M.T., *ibid.*, 3, 7, amplifying the statement in B.M. 75b.

person, and when the debtor ultimately refuses to pay what had been imposed upon him by Jewish law, he may be forced to do so through Gentile courts.

This is in consonance with Maimonides' own view, in opposition to that of his teachers, that loan contracts, if properly executed before Gentile authorities, establish valid claims in Jewish courts, provided there are Jewish witnesses to authenticate the signatures of the Gentile witnesses on the deed and to testify that the Gentile judge in question is not known to be accessible to bribery.[161] Only in case of a really impecunious debtor does Maimuni try to strike a balance between the legitimate interests of the creditor and the requirements of mercy toward the debtor. On the one hand, he states that the creditor, as the result of a geonic departure from ancient law, may demand from the debtor a solemn oath of manifestation that he possesses no concealed property and an equally solemn promise to apply all his future earnings (except for a month's food and a year's clothing for himself, but not for his family) toward the repayment of the debt. On the other hand, he demands that no such oath be administered to a debtor known to be poor and of good character, if this condition is recognized by both judge and public opinion. This liberating oath should be refused a well-known perjurer, who might readily take it in order to get rid of a debt. At the same time neither the creditor nor the marshal of the court is entitled to infringe upon the privacy of the debtor's home in a search for hidden assets.[162] However, the biblical law

---

[161] M.T., *ibid.*, 27, 1; Resp. 294–98. Cf. also the note to Resp. No. 155, quoting the text of a regulation enacted by a college of Egyptian rabbis, headed by Maimonides, that Jewish parties should refrain from repairing to Gentile courts. This, of course, was an old law which apparently had to be vigorously restated in the face of frequent violations by Maimuni's contemporaries in Egypt. Cf. also Ginzberg, *Genizah Studies*, II, 118, 127 f., and the excerpt from Hai Gaon's *Book of Judges' Morality*, ed. by S. Assaf, *Tarbiz*, VII (1935–36), 217 f.

[162] M.T., *ibid.*, 2, 1–4; Resp. Nos. 204, 228, 312. According to Moses of Coucy's SeMaG, Comm. 93, and *Haggahot Maimuniot, ad loc.*, the originators of this oath were the Saboraim. Cf. Tykocinski, *op. cit.*, pp. 67 ff. That this innovation had been widely accepted by the Jewish communities is emphasized by Maimuni: וכזה דנין ישראל בכל מקומותן. Maimuni amplifies it in many significant details: (1) the oath is to include the promise of payment from future earnings; (2) the burden of proof lies with the debtor that money found with him thereafter does not belong to nim (Maimuni quotes his "teachers' " opinion to this effect, but it is not mentioned, for instance, in Alfasi's *Responsa* No. 259); (3) only one oath is to be taken against the claims of many creditors; (4) it is left to the discretion of the judge to free an obviously honest debtor from an oath and to

demanding retention by the debtor (or constant restitution to him whenever needed) of all objects indispensable for daily use is interpreted to refer only to objects belonging to the debtor personally, not to those used by his wife and children. There are also recognized class differences, inasmuch as a defaulting debtor of the upper classes may claim, for instance, the retention of a regular mattress on his bed, one of the lower income groups only that of a mat. Finally, on grounds of sex morality Maimuni prohibits the seizure of such movables belonging to a widow, since their constant restitution by the creditor may lead to immoral relationships between them.[163]

These privileges of the plaintiff were, for the most part, limited to claims arising from loan contracts. Few of them were applicable to those other business transactions which, in order to secure income for capital, specifically avoided the term "loan." Nevertheless, one clearly sees that the Maimonidean restatement of talmudic law left sufficient means at the disposal of capitalists

---

refuse it to a notorious perjurer. It is questionable whether Maimuni wanted a period of ninety days, during which the debtor would live under ban to reveal his assets, to precede the administration of the oath, as demanded by Hai Gaon and others; cf. Tykocinski, *loc. cit.* The statements: מחרימין אבל מחרימין and ומחרימין תחלה are inconclusive, inasmuch as the former may have been replaced by the oath, and the latter is addressed to the public at large. Neither is any time limit set. At any rate, in Resp., *loc. cit.*, no bans are mentioned. In Resp. Nos. 177 and 203 the wife was protected against being divorced by an impecunious husband, who, through such an oath, tried to free himself from her marriage settlement. Curiously, Maimuni, in his desire to protect the innocent debtor in the case of insolvency, states in Resp. No. 299 that if threatened by the creditor to be dragged before a Gentile court where a declaration of bankruptcy would lead to his imprisonment, the debtor may swear that he is not indebted to the plaintiff at all. He should only make the mental reservation that he means to say that he owes him nothing until such time as he may have money to repay him. Cf. also M.T. Shebu'ot 3, 3 and the qualifying statements of Nahshon Gaon quoted by *Haggahot Maimuniot* thereon.

[163] C.M. on B.M. IX, 15; S.M. Comm. 199; M.T. Malveh ve-loveh 3, 1, 4–6, based on B.M. 113a–116a. Cf. also Resp. No. 177. The principle of differentiating between debtors according to rank, here (M.T. 2, 2) and elsewhere, is in keeping with the general rabbinic medieval concept of giving a poor man the things to which he had become accustomed. Lujo Brentano, in his stimulating lecture on "Ethics and Economics in History," has rightly pointed out that this doctrine of making allowances according to rank opened many a door for shady practice and concealed many legal subterfuges behind a cloak of respectability. Cf. *Der wirtschaftende Mensch in der Geschichte, Gesammelte Reden und Aufsätze* (Leipzig, 1923), p. 46, n. 2.

profitably to employ their funds in other persons' enterprises. The careers of the great Jewish bankers under Islam were little hampered by these prohibitive laws. None the less these laws fulfilled their main function of extending a measure of protection to those needy borrowers who negotiated loans only for purposes of subsistence.

The prohibition of usury affected still less the vast domain of Jewish credit extended to Gentiles. To be sure, similar limitations weakened also the Muslim and to a certain extent the Christian prohibitions of usury, but to Jews, the numerically smallest group, they opened the relatively largest range of "legitimate" activities. Let us assume, for the sake of illustration, that the population of a given district consisted of 70 percent Muslims, 25 percent Christians, and 5 percent Jews. A Muslim banker could deal more freely only with 30 percent of his compatriots, whereas his Christian colleague could extend credit on interest to 75 percent, a Jewish banker to 95 percent of the population. The few obstacles to such trade, moral rather than strictly legal, could be overcome without much difficulty, as may be seen in Maimuni's attempt to harmonize the various biblical and talmudic regulations. As a son of the highly intolerant age of the Almohades and the Christian Crusaders, he quotes without qualification the Sifre's interpretation of *la-nokri tashik* of Deuteronomy 23:21. Usually translated "unto a stranger thou mayest lend upon usury," the passage appears here as a positive commandment to extort interest from Gentile borrowers. This interpretation runs counter to the talmudic tradition to such an extent that Maimuni's juridical predecessors and successors almost unanimously repudiated this view. He repeats, on the other hand, the talmudic injunction to refrain from lending money to Gentiles altogether, unless one derives therefrom the only means of subsistence. Characteristically, he interprets in a restrictive rather than amplifying fashion the talmudic motivation that such transactions, because fostering the social relations between Jew and Gentile, may become prejudicial to the lender's orthodoxy. Instead of drawing the more general conclusion that all other commercial transactions should be discouraged on the same ground — an evident practical impossibility for the Jewish minority constantly living among Gentile majorities — he restricts even this regulation by exempting both a Jewish debtor and a scholarly creditor. There is no danger of the Jewish debtor, he says, coming under the social and intellectual influence of his Gentile creditor, because it is in the very nature of such relationships that the debtor avoids the creditor as much as possible. (One fails to see, however, why the Gentile debtor should not likewise avoid contact with his Jewish creditor and, being in an inferior position, fail to exercise any influence whatsoever.) A scholar may extend credit to a Gentile, because being deeply imbued with the spirit of Judaism, he is immune from such outside heterodox influences. Maimonides does not even use moral suasion, such as demanded by Amram Gaon, to make scholars abstain from such trade. Every Jew, moreover, may freely collect from Gentiles all types of "shade of usury."[164]

Like the other rabbis, Maimonides is, of course, deeply concerned about the possibility of evading the prohibition of usury from fellow Jews by using Gentiles as intermediaries. Evidently nothing could prevent a Gentile borrower from a Jew from lending that amount to another Jew at whatever rate of interest they might agree on. Maimonides declares that if this is done with the connivance of the Jewish creditor, it is a full-fledged usurious transaction. He insists that a Jew who borrows money on interest from a Gentile should not transfer his indebtedness to another Jew under the same conditions, because the second debtor would appear to pay him the interest. He should rather repay his loan and let the Gentile creditor lend the amount directly to the new debtor. This regulation was evidently intended to prevent Gentile capitalists from making use of Jewish bankers to employ their funds profitably by lending them to Jewish merchants. Such practices were then fairly prevalent between the nobles and their Jewish agents in western Europe and were actually legalized by the western rabbis, such as Meshullam. The general prohibition against forming partnerships with Gentiles, however, fortified by similar Muslim laws directed against partnerships between Muslims and infidels, at least prevented the formation of banking companies in which the

[164] C.M. on B.M. V, 7; S.M. Comm. 198; M.T. Malveh ve-loveh 5, 1–2; Resp. Nos. 115–16, based on Sifre on Deut. ed. Friedmann, No. 263 and B.M. 70b–71a. Cf. also RABD, *Haggahot Maimuniot* and the other commentaries, *ad loc.*, and Y.D., 159. Amram Gaon's responsum is printed in *Sha'arei ṣedeḳ*, IV, 2, 20, fol. 40a. Cf. also *ibid.*, No. 7, fol. 35b, where the gaon takes pains to persuade his inquirers not to excommunicate a creditor lending on interest to Gentiles.

Jewish partner would become the creditor of Gentile borrowers and the Gentile partner would grant loans to Jews.[165]

Viewing the totality of the Maimonidean restatement of the Jewish laws of usury, one easily perceives that these legal precautions hampered but slightly Jewish money lending to Gentiles and were far from eliminating Jewish money lending to Jews. Although the oriental Jews never became so one-sided in their economic endeavor as did European Jewry in medieval England, France, and Germany, a Hebrew author, writing a century later, could nevertheless with but slight exaggeration contrast Palestinian Jewry, deriving its main livelihood from the cultivation of fields and vineyards, with the Babylonian and Southern Italian Jews, "who can rely only upon usury." The prevailing high rates of interest of 30 percent and over per annum made this phase of banking, notwithstanding its economic as well as legal risks, most profitable and attractive in the period of Islam's great economic expansion. Despite its retrogression in the subsequent centuries, money lending still was, together with the related field of tax farming, the main source of economic and political power for individual Jews on top of the social ladder and through them greatly influenced the status of all Jewry in Muslim lands. Maimuni must

---

[165] M.T., *ibid.*, 5, 4–5, based on B.M. 70b–71. Other rabbis were more lenient; cf. the commentaries and Y.D. 169. For Meshullam's opinion, cf. Ginzberg, *Genizah Studies*, II, 200, 220. Cf. also Hoffmann, *Geldhandel*, p. 84. The rigid prohibition of partnership with Gentiles in M.T. Sheluḥin ve-shutefin 5, 10 is based on Bek. 2b, Sanh. 63b, but fails to take cognizance of those contradictory statements in the Talmud which induced some Tosafists to take a more lenient view. Cf. *Tosafot* on Bek. 2b; Sanh. 63b s. v. אסור; *Haggahot Maimuniot*; SeMaG Comm. 82 (ed. Venice, 1547, fol. 167d); *Oraḥ Ḥayyim*, 156. Maimuni's unqualified prohibition in M.T. (not so in C.M. on Bek. I, 1), in which he follows Sar Shalom Gaon and Alfasi, may have been influenced by a similar rigidity of the Muslim prohibition; cf. *Enc. of Islam*. s. v. Naṣara; Bergsträsser-Schacht, *op. cit.*, p. 45. Many geonic sources show, however, that these prohibitions by both religious laws were widely honored in the breach. Cf. Mann in JQR, n.s. X, 331 f. M.T. Malveh 5, 5 forbids a Jew to serve as guarantor for a debt contracted by another Jew from a Gentile on interest, because, if forced to pay, the guarantor would become the usurious creditor of a fellow Jew. This interpretation of B.M. 71b insofar corresponded with the practice under Islam that the creditor actually had the choice of approaching first the debtor or the guarantor. Cf. Sachau, *op. cit.*, p. 395. It is likely, therefore, that Maimuni understood the prohibition to cover also such a contingency, and not merely that in which the Gentile laws prescribed that the guarantor be sued first. Cf. De Boton's correct reply to Don Vidal's remarks. *ad loc.*

have realized that the laws, as restated by him, served as but a slight check on "productive" forms of credit and that he was reiterating but a pious wish of the ancient sages when he counseled the Jews to grant gratuitous loans to coreligionists, rather than loans on interest to Gentiles. This advice was clearly in line with Maimonides' general ethical postulates, which he addressed to exceptional individuals, and could have little influence upon the economic behavior reasonably to be expected from the masses. It is, for instance, quite on the same plane as his demand that a scholar should be very exact in computing his own obligations to others, but should be less exact about what others owe him; that in all his commercial dealings he should impose upon himself duties beyond those stated in the Torah and unfailingly keep his word, but be lenient and forbearing with others. "In general, he should be among the persecuted and not among the persecutors, among the offended rather than among the offenders." These ethical injunctions undoubtedly exercised some influence upon innumerable pious individuals who attempted to live up to these lofty expectations, but they coud not serve as a foundation for normative compulsory laws. They were still less effective in the realm of hard and fast reality.[166]

7. SLAVERY

Like his Muslim and most of his Christian contemporaries, Maimonides takes the institution of slavery for granted. To the medieval oriental, as to the ancient mind "slavery was a fixed and accepted element of life and no moral problem was involved." Living in a world in which slaves supplied a part of agricultural and industrial labor and the bulk of domestic employment, Maimuni regarded slavery as a natural, though "accursed," state, inflicted upon the individual through God's will. He certainly saw no reason to depart from the well-established attitude of the biblical and talmudic legislators. Many of their laws, to be sure, like

[166] M.T., *ibid.*, 5, 7, based on B.M. 70b; De'ot 5, 13, based on B.Ḳ. 93a; Yoma 86a, and so forth. The statement of Kalonymos ben Kalonymos in his *Masseket Purim*, IV, 13: אבל בני בבל ואיטליה של יון אין להם על מה שיסמכו אלא על הרבית (*c.* 1300) is partly borne out by numerous earlier sources quoted by Mann in JQR, n.s., X, 310 ff.; Björkmann, *op. cit.*, p. 89; Fischel, *op. cit.*; Louis Massignon, "L'Influence de l'Islam au moyen âge sur la fondation et l'essor des banques juives," *Bulletin d'études orientales de l'Institut français de Damas*, I (1931), 3–12.

numerous other regulations embodied in his *Code*, have a purely
theoretical import. He devotes about one-half of the entire section
on slavery to the position of "Hebrew" slaves. At the same time
he clearly indicates that such slaves disappeared from Jewish life
with the discontinuance of the observance of the Jubilee year,
i.e., the end of the First Commonwealth.[167] Nevertheless, his restatement of these obsolete talmudic laws throws characteristic light
on his views concerning both Gentile slavery and Jewish free labor,
between which Hebrew slavery occupies an intermediary position.

Maimuni does not consider at all the problem of philosophic
justification of slavery, such as had been attempted by a few
Graeco-Roman and Christian thinkers. For him it is simply a
matter of positive legislation, inasmuch as the Bible had enjoined
the Jews to exercise permanent dominion over the "Canaanite"
slaves, and not to grant them freedom, except in the case of serious
bodily injuries inflicted upon them by their masters. Like Plato
and Aristotle, he cannot conceal his personal contempt for the
slave, "the lowest among men." Discussing the various blemishes
which, if discovered by the purchaser after the acquisition of the
slave, make the sale null and void, he includes governmental requi-
sition, but not many defects of character. "If a slave is found to
be a thief, robber, kidnaper, constant fugitive, glutton, or the like,
he cannot be returned to the seller, because all slaves are expected
to possess all these bad traits." Nevertheless, Maimonides treats
slaves juridically as human beings rather than as chattels. Only
with respect to minor slaves does he repeat a formalistic decision

[167] *Encyclopedia of Social Sciences*, s. v. "Slavery," by W. L. Westermann
et al.; M.T. 'Abadim 1, 10, based on Ḳidd. 69a, 'Arakin 29a, etc. The talmudic
laws of slavery have been treated by Zadoc Kahn in his *L'Esclavage selon la Bible
et le Talmud*, Paris, 1867; David Farbstein, *Das Recht der unfreien und freien
Arbeiter nach jüdisch-talmudischem Recht*, Bern, 1896; Robert Salomon, *L'Esclavage en droit comparé juif et romain*, Paris, 1931. For Islam, cf. Juynboll, *op. cit.*,
pp. 202 ff., 234 ff.; Sachau, *op. cit.*, pp. 121 ff.; Bergsträsser-Schacht, *op. cit.*,
pp. 38 ff.; Mez, *op. cit.*, pp. 152 ff.; and, for the Jews under Islam, Mann in JQR,
n.s., X, 144 ff.; S. Assaf, "Slavery and Slave Trade among the Jews during the
Middle Ages" (Hebrew), *Zion*, IV (1938–39), 91–125. It is notable that, although
Maimuni was undoubtedly influenced by Alfarabi's condemnation of the primitive
tribes whom he, too, considered as "below the rank of men and above that of
monkeys" (M.N. III, 51; cf. Strauss in *Revue des études juives* C[bis], 27 f.), he
evidently did not adopt the Arab thinker's "natural" justification of slavery on
this score. The fact that many slaves, including Jewish victims of Mediterranean
piracy, hailed from civilized countries clearly militated against the facile equation
of slave with semihuman barbarian.

of R. Ashi that they are to be acquired through "drawing," like chattels. Adult slaves, possessing a will of their own, may be acquired in five different ways.[168] We shall presently see what important effects the slaves' independent will, as well as its legal limitations, had upon their economic function for Jewry under Islam.

How does one become a Gentile slave? Maimonides does not answer this question directly, but from various passages one may reconstruct the following possibilities: (1) birth from an unfree mother, regardless of the father (see below); (2) captivity in war, including piracy (these two sources of slavery were acknowledged in almost all slave-owning societies, including Islam); (3) captivity as the result of royal decree imposing servile status upon the king's own subjects for various sins of commission and omission, and especially for tax defaults (Maimuni restates here the talmudic recognition of a practice which had been fairly prevalent in Sassanian Persia, but which had been wholly abandoned under the rule of Islam); (4) self-sale of the slave; (5) the sale of children by an impoverished father; (6) the sale, by the courts, of an insolvent thief who is unable to pay the prescribed fine; (7) the initiatory ablution of a kidnaped child or foundling by a Jew, with the intent

[168] S.M. Comm. 235, based on Giṭṭin 38b; M.N. III, 39; M.T. Mekirah 15, 13, based on Tos. B.B. IV, 7, 403; M. Abot II, 8; Ḳidd. 11a, and so forth. Cf. also Ginzberg, *Geonica*, II, 106. Maimuni not only adds several categories to the talmudic designations of thief and קוביוסטוס, but also translates the latter by the harsh גונב נפשות (kidnaper). This explanation, although given also by Gershom and Rashi, is evidently incorrect. Etymologically it can only mean a dice player, as translated by Hananel and the Tosafists, *ad loc*. Cf. also Alexander Kohut, *Aruch Completum* (Vienna, 1926), VII, 56; Samuel Krauss, *Griechische und lateinische Lehnwörter* (Berlin 1898), p. 501. Maimuni neither hesitated to attach to the slave the opprobrium of professional kidnaping, instead of the milder charge of professional gambling, nor to add, on his own initiative, the generalization that all slaves are like that. M.T., *ibid.*, II, 1–4; Matenot 'aniyim 8, 17; 'Abadim 5, 1; C.M. on Ḳidd. I, 3, based on Ḳidd. 22b., and so forth. The משיכה of adult slaves is described, in accordance with talmudic law, as forcible seizure. In M.T. Zekiyah u-mattanah 2, 17, based on Ḳidd. 23a, Maimuni explains the effect of the decease of an heirless convert to Judaism upon the status of the latter's slaves. Adult slaves, able to make use of the free right of appropriation in such an ownerless (*hefḳer*) estate, become immediately free. "But minor slaves are like cattle and he who seizes them acquires them." Karo, in H.M. 275, 29, repeats verbatim Maimuni's statement, but omits the comparison with cattle. Muslim economists, for instance, Abul Fadl, sometimes enumerated slaves among the household animals. Cf. Mahmassani, *op. cit.*, p. 80.

to use him as a slave. Maimonides seems to have omitted only one ancient source of slave supply: the seizure of an insolvent debtor by his creditor, directly or through the intervention of a court. This institution, recorded also in ancient Israel, had come into disrepute in subsequent centuries, and Maimuni specifically repudiates it with respect to the Hebrew slave. His failure to mention it also in connection with Gentile slaves is very likely due to his feeling that the Jews would have to respect in these matters the legislation of those nations from which the slaves might be imported. Under Islam, in any case, all these methods, except the first two, had been suppressed by law. This consideration, indeed, may have influenced his reticence in discussing the origin of Gentile slavery, while he clearly states his views on the sources of Hebrew bondage. In practice the Jewish slaveholders undoubtedly derived their supply less through breeding — the reproductive power of the slaves was probably as low under Islam as it was in the other slave-owning communities — than through purchase. They bought them, directly or indirectly, from war lords operating along the empire's frontiers from Turkestan and Ethiopia to France and Germany. The Cairo-Fustat of Maimonides was speedily developing into the biggest slave market of the Near East.[169]

[169] M.T. 'Abadim 8, 20; 9, 1–4, in conjunction with *ibid.*, 1, 1–2, 5, based on numerous talmudic sources. The latter passages referring to a Hebrew slave undoubtedly allow the deduction *a fortiori* for Gentile slaves. Only the sale of an insolvent debtor (practiced in ancient Israel, but abolished under the Second Commonwealth; cf., for instance, II Kings 4:1, and Asher Gulak's *Toledot ha-mishpaṭ ha-ibri bi-teḳufat ha-Talmud* [*A History of Jewish Law in the Talmudic Period*] [Jerusalem, 1939], I, 149 f.), which is here strictly prohibited, may still have been regarded as permissible in a country which generally tolerated it. The reference in 1, 5 to the right of the Jewish community to enslave a misbehaving Jew, based on B.M. 73b, is evidently tied up with Hebrew slavery and has no practical importance for Gentile slaves. For 8, 20, cf. C.M. on Makshirin II, 7; M.T. Issurei biah 13, 7; 15, 26, and De Boton's question, *ad loc.* Cf. in general also Y.D. 67, 14–18, where this method of acquisition is totally ignored. To facilitate the transfer of Gentile slaves to Jewish masters, Maimuni interprets (in M.T. 'Abadim 8, 19; 9, 5) the equivocal discussion, in Yeb. 45b–46a, in a sense enabling the Jews to acquire full ownership over the slaves, although the "title" of their previous Gentile owners is necessarily limited to the latter's output alone. He must warn his coreligionists, however, that, if their newly acquired slaves hastened, immediately after the completion of the sale, to be initiated into Judaism for the purpose of obtaining their freedom, they would become free, unless the masters took the necessary precautions. But how should slaves know

As a matter of law a master is entitled to chastise his slave severely, but he must not kill him or injure him permanently. In the case of murder or manslaughter Jewish law extends to the slave the same protection as to an Israelite, namely capital punishment for the offender. This is the more remarkable as a lesser punishment is to be inflicted upon the Jewish murderer of a free Gentile. Following the Talmud, Maimuni qualifies the difference between chastisement and murder by stating that if the injuries cause the slave's death within twenty-four hours, the master is guilty of murder, but if death occurs after a day or more the master escapes prosecution. Maimonides adds, however, as his personal opinion that if the assailant used a knife, a sword, a stone, or merely a fist with the clear intent to kill, the ensuing death of the slave even after a year is punishable by the master's death.[170] Permanent injury, insofar as it involves the loss of the slave's eye or tooth (mentioned in the Bible) or of twenty-four other "visible" members of his body enumerated in the Talmud, leads to his enforced emancipation. The purpose of the law is that he should not "suffer from slavery and mutilation at the same time." Here Maimuni makes the significant exclusion from the talmudic list of injuries of castration and the cutting off of the slave's tongue, both of which are included by Alfasi and other rabbis. One can hardly escape the conclusion that Maimuni is guided here not merely by strictly legalistic considerations, such as the supposed

---

of this provision of Jewish law? According to M.T., *ibid.*, 8, 18, the slave, even while in the service of a Jewish master, must not be taught the Torah at all. Cf. *Sha'arei ṣedeḳ*, III, 6, 29; 36 (fol. 26b, 27b); and Karo's and De Boton's comments on M.T., *loc. cit.*

[170] M.T. Roṣeaḥ u-shemirat nafesh 2, 10–14, based upon Mekilta ed. Hoffmann, 21, 14, 20; Sanh. 52b, 86a, and so forth. This discrimination between murder of a Jew and a Gentile reveals less tolerance than the doctrine of the Hanafite school of Muslim jurisprudence, which demanded full retaliation for the murder of a *dhimmi* by a Muslim. But the other Arabian schools of Shafiyites and Hanbalites and, to a certain extent, of Malikites likewise, demanded different sanctions for the slaying of a believer and that of an infidel. Cf. Bergsträsser-Schacht, *op. cit.*, p. 46. Maimuni explains the preferential treatment of a Gentile slave over a free Gentile or "resident alien" (*ger toshab*) by the fact that "the slave has accepted Jewish commandments and joined the heritage of the Lord." He personally (יראה לי) emphasizes the psychological element of the intent to kill, rather than the time elapsing between the fatal injury and death. Cf. also David Hoffmann's note ('ק) to his edition of the *Mekilta*, p. 129.

invisibility of these injuries, which he himself emphasizes. The trade in eunuchs for the numerous oriental harems was such an integral part of the flourishing slave trade that Jewish dealers would have been greatly handicapped in competition with their Muslim and Christian rivals if the performance of the requisite operation had entailed the loss of the slave. Maimonides offers further protection to the master or dealer by stating that such loss may be decreed only by a court of superior learning. One wonders how frequently an impecunious slave, as a rule unfamiliar with Jewish law, had a chance to appeal to such a court. There were also other procedural difficulties (e.g., the slave's inability to testify) which greatly weakened this type of protection extended to slaves.[171]

Legally the master is also entitled to impose the hardest type of labor upon his Gentile slave. Maimuni stresses the point, however, that both piety and wisdom dictate that a Jew should be compassionate and charitable to his slave, not impose upon him too severe a yoke nor oppress him, but that he should let him share in his own food and treat him with dignity and humanity. Indeed Maimuni becomes rhetorical when he tries to emphasize the difference which ought to prevail between Jewish and Gentile

[171] C.M. on Ḳidd. I, 3; M.T. 'Abadim 5, 4–5, 17; M.N. III, 39, based on Ḳidd. 24–25. Cf. also C.M. on Nega'im VI, 7. The inclusion of castration is clearly outside the controversy of Ḳidd. 25a. It is so understood by Rashi and Alfasi, but Maimonides chooses to interpret it into the text and thus out of the list, without, of course, wishing to encourage the performance of such an operation, which he himself declares to be strictly prohibited by biblical law. Cf. S.M. Prohib. 361; M.T. Issurei biah 16, 10–11, based on Shab. 110b–111a. Asher b. Yehiel suggests a compromise formula with respect to an outwardly recognizable or unrecognizable form of castration. Cf. Karo's comments on 5, 4 and Y.D. 267, 28. For this reason the Jewish slave traders preferred to acquire slaves from Gentiles with the understanding that they be castrated before delivery. This procedure was specifically permitted by one of the geonim, cf. *Teshubot hageonim*, ed. by N. N. Coronel (Vienna, 1871), No. 78. Cf. also Assaf's remarks in *Zion*, IV, 100, n. 62, and the question raised by De Boton, *ad loc.*, with respect to the cutting out of the slave's tongue. Karo's intepretation of 5, 17 in a way favoring the slave is hardly tenable in the face of the final פטור מלשלמו, which shows that the first פטור does not refer to sacrifice, but to the obligation to liberate the slave. The milder view is taken by Nahmanides and others. Cd. *Haggahot Maimuniot, ad loc.*, and Y.D. 267, 40. Further procedural aggravations for the slave are the requirements of a deed of manumission on the part of the master, instead of automatic liberation, and the provision that the Gentile slave must prove that he had already been properly circumcised and subjected to the required ablutions.

slave owners, because cruelty and haughtiness is to be found among the Gentiles only, while "the descendants of Abraham, i.e., Israel," have pity upon all creatures. Indeed he feels that all the precepts concerning slaves, as restated in his *Code*, "reflect only acts of pity, mercy, and kindness to the poor."[172]

Such consideration applies especially to the Sabbath rest. Although, unlike animals, slaves have their own mind and will, one ought to guard them against work on Sabbath. In a statement quoted in his name, Maimuni also stresses the moral obligation to refrain from disturbing their Sabbath even in matters not strictly prohibited by law. For example, one should not order a slave to fetch an excess of water or awake him from his sleep. Chastising a slave on Sabbath is not only foolishness of ignorant persons, but also a great sin in the eyes of those who understand the intention of the Torah. It is characteristic of Maimuni that in this insistence upon the slave's Sabbath rest, as in his general injunction to treat slaves kindly, he advances merely ethical reasons. He totally neglects the economic arguments advanced by Bryson and his successors, who saw therein a great stimulus for the increased productivity of the slave's labor.[173]

A Gentile slave is, indeed, expected to observe a certain minimum of Jewish law. In the first place, every male slave ought to be circumcised as soon as possible. If an adult slave refuses to be circumcised within twelve months after his acquisition, he must be disposed of to a Gentile master. This extreme solicitude of the rabbis was due less to conversionist motives than to the wish to increase the slave's attachment to the family of the master and in some cases to prevent his turning informer to hostile outsiders. Maimuni allows, however, the keeping of an uncircumcised slave, if this had been made a condition by the previous Gentile owner, but the slave must in any case observe the seven Noahidic commandments, thus occupying in general the biblical position of a

---

[172] M.T. 'Abadim 9, 8 — a dramatic finale of the section dealing with slaves; M.N. III, 39. The emphasis upon Israel's exclusive descent from Abraham, is, of course, a pointed denial of the equality in rank of such descent of the Arabs. Cf. Outlook, p. 20.

[173] M.T. Shabbat, 20, 14; Ḳobeṣ 53a; Plessner, *op. cit.*, pp. 168 ff. For Maimuni's emphasis upon the obligation to enforce Sabbath observance upon a fully converted slave only, cf. *Teshubot ha-geonim*, ed. by Harkavy, No. 11. Cf. also the next note.

"resident alien." Refusal by the slave is punishable by immediate execution. Maimuni realizes, however, that this regulation was of little practical significance in his time, and that there were in Egypt and elsewhere numerous slaves belonging to Jews who adhered to their former pagan religion. The master could, in fact, find an easy subterfuge in the Muslim prohibition of converting any Muslim or "protected subject" to one of the non-Muslim religions. This prohibition could be interpreted as tantamount to a general condition, in advance of the acquisition, that the slave should not be converted to the master's creed.[174]

Once circumcised, a slave has in many ways the position of a free Jew, and the Jewish community is obliged to redeem him from captivity. An uncircumcised slave, however, does not enjoy this privilege, nor is he fully protected against murder and permanent injury. Even a circumcised slave, on the other hand, is not subjected to all the obligations of a full-fledged Jew. Like a Jewish

[174] S.M. Comm. 215 (cf. Heller's n. 6); M.T. Milah I, 1, 6; Melakim 9, 2, based on Ḳidd. 29a, Yeb. 48b, 'A.Z. 64b, Sanh. 56b. The fear of disloyal slaves is well reflected in the geonic responsa printed in *Teshubot ha-Geonim*, ed. by Harkavy, Nos. 11, 431. Cf. also *Sha'arei ṣedeḳ*, III, 6, 1; 20–21 (fol. 23a, 25b, 26a); Ginzberg, *Geonica*, II, 74, 81, 189 f., 197; Assaf, in *Zion*, IV, 92 f. RABD's excited objection that "we cannot now execute anybody," is beside the point, not only on strictly legalistic grounds, as stressed by Karo, *ad loc*. It seems that by immediately adding that "we accept 'resident aliens' only when the Jubilee year is being observed" Maimuni himself indicated clearly that the required observance of the seven Noahidic commandments had little bearing upon reality. Cf. also M.T. Issurei biah 14, 7–9, where Maimuni makes it perfectly clear that a slave purchased from a Gentile should be circumcised and, like a proselyte, taught the fundamentals of Judaism, provided he freely consents to do so. The period of twelve months is granted to obtain such consent, but where it is clearly stipulated that he should not be converted at all, he ought to be immediately resold to a Gentile. RABD objects to that, too; and other rabbis, such as Nahmanides take cognizance of the undeniable existence of numerous pagan slaves among Jews. Don Vidal, in his comment on M.T. Shabbat 20, 14, excuses his lengthy harmonistic discourse by the fact that this third type of unconverted slaves "is constantly found." In M.T. 'Abadim 8, 12, Maimuni himself seems to relax his stringent demands and to compromise with facts. The equation of governmental prohibition with a general stipulation in advance was subsequently made by Mordecai b. Hillel ha-Kohen on Yebamot No. 41, and adopted by almost all rabbis. Some later rabbis went a step further and expressed the opinion that, if a third person, through ablution, initiated a female slave into Judaism without the master's permission, he became personally responsible for the damage accruing therefrom to the master. This opinion was later recognized as authoritative by Isserles and others. Cf. Y.D. 267, 4, 11.

woman, he is exempted from many positive commandments, such as the duty to pray, to wear phylacteries, and to study the Torah. As a matter of fact, he must not study the Torah, even if he is desirous to do so.[175]

On account of this partial conversion of the slave to Judaism, the ancient sages had adopted a series of safeguards of a religious as well as Palestinocentric nature, which Maimonides does not hesitate to restate in a fashion which makes them appear as binding for his own day. One must not sell a slave, included in the Jewish fold, to a Gentile or a Jewish sectarian. In the case of contravention, the slave immediately becomes free.[176] The same sanction

[175] M.T. Matenot 'aniyim 8, 14; 'Abadim 5, 5; Talmud torah 1, 1, and so forth, based on Giṭṭin 37b, Ḳidd. 25a, 29b, Ket. 28ab, and other passages. With respect to the study of the Torah, cf. the somewhat less rigid stand of the geonim in Sha'arei ṣedeḳ, III, 6, 29; 36, fol. 26bf.; Ginzberg, Geonica, II, 75 f., 83 f. The vital distinction between the circumcised and the uncircumcised slave with respect to both redemption and freedom as a result of permanent injury seems to be derived from Maimonides' own interpretation of the sources.

[176] M.T. 'Abadim 8, 1–5, based on Giṭṭin 43b–44a. Of course, the rabbis realized that the Gentile purchaser would hardly respect the Jewish demand that the slave be given freedom. Maimuni therefore added the provision that the former Jewish master should try to repurchase the slave at a price up to ten times the amount which he had received. Through this interpretation he greatly limited the practical effect of this talmudic penalty. According to some of his geonic predecessors, a regular tenfold fine was to be imposed upon the transgressor, and the amount diverted to charitable causes within the Jewish community. Cf. Sha'arei ṣedeḳ, III, 6, 5; 19; 37 (fol. 23b, 26a, 27b) and Mann, in JQR, n.s., X, 145. Following some geonic teachers and Alfasi, moreover, Maimuni declared this penalty to be operative only if imposed by an ordained court. This provision nullified the entire sanction and removed a serious obstacle in the way of the Jewish slave traders who wished to dispose of their wares to Gentile masters, thus evoking, for example, Asher b. Yeḥiel's vigorous protest. Cf. Karo's comment, ad loc. Of course, the uncircumcised slave could freely be sold to a Gentile or into a foreign country, and hence most slaves were apparently uncircumcised. Another method of evasion was to mortgage the circumcised slave as security for a loan from a Gentile, with the understanding that in case of the master's refusal to pay the debt at a stipulated date, the slave should remain in the "creditor's" possession. To be sure, Jewish law demanded that the borrower stipulate that the new slaveholder should own merely the slave's products, and not the slave himself. But since, according to that law, all Gentile ownership of slaves was theoretically reduced to such control over the revenue, this condition was purely nominal. In practice, the Gentile who acquired slaves through such credit transactions would pay little attention to these minutiae of Jewish law. One wonders whether אפילו לכותי in 8, 5 refers to a real Samaritan, as interpreted by Karo. According to ibid., 6, 6, the Samaritans are to be treated

applies to the sale of a slave from Palestine to a Jew residing in a foreign locality, even to neighboring Akko. The Jewish purchaser abroad is to be forced by the courts to emancipate the slave. Furthermore,

> if a slave declares his intention to emigrate to Palestine, we force the master to emigrate with him, or to sell him to another master who is willing to take him to Palestine. If a Palestinian master wishes to go abroad, he can take along his slave only with the latter's consent. This law is to be enforced at any time, even today when the country is in Gentile hands.

One can hardly imagine that such a law was at all operative in a period when an insignificant minority of the Jews resided in the country of their forefathers. Maimuni's Egyptian coreligionists would have been wholly at the mercy of their slaves' whimsical desires to settle in Palestine, had it not been for the prevailing difficulty in obtaining court action in favor of slaves and the undoubtedly widespread practice of refraining from circumcising at least those slaves who were intended for resale to uncircumcised masters.[177]

---

altogether like Gentiles. It is more likely that Maimuni wished to prohibit the sale of circumcised slaves to Karaites, whom he placed practically on a par with the ancient Samaritans. He thus incidentally answered in the affirmative a question left open in the Talmud.

[177] M.T., *ibid.*, 8, 6–9, based on Giṭṭin 43b–45a and Ket. 110b. Maimuni interprets the לאתויי עבדים in Ket. in a subjective rather than objective sense, as Rashi and others understood it, thus making masters dependent on their slaves' wishes. He decides also, in S.M. Prohib. 252–55; M.T., *ibid.*, 8, 10–11, that a fugitive slave from abroad should be treated in Palestine as a full-fledged proselyte and merely made to promise to indemnify his master when able to afford it. This interpretation is given also by Jacob Tam, notwithstanding Joseph b. Yom Tob's self-evident objection that, in this case, "all slaves could get rid of their masters by fleeing to Palestine." Cf. *Tosafot* on Ket. 110b s. v. הכי. However unrealistic this interpretation may be, it helped to explain away the still more radical demand of the Deuteronomist (23:16) that no fugitive slave be returned to his master. The rabbis reduced this highly humanitarian postulate to the case of either a slave fleeing from a Gentile owner or one deserting a Jewish slaveholder abroad, after a pledge to make good the loss. Cf. Onkelos' translation of, and Rashi's, Ibn Ezra's and Nahmanides' comments on that biblical passage. It is to be noted that Maimonides' extreme views are shared by most of his successors; cf. Y.D. 267, 82–85, and the commentaries thereon. The evidence collected by Mez (*op. cit.*, p. 162) indicates that the masses of runaway slaves constituted a serious problem in the tenth-century caliphate.

Of great interest is the position of the slave in family matters. Although a member of the Jewish community, the circumcised slave is by no means a member of the Jewish *familia*. For Maimuni a slave is not fully human in matters of sex. While deciding in the affirmative the controversial point as to whether homosexuality and sodomy are capital crimes in the case of slaves, he nevertheless states peremptorily that legal matrimony may be established only between Jews or between Gentiles, but not between slaves or between slaves and Jews. The prohibition of incest, consequently, does not apply to them and "as long as he is a slave he may marry his own mother." A master may freely give his female slave to his own or to another man's slave; in fact, he may without scruple give her simultaneously to two slaves, "because they are like cattle." Children of slaves follow the status of the mother. If the mother is a full-fledged Jewess, the slave's paternity has no effect upon the civil standing of the child. But if the mother is a slave, the child likewise becomes a slave. In contrast to other illegitimate children, who in Jewish law enjoy full equality in regard to inheritance from their father, the child of a female slave and a free Israelite has no rights of inheritance at all. Moreover, the existence of such a child does not free the wife of its father (including its own mother after her liberation and lawful marriage) from the obligation of the levirate marriage, because it is regarded as legally nonexistent.[178]

It is not likely that the conditions were vastly different two centuries later. See also Mann, *Texts*, II, 91; and Raphael Mahler, "Studies in the Socio-Political Conditions of the Babylonian and Persian Jews in the So-Called Geonic Period" (Yiddish), *Jiwobleter*, XI (1937), 178, note 14.

[178] C.M. on Temurah VI, 2; Ḳidd. III, 12; M.T. Issurei biah 12, 11–14; 14, 17–19; 15, 3; Yibbum va-ḥaliṣah 1, 4; Ebel 2, 3; 'Abadim 9, 1, based upon Sanh. 58b, Niddah 47a, Yeb. 45ab, 78ab, Ḳidd. 68ab. In M.T. Ebel 12, 12, based on Berakot 16b, Maimuni states generally that one does not mourn a deceased slave in the usual way, nor does one console his master through the recitation of the usual formula, "but one says to him, as one would say over the loss of his ox or donkey: may the Lord replenish thy deficiency." In 'Abadim 9, 1 he emphasizes the fact that it makes no legal difference whether the mother of the master's child is his own or somebody else's slave. This is in line with M.T. Gerushin 10, 19; Naḥlot 4, 6, where he expressly combats various opinions of his predecessors who wished to establish some such difference. They evidently tried to compromise on a social phenomenon which they did not wish to encourage, but some hardships of which they tried to mitigate. They were also concerned

Through these harsh regulations, Maimuni, in some respects going beyond the talmudic law, tries to discourage sex relationships between the Jews and their Gentile slaves. This was particularly important in the Muslim countries, where slaves were generally included in the harems of the most prominent dignitaries of the state and mosque, and where the majority of the caliphs themselves were descendants of female captives. Just as under Sassanian Persia Jews consistently fought for the preservation of their family purity by suppressing incestuous relations, which were widely prevalent among their Persian neighbors, so also under Islam they placed the cohabitation with female slaves under stringent sanctions. Public opinion often effectively interfered where the slightest suspicion appeared justified, and an interesting case of this kind is recorded in a Maimonidean responsum. Maimuni must admit that the convicted lawbreaker cannot be sentenced to flagellation, according to biblical law. Nevertheless, he tries to impress the severity of the transgression upon the mind of the reader by pointing out that one thus despoils one's own offspring by making them slaves and infidels. Even in the use of the intermediary type, the *shifḥah ḥarufah*, whom he defines as "turning from the state of slavery to the state of marriage," sexual intercourse is to be punished by adminis-

---

with the effects of such extramarital relations upon the laws of divorce and levirate marriage. Maimuni declines to follow even the intermediary solution suggested by Alfasi. Cf. Don Vidal's comments on Naḥlot 4, 6, and the sources quoted by Schwarz in MbM, I, 351 f. Cf. also the conflicting opinions discussed in the commentaries on Y.D. 267, 69, and, for punishments far transcending in severity the rabbinic type of flagellation suggested by Maimuni, *Sha'arei ṣedeḳ*, III, 6, 13; 38; 42 (fol. 25a, 27a, 28b); and the sources cited by Tykocinski, *op. cit.*, pp. 174 ff. Maimuni himself cannot quite escape the impact of reality, however. In Resp. No. 154 he advises his inquirers to induce a young Jew suspected of illicit relations with one of his female slaves to liberate and marry her, although he clearly realizes that he thereby runs counter to a talmudic law. He does it, he contends, merely "for the welfare of the penitents." That the Jewish public was not inclined to rely wholly upon these legal prohibitions is evidenced by several extant marriage contracts (from a Muslim environment of a later age) in which the bride makes the bridegroom promise that during her lifetime he will not take another wife, wife-slave, or concubine, except with her consent, and that he will not "have in his employ a female slave that is objectionable to her." Cf. Louis M. Epstein, *The Jewish Marriage Contract* (New York, 1927), pp. 272 f., and, for the connection between these safeguards and the Maimonidean views on concubinage, the same author's "The Institution of Concubinage among the Jews," *Proceedings of the American Academy for Jewish Research*, VI (1934–35), 182 f.

tering flagellation to the slave and forcing the Jewish male to offer a sacrifice. This is, he points out in his *Guide*, one of the few transgressions in which an inadvertent act is as severely punished as one performed with premeditation, because of the great frequency of the temptation. He well epitomizes his views in another connection in the following epigram: "slaves do not exist for sexual purposes, but for work."[179]

Thus having legally eliminated concubinage, one of the major factors of almost all slave-owning societies, from Jewish slaveholding — of course, not from the Jewish slave trade supplying concubines to non-Jews — Maimuni centers his attention upon other, more strictly economic functions of slaves. Unfortunately the factual material in his writings and in those of his predecessors under Islam is too scarce to allow for a satisfactory explanation of the role of slave economy in the Jewish economic structure. Jewish slaveholders could employ their slaves in agriculture and industry. But it seems that, perhaps even more than their Muslim contemporaries, they found it unprofitable to make extensive use of slave labor in these spheres. Free labor was relatively cheap, the cost of slaves rather high. Combined with the widespread scarcity of capital, it made the investment of 200 dirhems and over for each slave even less remunerative to Jews, who could easily lend the equivalent amount to their Gentile compatriots at a high rate of interest. The security of the investment suffered from widespread diseases and high mortality rate, especially in the slave population. The responsibility for the maintenance of a slave in his old age, in his years of illness, and in particular during the seasonal inactivity in agriculture or in the frequent industrial crises, made his productive employment profitable only in those exceptional periods when the wages of the free laborers were considerably above sheer maintenance levels. The absence of latifundia and large-scale industries in the Muslim world generally prevented the rise of slave labor *en masse*.

It seems that the Gentile slaves belonging to Jews were somewhat more extensively employed in commerce. The rabbinic principle that "the slave is like the master's hand," like the simile

---

[179] Resp. No. 154, cf. the last note; C.M. on Keritot II, 4–6; M.T. Issurei biah 3, 14–17 (insisting upon the rabbinic type of chastisement for the adult male offender); 12, 13; M.N. I, 39; III, 41, based upon Ker. 10b–11b, and so forth; M.T. Mekirah 15, 12, possibly paraphrasing Mar Samuel's homily on Lev. 25:46: לעבודה נתתיו ולא לבושה in Niddah 47a. Cf. also the sources quoted by Assaf, in *Zion*, IV, 98 ff.

of the Arabian economists that commercially employed slaves are like "legs" upon which rests the burden of the enterprise, made such an unfree employee a most useful instrument in the transaction of business. Any arrangements made by the slave in the name of his master were binding upon the other party, but could be repudiated by the master by a simple declaration to this effect. Unlike Roman and Muslim law, the rabbinic regulations did not allow for the Gentile slave managing an independent enterprise in his own behalf. Maimonides' intimation of the possibility of establishing a sort of *peculium* for the Hebrew slave merely puts into bolder relief his uncompromising insistence upon the talmudic principle that "all that the [Gentile] slave acquires is acquired for the master." Even gifts do not belong to the slave, unless the donor specifically stipulates that they shall not belong to the master. The slave's usefulness was further enhanced by the master's limited liability for damages caused by his slave to third persons. In most cases the slave alone was held responsible, even though the amount of the damage could not be collected from him until after he had obtained his freedom and amassed earnings of his own. On the other hand, damages inflicted upon the slave were immediately collectible for the benefit of his master.[180]

In general, however, slaves were principally used in domestic employ in Jewish as well as in Muslim houses. C. H. Becker is essentially right in stating that, under Islam, slavery as a whole was principally "a morally elevated solution of the problem of domestic help." In the case of the Jews, we learn from an earlier responsum that they favored the employment of Gentile slaves, because it kept the Jewish women away from the wells and other places, where morally objectionable persons used to congregate. It was this prevalent domestic employment which made the partial conversion of the slaves to Judaism so extremely desirable and

---

[180] C.M. on B.M. VIII, 3, based on B.M. 99a, and so forth; M.T. Mekirah 30, 2, following Hai Gaon's interpretation of the often-reiterated talmudic principle that "all that the slave acquires is acquired for his master," Pes. 88b, and so forth, which is literally the same as Justinian's *quodcunque per servum acquiritur, id domino acquiritur.* Cf. also M.T. Sheluḥin ve-shutefin 2, 2, based on M. 'Erubin VII, 6; Ḳidd. 41b, and so forth. M.T. 'Abadim 2, 7 end; 5, 2 in conjunction with *ibid.*, Gezelah va-abedah 17, 13; Zekiyah u-mattanah 3, 12–15; C.M. on Ḳidd. I, 3, based on B.M. 12ab, Ḳidd. 23ab, and so forth. M.T. Ḥobel u-mazziḳ 4, 21–22, repeating B.Ḳ. VIII, 4, and adding the comparison with an insolvent debtor.

which also served to arouse sexual appetites among the masters —
lonely mistresses were not supposed to acquire any male slaves
at all — appetites which had to be combated by those numerous
legal and moral injunctions restated by Maimonides.[181]

It is also in the inheritance of such domestic slaves by more than
one heir, rather than in their belonging to a commercial or industrial
company, that we may see the origin of some of those partnerships
in the ownership of slaves which gave rise to numerous complicated
legal problems. This was particularly the case when one of the
partners decided to liberate the slave, while the other partner or
partners refused to do so. The result was a hybrid legal creature,
a half-free slave, a three-quarters or five-eights free slave, and the
like. The Mishnah had already considered the position of these
complex beings and demanded that their masters be forced to
liberate that part of them which was still enslaved. Perhaps under
the influence of the extensive Muslim discussions on the *muba'ad*,
Maimonides and his contemporaries debate rather frequently the
legal consequences of such partial slavery in various walks of life.
When one such complicated case was brought to Maimuni's attention, he answered in a strictly legalistic vein.[182]

The juridical features of slaveholding had many economic
effects. Originally treated in the Bible as a sort of immovable property, the slaves were placed on a par with movables with respect
to the new legal transactions introduced in the talmudic age. The
result was that in Maimuni's treatment they have traits of both
types. While basically treated as movable property, they are frequently exempted from the operation of the laws affecting this by
being "compared" with land. That is why the theft of a slave is not
subject to the usual fine of the double amount; robbery is not
punished by the excess fine of one-fifth; a partial denial of a claim

[181] C. H. Becker, *Islamstudien*, I, 60; *Sha'arei ṣedeḳ*, III, 6, 6, fol. 23b; *Teshubot
ha-geonim*, ed. by Harkavy, No. 431; Assaf, in *Zion*, IV, 107, n. 113; M.T. 'Abadim
1, 2; 9, 6, based on B.M. 71a. Maimuni's personal view that a woman should be
allowed to acquire male slaves below the age of nine is rejected by Jacob b.
Asher and his successors, on the ground that this purchase might be preparatory
to illicit relations some time later. Cf. Y.D. 267, 19. But they evidently did not
object to her raising male slaves born in her household and possibly allowed her
to keep such slaves as she might have inherited from somebody else.

[182] Cf., for instance, C.M. on Pes. VIII, 1; IV, 5; M.T. Ḥobel u-mazziḳ, IV, 12;
'Abadim 7, 4, 7–8, based on Pes. 87–88; Giṭṭin 41–43; Resp. No. 317. Cf. also
Ibn Gaon's, Karo's and De Boton's comments on M.T.; Y.D. 267, 60, 62–63;
Levi ibn Habib, *Responsa*, No. 85; and, for Islam, Juynboll, *op. cit.* p. 205.

on the defendant's slaves need not be affirmed by a biblical oath. In principle, the regulations concerning the responsibility of the depository or guardian for property intrusted to him should not be applied to slaves given in trust. Nevertheless, Maimuni expresses his personal opinion, supported by that of his teachers, that the guardians should at least be responsible for overt negligence. More strictly adhering to Bible and Talmud, however, he declares that one who kills a slave must indemnify his master by paying him the lump sum of 30 *sela's*, regardless of the value of the slave. Since he had estimated an ancient *sela'* as the equivalent of 6⅓ dirhems, the total indemnity amounted to 190 dirhems. This sum was below the usual price of 200 dirhems and over for an unskilled slave and wholly incommensurate with the cost of a skilled worker or a beautiful woman, which sometimes went into thousands of gold denars.[183] Combined with the perennial problem of fugitive slaves, this weakening of the protective laws for the owner must have made slaveholding for purposes of production even more precarious. Only in domestic employ, where the master's security was considerably enhanced by greater facility of surveillance and where for obvious reasons the permanence and psychological attachment of the slave to the family added strong noneconomic imponderables, did slave tenure remain a widespread feature of Jewish life. The wealthy Jewish bankers, landowners, and state officials, in particular, required the conspicuous display of a large retinue of slaves to impress their Gentile and Jewish compatriots with their superior status and power.

Still less significant was the economic role of the freedmen. Following the Talmud, Maimonides rather frequently refers to the legal status of the freedman and the freedwoman. On the whole,

[183] M.T. Mekirah 2, 1–4 (C.M. on Ḳidd. I, 3); Ṭo'en ve-niṭ'an 5, 1; 10, 4; Genebah 2, 2; Gezelah va-abedah 8, 14; Sekirut 2, 1; Nizḳei mamon 11, 1, based on numerous talmudic sources. Cf. also *Teshubot ha-geonim*, ed. by Harkavy, Nos. 435, 536 ("The slave resembles land and resembles movables"); Gulak, *Yesodei*, I, 38, 92 ff.; and n. 103 above. The prices of slaves seem to have been rising from the eighth to the tenth centuries, when a Nubian female slave was valued at 300 gold denars and a white slave girl at 1,000 denars and over. Cf. Mez, *op. cit.*, pp. 153 f. In the recorded cases of redemption of Jewish captives, the price paid in the eleventh century averaged about 25–33½ gold denars each. Cf. Jacob Mann, *Jews in Egypt*, I, 87 ff., 244; II, 316 f.; Mann, *Texts and Studies*, I, 136 ff., 348 f., 366 ff. In the case recorded in the Maimonidean Resp. No. 379, the undoubtedly exceptional sum of 100 denars was agreed upon between the community of Alexandria and the captive's owner. Cf. also n. 186 below.

their position resembled that of proselytes. In almost all respects treated like full-fledged Jews, they were subject to certain limitations with respect to high offices and the connubium with priests. Other modifications of the law arose from their lack of legal family connections antedating their emancipation. Like the proselytes, for example, they were not supposed to recite "the confession of the tithe," because it included a passage concerning the soil which God had "given us." But they were allowed by Maimuni to refer to the God of "our fathers" in their prayers over the "first fruits." If they did not leave offspring conceived after their manumission, their inheritance became *hefḳer*. Unlike Roman and Muslim law, Jewish law did not retain the permanent relationship between master and freedman in the form of patronage. The freedman was altogether a free citizen, largely equal in rights to all the others. Economically, however, he had a struggle for existence. The humanitarian provisions of Deuteronomy 15:14, which had tried to offer him a minimum of security by obligating the master to provide him with certain necessaries for the new start in life, referred only to the Hebrew slave. The manumitted Gentile slave was frequently worse off than while in slavery, especially if he was released at a period of reduced capacity for work.[184]

All these discussions seem to have had little relation to reality, however. Unlike the Muslim jurists, the rabbis viewed with disfavor the emancipation of Gentile slaves. Perhaps influenced by

[184] M.T. Issurei biah 13, 12; 14, 11, 19; 19, 15–16, based on Yeb. 47b–48a; Ḳidd. 69ab, and so forth. M.T. Ma'aser sheni 11, 17; Bikkurim 4, 3; C.M. on Ma'aser sheni V, 14; Bikurrim I, 4. The latter, referring to the milder decision in j. Bik. I, 4, 64a, mentions only the proselyte, but undoubtedly includes also the freedman. M.T. 'Abadim 3, 14; 5, 3; 6–7, based upon numerous talmudic sources. All money owned by the slave and even all his clothes except those worn by him at the time of his manumission were adjudicated to his master by a gaon in *Sha'arei ṣedeḳ*, III, 6, 31, fol. 27a. The complex regulations concerning the deed of emancipation are explainable in the light of the high legal status enjoyed by the freedman. To eliminate all disputes, especially in family matters, this deed had to be issued, like a writ of divorce, by Jewish rather than Gentile courts (*ibid.*, 5, 5). Various legal sanctions increased the self-interest of the liberated slave in obtaining a proper legal deed. For example, a manumitted slave was open to assault without being able to collect damages, as long as he could not produce his deed of manumission. Neither could his former master raise the claim, since he had lost his ownership over the slave through his declaration, however informal. M.T. Nizḳei mamon 11, 1; Ḥobel u-mazziḳ 4, 11, deciding an open question in Giṭṭin 42b against the freedman. Cf. Don Vidal's, Karo's, and De Boton's comments.

considerations of racial purity, they did not wish to see large-scale absorption of Gentiles into the Jewish community via slavery and emancipation. At any rate, Maimuni reëchoes the talmudic statement that the Levitical lawgiver's injunction: "They shall be your bondmen for ever" (Lev. 25:46) is to be regarded as a positive commandment, and that any uncalled-for manumission of slaves constitutes a violation thereof. To be sure, Maimuni countenanced the liberation of a female slave, with a view to subsequent marriage, as preferable to illicit relations. Neither was the liberation of slaves after the master's death as a reward for faithful lifelong services altogether discouraged. Like his predecessors, Maimuni insists that a testator's will to this effect be liberally interpreted in favor of the slaves. But, on the whole, his and the other rabbis' intrinsic opposition to the emancipation of slaves must have greatly diminished the number of freedmen in the Jewish community. That is probably why our sources have so few references to freedmen. They seem never to have attained a position nor constituted a socio-economic problem in medieval Jewry at all comparable with those of their brethren under Islam.[185]

There was one aspect of Hebrew slavery which made it significant also in the medieval period: the redemption of captives. The Maimonidean statement that a Jew may become master over his fellow Jew if a royal decree allows the putting in bondage of an insolvent or recalcitrant taxpayer was of no practical significance.

[185] S.M. Comm. 235; M.T. 'Abadin 6, 4; 9, 6, based on Giṭṭin 38b, 40a, Soṭah 3a, and so forth; Resp. No. 154, discussed in n. 178 above. The explanation here suggested, viz., the fear of the influx of too many foreign elements, seems to be more satisfactory than that based upon the assumption that the legal curtailment of the owners' right to emancipate their slaves under the Roman Empire influenced also the ancient rabbis. Cf. Krauss, *Archäologie*, II, 98, 497, n. 677. Only so can we understand the consistent approval of the alleged biblical prohibition by the Jewish teachers both in Persia and under Islam. Their attitude is, indeed, in striking contrast to the injunctions of Mohammed and the leading Muslim jurists, who favored, morally as well as legally, the manumission of slaves. Cf. Koran 4, 94, and so forth; Juynboll, *op. cit.*, p. 205; Bergsträsser-Schacht, *op. cit.* p. 41. For Maimuni's realization of the importance of the ethnic element in connection with slavery, cf. n. 187 below. Characteristically, in M.T. 6, 4, Maimuni repeats the talmudic phrase פלונית שפחתי, thus leaving somewhat unclarified the position of the male slave similarly liberated through the will of his master. Like Alfasi, Maimuni interprets the קורת רוח in the Talmud in a rather restrictive sense. Rashi on Giṭṭin 40a s. v. ועושין is still more liberal. Cf. also De Boton's comments. For some geonic sources, cf. Mann, in JQR, n.s., X, 149 f.

Apart from Maimonides' own qualification that such an appropriated Jew should be treated as a slave only when he misbehaves, there existed, to the present author's knowledge, no such royal decree in any Muslim country. However, Jewish captives taken in the frequent wars or seized by Mediterranean pirates abounded, and here were applied those laws concerning the redemption of captives which Maimonides relates to Hebrew slavery. In the case of a Jew's self-sale to a Gentile, the nearest relatives were obliged to ransom him. If they were unable to do so, more distant relations and finally all Jews were obliged to redeem him. Those who paid the ransom were immediately to set him free. In another connection Maimuni states that a Jew who sells himself or his children into bondage or is seized by a Gentile creditor for debts should be ransomed twice and no more. A circumcised Gentile slave is likewise to be redeemed, but he ranks below the ten categories of free Jews, who enjoy successive priority if the available funds prove insufficient for the redemption of all. Although, in a similar division into ten categories of Jews enumerated in the Mishnah in regard to connubium with Jews, the freedman is placed sixth, he is but tenth in rank in the case of redemption. The free proselyte is ninth, because he had never lived in the "accursed" state of slavery. In any case, the redemption of captives has precedence over any other form of charity, and "there is no greater commandment" than this. However, one must not pay a higher ransom for the captive than his market price, in order not to whet the appetite of the pirates; nor should one help him to escape, because this would lead to increased vigilance over, and harsher treatment of the remaining captives. Numerous extant, more or less contemporary documents, especially from Maimuni's own community of Fustat, unmistakably reveal that Jewry as a whole took these injunctions very seriously and time and again strained all its resources in order to redeem from captivity Byzantine and other coreligionists.[186]

[186] C.M. on Giṭṭin IV, 6; Horayot III, 7; M.T. 'Abadim 1, 8; 2, 7; Matenot 'aniyim 8, 10–18, based on Giṭṭin 45a, Horayot 13ab, etc. For the ransom of captives, see n. 183 above. We also possess an autograph letter of Maimonides addressed in 1173 to various communities and requesting their leaders to assist a special messenger dispatched for the collection of such funds. Cf. S. H. Margulies, "Zwei autographische Urkunden von Moses und Abraham Maimuni," *Monatsschrift für Geschichte und Wissenschaft des Judentums*, XLIV (1900), 8 ff. Cf. also Resp. Nos. 223 and 379.

8. FREE LABOR

Free labor, in contrast to slavery, appears to Maimuni as almost exclusively Jewish. We have practically no reference to Gentile laborers for Jews. Even domestic service, which in the Christian Middle Ages was predominantly in the hands of non-Jewish servants, seems under Islam, as in the talmudic era, to have been performed by Jews. This distinction is vital in the consideration of all Maimonidean views on the subject, because free labor is thus distinguished from unfree labor not only as a class, but also as an ethnic and religious group. Maimuni, indeed, places the employment of fellow Jews in domestic service among the highest forms of charity:

The sages have enjoined us to keep as one's domestics poor Jews and orphans rather than slaves; it is better to employ the former so that the descendants of Abraham, Isaac, and Jacob should derive the benefit of one's fortune, and not the descendants of Ham. He who increases the number of his slaves from day to day increases sin and iniquity in the world, whereas the man who employs poor Jews in his household increases merits and religious acts.[187]

Learning a trade and teaching it to one's children is declared by Maimonides to be one of the major obligations of every Jew. Commenting on the famous passage in the *Sayings of the Fathers*: "Love work and hate mastery, and make not thyself known to the government," he states that these three virtues have been juxtaposed

[187] M.T. Matenot 'aniyim 10, 17; C.M. on Abot I, 5, based on Pes. 60b. Cf. also Outlook, pp. 101 ff. Although Maimuni expresses here but a commonplace opinion of the medieval commentators of that Mishnah in Abot, such as Meshullam, Rashi, Jonah Gerondi, and Simon Duran, he formulates it more sharply and evidently wishes to warn his readers against an existing evil. Apart from this general moral injunction, Maimonides, following Tos. Pe'ah III, 1, 20; and j. Pe'ah II, 7, 17a, states that one must not employ Gentile laborers during harvests, because they are not familiar with the laws concerning the gleanings and corners which are to be given to the poor, cf. M.T., *ibid.*, 2, 10. The reference to corners seems to be Maimuni's own addition, evidently in reference to the latitude left the owner in assigning the corner, according to *ibid.* 1, 15. Here and in C.M. on Pe'ah I, 2, Maimonides demands that the owner should leave more than the legally required one-sixtieth of the area whenever the "corner" would become too small to be of any use, when the number of the poor in the community is very large, or when the crop is unusually bountiful. The exercise of such discretion naturally was to be left to the owner himself, or, if necessary, to his Jewish employees, but not to his Gentile workers.

here because they are vital for the welfare of religion and the world. "A man without work gets into difficulties and [ultimately] robs and cheats." In a style reminiscent of modern Jewish apologias, he emphasizes the fact that there were wood choppers and water carriers among the greatest sages of Israel, although his intention is to demonstrate that poverty and hard work should in no way diminish one's devotion to learning. Vocational education is placed on a par with that in Torah and wisdom. If a father, exercising his "legitimate" right of chastisement, accidentally kills his obstreperous son who refuses to be educated along any one of these three lines, he need not suffer exile to one of the asylum cities, the usual fate of accidental slayers. Thus the obligation to work is coupled in rabbinic theory with a sort of moral, if not legal right to work, emanating from the obligation of every Jew, as well as of the community at large to supply employment to needy coreligionists.[188]

As a medievalist Maimuni believes in the objective price of labor. Discussing the legal compensation for working time lost on account of physical injury, or the reward due to the finder for the time spent in returning a lost object to its owner, he states that payment is to be made in the former case to the extent of the *lucrum cessans*, in the latter case only in the amount which is necessary to induce this particular individual to abstain from his regular work for that period of time. While undoubtedly allowing for differences in local wages, he assumes that such compensation may be estimated in each locality with reference to the work in question and need not be computed on the basis of more individualistic considerations. He illustrates the operation of this principle by the example of a money changer and a smith, whose general earning capacity may be the same, but where abstention from work is worth more to the hard-working smith.[189]

[188] C.M. on Abot I, 10; Makkot II, 2–3; M.T. Talmud torah 1, 9; Roṣeaḥ u-shemirat nafesh 5, 5 amplifying Ḳidd. 30b, Makkot 8b, and so forth. Cf. also Rosin, *op. cit.*, p. 125. For somewhat similar teachings of Avicenna, Alghazali, and others, cf. Plessner, *op. cit.*, pp. 47, 86; Mahmassani, *op. cit.*, pp. 67, 83. Nowhere in Maimuni or in these Arabian thinkers do we find a theoretical evaluation of labor as a basic element of value, such as visualized by Aristotle before and Ibn Khaldun after them.

[189] There is a characteristic difference in Maimonides' formulation of the following passages in his Code: M.T. Ḥobel u-mazziḳ 2, 11, discussing the compensation for enforced idleness caused by physical injury, and in Sheluḥin ve-shutefin 6, 2, referring to the compensation for the active partner (cf. n. 153 above), we find the phrase כפועל בטל של אותה מלאכה שבטל ממנה, which evidently

None the less, he favors complete contractual freedom. Disregarding here, as often elsewhere, the pressure of economic inequality, he regards the parties to the contract as absolutely free and equal. That is why, in his opinion, one may employ a free Israelite to perform services which one must not impose upon a Hebrew slave. The ancient protective laws for the latter do not apply to the hired worker, "because he is doing the work of his

---

indicates the loss of all earnings by an average worker of this type and is a literal repetition of Abbaye's statement in B.M. 68ab, and so forth. A similar reasoning is expressed, *ibid.* 8, 1, by שכר עמלו מזונו בכל יום כפועל בטל. In M.T. Gezelah va-abedah 12, 4, however, Maimuni changes the same statement in B.M. 31b to read: כפועל בטל שיבטל מאותה מלאכה שהיה עוסק בה, and explains it specifically to mean that a man returning lost property has no right to demand full compensation for one's normal earnings during the time so consumed, but must deduct the difference between the value of time spent in work or in idleness. C.M. on B.M. II, 9, may be interpreted in the same way. In M.T. Sanh. 23, 5, Maimuni completely rephrases Abbaye's identical statement in Bekorot 29b by ואמר להן תנו לי מה שיעשה תחתי עד שאדון לכם או תנו לי שכר בטלתי, indicating that a judge who is forbidden to charge anything for his judicial function may nevertheless demand compensation to the extent of either the cost of a substitute or that of his own idleness. The latter formula being rather equivocal, one may best explain it in the light of Maimuni's own interpretation in C.M. on Bek. IV, 6. After mentioning the controversy over the meaning of Abbaye's statement, he advances the following explanation, which he underscores as being "wonderful and true." (1) One must not make such estimates on the basis of the particular individual's capacity for work and daily earnings, but on that of the customary earnings in his line of employment. (2) One must also take into consideration the amount of labor usually required in that occupation and the ensuing benefit of idleness. Since the labor of a smith is incomparably harder than that of a money changer, the benefit of rest to the former is so much the more substantial. Assuming that both earn on the average two drachmas a day, you would have to pay for enforced idleness perhaps as much as a drachma and a half to the money changer, and only one half a drachma to the smith. It is evident that Maimuni follows here a clear line of demarcation: the compensation (unless otherwise stipulated in advance) should be reduced to a minimum, if the time is spent in the pursuit of a pious cause, such as the administration of justice or the return of a lost object to its owner; but it should make good the entire loss in earnings sustained by an innocent victim of assault or by an active partner devoting all his time to the company's business. The latter provision was doubly necessary to counteract evasions of the anti-usury legislation, which might have been the original purpose of those silent partnerships. In this interpretation Maimonides runs counter not only to the obviously uniform meaning of Abbaye's statement in all four connections, but also to the opinions of his predecessors, including Hananel, Alfasi, and Rashi. Cf. also *Tosafot* on Bek. 29a s. v. כפועל; the commentaries on M.T.; H.M. 9, 5; 265; Y.D. 177, 2 (generally following Maimonides) and the commentaries thereon.

own free will and on his own decision." With respect to the amount of wages, in particular, there are no legal restrictions upon either employer or employee. Either of them may also freely stipulate the conditions under which the contract should be operative, because all conditions are valid in labor contracts, as in sales contracts. Basically "hiring is but a sale for a definite period." On the other hand, though assuming that there exists an objective price of labor, Maimuni exempts wage contracts from the operation of the laws governing the "just price." In regard to wages, free workers are placed in the same position as slaves, to whom, for reasons discussed above, the ancient laws of "misrepresentation" had never been applied. That is why the underpayment of wages by more than 16.66 percent of the market price does not nullify the contract, whereas a similar underpayment (or overcharge) for the leasing of animals or vessels would immediately have that effect. Bound by a long chain of historic evolution, Maimonides could not radically alter these provisions. His own attitude, nevertheless, becomes apparent when he tries, as a matter of personal opinion, to extend the protection of these laws at least to artisans contracting with customers for a specific job. Artisan associations, moreover, are given the right to regulate their trade in accordance with custom and under the supervision of the community as a whole. In another connection he expresses his moral rather than legal conviction that workers "ought to receive their pay in accordance with their work."[190] Two other significant restrictions of the rights of employers, upon which all rabbis had agreed since the days of the

[190] M.T. 'Abadim 1, 7; Sekirut 7, 1; Mekirah 13, 15–18; 14, 10–11, based on B.M. 56b, and so forth. Cf. notes 104 and 110 above. Maimuni's inclusion of the contracting artisans in the class of those subject to the laws of "misrepresentation" was accepted by the subsequent codifiers as authoritative, despite the objections raised by Nahmanides and Ibn Adret. Cf. Don Vidal's comments on M.T. Mekirah 13, 15; and H.M. 227, 36. For Maimonides' personal view, cf. M.N. III, 42. His insistence upon the validity of contractual conditions beyond and above custom comes to the fore also in the following provision of M.T. Sekirut 5, 6: when hiring a beast of burden one must not load upon it more than the stipulated weight, even if an animal of that sort usually carries heavier loads. An excess load of but one-thirtieth of the contractual burden calls for special remuneration to the owner of the animal, while a greater excess makes the contractor responsible for the animal's breakdown. Nahmanides and others argue that such responsibility exists only where the overloading exceeds the customary (not contractual) load by more than one-thirtieth. Cf. Don Vidal's comment, *ad loc.*, and H.M. 308, 5–6.

Mishnah, operated in favor of workers rather than middle-class artisans. They referred to the hours of labor and the entrepreneur's obligation to feed his employees in part or in full. In both of these matters local custom was declared to be supreme, except where there existed express stipulations in the contract. Even if the employer agreed to pay wages higher than those customarily paid to workers in that particular occupation, he could not exact overtime work, if the workers were unwilling. Neither could he refuse them the type of food customarily expected from him, unless he made his intention perfectly clear before the conclusion of the contract.

Maimonides also describes at great length the mutual obligations of employer and employee in the execution of such "freely" arranged contracts. The employer's most important obligation, as emphasized already by the biblical legislator, consists in the prompt payment of wages. In this respect, says Maimuni, there is but slight difference between a Jewish and a Gentile laborer. The retention of due wages for a single night constitutes a violation of one positive and one negative commandment in the case of a Jewish laborer, and that of one positive commandment in the case of a Gentile worker. In no case is this transgression punishable by flagellation, however, because it is subject to financial restitution. Permanent refusal to pay wages constitutes a violation of four negative commandments and one positive commandment and is exaggeratedly likened to cold-blooded murder.[191] To be sure, the employer may mitigate

[191] M.T. Sekirut 9, 1; 11, 1-2, based upon B.M. 73a, 111ab. While in both passages Maimuni merely repeats the Mishnah's protective laws, we find in them curious deviations. He evidently agrees with *Tosafot* on B.M. 73a s. v. השוכר that contracts may abrogate custom, but ignores the problem of legal presumption concerning the hours of labor where there is no clearly established local custom. Like Alfasi, he fails to repeat Simon b. Lakish's statement, in B.M. 73b, that the normal hours of labor extend from sunrise to sunset and that the laborer's walking time to his place of work is included in that working time, but not his walk home after work. This provision was subsequently included by Jacob b. Asher and Moses Isserles in H.M. 331, 1. The explanation frequently offered (for instance, by Moses Rivkes in his comments thereon) that Maimuni would not mention such a rare case is rightly rejected by Rosanes, *ad loc.* It is much more likely that Alfasi and Maimuni disregarded this passage because it so obviously conflicted with the system prevailing under Islam. Maimuni may also have had in mind his pet advice to all Jews to devote as little time as possible to earning a living and as much as possible to the study of the Torah. Cf. n. 32 above. The apparently innocuous repetition in 11, 1 of the Mishnaic phrase with respect to the *ger toshab*, assumes different meaning in the light of Heller's comment on S.M., p. 63, n. 3. It may perhaps be explained by Maimuni's contention

the harshness of the law by hiring the worker for longer periods, such as a week, a month, a year, or even seven years, since the wages fall due at the end of the contractual period, unless different dates are arranged in advance. Unfortunately Maimuni's repetition of these talmudic laws gives us no indication of the contemporary practice, which probably ranged from daily to annual contracts. According to certain Muslim schools as well as some later rabbis, a triennial contract was the maximum allowed by law. An even more effective means of evasion is the hiring of workers through an agent, or manager. If the latter makes it clear to the worker that the employer is to pay the wages, he is not responsible for the delay, whereas the employer is not responsible because he himself did not do the hiring.[192]

For the protection of the worker, certain general rules are suspended with respect to both breach of contract and proof of the worker's claims. While the complicated regulations concerning withdrawal from a contract sometimes favor the employer, especially if unforeseen circumstances make the work unnecessary before it is started, it is the worker alone who may give up the work without giving any reason in the middle of the contractual period. The worker may even demand the proportionate payment of wages for the time he has worked or, if he is a contractor, the payment of the stipulated sum, proportionately reduced by the amount of work still needed for the completion of the job. Only in emergencies, such as threatened deterioration of the material or provisions for burials and weddings, may the employer engage another worker at higher wages and deduct them from the amount due to the first laborer, who had quit his work without legitimate excuse. The reason for this preferential treatment of the worker is offered through the ancient homily, "because the sons of Israel are My slaves and not slaves of slaves." The usual rules of evidence, whereby the plaintiff must fully prove his claim while the defendant

---

that the *ger toshab* had disappeared from Jewish life since the discontinuation of the Jubilee year observance. Cf. M.T. 'Akum 10, 6; Issurei biah 14, 7–8, based on 'Arakin 29a, and so forth, and the objections to this interpretation raised by RABD and others. Since uncircumcised Gentile slaves, to some extent falling into this category (cf. M.T. Milah 1, 6; n. 174 above), could not be considered by the Mishnah in connection with hiring free labor, Maimuni was induced to extend its range to cover all free Gentile workers.

[192] M.T. Sekirut 11, 2, 4, based on B.M. 110b–111a. Cf. Isserles H.M. 333, 3; Farbstein, *op. cit.*, pp. 43, 57.

need merely take the rabbinic type of oath that he had made the required payment, are reversed in the case of litigations over wages. A laborer hired in the presence of witnesses and claiming his wages at the proper time may obtain his due by swearing that he never received payment. The reason here given is that the employer is too busy with his numerous workers and may more easily make a mistake than the laborer, whose mind is set upon his earnings.[193]

The employer need not furnish food to the laborer, except when local custom prescribes it, but he must allow him, while working on the field, to eat from its produce. The worker ought not to be treated worse than one's ox or donkey, whose muzzling is so strictly prohibited by the Deuteronomic lawgiver. To be sure, the original humanitarian intention of Deuteronomy 23:25–26 was to prevent starvation by enabling any passer-by to help himself from the agricultural produce. In the more capitalistic age of the Talmud or Islam, such infringement upon private ownership appeared untenable. That is why the law was first limited to apply only to workers employed in the cultivation of that particular parcel of land. It was then hedged around by so many restrictions as to become practically meaningless. Restating talmudic law, Maimuni excludes orchards and most truck gardens, limiting this privilege of the worker to the consumption of grapes and grain. The latter could hardly be eaten without being baked into bread at home, but the laborer was forbidden to remove anything from the spot. Neither was he entitled to share it with his family, unless his wife or children happened to work together with him in the field. The employer was free, moreover, to curtail the laborer's right through contractual agreement. The law thus had a moral rather than a practical effect. Similarly the waiter on table, says Maimuni, although not participating directly in the meal, should as a matter of humanity, be given a taste of every dish. That he considers it, however, a favor rather than a right, is clearly illustrated by the example of the benediction over wine which the waiter is to repeat

---

[193] C.M. on B.M. IX, 12; Shebu'ot VII, 1; M.T., *ibid.*, 9, 4; 11, 6, 9, based on B.M. 76b, 112b, Shebu'ot 45ab. Maimonides' decision that the worker's oath is of the biblical kind is in line with his general conviction that all oaths recorded in the Mishnah are of that type. Cf. n. 131 above. The homily on Lev. 25:55 is given as the reason for the worker's privileged position in B.Ḳ. 116b, B.M. 10a. Cf. *Tosafot* on the latter s. v. יכול. Nevertheless, some of Maimuni's predecessors took a stand less favorable to labor even in cases where the work could suffer delay. Cf. Ginzberg, *Geonica*, II, 157, 164 f.

before drinking each cup, since "his drink is dependent on their [the masters'] will and not on his."[194]

On the other hand, the laborer should be extremely careful in fulfilling his obligations toward the master. "He who interrupts his work in order to eat, or eats before the completion of his work, breaks a negative commandment." He is to work with all his strength, emulating the example of Jacob, who was ultimately rewarded with earthly fortune. He must neither starve himself by giving most of his food to his family nor do extra work at night and thus diminish the return of his labor during the day. "Just as the employer is enjoined not to rob the wages of his employee nor to delay their payment, so is the poor [worker] enjoined not to despoil the employer of the work due him, not to waste a moment here and a moment there and dishonestly spend the whole day, but to check carefully his working time." Indeed, the rabbis exempted the laborer from all benedictions before and from some benedictions after the consumption of food, so as not to interfere with the full utilization of his working time.[195]

Employment in certain activities does not in itself exempt the workingman from the general rules affecting his position as a citizen. Lay workers employed in the sanctuary, for example, are not entitled to consume any of the sacred food, although provisions for food may be included in their contract. In such case the Temple administration is to pay them in cash the equivalent of their food. In building the Temple with the help of lay laborers, one ought not to use lumber or stones belonging to sacred property (*hekdesh*) nor devote the building in advance to sacred uses. In either case the workmen may find themselves guilty of the serious crime of sacrilege by making the slightest profane use of sacred objects, such as enjoying the shade of the structure on a hot day or leaning on a stone or beam during their work. To safeguard the workers against unconscious sacrilege due to mistaken measurements, one ought to draw up a contract stipulating payment for each ell of twenty fingers, but actually to pay per ell of twenty-four fingers. The

[194] C.M. on B.M. VII, 2–7; Ma'aserot III, 1–3; M.T. Sekirut 12, 1–14; Ma'aser 5, 9–13, based on B.M. 87a–93a, and so forth. M.T. Berakot 7, 7, based on Ket. 61ab, Ḥullin 107b. Cf. Karo's comments, *ad loc.*, and Oraḥ Ḥayyim 169; 170, 18, 21.

[195] M.T. Sekirut 12, 3; 13, 6–7; Berakot 2, 2, based on Tos. B.M. VIII, 8–9, 388; Berakot 16a. Cf. Don Vidal's and Karo's remarks on these passages. Cf. also S.M. Comm. 19; and Outlook, p. 21

ensuing loss to the worker of 20 percent of his wages is infinitely less important than the possibility of unwittingly committing a grievous sin. Should a priest offer to his laborers (or guests) a meal of the heave offering belonging to him, they are obliged, like other laymen mistakenly consuming sacred food, to pay a fine amounting to five-fourths of the value of the offering, but may demand compensation to the full value of their meal in ordinary food. Forestalling the objection that such a penalty would operate to the disadvantage of the innocent laborer, Maimuni argues from the economic standpoint, that nonconsecrated food would normally exceed in monetary value the heave offering, the consumption of which is limited to a minority of citizens and hence creates but slight demand.[196]

These regulations referring to sanctuary and priestly dues were of purely theoretical importance in Maimonides' day, and are cited here only because of the characteristic light they shed upon the Maimonidean views on the status of labor within the ceremonial system. Of more contemporary interest is, for example, Maimuni's acceptance of the talmudic assumption that many craftsmen and workingmen are frequently away from their families for a long time. Discussing their marital duties, he repeats the talmudic regulation that while men of leisure are expected to cohabit with their wives every day, artisans, such as tailors, weavers, and masons, are supposed to do it twice a week if their place of work is in the same town, and once a week if they work in a different locality. Donkey drivers are to comply with that duty once a week, camel drivers once a month, and sailors only once in six months. Scholars are advised, for the purpose of erotic self-control and for the conservation of their strength, rather than under economic stress, to refrain from exercising their marital rights more than once a week.

[196] C.M. on Kelim XVIII, 9; Terumot VI, 3; M.T. Me'ilah 8, 1, 4; Terumot 10, 10, based on Me'ilah 13a; Men. 98a, j. Terumot VI, 3, 44a. The latter passage is quoted by Samson of Sens in his commentary on M. Terumot VI, 3, as a question of fact, while Maimuni in M.T. interprets it as referring to the economic effect of a diminished demand. In his own remarks in C.M., he merely points out the additional religious responsibility of the priest for misleading his laborers. In his zest to forestall all possible sacrilege, on the other hand, he fails to mention the economically important exception permitting the use of larger measures in contracts affecting precious workmanship by gold and silversmiths. This exception, stated in Men. 96a, had scriptural backing in Job 37:22, according to *Tosafot*, *ibid.*, s. v. הדר. Cf. Karo's comments, *ad loc.*

That is why a woman may object, if her husband wishes to change his calling to the disadvantage of his family ties or to undertake extended commercial journeys to distant localities. She must not object, however, if her scholarly husband finds it necessary for the pursuit of his studies to absent himself for a period of two or three years. Neither may she prevent her "rentier" husband from pursuing a scholarly career.[197]

Maimonides discusses various classes of labor, some of which offer peculiar legal problems. He refers, for example, to shepherds supervising an entire herd, who employ assistants with various specific assignments. In such case, Maimuni states, the responsibility for damages inflicted to a neighbor's property rests with the assistant in charge of the guilty animal, rather than with the general manager of the herd. The talmudic terms *soker*, *ḥoker*, and *mekabbel* are illustrated by various forms of farm tenancy, insofar as the first two represent tenants who pay to the owner stipulated amounts in money or in kind, while the third term refers to share-croppers. Sometimes applying the term *mekabbel* as a more generic denomination for all farm tenants, Maimuni goes to great length in expounding the talmudic laws governing their relationships with the landowners and their responsibilities toward outsiders. It is difficult to say to what extent these regulations reflected the economic realities in Maimonides' time. The material in his *Responsa* and in those of his predecessors is too meager to allow definite historical conclusions. In state-capitalistic Egypt, in particular, farm tenancy was largely a matter of state regulation. There was an increasing accumulation of crown lands on which the farmers served as "emphyteutic" tenants, paying a combination of rent and tax. There was more opportunity for the Jews to engage in

---

[197] C.M. on Ket. V, 6; M.T. Ishshut 14, 1–2; De'ot 5, 4; Issurei biah 21, 11, based on Ket. 61b–62b, etc. Maimuni's decision in favor of the majority opinion, against the evident context of the Talmud and the interpretation of Alfasi, merely adds another illustration to his glorification of scholarly pursuits. Cf. Don Vidal's comment on 14, 2. It is interesting that taking a clue from מפנקי דמערבא in Ket. 62a, Maimuni renders the class of טיילים of the Mishnah by "the strong pampered persons who have no work to do which would weaken their bodies, but eat and drink and sit at home." Jacob b. Asher added the characteristic "and do not pay taxes," while Karo reverts to the original undefined term of "men of leisure" in the Mishnah. Cf. *Eben ha-'Ezer* 76, 1. All of these definitions clearly are reflections of changing contemporary conditions.

large-scale tax farming and in collecting agricultural revenue in kind for the state than in leasing their own lands to Jewish or non-Jewish tenants.[198]

Some forms of labor connected with the performance of a civic duty constituted another sociological problem. Theoretically of a gratuitous nature, these civic labors often required all or most of the time of their devotees and before long became remunerative full-time occupations. Such was the case, especially, with teachers. Maimuni repeats the talmudic regulation that only the Written Law may be taught for a remuneration in those places where payment is customary, but that instruction in the Oral Law should always be given without pay. This difference, which had probably originated from the need of paying for the services of the numerous elementary teachers after the spread of popular education in Jewish antiquity, was rationalized as a distinction between teachers of Scripture, who receive their pay only for supervising the children, keeping them out of mischief, and for the incidental instruction in accents and vocalization, and the intellectual élite giving academic instruction. Maimuni severely attacks those "great men whom greed had blinded and they denied the truth, permitting themselves to charge a fee for judging and teaching under false excuses." He nevertheless emphasizes the obligation of every father to pay for the elementary instruction of his son. In one of his *Responsa* we find a curious personal animus, revealing undisguised hostility to the entire teaching profession in the elementary schools of his day. Replying to an inquirer, he denies the right of elementary teachers to obtain a reward for appearing at court as witnesses, since "they waste so much time every day with futile matters." In contrast, the scribes of the court are entitled to charge for the time lost by appearing in court or rendering services such as writing deeds and the like. Maimuni argues that their reward is not for offering testimony, but for their notarial work.[199]

[198] C.M. on B.Ḳ. VI, 2; B.M. IX, 2; M.T. Sekirut 8, 1–14, and so forth. Cf. Becker, *Islamstudien*, I, 211 ff.

[199] C.M. on Nedarim IV, 3; M.T. Talmud torah 1, 3, 7, based on Ned. 36b–37a; j. Ned. IV, 3, 38c; Resp. No. 194. Maimonides, true to his general opposition to the growing commercialization of learning, does not allow the teacher of Oral Law to charge even the accepted minimum wage for time spent in teaching. This is doubly remarkable since he was forced to permit such charges to judges for the time spent in the exercise of their function. Cf. n. 189 above. Other medieval rabbis were more lenient. Cf. the commentaries on M.T., *loc. cit.*; Nissim's comments on Ned. 37a; Y.D. 246, 5.

Reviewing the entire structure of rabbinic labor legislation, as summarized by Maimonides, one can hardly escape the feeling that much more attention was paid to the problems arising from farm tenancy and contracting than to employee labor in the stricter sense. Undoubtedly in the talmudic period the classes of farm tenants, artisans, and men engaged in some form of transportation numerically exceeded those of free wage earners. Subsequently the first of these groups must have greatly declined, while the number of Jewish craftsmen of all kind, as well as of donkey and camel drivers, shipowners, and so forth doubtless increased steadily during the first centuries of Islam's marvelous expansion. There is every reason for assuming that the number of free Jewish employees in all these occupations, as well as in the manifold commercial under-takings, was likewise on the increase. Nevertheless, the medieval rabbis seem reticent in expanding the few talmudic regulations governing their economic status. Besides repeating the old laws, with minor adaptations to the new situation, the jurists are, on the whole, satisfied with general moral injunctions emphasizing justice as the paramount principle in the relationships between employer and employee. However, by removing these relationships from the realm of communal price fixing and the operation of the principle of "just price," the road was opened to the largely uncon-trolled fluctuations in supply and demand, with all the concomitant evils for the laboring masses. There was, of course, a major antidote: the force of custom. The prevention of glaring abuses by the force of such unwritten laws may perhaps explain, in part, the extreme paucity of references to controversies over labor contracts in the Maimonidean or the geonic responsa. This paucity may also have been due, however, to reluctance on the part of laborers to go to court and air their grievances before the official judges. The rab-binic insistence upon the parties' personal appearance before the judges, although greatly enhancing the efficiency of Jewish courts, doubtless worked to the disadvantage of the employees. Their generally lower standard of education and slighter familiarity with the intricacies of Jewish law, coupled with their inability to go to court without losing some of their precious working time, must have encouraged more than one worker to forego his rights, rather than to enter such an uneven contest. There may also be more than a grain of truth in the reiterated accusations, voiced by Sahl ibn Masliah and the other Karaites, that the judges, partly dependent upon the good will of the communal leaders, were not always above reproach in their dealings with poor plaintiffs against rich defendants. Did not Sherira Gaon himself attack those unscrupulous students of Jewish law who, literally applying the irate talmudic utterances concerning the *am ha-areṣ*, felt entitled to treat lightly the property rights of the uneducated masses?[200]

A definite answer to all these complicated problems must await the publication of many more sources, still hidden in the manuscript collections of the world's great libraries. It seems, nevertheless, that in Maimonides' day the inner Jewish class conflict was not so sharp as to require the direct attention of the Jewish leaders. Besides being overshadowed by the compulsory solidarity imposed upon a struggling religious minority, sensitive to all changes in Muslim society and exposed to the whims of its rulers, this conflict seems to have been greatly mitigated by the prevailing scarcity of labor, at least in periods of expansion. The rising prices paid for unskilled and skilled slaves, in the face of the prevalent shortage of capital and the high rates of interest, justifies the conclusion that the wages paid to free laborers must likewise have been comparatively high and the conditions under which the work was to be performed more or less tolerable. Maimonides, by restating the minimum protective laws concerning the immediate payment of wages, the relaxation of the strict rules of evidence, and so forth, and by generally invoking the sanctions of religion upon those who wronged the poor, undoubtedly felt entitled to leave the details to the deep-rooted respect for the customary and to the individual discretion of judges and elders in the Jewish community.

9. CONCLUSION

The present analysis of Maimonides' economic views lays no claim to being exhaustive. Entire branches of economic life, such as public finance and social work, which occupy a conspicuous place in Maimuni's legal economic teachings, could not be dealt with at all. Neither has the economic position of women and children in and outside the family been treated, although for Maimuni's

---

[200] S. Pinsker, *Liḳḳute ḳadmoniot* (Vienna, 1860), Appendix, pp. 31 f.; *Sha'arei teshubah*, No. 23.

contemporaries of the school of "Bryson" the status of women and children constituted, next to money and slavery, the chief topic of interest in the science of domestic economy.[201] It seems, nevertheless, that the present survey of the rabbinic doctrines concerning private ownership and just price, money and banking, slavery and free labor may give a fairly comprehensive idea of medieval Jewry's basic attitudes to economic endeavor. These attitudes, as reflected in the mind of the greatest medieval Jewish jurist and philosopher, were clearly the result of endless compromises between a powerful tradition, changing economic realities, and, to a certain extent, the exigencies of non-Jewish society and legislation.

One aspect of these compromises stands out boldly: the gap between certain phases of the accepted economic theory and those of the corresponding practice. In theory one might postulate comprehensive economic regulation by communal authorities, with price fixing for all commodities as its major objective; in practice one had to limit even the juridical demand to the field of necessaries and to recognize the existing reality that the Jewish community under Islam exercised no control whatsoever over the prevailing price structure. In theory one might insist that, even in the total absence of authoritatively fixed prices, producers as well as traders be satisfied with the "legitimate" profit of one-sixth (in certain branches of commerce, such as money changing, some rabbis insisted upon a maximum profit of less than one-sixth); in practice one had to allow for the largely uncontrolled operation of the laws of supply and demand, characteristic of the semicapitalistic economy of the period. While the traditional view of the essence and function of money, as accepted and amplified by Maimuni and his confreres, had already been a mixture of the nominalist and metalistic theories, various aspects of the growing money trade called for increasing modifications of the legal theory and practice, in order to facilitate the flow of money through the channels of bank deposits, transfers, and the extension of credit. The undiminished theoretical resistance to "usurious" credit transactions among Jews was, of course, no obstacle to the development of extensive Jewish banking with a non-Jewish clientèle. Even money lending to Jews on interest, however, was made possible through various legal subterfuges,

[201] The present author intends to deal with some of these problems in another essay on "The Political Theories of Maimonides."

which, although largely ignored in legal theory, effectively enabled numerous bankers and petty money lenders to evade the prohibition without serious inconvenience. Maimuni and his fellow rabbis might still deal with the problem of slavery from the standpoint of unadulterated talmudic law, but they put up no determined resistance to the increasing transformation of certain sections in Jewry from slave-owning to slave-trading communities. The talmudic legislation, which had well met the needs of the predominantly rural Jewish mass settlements in ancient Palestine and Babylonia, utilizing to some (though relatively minor) extent the productive power of slave labor, evidently became obsolescent in many details, as well as in fundamental approach, under the new social conditions of the Caliphate. But since, like its even more obsolete parts dealing with Hebrew slaves, it offered but few practical hindrances to the growing employment of Gentile slaves in the domestic service of the increasingly urbanized Jewries under Islam, and to the commerce in slaves in which some Jews, especially in the western countries, began to participate even beyond their numerical strength in population,²⁰² it could be restated by rabbis such as Maimonides without conspicuously clashing with the existing reality. The talmudic provisions for free labor, on the other hand, could be taken over and adjusted, with but few modifications, to the productive system under early Islam.

These modifications of a long-regnant theory and law, however camouflaged behind the veil of reinterpretation, rarely necessitated direct abrogation of the accepted talmudic norms. Such was the case, for example, in the new methods governing the issuance of a power of attorney and the 'iska partnerships. For the most part, adjustments were easily made by leaving open sufficient outlets into which the new economic stream could be diverted without undermining the existing structure. Moreover, the adjustment of law to life proceeded not only along the customary lines of scholarly and judicial interpretation, but curiously, sometimes, also by a

²⁰² Eugen Täubler has rightly emphasized the fact that the role of the slave trade in the nascent Jewish communities of the Merovingian and Carlovingian empires has been greatly exaggerated, but he seems to have gone too far in the opposite direction. Cf. his "Zur Handelsbedeutung der Juden in Deutschland von Beginn des Städtewesens," *Festschrift Martin Philippson* (Leipzig, 1916), pp. 381 ff.; Baron, *History*, III, 95 f., n. 3; and the data assembled by Assaf, in *Zion*, IV, 109 ff.

most literal adherence to the old regulations in the face of changing reality. Medieval rabbis merely had to restate, for example, the ancient talmudic exemption of sales affecting land, slaves, or deeds from the operation of the laws of "misrepresentation" and just price. By ignoring the vital difference between its original import and its significance for the contemporary world, they greatly facilitated the untrammeled contractual freedom in three major domains of economic life. Originally land was not considered as ordinary commodity, but as family property which was disposed of only in emergencies. Slaves, whether engaged in agricultural production or in domestic employ, were likewise in the permanent possession of their masters and were sold by them only under exceptional circumstances. To hamper these transactions, which as a rule had all the earmarks of forced sales, by restrictive price regulations would have injured rather than benefited those whom the lawmakers wished to protect. Deeds, too, were commercially insignificant in the relatively primitive economy of early tannaitic Palestine and served as instruments of court evidence much more than as media of business transactions. By simply *not* changing the existing law, the medieval rabbis thus succeeded in greatly liberalizing the restrictive provisions of *ona'ah* and in removing what otherwise would have become a serious barrier to the advanced mercantile relations of the semicapitalistic caliphate. A final safety valve existed, moreover, in the elastic application of the ancient principle that "the law of the kingdom is law." Just because this principle was subject to a great variety of interpretations, it could be invoked to support modification, or even temporary abrogation of the traditional law, whenever this conflicted with both the state laws and Jewish economic interest. Since the major transformations in the economic system of the countries of Jewish settlement, which were largely responsible also for the changing economic needs of Jewry, were constantly reflected in the legislation of these countries, Jewish leadership had at its disposal a considerable mass of state laws which could be substituted for certain inconvenient vestiges of tradition. With all their insistence upon Jewish judicial autonomy, the rabbis professed respect for royal decrees, particularly in matters affecting taxation. None the less, wherever Jewish interests conflicted with the interests of the state or its rulers, the nimble dialectical interpretation of the rabbis could easily fall back upon the supremacy of the divine law of Judaism over the human law of the kings.[203]

A combination of all these methods sufficed to maintain a sort of equilibrium between the universally accepted theory and the varying actual practices. Nor should one equate these endeavors with sheer opportunism. In the final analysis it was not only important for the very preservation of Judaism that the formalistic continuity of tradition and the authority of the ancient sources of Jewish law be strictly upheld, but the underlying purposes of this law in its economic aspects, namely, the preservation of a proper balance between the interests of society and the rights of the individual and the meeting of the exalted requirements of "justice," could thus the more easily be realized. With all its compromises and enforced inconsistencies, the rabbinic solutions of the economic problems facing medieval Jewry proved to be astoundingly workable over a period of many generations. Thus equipped with a law and an economic theory, which combined millennial continuity in fundamentals with great elasticity in details even at the expense of logical consistency, the Jewish people was best prepared to face the constant changes in the outside world without losing its own identity. If, in the vast domains of its economic pursuits, even more than in those of its political and cultural evolution, the Jewish people had largely become the "object" of often world-wide historical processes, it succeeded, largely through this staunch adherence to its traditional, but pliable law, permeating its self-governing communal organism, in salvaging a considerable measure of autonomous control over its historic destiny.

[203] An analysis of the complex problems of the rabbinic recognition of *dina de-malkuta* and its limitation, which played a vital role in the political theory of the rabbis, must also be relegated to the forthcoming essay mentioned in n. 201 above.

CHAPTER SEVEN

THE MEDICAL WORK OF MAIMONIDES

By MAX MEYERHOF

THERE is a curious superstition among the crowded and exceedingly poor population of the Jewish quarter in the heart of the great city of Cairo in Egypt. When a member of a family is seriously ill and medical advice has given no immediate results, they carry the patient to the old synagogue of Maimonides, called Rab Moshe, which has lately been rebuilt, and leave him to sleep in a cellar under the main prayer room of the synagogue for one or more nights. A patient of mine told me not long ago that his wife, when pregnant, spent a night in a part of the cellar reserved for women, and that she saw in a dream the venerable Maimonides, who blessed her with a small torah roll which he held in his hand. A lady friend, learned in the interpretation of dreams, told her that she would certainly have a son, and so it happened. It is said that when King Fuad I of Egypt was seriously ill, in the spring of 1935, the loyal inhabitants of the Jewish quarter borrowed some of the ruler's clothes from the royal palace and took them to the prayer room of the Rab Moshe synagogue, where they kept them for a week. They are convinced that the marked improvement in the king's condition observed after that time was due to the blessing of the great physician, Maimonides. It is obvious that this custom is a relic of the "incubation," or temple sleep, of heathen times, which was deeply rooted in the life of the Greeks, who had a particular belief in the efficacy of sleeping in the temple of Aesculapius (Asclepios), the God of Healing. The same custom exists in certain Christian churches and Mohammedan mosques in Cairo. It is not long since it was abolished in the mosque of Sultan Qalâwûn, who had earned his reputation as a healing saint by founding, at the end of the thirteenth century, a magnificent hospital, not far from Maimonides' synagogue. It is noteworthy that Christian and Muslim patients share the belief in the healing power of the Maimonides synagogue, and they are sometimes admitted to pass the night under the protection of his spirit.

1. MAIMONIDES' MEDICAL BACKGROUND

This superstition is, unfortunately, all that is left of Maimonides' medical work in the city where he gained world fame as theologian, philosopher, and medical practitioner. No other relics of his activities are left, and all the manuscripts of his medical works are scattered abroad in the libraries of Europe and America, leaving none extant in Egypt. In general, not much is known of Maimonides' personal medical experience, the best information, though not always trustworthy, being supplied by Muslim biographers, writing in Arabic. In particular, nothing certain is known of the period during which Maimonides was studying medicine. We are obliged to search for a few brief references in his medical and philosophic writings in order to get an idea of it.

When his native Cordova had fallen into the hands of the fanatical Almohades in 1148, he was obliged to live an errant life in southern Spain and northern Africa, traveling from place to place with his family, until he reached his twenty-fourth year. Although during this period of about ten years he composed his first philosophic and rabbinic works, it is improbable that he found time to reside with a physician, as was usual in his days in order to obtain practical instruction in the medical arts.[1] He must have done this in the subsequent period, during his family's seven years' stay in Fez, Morocco (about 1158–65). Indeed we find in his writings frequent allusions to his intercourse with medical men of *al-Maghrib* ("the West") or *al-Maghrib al-Aqsa* ("the Extreme West" of the Mohammedan world), but only a few references to Andalusian (Spanish) physicians. For example, in the unique Istanbul manuscript of Maimonides' glossary of drug names (with which we shall deal below, under item 10), the expression, "in our land, al-Maghrib,

---

[1] The allegation made by Leo Africanus and often repeated by other historians that Maimonides had been a pupil of Ibn Zuhr (Avenzoar) and Ibn Rushd (Averroës), the two greatest medical and philosophic authorities of thirteenth-century Spain, has been definitely disproved by S. Munk in his "Notice sur Joseph ben-Iehouda," *Journal asiatique*, XI (1843), 31.

such-and-such a drug is called by such-and-such a name, but the
Egyptians call it . . .," is repeated nearly a hundred times. A variant
appears in the same manuscript under No. 380 of his alphabetical
drug list, concerning the plant *Thapsia garganica*: "What I saw
among the physicians of al-Maghrib are reddish-white roots, which
they call *al-yantûn*."

The most important passage shedding light on his medical
career in Morocco is to be found at the end of his *Treatise on Asthma*,
with reference to a discussion on the death of a highly placed
patient, the Almoravide Prince, 'Ali ibn Yûsuf ibn Tashfîn, who
had died in 1142 from a wrongly treated attack of asthma. Maimonides names, as those who furnished him with information, the sons
of two prominent physicians, who themselves were excellent prac-
titioners. They were Abû Bakr Muḥammad ibn Zuhr, son of the
famous Abû Marwân ibn Zuhr (Avenzoar), and Abû Yûsuf, son
of the Jewish physician and poet, Ibn al-Mu'allim. They gave
Maimonides a report on the opinions of their fathers, who had
taken part in the last consultation on the prince's case in the Moroccan town of Marrâkesh. While the names of no other physicians
acquainted with Maimonides have thus far become known, it is
evident that the young and ardent scholar must have known all
Jewish and many Muslim physicians practicing in Fez. On the
other hand, it is also possible that he never had any formal training
in medicine, but prepared himself through study of medical writers
and then supplemented this theoretical knowledge by his personal
experience with patients. Such self-study was not at all uncommon
in the medieval world. A century before Maimonides, a long and
heated debate took place between the most prominent Muslim
physician of Egypt, 'Alî ibn Riḍwân (d. 1061), and the Mesopo-
tamian Christian practitioner, Ibn Butlân (d. 1067), the former
vigorously defending the possibility of obtaining complete medical
education by the study of books without a master, while the latter
condemned it as a bad method.[2]

In any case, it is certain that Maimonides, simultaneously with
his theological and philosophic studies, was an eager reader of the
old medical writers. We find in his works a profound knowledge
of the writings of the two greatest Greek physicians, Hippocrates

[2] L. Leclerc, *Histoire de la médecine arabe*, I, 525 ff; J. Schacht and M. Meyerhof, *The Medico-Philosophical Controversy between Ibn Butlân and Ibn Ridwân*,
Cairo, 1937.

and Galen. The scientific works of these and some other Greek medical writers had been available in Arabic translations, prepared, from the ninth century on, by Ḥunayn ibn Isḥâq and his pupils under the patronage of the Abbasid caliphs in Baghdad and their grandees. Although Maimonides was not acquainted with the Greek language, we find in his writings many Greek names, particularly those of plants and drugs. These are mostly extracted from the Arabic version of Dioscorides' *Materia Medica*, the most famous book of antiquity on simples, which had been translated by Ḥunayn and corrected, in tenth-century Cordova, by the Jewish physician and minister, Hasdai ibn Shaprut, with the help of a Christian monk and certain Muslim pharmacologists.[3] Maimonides was also well acquainted with many of the numerous writings of Muḥammad ibn Zakariyyâ' ar-Râzî (Rhazes of the Latin world). In his treatises on hygiene, he often quotes Rhazes' book *On the Use of Aliments and Protection against Their Dangers*.[4] Still more frequently does he refer to Ibn Sînâ (Avicenna), the great Persian physician and Aristotelian philosopher, whose enormous medical encyclopedia, the *Canon Medicinae*, had been brought to Spain during the eleventh century and was as eagerly studied there as in the East. Most of the other medical writings cited by Maimonides are those of authors from Spain, e.g., Ibn Wâfid, Ibn Juljul, at-Tamîmî, Ibn Zuhr (Avenzoar), al-Ghâfiqî and the Jewish physician, grammarian and philosopher, Ibn Janâḥ. He quotes, moreover, the aforementioned Egyptian physician, Ibn Riḍwân.

Equipped with such theoretical knowledge of medicine, Maimonides left Morocco, in April, 1165, and reached Cairo at the end of the same year. He settled in Fustat, the old city which had become a southern suburb of New Cairo following the foundation of al-Qâhira, the splendid capital of the Fatimid caliphs. There he fell on sad times, losing his father in 1166 and soon after his younger brother, David, who had been the material mainstay of the family. After these mishaps, Maimonides was ill for a whole year, and then decided to practice medicine for a living.

We are much better informed of Maimonides' medical activities in Cairo, as three authors of Arabic bio-bibliographical works have furnished us a number of interesting details. They are 'Abd al-Laṭîf

[3] For details, cf. Meyerhof, "Esquisse d'histoire de la pharmacologie et botanique chez les Musulmans d'Espagne," *Al-Andalus*, III (1935), 1–41.

[4] *Kitâb manâfi'al-aghdiya wa-daf'maḍârrhâ*, Cairo, 1305 A.H.

of Baghdad, a famous practitioner who undertook the journey to Cairo specially to make the acquaintance of three prominent men, one of whom was Maimonides; Ibn al-Qifṭî (d. 1248), who was a personal friend of Maimonides' favorite pupil, Joseph ben Yehûda; and Ibn Abî Uṣaybi'a (d. 1270), who was a colleague of Maimonides' son, Abraham, at the Nâṣirî Hospital in Cairo. Also the Christian historian, Barhebraeus (d. 1286) has repeated a number of Ibn al-Qifṭî's statements. The latter describes, for example, the beginnings of Maimonides' career as court physician:

He settled in Fusṭâṭ amongst the Jews, manifested his faith, inhabited a place called *al-Maṣîṣa* and earned his livelihood by commerce in precious stones and similar trades. The people used to read with him the sciences of the ancients [i.e., philosophy, mathematics and the like] — this was in the last years of Alide (Fatimid) rule in Egypt — and wished to give him employment among the physicians [of the court?]; they wished to send him to the Frankish king at Ascalon, because the latter had asked them for a physician, and so they chose him. But he refused to do this service and to join in this affair, and persisted in his refusal. When al-Mu'izz [i.e., Sultan Nûr ad-Dîn] became the master of Egypt and the Alide (Fatimid) rule was thrown down [in 1171] the Qâḍî al-Fâḍil 'Abd ar-Raḥîm ibn 'Ali al-Baisânî took him over and fixed for him an allowance. So he joined the other physicians and did not separate himself with his opinion on account of his partnership, nor did he follow a fixed line in treatment and regulation of diet.[5]

We may conclude from this somewhat unclear passage that Maimonides was then not yet an independent practitioner. This is quite understandable, since he had been a pure theorist during the first thirty years of his life.

Maimonides must have witnessed the great conflagration at Fustat, when the town was completely destroyed by the Egyptians at the approach of the Crusaders in November, 1168. It seems,

[5] Page 318 ll. 9 ff. The assertion of Ibn al-Qifṭî concerning Maimonides' participation in the trade in precious stones is evidently erroneous; the author probably confused him with his brother David. The king of Ascalon probably was Amalric of Jerusalem rather than Richard Coeur de Lion, who came to Palestine twenty years later. The works of these Arabian authors were first utilized by M. Steinschneider in his youthful study on the medical writings of Maimonides. After a long interval, Pagel, Münz, and the present author have written on the same subject, while the octocentennial celebrations in 1935 have produced a veritable avalanche of publications, including two important papers by Alexander Marx, based on original and partly new Hebrew and Arabic material.

however, that it was very quickly rebuilt, and Maimonides again made it his home. In 1171, the Caliph Al-'Âdid was deposed in the name of Nūr ad-Dîn by the young and energetic general Salâḥ ad-Dîn, the famous Saladin. The latter's Vizier, the Supreme Judge Abd ar-Raḥîm ibn 'Alî al-Baysânî, was so impressed by Maimonides' reputation and science that he took him into his service. Upon the Vizier's recommendation, Saladin, too, appointed him as one of his court physicians.[6] We may mention at this juncture that al-Aḍid, as well as Saladin and his successors, had many Jewish court physicians. Ibn Abî Uṣaybi'a, for example, mentions Ibn Jumai' and his pupil, Abu 'l-Bayân Sadîd, in the service of Saladin and authors of medical treatises; Ibn Shaw'a and Al-Quḍâ'î, surgeons and oculists in the service of Saladin and his son, Al-'Azîz; Abu 'l-Ma'âlî, physician-in-ordinary to Saladin and his son, Al-Âdil; and Ibn Abî' l-Bayân, court physician to the same sultan. Maimonides must have known all these men, but he never mentions their names in his medical writings. He certainly had authority over them in his capacity of (unofficial) religious leader of the Jewish community in Cairo. His reputation as a physician grew rapidly in Egypt and the neighboring countries, while his fame as a theologian and philosopher very soon became world-wide.

Maimonides apparently had no hospital service at his disposal and therefore was not able to give practical instruction to medical students. But it is certain that he had pupils to whom he lectured on the Greek and Arabic medical authors.[7] In time, Maimonides' duties as physician, religious chief, and philosopher in contact with scholars of many lands became overwhelming. In the famous letter which he wrote in 1190 to his pupil, Joseph ben Yehuda (Ibn Aknin), he refers to his occupations in the following terms:

I inform you that I have acquired in medicine a very great reputation among the great, such as the Chief Qâdî, the princes, the house of Al-Fâḍil [his above-mentioned protector] and other grandees, from whom I do not obtain a large fee. As for the ordinary

---

[6] Ibn Abî Uṣaybi'a (II, 117, l. 22) relates it in the following words: "Sultan Al-Malik an-Nâṣir Ṣalâh ad-Dîn held him in esteem and consulted him; and so did his son Al-Malik al-Afḍal 'Alî."

[7] This has been contested by some authors. But Ibn Abî Uṣaybi'a (II, 247, ll. 7 f.) expressly states that his own father, Al-Qâsim ibn Khalifa, had "studied under other of the prominent old physicians who were at that time in Cairo, as for instance the Chief Mûsâ of Cordova the author of famous works, and others of his rank."

people, I am placed too high for them to reach me. This obliges me continually to waste my day in Cairo visiting the [noble] sick. When I return to Fustât, I am too tired for the rest of the day and night to pursue my study of medical books, which I need. For you know how long and difficult this art is for a conscientious and exact man who does not want to state anything which he cannot support by argument and without knowing where it has been said and how it can be demonstrated.[8]

Saladin died in 1193, and, after a protracted quarrel among his sons, his eldest son, Al-Afdal Nûr ad-Dîn 'Alî, a pleasure-loving profligate, took possession of the throne of Egypt, which he held for only two years (1198–1200). He appointed Maimonides as his chief court physician — probably at the recommendation of the latter's brother-in-law, Abu 'l-Ma'âlî, who was secretary to the sultan's mother. During this period Maimonides was obliged to render even more strenuous services at the court, which was undoubtedly located in the main palace of the Citadel built by Saladin. Another famous letter, addressed by Maimonides to Rabbi Samuel ibn Tibbon (in France) in 1198, gives an impressive account of his duties:

You will expose yourself in vain to the dangers of the journey, as you will not find a moment during the day or night to discuss with me. The Sultan resides in Cairo and I dwell in Fustat, and the distance between the two places is a double Sabbath-day's journey [about a mile and a half]. My duties to the Sultan are heavy. I must visit him early in the morning; if he feels weak or any of his children or the inmates of his harem are ill, I cannot leave Cairo but have to spend the greater part of the day in the Palace. Also, if any of the officials falls ill, I have to attend him, and thus spend the whole day there. In brief, I repair to Cairo every day in the morning, and even if nothing unusual happens, I do not return to Fustat till after the noon hour. Then I am fatigued and hungry, and I find the courts of my house full of people, prominent and common, gentlemen, theologians, and judges, waiting for the time of my return. I dismount from my animal, wash my hands, go forth to them and entreat them to wait for me while I take a slight refreshment, my only meal in twenty-four hours! After that, I attend to the patients and prescribe for them. Patients go in and out until nightfall, or, I assure you, sometimes until two hours in the night. I talk to them lying on my back because of weakness. When the night falls, I feel so weak, I cannot speak any more. Thus no Israelite can have a private discussion with me, except on the Sabbath . . . .

[8] Here and in the next letter I follow the translation given by Professor Marx.

Notwithstanding this overwhelming amount of practical work, Maimonides found time to compose for the Sultan the two valuable treatises on hygiene, of which we shall speak below under items 8 and 9, and for the Qâḍî al-Fâḍil the *Book on Poisons* (item 7). Shortly thereafter he received a visit from 'Abd al-Laṭîf of Baghdad. The latter's criticism of Maimonides' character, that "he was a man of great merits, but tainted by ambition and by excessive readiness to pander to the great," is clearly unjustified. Owing to his high scientific standing and medical reputation, he had to give advice and treatment to highly placed personages, but, as we have seen from his letter, this was very much against his personal inclinations. The continuous strain very soon had a deleterious effect on Maimonides' health. We learn from the last of his medical treatises that he fell ill in 1200 and was unable to appear at the sultan's court. He also must have been a witness of the calamities which befell Egypt during the following years (1201–3), when a terrible drought was followed by famine, a widespread epidemic of plague, and an earthquake. He died in Cairo on December 13, 1204, at the age of sixty-nine.

If we consider his medical writings, which are our main concern here — without taking into consideration the numerous allusions to medical matters in his theological and philosophic works — we must admit that most of them are neither very original nor reflect the achievements of a great and independent practitioner. In comparison with the multitude of medical workers under medieval Islam, the number of independent thinkers is very small indeed. This is due mostly to the scholastic bent which medicine had inherited from the late Hellenistic period. With the exception of Rhazes, who was an outstanding clinician of great merit, most of the doctors of the tenth to the thirteenth centuries contented themselves with systematically arranging the knowledge transmitted by the Greeks, adding merely the experiences and remedies of their times and lands.[9] Maimonides composed all his medical writings in Arabic, probably using Arabic characters, as he had nothing to hide from the Muslims. On the other hand, he wrote his theological and philosophic works, particularly his *Guide for the Perplexed*, either in Hebrew or in Arabic with Hebrew letters, in order to conceal his ideas from his non-Jewish public. Moreover, it is probable that he prepared most of his medical treatises for Muslim or Christian

[9] Cf. Meyerhof, "Science and Medicine," *Legacy of Islam*, Oxford, 1931.

pupils and therefore preferred to use the Arabic language, the more so since medical terms had as yet to be created in Hebrew. This hard task was to be accomplished, with considerable difficulty, by a series of translators during the following century.

Maimonides' position in Arabic medical literature is characterized by his dependence on his medical predecessors and by the apparent fact that most of his works follow certain well-known patterns. The basis of his medical knowledge is Greek rather than Arabic. Three of his books (items 1–3 below), evidently compiled as memoranda for himself and others, are entirely from Greek sources, though in items 2 and 3 he added commentaries of his own. The next six books (items 4–9 below) are mostly short treatises, each composed at the request of a sultan or another person of high rank. The book on poisons and the book on sexual intercourse belong to a very well-known type, for such treatises were in great favor with princes and other prominent personages. Ibn Abî Uṣaybi'a enumerates several hundred works of this kind, composed between the ninth and thirteenth centuries. The treatises on hemorrhoids and asthma reflect practical knowledge, though they do not omit the experiences of previous Greek and Arab writers. The two treatises (items 8 and 9 below), written for the Sultan Nûr ad-Dîn 'Alî are the most remarkable of the entire collection because they give, in concise form, a compendium of the hygiene of body and soul, transcending the limits of the usual works of this type. It is therefore by no means surprising that these two pamphlets, in medieval Latin translation, met with extraordinary success in the European medical world. The last book of our series follows a literary pattern, well-known and much in favor with physicians in Spain and Morocco, but also known in medieval Europe; it is the literature of synonyms of drugs, or of glossaries of drug names in several languages. Maimonides composed this little glossary for non-Jewish pupils or friends. It is, as it were, a paramedical work, a piece of medical philology.[10]

[10] Cf. Renaud and Collin, *Tuḥfat al-Aḥbâb; glossaire de matière médicale marocaine*, Paris, 1934; Meyerhof, *Al-Andalus*, III, *loc. cit*. We have intentionally omitted here the numerous apocryphal medical works wrongly attributed to Maimonides. The most quoted among these are the *Book of Medicine (Sefer ha-Refuot*, in Hebrew) [published by M. Grossberg (London, 1900); and the "Prayer of the Physician Maimonides," first published in German in the *Deutsches Museum*, I (1783), 43 as translated "from a Hebrew manuscript of a famous Jewish physician of the twelfth century," and reissued by Ludwig

2. THE TEN TREATISES OF MAIMONIDES

We shall now turn to a brief discussion of Maimonides' ten known treatises, which for the most part, are not mentioned by Ibn al-Qiftî and Ibn Abî Uṣaybi'a. While it is very likely that they were all written between the years 1180 and 1200 in Cairo, the exact date of their composition is mostly unknown. We begin with the three books which consist of extracts from, or commentaries on Greek medical works.

1. *The Extracts* (*Al-Mukhtaṣarât*), viz., from the medical works of Galen. This is the book on which 'Abd al-Laṭîf of Baghdad wrote slightingly,

He [Maimonides] composed a selection from the *Sixteen Books* of Galen and from five other books. He adopted the rule of not changing anything of the wording of the books from which he made extracts, except for a conjunction or a particle; he contented himself with mere selection of texts which he wished to insert in this extract.

It is evident that 'Abd al-Laṭîf had no knowledge of Maimonides' other medical writings. The latter expressly states in the Introduction to his *Aphorisms* (No. 3) that in *The Extracts* he had intended to prepare a selection from Galen's works for students, without any change in the text. There is no complete Arabic manuscript of these *Extracts* in existence, but several Hebrew translations are available, though still unpublished.[11]

2. *Commentary on Hippocrates' Aphorisms* (*Sharḥ Fuṣûl Abuqrâṭ*). These famous *Aphorisms* had been translated into Arabic by Ḥunayn Ibn Isḥâq (d. 873). Maimonides wrote a commentary

---

Philippson in his *Allgemeine Zeitung des Judentums*, XXVII (1863), 49–50. It then appeared in Hebrew in the *Ha-Meassef*, VI (1790), 242–44, as Isaac Euchel's trans. of a composition by Marcus Herz. There also exist other translations into German (by Toeplitz and others), as well as into French, Dutch, and English. English versions appeared in the *Voice of Jacob*, I, No. 7 (1841), 49–50 and in *Medical Leaves*, I (1937), 9. Cf. also G. Deutsch, "Jew and Gentile" in his *Scrolls*, Boston, 1920, III, 93–95; S. Seeligmann, "Morgengebed van den arts naar Maimonides," *Vrijdagavond*, V (1928), 404–6; Emil Bogen, *The Daily Prayer of a Physician*, Chicago, 1929 (reprinted from *The Journal of the American Medical Association*, XCII, 2128)].

[11] Steinschneider, *Hebräische Uebersetzungen*, pp. 762 ff.

on this translation, as many other Arab medical writers had done before him. There are two incomplete manuscripts of this book extant in Arabic, but a good Hebrew translation was made by Moses b. Samuel ibn Tibbon, from a manuscript of which Steinschneider edited the Introduction. Maimonides' professed intention was to follow generally the commentaries of Galen on this work, but from time to time to voice also his own opinions.[12] He reveals himself here as a severe critic. He does not accept all the sayings of the "Divine" Hippocrates as sacred, but distinguishes between the useful and useless, clear and obscure, true and false aphorisms. Indeed the *Aphorisms* are considered by modern philologists as an inadequate collection of sayings by physicians of the Coian and Cnidian schools and in no wise as the work of Hippocrates or any other single man.

3. *The Medical Aphorisms of Moses* (In Arabic: *Fuṣûl Mûsâ fî 't-Ṭibb*; in Hebrew: *Pirkê Môshê*). This is the bulkiest medical book composed by Maimonides and is also, for the most part, a compilation from the works of Galen and other Greek medical writers.   The book is subdivided into twenty-five discourses (*maqâlât*), in accordance with the system of most great Arabic treatises on medicine. The first three discourses, or chapters, treat of anatomy, physiology, and general pathology; the next two of symptomatology and diagnosis; and the following three of etiology and therapeutics. Chapters X–XII comprise the Galenic doctrine of fevers; XII–XIII the application of bleeding, purging, and vomitives; XIV surgery; XV diseases of women; XVII–XX hygiene, exercise, baths, and diet; XXI–XXII the pharmacopeia; XXIII the misinterpreted doctrines of Galen; and XXIV a record of the rare and interesting cases described by Galen in his works. Chapter XXV, the last discourse in the book, is very long. In it Maimonides criticises Galen's opinions and cites more than forty passages in which the great physician contradicted his own sayings (e.g., when he recommended in one place absolute rest for hemoptysis and, in another, movement of the lower limbs). Finally, in a long

---

[12] Idem, "Die Vorrede des Maimonides zu seinem Commentar über die Aphorismen des Hippokrates," *Zeitschrift der Deutschen Morgenländischen Gesellschaft*, XLVIII (1894), 211–34. The entire Hebrew text has been published by M. Z. (Bocian) Hasidah in his *Hassegullah*, Nos. 1–30, Jerusalem, 1934–35 (mimeographed).

exposition, Maimonides refutes Galen's teleological opinions concerning the origin of the world and defends the biblical cosmogony.[13]

There are several Arabic manuscripts of this work extant, the best being that of the Gotha Library. This precious text was copied from a copy by Abu' l-Ma'âlî Yûsuf ibn 'Abdallâh, son of Maimonides' sister, who claimed to have finished the copy of the twenty-fifth discourse in August, 1205, eight months after the death of the author, the latter having been unable to correct it as he had the preceding twenty-four discourses. So we must conclude that Maimonides composed his *Aphorisms* during the last ten years of his life, and that he had just finished the rough draft of the last discourse when death overtook him. Another good copy of the *Aphorisms* is extant in the Leyden Library. It was copied by a Jewish scholar at Toledo in 1324. An edition of the entire text of the *Aphorisms* is one of the great desiderata of Jewish and Arabic medicine.

The Arabic Introduction to the *Aphorisms* has recently been published by Kahle.[14] Maimonides makes express mention of the

[13] The Hebrew text (Zerahiah ben Isaac's translation) of Chapter 40, Book XXV, has been published by Moritz Steinschneider in his monumental work *Al-Farabi (Alpharabius) des arabischen Philosophen Leben und Schriften* (St. Petersburg 1869) pp. 230–38. In the first half of this chapter, Maimonides attacks Galen as a philosopher, stating that he was a most prominent medical scholar and well versed in mathematics and logic, but that he was inferior to Aristotle and other philosophers in the exact criticism of syllogisms. Maimonides exhibits, on this occasion, a remarkable knowledge of Galen's philosophical works (most of which were lost a few centuries after his death), and especially of his book *De demonstratione*, the fragments of which had been transmitted to the Arabs by Ḥunain ibn Isḥāq. Maimonides then quotes against Galen the great Muslim Aristotelian philosopher Abū Naṣr al-Fārābī (d. 950) who reproaches the Greek physician with having wrongly included in his last-named book the syllogisms of existence. After this discussion Maimonides quotes a passage from Galen's famous book *De usu partium* on account of Galen's attack against the Bible and the Mosaic tradition. I have used the Arabic original text as preserved in MS Gotha no. 1937, the best of all the existing MSS, in a photostat belonging to the Jewish Theological Seminary of America and kindly loaned me by Professor Alexander Marx. Galen's passage exists in Greek (Kühn's edition of Galen's *Works*, III (Leipzig 1829) 904–7; and G. Helmreich's edition of *De usu partium*, II (Leipzig, 1909), 158–59, but has never been translated into a modern language. An extract from the last *Maqala* has been published by me, in collaboration with Dr. Joseph Schacht, Professor of Semitic Languages in the Egyptian University, in the *Bulletin of the Faculty of Arts, the Egyptian University*, 1939.

[14] In the Arabic appendix to H. O. Schröder's *Galeni in Platonis Timaeum commentarii fragmenta*, Leipzig and Berlin, 1934.

fact that he did not compose these aphorisms, but merely selected them, and that he did not follow the wording of Galen, as he had done in *The Extracts*, but tried to put the opinions of the great Greek physician in comprehensible form. He states modestly that he selected the aphorisms for his own use and for the use of other men who were not more learned than himself. He has sometimes inserted his own opinions, however, and quoted, very rarely, from Arab medical authorities, e.g., from Ibn Zuhr (Avenzoar), the Hispano-Moorish physician Muḥammed at-Tamîmî (eleventh century), and the Egyptian Ibn Riḍwân, one of the greatest Arabic authorities on Greek medicine.

The *Aphorisms* have been translated into Hebrew by the famous Nathan ha-Meathi, and a second time by Zerahiah ben Isaac ben Shealtiel Hen. Only the first version has been published (Lemberg, 1834–35 [supplemented by S. Sachs in *Ha-Teḥiyya*, Berlin, 1850, I, 33–35] and Wilno, 1888); but these printed versions are inadequate and full of mistakes, and a new edition is badly needed. The Latin translation is much better. It was made during the thirteenth century and printed in Bologna, 1489, Venice, 1497 and 1500, and in recast form in Basle, 1579. These translations made the name of Maimonides famous in the European world, and we find him frequently quoted, principally in the French medical literature of the time, under the stereotyped formula: *Dixit Rabbi Moyses*.

The next six treatises have been partially edited by the German Rabbi, Dr. Hermann Kroner, who devoted twenty years of his life and much money to the task of collecting Arabic and Hebrew manuscripts and editing them with German translations and commentaries. If these editions do not always comply with the exigencies of modern philology, it must be remembered that Kroner lived in a very small town in South Germany, far from public libraries and the scientific aid of universities. His merit is very great, and his untimely death (in 1930) has deprived us for a long time to come of two important editions. I wish to pay my tribute here to the memory of this indefatigable scholar.

4. *On Hemorrhoids* (*Fi' il Bawâsîr*). This short treatise was composed by Maimonides for the use of a young man of a noble family in Cairo. Dr. Kroner edited the Arabic text in Hebrew letters in 1911, having consulted altogether three Arabic manuscripts and four manuscripts of the anonymous Hebrew translation of this treatise. He also studied previous Arabic treatises on hemorrhoids

and the book on the same disease, written in Hebrew by a Spanish Jew, Solomon b. Joseph ibn Ayyub (Beziers, France, 1265). Maimonides divides his abstract into seven chapters, which deal with the normal digestion,[15] the aliments harmful to sufferers from hemorrhoids, the useful aliments, general and local treatment by remedies: half baths, oils, fumigations, and so forth. He disapproves of bleeding or operation except in cases of great severity. Maimonides' merit in this treatise is in his having insisted on the causative effect of bad digestion, particularly constipation, and his having prescribed an efficacious diet, mostly of a vegetable nature: tamarinds, myrobalans, spinach, and marshmallow being among the plants recommended.

5. *On Sexual Intercourse* (*Fi' l-Jimâ'*). This is a treatise on sexual hygiene, written by Maimonides at the request of a nephew of Saladin, the Sultan al-Muẓaffar 'Umar ibn Nûr ad-Dîn, who reigned at Ḥamâ in Syria from 1179 to 1192. Dr. Kroner edited in 1906 the Arabic text in Hebrew characters with a German translation, followed by a commentary and two Hebrew translations of a shorter version. The latter was published by him in 1916 in the Arabic original, accompanied by a new translation. He also made reference to the many previous and subsequent treatises on the same subject, written by Arabic physicians.[16] It comprises nineteen chapters on the nature of men, the utility and harmfulness of sexual intercourse, the remedies for and against excitement to sexual intercourse, on all kinds of cosmetics and on aphrodisiac and narcotic recipes. The minor text is an abridged edition, mostly consisting of recipes, the number and variety of which are surprisingly great. The Hebrew translation of this treatise was made by the above-mentioned Zerahiah ben Isaac ben Shealtiel. It was also translated, during the Middle Ages, into Latin, but the Latin versions exist only in unpublished manuscript copies.

6. *Discourse on Asthma* (*Mâqâla fi'r-Rabw*). This treatise was composed by Maimonides about 1190 for a patient of high rank. Dr. Kroner intended to edit this pamphlet, and had begun preliminary work on the Arabic and Hebrew manuscripts when he died.

---

[15] *See* Appendix I.

[16] Hermann Kroner, *Ein Beitrag zur Geschichte der Medizin des XII Jahrhunderts*, Oberdorf-Bopfingen, 1906; also, "Eine medizinische Maimonides-Handschrift aus Granada," *Janus*, XXI (1916), 203–47. [A second manuscript of the shorter version has recently been recovered. Cf. *Register of the Jewish Theological Seminary of America*, 1940, p. 51.] See Appendix II.

According to Steinschneider, this treatise was translated in 1302 from Arabic into Latin (*Tractatus contra passionem asthmatis*) by the French scholar, Armengaud de Blaise, at Montpellier. Later, it was translated from Latin into Hebrew by Samuel ben Benveniste and Joshua Shaṭibi, two Hispano-Jewish translators of the fourteenth century.[17]

The contents of the treatise are as follows: In the introduction, Maimonides relates the complaints of the patient, viz., stenocardiac symptoms and violent headache, which prevented him from wearing a turban; the patient asked whether he had not better have a change of air and transfer his residence from Alexandria to Cairo. Maimonides explains in thirteen chapters, first, the general rules regarding diet and climatic conditions, then the special diet suitable for sufferers from asthma. This is followed by recipes and a review of the aliments and climates of different countries of the Near East. He emphasizes, very soundly, the healthiness of the dry Egyptian climate for asthmatics, adding that one can bring this disease to an end in Egypt by diet only, without the use of remedies. He insists on the danger of the use of strong remedies for asthma, referring to the previously mentioned case of the Amîr (Prince) 'Alî ibn Yûsuf ibn Tashfîn of Morocco, who died in 1142 because he took too strong a dose of theriac administered by his doctors.

7. *On Poisons and the Protection against Deadly Remedies* (*Kitâb as-Sumûm wa'l-Mutaḥarriz min al-Adwiya al-Qattâla*). This is a treatise composed by Maimonides in 1199 at the request of his noble protector, the Vizier and Supreme Judge (*al-Qâḍî al-Fâḍil*), 'Abd ar-Rahîm ibn 'Alî al-Baysânî. For this reason Maimonides himself called his little treatise *The Missive for al-Fâḍil* (*Ar-Risâla al-Fâḍiliyya*). The Arabic text is extant in several manuscripts which had already been prepared for publication by Dr. Kroner at the time of his death. It was translated into Hebrew by Moses ben Samuel ibn Tibbon and (probably) by Zerahiah ben Isaac, and from Hebrew into Latin, under the title: *Tractatus de venenis*, by Armengaud de Blaise, whom we already know as the translator of the book *On Asthma*. From the Hebrew text stem also Rabbinowicz's

[17] Steinschneider, "Die europäischen Uebersetzungen aus dem Arabischen," *Sitzungsber. der Kais. Aka. der Wiss. in Wien*, CLI (1905), 33; also, *Hebräische Uebersetzungen*, p. 767. [The Hebrew translation has recently been published by Suesskind Munther as Vol. I of Maimonides' *Ketubim refuiim*, Jerusalem, 1940.]

French translation of 1865 and Steinschneider's German rendition of 1873, both inadequate.[18] I was fortunate enough to obtain from Dr. Kroner, not long before his death, a summary of the Arabic original of this treatise, from which I extract the following data. The Arabic text is divided into an introduction and two main parts, or sections. In the introduction, Maimonides praises the vizier and his feats in peace and war and mentions Al-Fâḍil's orders to import from remote lands the drugs lacking in Egypt for the preparation of two important antidotes, the *Great Theriac* and *Mithridates' Electuary*. None of the ingredients for their compounding, except opium, had been available in Egypt. Al-Fâḍil, having procured the necessary drugs, ordered the distribution of these two costly medicines to any person suffering from poisoning. In the month of Ramaḍân, 595 A.H.,[19] Al-Fâḍil asked Maimonides to compose a short treatise on the treatment of cases of poisoning by venomous animals before the arrival of the physician or until the patient might reach the dispensary where the theriacs were kept. Maimonides reminds his patron of the great number of treatises on poisons, written by Arab authors, and proposes to give extracts from them, while mentioning a limited number of remedies only in order to make possible quick help in urgent cases.

The first section deals, in six chapters, with the bites of snakes, the stings of scorpions, bees, wasps, spiders (tarantulas), and the bites of mad dogs. Maimonides warns against dressing the wounds and advises letting the blood flow from them in order to carry away as much as possible of the poison. He also recommends a vegetable diet and the drinking of strong wine — treatment which entirely corresponds with our present-day conceptions. He emphasizes the length of the period of incubation of canine hydrophobia, which may deceive the doctor and patient, and lays stress also on the danger of the bite of man. The second section, in four chapters, treats of poisons and poisonous remedies, referring particularly

[18] I. M. Rabbinowicz, *Traité des poisons de Maimonide*, Paris, 1865, reprinted in Paris, 1935; Steinschneider, "Gifte und ihre Heilung, eine Abhandlung des Moses Maimonides," *Virchow's Archiv f. pathologische Anatomie*, LVII (1873), 62–120; [Louis J. Bragman, "Maimonides' Treatise on Poisons," *Medical Journal and Record* of July 21 and August 4, 1926].

[19] Corresponding to July, 1199 A.D. During the hot summer months cases of bites and stings by venomous reptiles and insects are very numerous in Egypt. The First Aid Society of Cairo, for example, had to treat daily during July, 1935, several hundred patients stung by scorpions.

to verdigris, arsenic, litharge, hyoscyamus, the Solanaceae, mushrooms, cantharides, and the like. He gives very good descriptions of the symptoms of poisoning, e.g., redness of the face after belladonna poisoning and hematuria after the ingestion of Spanish flies. The very complicated theriacs of olden times (one of the simplest contained forty-two different drugs!) are not now esteemed efficacious remedies. In the Middle Ages, however, Maimonides' *Tractatus de venenis* was considered a great boon and it was often quoted in the works of the French physicians and surgeons, especially at the School of Montpellier.

I hope that a way will be found to publish Dr. Kroner's posthumous work comprising the text, commentary, and translation of this short and attractive medical pamphlet of Maimonides.

We now turn to two treatises, written by Maimonides during the same period of his life, when he was, from 1198 to 1200, chief physician-in-ordinary to the Sultan Al-Afḍal Nûr ad-Dîn 'Ali, Saladin's eldest son. I consider these two abstracts as the most original and most mature medical works of the great Jewish scholar. Their Latin versions exercised considerable influence on medical thought in medieval Europe.

8. *On the Regulation of Health* (*Fî Tadbîr as-Ṣiḥḥa*). Maimonides wrote this treatise in the first year of the reign of Sultan Al-Afḍal (i.e., a few months before his treatise *On Poisons*), at the request of the ruler himself. The Sultan, as we have stated before, was a frivolous and pleasure-seeking man of thirty, subject to fits of melancholy, due to his life of inordinate luxury, his intrigues, and his warlike adventures with his own relatives and the Crusaders. He complained to his physician, Maimonides, of constipation, dejection, evil thoughts, premonition of death, and bad digestion. Maimonides replied with the treatise in question, which very soon acquired a great reputation. It exists in numerous Arabic manuscripts. On these Dr. Kroner has based his edition of the Arabic text, with translation and commentary.[20] Moses ben Samuel ibn Tibbon made a Hebrew translation from the Arabic in 1244, and this version was printed several times during the nineteenth century (Prague, 1838; Jerusalem, 1885, and Warsaw, 1886). Two Latin versions were also made, one of them by the famous translator, John of Capua, a converted Jew (thirteenth century). The Latin translation, very well known in Europe, was printed before 1484 in Florence,

---

[20] In *Janus*, XXVII–XXIX, 1923–25.

under the title *De regimine sanitatis ad soldanum Saladinum*, and five more times during the sixteenth century. A German translation, published in Vienna by Winternitz in 1843, is very inaccurate and was severely criticized by Steinschneider.[21]

Maimonides composed his treatise for the Sultan in four chapters. The first is a short abstract of Dietetics, mostly from Hippocrates and Galen. He discusses the qualities of various aliments, especially different kinds of meats. He does not agree with Galen, who advised against the use of fruits because their effect on himself had been to cause fever. What is good for one individual may be bad for another, says Maimonides. In Chapter II he gives advice concerning hygiene, diet, and remedies for patients in the absence of the physician. Chapter III is the most interesting, as it shows Maimonides, as doctor, in the new capacity of "hygienist of the soul." After having dealt with laxative remedies and diet, according to Galen and Avenzoar, Maimonides describes in vivid language the oscillations of psychic conditions in individuals of labile mind — probably a description of the psyche of his august patient! He then contrasts with this picture that of a man with philosophical education who keeps his moral balance despite every accident.

It is the truth, if philosophers call the goods of this World and its evils imaginary goods and evils.... How often does there fall to someone's share a great fortune or a powerful position, and it is this that causes the decay of his body and the deterioration of his soul and character, shortens his life, and alienates him from his Creator, the Most High! What an eternal misfortune is this for him! On the other hand, how often does someone lose his fortune or his power, and it is this that strengthens his body, perfects his soul with moral qualities, prolongs his life, brings him nearer to the Lord, and incites him to devotion to His service. What an eternal happines is this for him! [Your Majesty's] humble servant utters this according to the opinion of some ancient physicians, philosophers, and propounders of divine laws before the rise of Islam.[22] Generally speaking, most of what the common people think to be happiness is in reality misfortune, and what is thought to be misfortune is happiness.

After that, he exhorts the sultan not to worry about things past or things that may come or not come, but to preserve his equa-

---

[21] Cf. Steinschneider in *Oesterr. Blätter, loc. cit.* Kroner, too, has made use of these MSS in various publications. [A facsimile of the Florence edition, usually dated about 1477, has been published by A. Freimann in Heidelberg, 1930].

[22] The concluding words contain a circumspect allusion to the Bible.

nimity and imperturbability.[23] In the fourth chapter Maimonides summarizes his prescriptions in seventeen paragraphs, dealing with the hygiene of climate, dwelling, occupation, baths, sexual intercourse, wine-drinking, with catching colds, and with spoiled aliments and diet. At the end there comes a discourse on the various kinds of meat. The whole treatise is a short but complete abstract of hygiene in a very comprehensible form. It is therefore easy to understand how this medical book of Maimonides met with such great success.

9. *Discourse on the Explanation of Fits* (*Maqâla fî Bâyân al-A'râd*). This is probably the last of Maimonides' medical writings — Kroner calls it his *medizinischer Schwanengesang* — as it was composed in the year 1200, shortly before the Sultan Al-Afḍal was deposed and four years before Maimonides' death. Evidently the ruler had not changed his unsuitable mode of life and continued to suffer from fits of melancholic dejection. He sent to Maimonides, who was ill in Cairo, a detailed report of the consultation of his other physicians, asking for opinion and advice. Maimonides' answer is contained in this short abstract, which he addressed to "the King of Riqqa." I conclude from this title that the sultan had taken up his residence in a palace at or near the village of Riqqa in Upper Egypt, not far from the oasis of Al-Fayyûm. Dr. Kroner has edited the Arabic text of the little treatise and a fragmentary Hebrew translation, with a German version and commentary. This was the last edition of a Maimonidean medical work completed by Dr. Kroner.[24] John of Capua also translated this treatise into Latin, probably from a Hebrew version unknown today, under the title [first appearing in the edition of Pavia, 1501]: *De causis apparentium accidentium domino et magnifico soldano* . . . . It was printed as an appendix to [or as Chapter V of] *De regimine sanitatis*.

Maimonides' letter comprises twenty-two paragraphs or sentences, the first eighteen of which are devoted to answering, one after another, the points raised by his colleagues' advice. He confirms most of their prescriptions — potions, wine, laxative remedies (rhubarb), baths, exercise, and a principally vegetable diet with a predominance of fruits. He warns against the use of vomitive drugs, but in a very gentle manner, without showing contempt for the

[23] See Appendix III.
[24] Kroner, "Der medizinische Schwanengesang des Maimonides, "*Janus*, XXXII (1928), 12–116.

opinions of his colleagues. We know, by the way, from a passage
in Maimonides' biography in Ibn al-Qifṭī's *History of Learned Men*
that, although reserved in his relations with other medical men, he
was a perfect colleague.[25] In paragraphs 19–20 Maimonides discusses
generalities concerning the best regimen in cases like that of the
sultan. We find there the remarkable passage: "I have had occasion
to treat some patients whose disease followed the way of the kings
suffering from melancholy, viz. that it turns into *mania*, that is
raving madness." In the twenty-first paragraph Maimonides gives
a very detailed regimen for the daily life of the sultan, hour by hour.
He advises the ruler to rise with the sun, to take a little hydromel,
after that to ride for several hours, and to consume a light meal,
mostly consisting of fruits, followed by a siesta to the low voice of
a singer, accompanied by his stringed instrument. After that should
come reading and agreeable conversation, then drinking of a little
wine with *bugloss* (*Anchusa officinalis*), a remedy which, very much
in favor with the Greek physicians, was known to them under the
name of *euphrosynê* ("cheerfulness"), because it was thought to
cheer the hearts of melancholic patients. This is to be followed by
a light supper, and once more music for two hours, until sleep
overtakes the royal listener. This regimen is followed by much detailed advice concerning the different kinds of diet, baths, exercise,
sexual intercourse, and so on, varying for winter and summer. The
twenty-second paragraph contains the conclusion, in which Maimonides proclaims his confidence in the intelligence of the ruler,
who will know how to employ the given prescriptions. Then follows
another curious passage:

May our Master not blame his humble servant because he has
prescribed in this discourse the preparation of wine and the use
of music, which are abominated by the religious law. For the
humble servant does not prescribe the use of these [forbidden]
things, but he merely mentions all the things that are required
by medical art . . . . Religion prescribes all that is useful and forbids
all that is harmful in the next world; while the doctor indicates
what is useful and warns against what is harmful in this world.

Kroner believed that in these words was hidden a conflict between
Maimonides, the physician, and Maimonides, the theologian; but,
in our opinion, he merely had to be very cautious in his prescription
because the presence of an unbeliever at the court doubtless did

[25] See Appendix IV.

not please the pious Muslim councilors of the Sultan. He had to be careful not to hurt their religious feelings.[26]

10. *Glossary of Drug Names (Sharḥ Asmâ al-'Uqqâr).*[27] This medical writing by Maimonides was known only to Ibn Abî Uṣaybi'a and is mentioned by him in his great *Sources of Information on the Classes of Physicians.*[28] I myself believed it to be an apocryphal book up to the time when, a few years ago, I was informed by Dr. H. Ritter, in Istanbul, that this book exists in Arabic manuscript No. 3711 in the Aya Sofia Library. In this book Maimonides reveals an unknown side of his vast learning, namely, that of a philologist and linguist. The manuscript itself is very remarkable because it was written by the famous Arab pharmacologist and botanist, Ḍiyâ' ad-Dîn 'Abdallâh, better known as Ibn al-Bayṭâr, the author of the greatest Arabic treatise on the simples. He was born in Malaga (Spain) and emigrated to Egypt about 1220, i.e., sixteen years after the death of Maimonides. That the copy of Maimonides' treatise on drug names was made by Ibn-Bayṭâr himself is certified on the cover of the Istanbul manuscript by his pupil, Ibn as-Suwaydî, a distinguished physician of the thirteenth century, and by Khâlîl ibn Aybak aṣ-Ṣafadî, a well-known scholar and historian of the fourteenth century, who were both among the owners of this precious and unique manuscript. It is impossible to decide at exactly which period of his medical career Maimonides would have been likely to compose such a treatise. It appears certain, however, that he wrote it in Cairo, because he frequently refers to names of plants and drugs which were, and still are in use in Egypt. He must have composed it for the use of his Muslim friends and pupils in Egypt and Palestine. I suppose, moreover, that Ibn al-Bayṭâr copied the treatise soon after his arrival in Egypt and not from the author's copy, because he not only made many mistakes in copying, but also left uncorrected many mistakes

---

[26] Cf. Kroner, *Der Mediziner Maimonides im Kampfe mit dem Theologen,* Oberdorf-Bopfingen, 1924; Meyerhof,"Zwei hygienisch-dietätische Abhandlungen des Maimonides," *Der Morgen,* IV (1928), 620–24. It is generally known that wine is forbidden to Muslims, but it is less well known that the same prohibition applies to music. The very strict followers of Islam, e.g., the Wahhabites in Arabia, prohibit any kind of musical entertainment.

[27] The meaning of the word *sharḥ* is commentary, but this Maimonidean work is less a commentary than a glossary, as the long list of names is rarely accompanied by an explanation of their meaning.

[28] Cairo edition, II, 117 last line.

of previous copyists. Ibn al-Bayṭâr evidently was still far from the great exactitude and experience in drug names which he showed later in his great *Collection of Simple Drugs*, which he composed in the years preceding his death in 1248. But, in general, the manuscript is sufficiently correct to permit an edition of the text, accompanied by a translation and commentary in French.[29]

The Arabic text begins with the following words: "My aim in this discourse is the explanation of the names of simple drugs which are extant in our time, known among us, used in medicine, and cited in the medical books." The author adds that he will omit the remedies that have only one well-known name and those that are too rare; he will also try to avoid repetitions and all circumstantial descriptions, in order to shorten the glossary as much as possible. He quotes as his forerunners in this work only Spanish physicians: Ibn Juljul, Ibn Janâḥ, Ibn Wâfid, Ibn Samjûn, and Aḥmad al-Ghâfiqî. He intends adding popular names from "the Westland" (Morocco). Then follow 405 short paragraphs containing, in alphabetical order, about 2,000 names of drugs, mostly of vegetable and more rarely of mineral or animal nature. Maimonides generally gives first an Arabic name, which, however, is very often of Greek, Syriac, or Persian origin; after that, several other Arabic and Syriac names, and then names in Greek, Persian, Berber, and Spanish. These latter names, as usual among the Spanish Arabs, are given under the title of "names in the foreign language of Andalusia." They are often mutilated by the copyists, but I was able to restore most of them with the help of Simonet's invaluable glossary. For the restoration of mutilated Berber names, the recently published glossary of Moroccan *Materia Medica*, by Renaud and Colin, proved very useful. It is strange that Maimonides did not mention a single Hebrew name of a plant or drug, although such names occur rather frequently in his theological writings and have carefully been collected by Löw in his great *Flora of the Jews*. This is even more remarkable since Maimonides' older Muslim contemporary, the

---

[29] [This edition and trans. by the present writer appeared in Cairo, 1940, under the title, *Šarḥ Asmâ' Al-Uqqar (L'Explication des noms de drogues). Un glossaire de matière médicale* ...]. Cf. also Meyerhof and Sobhy, *The Abridged Version of the Book of Simple Drugs,* ... Cairo, 1932–38; Meyerhof, "Sur un ouvrage médical inconnu de Maimonide," *Mélanges Maspéro,* Cairo, 1935, Vol. III; Meyerhof, "Sur un glossaire de matiére médicale composé par Maimonide," *Bulletin de l'Institut d'Egypte,* XVII (1935); Meyerhof, in *Al-Andalus, loc. cit.* See Appendix V.

famous geographer, Al-Idrîsî, in his hitherto unpublished "Book on Simples" (MS, Fâtiḥ Library, No. 3610, Istanbul) gives plenty of Hebrew drug names, which he probably copied from the works of Jewish scholars in Sicily. The absence of Hebrew names very likely proves that Maimonides composed his book mainly for the use of non-Jewish friends and pupils.

Close examination of the text again reveals Maimonides' vast knowledge of Arab medical literature, from which he took the approximately 2,000 names that occur in this small but very important abstract. He utilized the drug books of his predecessors in Spain and Morocco, but very often supplemented their knowledge by information which he had obtained from the common people in Morocco. He must also have inspected the stocks of drugs kept by medical men there, as he often quotes what he had seen of roots and dried flowers in their stores. He continually repeats "in our land, *al-Maghrib*," thus showing that he felt at home in the West, the land of his study during his youth. He sometimes adds: "In Egypt or Syria, they call this plant . . . ." The following short paragraph concerning the plant waybread (*Plantago major L.*) may serve here as an illustration:

Lisân al-ḥamal ("ram's tongue"). It is *lisân al-kalb* ("dog's tongue") and *dhanb al-fâr* ("mouse-tail"), and it is also called bard wa-salâm ("cooling and health"). Its name in the foreign language of Spain is *plantagine*, and that is what the common people of Morocco call *al-maṣṣâṣa* ("the sucking one"). It is the same as *karkûs*.

The last name is a mutilation of the Persian *khargûsh* ("Ass's ear"), which is, in fact, the name of *Plantago major*.

3. SUMMARY

To sum up, Maimonides' medical work is very varied, comprising extracts from Greek medicine, a series of monographs on individual diseases and cases, and a glossary of drug names, which required extensive knowledge of Arab medical literature and familiarity with several languages. Maimonides, as a medical writer, was less original and less a pioneer than in his theological and philosophical writings. Several of his works, however, gained an excellent reputation in the medieval medical world, and the name of *Rabbi*

Moyses became as famous in medicine as in theology and philosophy. It may be that his personal prestige, established by numerous successes in practical treatment, contributed to spreading abroad the fame of this great and versatile scholar.

APPENDIX

At the request of the editor, I add to my discussion a few translations from original Arabic medical texts of Maimonides. I extracted the first four from the late Rabbi Hermann Kroner's editions in the journal *Janus*; and section V from the unedited Istanbul MS. I have prepared an independent translation of all these texts, including such as had previously been translated into a European language, which, I hope, will correct some errors and misunderstandings of former translators. All these texts are illustrative of Maimonides' universal erudition and of his medical thought, which was so largely dependent on Greek and early Arabic tradition. But they show at the same time his high ethical standards, his professional honesty, his serious scientific conception of the medical arts, his feeling of fellowship toward his colleagues, his modesty, and, last but not least, his delicate position as physician-in-ordinary to an absolute ruler who had to be handled with particular tact and devotion, so as to avoid outbreaks of tyrannical humor caused by his diseased mind. I have intentionally chosen such sections in Maimonides' medical discourses as are easily understandable to the layman.

I. From Maimonides's Discourse on Hemorrhoids

[*Chapter I: General Considerations on the Regulation of the Digestion*]

You must know that the most frequent and the most severe diseases take their origin from bad digestion in the stomach, because, when the digestion of the aliments is disturbed in the stomach, this disturbance is continued during the second digestion, which takes place in the liver, and during the third digestion, which is accomplished in the other organs. The disturbance of the digestion is caused, as far as nutrition is concerned, by one of the following four causes: either by the quantity of the aliments, or by their quality, or by the bad regulation of their order (order of diet), or by the irregularity of the time of nutrition. We will explain them one after another.

Concerning the quantity of aliments, this means the overabundant ingestion of solid and liquid aliments. For good aliments, even such of the best quality, if the stomach is overloaded and glutted with them, cause indigestion. The first rule must be that a man must not satisfy his appetite to the point where he lifts his hand [from the meal, i.e., ends his meal], but to leave a remainder of appetite and to take care not to extend his stomach to the point where it swells like a tumor. For there are people who have such a strong appetite as to cause a distention of the stomach to this size, and who continue to have appetite even then.

Concerning the quality, that means that the aliments must not be of bad quality. For bad aliments, even if digested as well as possible, do not produce healthy blood. It must be the first rule to avoid the aliments of manifest heat[ing property] like mustard, and those of manifest cold temper like cucumbers, as well as those in which is manifest bitterness like celery, brinjal (aubergine), and colocasia, or manifest acridity like onions, garlic, and radish, and those who are sour like vinegar and lemons. In general it is better to prefer aliments which are predominantly tasteless or sweet or greasy like the ordinary kinds of bread, meat and eggs, honey, sugar and the like. In the same manner one must avoid all the aliments which have a fetid flavor like seasoning [kâmakh], saltfishes [sîr], roast-meat and the like of altered dishes. Likewise, cooked dishes which were kept overnight and have begun to become altered, and altered fruits and oils; against all this we must be always on our guard. Galen said in the well-known sentence: *Altered dishes and drinks produce putrefactions [in the organism] in the same manner as caused by deadly poisons.*

Concerning bad regulation that means that dishes are taken first which should be taken at the end. So the best and safest way is to choose one dish only and, if several cannot be avoided, the very lightest ought to be the first to be taken, and those of difficult digestion ought to be taken last. So boiled vegetables should precede eggs, eggs precede the flesh of birds [poultry], poultry precede mutton, and in this way aperient dishes should always precede constipating ones: e.g., dishes prepared with lemons should precede such dishes as are prepared with sumach [tanner's sumach] or pomegranates. To this chapter also belongs, moreover, the regulation of drinking water, in this sense, that drinking of cold water before the meal is very harmful and provokes serious diseases. Drinking of water during the meal is less harmful, but disadvantageous to the digestion of aliments. The best moment to be chosen for drinking is one hour after the meal.

As to the time of taking [solid aliments] they should not be taken before the time of real hunger, and one has to beware of ingestion of aliment over aliment. The best thing is to take meals only after some exercise or movement which excites a little the bodily heat. On the contrary, beware of movement after the meal until digestion is finished. Every movement after the meal is harmful to the digestion, viz., the movement of exercise, of coition, the bath, and mental excitements. If one follows these principles which we have established concerning ingestion of meals and drinks, that will be quite sufficient to keep the digestion generally in good condition.

II. *Introduction to Maimonides's* Discourse on Sexual Intercourse

Says Mûsâ ibn 'Ubaidallâh, the Israelite of Cordova: Our Lord His Majesty — may Allah make His power last long! — ordered me to compose for him a treatise on behavior which would help to increase his sexual power, as he mentioned that he had some hardship in this way. At the same time he informed the humble servant of the falling away of the lord's body so that he is near to abate in his flesh; and that his temper is a little inclined to heat. He mentioned, moreover, that he does not wish to depart from his custom concerning sexual intercourse and wishes for that purpose a regulation, being alarmed by the abatement of his flesh, as He desires an augmentation [of the sexual power] on account of the increasing number of female slaves. He informed me that what he wants is a regulation easy of execution and of little difficulty. The humble servant complied with the order and tried to collect the remedies and aliments which are useful for the given purpose, taking into consideration those which exist and are easily supplied in this town, and which are not of too hot temper, according to what was mentioned about it. It is well known to the physicians that there are aliments which are much more useful for this purpose than remedies, as the sperm is a residue from the aliments left over and above what has been required for the organs during the third digestion. For this reason the body becomes lean if there is some waste and squandering, to say nothing of the harm done by squandering [of body economy].

III. *From Maimonides's* Regimen Sanitatis

[*Introduction and End of Chapter III*]

In the Name of Allah the Merciful Compassionate! Lord, Ease (Our Burden)!

There reached the humble servant Mûsâ ibn 'Ubaidallâh, the Israelite of Cordova, the order of His Royal Lordship the Majesty Al-Afḍal — may Allâh elevate Him! — authorized and confirmed by a messenger, ordering him to compose a regulation reliable for the cure of the diseases which recently befell our master — may Allâh remove diseases from his high abode and make health and welfare His everlasting companions! The messenger transmitting the high order mentioned that our lord complained about dryness and induration of his bowels so that they move only with great difficulty. Likewise he mentioned that he is beset sometimes by dejectedness, evil thought, unsociableness, and foreboding of death, that he suffers often from indigestions and that his digestion is sometimes weak. That is what he (the royal messenger) mentioned. The humble servant intends to compose this regulation in four chapters:

Chapter I: *On the Regulation of Health in General* concerning all people, in an abridged discourse.

Chapter II: *On the Regulation of Diseased People in General* where no physician is present, or an inadequate doctor who is not firm in his knowledge.

Chapter III: *On the Regulation of Our Lord in Particular*, according to the attacks about which he is complaining.

Chapter IV: It comprises subdivisions which contain *Prescriptions in General and in Particular for Healthy and Diseased People in Any Place and at Any Time.*

He who reads this discourse and in general all the writings which I composed, ought not to criticize the repeated mention in some of their chapters of things which were mentioned already in my former output. For all my discourses [treatises] have been composed by personal demand, and not with the purpose of giving all people instruction in the medical art. We ask from Allâh help to find the right!

[End of Chapter III, following the short passage translated above]

The aim of this discourse is by no means to explain or to comment on the truth of these matters or teaching of their methods, as many such things have been composed at all times and for all educated peoples who are interested in the sciences. The humble servant only gave advice by these regulations in order to explain how the soul may become accustomed to resist passion by considering the ethical books, the literature on the rules of the religious law, and the sermons and wise sayings of the sages, until the soul is strengthened and sees the right as right and the idle as idle. In this way the passions diminish, the bad thoughts disappear, the unsociableness is removed, and the soul is gladdened in spite of all the conditions which may happen to a man.

This is a very salutary consideration, which diminishes evil thought, affliction, and sorrow; and they may disappear entirely, if a man sets up the following consideration as a mark to his spiritual eye; namely, in all human thought and faint-heartedness caused by reflection and continually renewed affliction, sorrow, and sadness, there is no doubt that there are two causes in question: either he thinks about the condition of things passed away, like a man who frets about his lost fortune or who mourns over the death of someone he loved; or he thinks about events which he expects and whose development he fears, like a man who expects the occurrence of a misfortune. It is however well known, taking intellectual consideration, that thought about things which have passed away and are accomplished is of no use in any direction, and that grief and sorrow about passed things belong to the characteristics of inferior imaginative power. There is no difference between a man who is sorry about his lost fortune and the like and a man who is grieved because he is an ordinary mortal and not a king or a star and such like and similar inaccessible things. Likewise it is necessary to abandon the thoughts leading to oppression of the soul concerning things whose development is expected in the future. The way to consider the events of life is of necessity as follows: all that man can expect falls within the range of what possibly may happen or may not happen. Inasmuch as you are distressed and grieved about what is expected of such events, so the soul should be cheered by the hope that the contrary of the expected events may happen, as the expected events and their contrary are within the range of possibility. These are all the necessary considerations submitted by the humble servant in this chapter.

IV. *From* The Explanation of Fits

[*Introduction and Paragraph 1*]

There reached the most humble servant the letter containing the explanation of all those attacks which befell our lord — may Allâh make everlasting his days! — and the interpretation of all those attacks, and the time of their occurrence, and information on all the particulars about which the physician needs inquiries, as well as the remarks after, and the reflections on every one of these attacks at any time. Written down, moreover, in it was the advice of the physicians concerning treatment, and stating where they agreed as well as where they differed.

Now, the most humble servant knows certainly that this letter has been beyond doubt dictated by our lord, and the servant swears by Allâh the Most High that even the most prominent physicians of our time fall short of the necessary knowledge to classify the complaint in question; how then could they explain it and dispose of it? Therefore the most humble servant made up his mind to give such an answer to the Ruler of Riqqa — may Allâh make lasting his shadow! — as would be given by a physician to a physician, and not like the answer of a doctor to a layman.

As the complete knowledge of our lord concerning those attacks and their causes is well known to the humble servant and as he has actual knowledge of the fits which are now continuing and the checking of which he eagerly desires; and as our lord informed the humble servant about what was the advice of each of the several physicians and ordered him to give his opinion on each physician's advice, he obeys this order.

[Paragraph I] Concerning the saying of one of the physicians: "If blood came now out of the pores of the veins [viz., hemorrhoids] as it came already sometimes before, the present attacks would be removed," this opinion is true, and there is no doubt about it. For that blood which comes is a sediment and refuse of the blood, which is expelled in a kind of crisis by nature on account of its badness. On the contrary, the doctor who advised helping the opening [dilation] of the veins by a hipbath or by sitting on cataplasms is wrong, and the humble servant does not advise this proceeding for several reasons which he will explain: (1) Those remedies which are carried or in whose infusion the patient has to sit are hot and sometimes heating to the temperament and burning to the humors [of the body]. (2) When those veins are opened naturally, they are opened as far as is required; but when we open them by the help of remedies, they are opened more than required and the flow of blood is excessive and difficult to stop. This even happens sometimes when it comes spontaneously, and it [the hemorrhage] may be so excessive that it is impossible to stop it. (3) When these veins open spontaneously, there comes out from them mostly what has to be eliminated, because nature had expelled it to the remotest parts [of the body] where the expulsive power eliminates it. On the other hand, when we open them [by remedies] there comes out that which does not require elimination; if some of what is fit for elimination comes away, nevertheless, most what comes away is what does not require elimination. In general, I never have recourse to this proceeding except in cases where that region [i.e., the anal] is swollen and very painful; then sometimes I try to contract it by remedies until all the blood which had been driven to that place and had caused its swelling flows out. In this case our proceeding is like that of the surgeon who incises a swelling, the covering of which nature is unable to open, in order to empty its contains. So our lord must not at all proceed thus, but if [the blood] comes spontaneously, as happens sometimes, he must not have it stopped, except when its flow is excessive, with recourse to Allâh!

V. *Introduction and First Ten Paragraphs from Maimonides's* Glossary of Names of Drugs

The Book of the Explanation of the Drug, composed by the Master and Chief Abû 'Imrân Mûsâ ibn 'Abdallâh [*sic*!] the Israelite from the Maghrib [i.e, "Land of the West"]

He says: My aim in this book is the comment on the names of such drugs as exist in our time and are known to us and are in use in the Art of Medicine and met with in the medical books. I shall mention among the known simple drugs only those to which has been given more than one synonym [name], either in different languages, or by more than one in one and the same language. For one and the same remedy may have different names for people speaking one and the same language, either by a coincidence in the origin of the denomination or by a difference of the terminology with the inhabitants of different regions. I shall not mention, moreover, any very well known remedy to which the physicians do not give more than one name, Arabic or foreign. For the aim of this discourse is not to acquaint the reader with the different kinds of remedies by their description or the mention of their use, but the explanation of some of their names by other names. Likewise I shall not mention remedies which are well known and verified, such as, for instance, the fig, the grape, and the like, only on account of their Greek names, as they are mentioned in the books which came down to us and whose authors discussed and explained the matter. I make an exception where that Greek name preponderates among a great number of synonyms for the drug in question. I shall not mention, moreover, any remedy which bears rare and unknown names and which is not particularly useful in medicine.

I arrange the mention of remedies according to the letters of the alphabet, but I shall avoid repetitions. For example, when a remedy bears two names, one of them beginning with letter *Alif* and the other with *Bâ'*, I shall classify both names in the chapter *Alif* without repeating them in chapter *Bâ'*. All this with the purpose of abridging and facilitating record keeping. Even if the search for a certain name is in this way a little more burdensome, it is a powerful help toward retaining in the memory all the names of that remedy. My aim in this discourse is to reduce its size in order to facilitate keeping it [easier to use] and so to increase its utility. The first of the names of any remedy which I give is [usually] the best known [to the public] and therefore less known to the specialist, as many remedies are better known to the physicians by their foreign names than by their Arabic ones.

I am relying for the explanation of these names on the book of Ibn Juljul, his *Drug-Comment*; on that of Abu'l-Walîd ibn Janâḥ; on the *Collection* which was composed by al-Ghâfiqî, one of the more recent of the Andalusian authors; and on the discussions by Ibn Wâfid and Ibn Samjûn. I have added to it what is well known to the public in the Maghrib and in which the opinion of the medical authorities is in agreement. There where we had to state controversy of opinion between the commentators, and where one of the two comments seems to be more obvious, the comment mentioned will be that of the author which is the more reputed in our land, and in cases of differences of opinion I shall mention the preponderating opinion. Allâh helps us to find the truth!

VI. *Chapter Alif*

1. *Utrujj* [lemon, citron]. It is "the Median apple."
2. *Arz* [pinetree, cedar]. It is the "male" of the pinetree, whose fruits are not edible and from which is extracted the vegetable tar. The cypress is akin to the pinetree.
3. *Afsintîn* [wormwood, absinth]. It is often called in the medical books "Roman dodder" [*kushûth rûmî*]. It is called in the foreign dialect of Andalusia [i.e., Spanish] *yerba baṭra* and they call it also *ushainîsa* [*ajenjo*=absinth].
4. *Anzarût* [sarcocolla-resin]. It is called also *'anzarût*; it is "the Persian collyrium" [eye-salve], and its name in Greek is σαρκοκόλλη.
5. *Isfanj al-Baḥr* [sponge]. It is "the foam of the sea," and it is also called "the cream of the sea," and "the cloud." It is called, moreover, "the cloudy," and the name under which it is known to the common people of the Maghrib is "the absorber," and they call it also "the sea-wool."
6. *Usṭûkhûdûs* [stoechas, lavender]. What the doctors in the Maghrib and in Egypt use is the plant called by the common people of the Westland *ḥalḥâl*, and *washâ'î' ash-shaikh*, which is the same as "the old man's spindles." It is also called *arshanîsa* and "the *ahâniya* [?] — ear." But I heard from people who make careful scientific researches on plants that this is not the real στοιχάς mentioned by Galen, but a drug with similar properties. The real *Stoechas* has broader leaves than the other and thicker ears; it grows in the vicinity of Toledo.
7. *Iklîl al-Malik* ["king's crown," i.e., melilot]. It is "the love-plant," and its name in Berber language is *tîrâzan* and that is [the same as] *ad-dâr-shâh* [Persian: "king's wood"]. It is that which is called in Spanish *coronilla* [*del rey*]. It has two species: one produces pods having the form of scorpiontails; it is called "scorpioid melilot." I heard that those roots which are imported from Syria, which are an antidote against the sting of scorpions and are called "snake-root," are the roots of this kind of melilot.
8. *Idhkhir* [lemon-grass] *Andropogon Schoenanthus L.* It is well known with us in the Maghrib as "Mecca-straw," and its ear is called *jawz jînâ* [mutilation of Persian *gôr-giyâh*= "wild ass's herb"].
9. *Athl* [Oriental tamarisk]. This is a very well-known tree, known under this name in Egypt. It is [called] "the bright-green" and *as-samsâr*. But it is said that *as-samsâr* is the wood of the box-tree. *Athl* is a kind of tamarisk [*ṭarfâ*]. Its grain (gall) is called by the inhabitants of Egypt "the palatable."
10. *Âs* [myrtle]. Its name, which is known by the inhabitants of the Maghrib, is *ar-raiḥân* ["the odoriferous," or "basilic"]. The common people of Egypt call it *al-marsîn* [from the Greek μυρσίνη].

BIBLIOGRAPHY

Barhebraeus (Ibn al-'Ibrî), *Ta'rîkh Mukhtaṣar ad-Duwal*. Beirout, 1890, pp. 417–18.

Bogen, Emil, *The Daily Prayer of a Physician*. Chicago, 1929. Reprinted from *The Journal of the American Medical Association*, XCII, 2128.

Bragman, Louis J., "Maimonides' Treatise on Poisons," *Medical Journal and Record*, July 21 and August 4, 1926.

Brockelmann, Carl, *Geschichte der arabischen Literatur*. Weimar, 1898, I, 489; and Supplement, Leiden, 1937, II, 899.

Cahiers juifs, juillet-octobre, 1935, "Maimonide, sa vie et son oeuvre.".

Castiglioni, Arturo, "Mosè Maimonide, medico e filosofo nell' ottavo centenario della sua nascita (1135–1935)," *Rassegna Clinico-Scientifica*, 1935, No. 4.

Choulant, L., *Handbuch der Bücherkunde für die ältere Medizin*. Leipzig, 1841, pp. 378–80.

Communauté Israélite d'Alexandrie, *Maimonide, huitième centenaire*. Alexandria, 1935.

Deutsch, G., "Jew and Gentile." In *Scrolls*, Boston, 1920, III, 93–95.

Elbogen, Ismar, *Das Leben des Rabbi Mosche ben Maimon. Aus seinen Briefen und anderen Quellen*. Berlin, 1935.

Epstein, I., Editor, *Moses Maimonides 1135–1204. Anglo-Jewish Papers in Connection with the Eighth Centenary of His Birth*. London [1936]. Includes W. M. Feldman, "Maimonides as Physician and Scientist," pp. 109–34.

Fischer, L., "Der Arzt Maimonides, einer der grössten Philosophen aller Zeiten," *Wiener medizinische Wochenschrift*, 1935, Nos. 14–15.

Fishman, J. L., Editor, *Rabbenu Moshe b. Maimon* (R. Moses Maimonides): A Collection of Essays [Hebrew]. Jerusalem, 1935. Includes H. Heller, "Maimonides as Physician and Healer," pp. 328–40.

Gabrieli, Giuseppe, "Biografie e bibliografie di scienziati arabi. II. Maimonide," *Archivo di Storia della Scienza*, V (1924), 12–15.

Gershenfeld, Louis, "Moses Maimonides," *Medical Life*, XLII (1935), 1–34.

Grossberg, Menasseh, *Sepher Rephuoth. The Book of Medicine by Maimonides, etc.* London, 1900.

Haaretz [A Hebrew Daily]: Special Maimonides Jubilee Issue, Jerusalem, 1935. Cols. 85–104: Essays on Maimonides as a physician by A. M. Maze and W. Schweinsheimer.

Ha-Refuah, In Memory of Maimonides [by different authors, in Hebrew]. Jerusalem, 1935.

Ha-Rofe ha-ibri [A Hebrew Medical Periodical], No. 4, New York, 1936, pp. 114–44: Essays on Maimonides by H. Keller, S. R. Kagan, and S. Mebel.

Hasidah (Bocian), M. Z., Editor, "Maimonides' Commentary on the Aphorisms of Hippocrates" [Hebrew]. *Hassegullah*, Nos. 1–30, Jerusalem, 1934–35.

Heschel, Abraham, *Maimonide*. Paris, 1936.

Ibn abî Usaybi'a, '*Uyûn al-Anbâ' fî Ṭabaqât al-Aṭibbâ'*, ed. by A. Müller. Cairo and Koenigsberg, 1882–84, II, 117–18.

Ibn al-Bayṭâr, *Traité des simples par Ibn el-Beithar*. Trans. by L. Leclerc. 3 vols., Paris, 1877–83.

Ibn Al-Qifṭî, *Ta'rîkh al-Ḥukamâ*, ed. by J. Lippert. Leipzig, 1903, pp. 317–19.

Kroner, Hermann, *Ein Beitrag zur Geschichte der Medizin des XII. Jahrhunderts.* Oberdorf-Bopfingen, 1906.

——"Die Haemorrhoiden in der Medizin des XII. und XIII. Jahrhunderts," *Janus*, XVI (1911), 441–718.

——*Die Seelenhygiene des Maimonides.* Stuttgart, 1914.

——"Maimonides als Hygieniker." In M. Grunwald, *Die Hygiene der Juden*, pp. 243–61.

——"Eine medizinische Maimonides-Handschrift aus Granada," *Janus*, XXI (Leiden, 1916), pp. 203–47.

——*Zur Terminologie der arabischen Medizin und zu ihrem zeitgenössischen hebräischen Ausdrucke.* Berlin, 1921.

——"Fî Tadbîr aṣ-Ṣiḥḥat," *Janus*, XXVII–XXIX (1923–25), 8 fascicles.

——*Der Mediziner Maimonides im Kampfe mit dem Theologen.* Oberdorf-Bopfingen, 1924.

——"Die Sexualhygiene in der Medizin des Maimonides," *Monatsschrift für Harn-Krankheiten und sexuelle Hygiene*, II (1928), 133–37.

——"Der medizinische Schwanengesang des Maimonides," *Janus*, XXXII (1928), 12–116.

Laignel-Lavastine, "Moïse Maimonide et sa place dans l'histoire de la médecine," *Revue "Ose,"* X (1935, fasc. 4), 1–16.

Leclerc, Lucien, *Histoire de la médecine arabe.* Paris, 1876, II, 57–64.

Lévy, Louis-Germain, *Maimonide.* Paris, 1911.

Levy, Reuben, "The 'Tractatus de causis et indiciis morborum' attributed to Maimonides." In *Studies in the History and Method of Science*, ed. by Charles Singer, Oxford, 1917, pp. 225–34.

Llamas, P. José, *Maimonides, Siglo XII.* Madrid [1935].

Löw, Immanuel, *Die Flora der Juden.* Vienna, 1934, IV, 201–11.

Macht, David Israel, "Moses Maimonides," *Johns Hopkins Hospital Bulletin*, XVII (1906), 332–36.

Marx, Alexander, *Moses Maimonides.* New York, 1935. In *Maimonides Octocentennial Series*, Vol. II.

——"Texts by and about Maimonides," *JQR*, XXV (1935), 371–428.

Mendelson, Walter, "Maimonides, a Twelfth Century Physician," *Annals of Medical History*, V (1923), 250–62.

Meyerhof, Max, "Zwei hygienisch-diätetische Abhandlungen des Maimonides," *Der Morgen*, IV (1928), 620–24.

——"Notes sur quelques médecins juifs égyptiens, qui se sont illustrés á l'époque arabe," *Isis*, XII (1929), 113–31.

——"L'Oeuvre médicale de Maimonide," *Archivio di Storia della Scienza*, XI (1929), 136–55.

——"Sur un ouvrage medical inconnu de Maimonide," *Mélanges Maspéro*, Cairo, 1935, III.

——"Sur un glossaire de matière médicale composé par Maimonide," *Bulletin de l'Institut d'Egypte*, XVII (1935).

——"Esquisse d'histoire de la pharmacologie et botanique chez les Musulmans d'Espagne," *Al-Andalus*, III (Madrid, 1935), 1–41.

Meyerhof, Max, "Mediaeval Jewish Physicians in the Near East, from Arabic Sources," *Isis*, XXVIII (1938), 432–60.

——"Jewish Physicians under the Reign of the Fatimid Caliphs in Egypt," *Medical Leaves*, 1939, pp. 131–39.

——"Šarḥ Asmā' Al-'Uqqār (L'Explication des noms de drogues): Un glossaire de matière médicale composé par Maimonide. Text publié pour la première fois d'après le manuscrit unique avec traduction, commentaires et index. Cairo, 1940.

Meyerhof, Max, and G. P. Sobhy, *The Abridged Version of the Book of Simple Drugs of Aḥmed ibn Muḥammad al-Ghāfiqī, by Gregorius Abu'l Faraǧ* (Barhebraeus). 3 Parts, Cairo, 1932–38.

Millán, A. C., *Maimonides*. Madrid, 1903.

Mittwoch, E., "Ibn Maimun." In *Encyclopaedia of Islam*, II (1927), 400–1.

Munk, S., "Notice sur Joseph ben-Iehouda . . . disciple de Maimonide," *Journal Asiatique* (1843), No. 11, pp. 30–31.

Munther, Suessman, *Moshe ben Maimon (Maimonides) Ketabim refuiim (Medical Works)*, edited and arranged according to Hebrew and other manuscripts with introductory remarks, commentary, key, and list of references. Vol. I: *The Book of Asthma*, Hebrew translation by the physician Rabbi Shemuel Benvenishti, the Saragossan (about 1300). Jerusalem, 1940.

Münz, J., *Maimonides (the Rambam). The Story of His Life and Genius.* English trans. from the German, Boston, 1935, pp. 177–205.

Neuburger, Max, *Geschichte der Medizin.* Stuttgart, 1911, II, 222.

Pagel, I., "Maimuni als medizinischer Schriftsteller," MbM, I, 231–47.

Philippson, Ludwig, "Tägliches Gebet eines Arztes vor dem Besuche eines Kranken," *Allgemeine Zeitung des Judentums*, XXVII (1863), 49–50. Also in *Weltbewegende Fragen*, Leipzig 1869, II, 159–60.

Rabbinowicz, I. M., *Traité des poisons de Maimonide.* Paris, 1865; 2d ed., Paris, 1935.

Ratner, "Maimonides als hygienischer Schriftsteller," *Hygienische Rundschau*, (1915), 769–74.

Renaud, H. P. J. and G. S. Colin, *Tuḥfat al-Aḥbâb: glossaire de la matière médicale marocaine.* Paris, 1934.

Ritter and Walzer, "Arabische Uebersetzungen griechischer Aerzte in Stambuler Bibliotheken," *Sitzungsberichte der Preuss. Akademie der Wissenschaften. Phil.-Hist. Klasse*, Berlin, 1934, p. 836.

De Sacy, S., *Relation de l'Egypte par Abd-Allatif, médecin arabe de Bagdad.* Paris, 1810, pp. 490, 466.

Savitz, Harry A., "Maimonides' Hygiene of the Soul," reprinted from *Annals of Medical History*, n.s., IV (1932), 80–86.

Schröder, H. O., *Galeni in Platonis Timaeum commentarii fragmenta.* Appendicem arabicam add. P. Kahle. Leipzig and Berlin, 1934.

Seeligmann, S., "Morgengebed van den arts naar Maimonides," *Vrijdagavond*, V, 1928, 404–6.

Steinschneider, Moritz, "Medicinische Schriften von Maimonides," *Oesterreichische Blätter für Litteratur und Kunst*, II (1845), 89–92, 109–12, 118–19, 123–26, 442–46, 452–55.

Steinschneider, Moritz, "Moses Maimonides." *Catalogus Librorum Hebraeorum in Bibliotheca Bodleiana*, Berlin, 1852–60.

———"Kaiser Friedrich II über Maimonides." In *Hebräische Bibliographie*, Berlin, VII (1864), 62, 136.

———"Maimonides, Iggeret ha-Sodot," *ibid.*, IX (1869), 116.

———"Gifte und ihre Heilung, eine Abhandlung des Moses Maimonides," *Virchow's Archiv für pathologische Anatomie*, LVII (1873), 62–120.

———"Maimonides," *Magazin für die Wissenschaft des Judentums*, XIX (1892), 86–88.

———*Die hebräischen Übersetzungen des Mittelalters*. Berlin, 1893, pp. 762–74.

———"Die Vorrede des Maimonides zu seinem Commentar über die Aphorismen des Hippokrates," *Zeitschrift der Deutschen Morgenländischen Gesellschaft*, XLVIII (1894), 218–34.

———*Die arabische Literatur der Juden*. Frankfort, 1902, pp. 213–21.

———"Die europäischen Übersetzungen aus dem Arabischen," *Sitzungsberichte d. Kais. Akademie der Wissenschaften in Wien*, CLI (1905), 33.

Toeplitz, P., "Das Gebet eines jüdischen Arztes," *Israelitisches Familienblatt*, V (1902), No. 36.

Valenzuela, R. V., "A Maimonides, en el VIII centenario de su nacimento," *Trabajos de la Cátedra de Historia Crítica de la Medicina*, IV (1935), 285–94.

Winternitz, *Diätetisches Sendschreiben des Maimonides an den Sultan Saladin*. Vienna, 1843.

Wolfenson, Israel, *Mûsâ ibn Maimûn, haiyâtuhu we-mussannafâtuhu*. Cairo, 1355–1936.

Wüstenfeld, Ferdinand, *Geschichte der arabischen Aerzte und Naturforscher*. Göttingen, 1840, pp. 109–11.

Zeitlin, Solomon, *Maimonides, a Biography*. New York, 1935.

INDEX